AQA A-level History

Britain 1851–1964
Challenge and Transformation

Mike Byrne

Nick Shepley

Approval message from AQA

This textbook has been approved by AQA for use with our qualification. This means that we have checked that it broadly covers the specification and we are satisfied with the overall quality. Full details of our approval process can be found on our website.

We approve textbooks because we know how important it is for teachers and students to have the right resources to support their teaching and learning. However, the publisher is ultimately responsible for the editorial control and quality of this book.

Please note that when teaching the **AQA A-level History** course, you must refer to AQA's specification as your definitive source of information. While this book has been written to match the specification, it cannot provide complete coverage of every aspect of the course. Please also note that the practice questions in this title are written to reflect the question styles of the AS and A-level papers. They are designed to help students become familiar with question types and practise exam skills. AQA has published specimen papers and mark schemes online and these should be consulted for definitive examples.

A wide range of other useful resources can be found on the relevant subject pages of our website: www.aqa.org.uk.

DYNAMIC LEARNING

HODDER EDUCATION
AN HACHETTE UK COMPANY

Acknowledgements

The Publishers would like to thank the following for permission to reproduce copyright material:

Photo credits: **p.v** l © TopFoto, r © TopFoto; **p.vi** © Mary Evans Picture Library; **p.vii** © TopFoto; **p.viii** © Robert Hunt Collection / Imperial War Museum / Mary Evans Picture Library; **p.1** © TopFoto; **p.10** © Print collector / HIP / TopFoto; **p.12** © TopFoto; **p.14** © Illustrated London News; **p.35** © TopFoto; **p.37** © TopFoto; **p.40** © INTERFOTO / Alamy; **p.49** © Liszt collection / Alamy; **p.54** © TopFoto; **p.63** © Library of Congress Prints and Photographs Division / LC-USZ62-8054; **p.66** © World History Archive / Alamy; **p.73** © Library of Congress Prints and Photographs Division / LC-USZ62-8054; **p.88** © Punch Ltd; **p.96** © The Granger collection, N C / TopFoto; **p.102** © The British Library Board (shelfmark 081685); **p.111** © Pictorial Press Ltd / Alamy; **p.112** © Heritage Image Partnership Ltd / Alamy; **p.120** © Punch Ltd; **p.121** © World History Archive / Alamy; **p.132** © World History Archive / TopFoto; **p.133** © The Granger Collection, NYC / TopFoto; **p.143** © World History Archive / TopFoto; **p.148** © 2003 AP / Topham Picturepoint / TopFoto; **p.150** © Marx Memorial Library / Mary Evans Picture Library; **p.157** © Mary Evans Picture Library; **p.161** © Robert Hunt Collection / Imperial War Museum / Mary Evans Picture Library; **p.171** © Brooke / Topical Press Agency / Getty Images; **p.183** © Robert Hunt Collection / Imperial War Museum /Mary Evans Picture Library; **p.188** © Mary Evans Picture Library / Alamy; **p.190** © 2004 UPP / TopFoto; **p.190** © Lordprice Collection / Alamy; **p.202** © Gerald Wilson / Mary Evans Picture Library; **p.204** © Illustrated London News; **p.210** © Gerald Wilson / Mary Evans Picture Library; **p.212** © Corbis; **p.220** © PA Photos / TopFoto; **p.223** © Photoshot; **p.225** © Illustrated London News Ltd / Mary Evans Picture Library; **p.238** © TopFoto; **p.239** © Roger Mayne / Mary Evans Picture Library; **p.245** © Illustrated London News Ltd /Mary Evans Picture Library; **p.252** © Gulliver Photos / Mary Evans Picture Library.

Acknowledgements: **pp.16,33**: Paul Adelman: from *Gladstone, Disraeli and Later Victorian Politics* (Longman, 1974); **p.33**: David Cooper: from *Years of Expansion: Britain 1815–1914*, ed. M Scott-Baumann (Hodder & Stoughton, 1995); **p.48**: adapted from a speech by Gladstone in 1871 from a report in *The Times*, 30 October 1871; **p.70**: © Edgar Feuchtwanger, 1985, 'Democracy and Empire: Britain 1865-1914', Bloomsbury Academic, an imprint of Bloomsbury Publishing Plc; **p.70**: Clive Behagg: from *Labour and Reform: Working-Class Movements 1815–1914* (Hodder & Stoughton, 1991); **p.75**: David Lloyd George: from *Great Lives Observed: Lloyd George*, ed. Martin Gilbert (Prentice-Hall, 1968); **p.91**: Adapted from *The Edwardian Crisis: Britain 1901–1914* by David Powell, Macmillan, 1996, pp.39-42; **p.91**: © Edgar Feuchtwanger, 1985, 'Democracy and Empire: Britain 1865-1914', Bloomsbury Academic, an imprint of Bloomsbury Publishing Plc; **p.91**: Robert Blake: *The Conservative Party from Peel to Churchill* (Eyre & Spottiswoode, 1970); **p.112**: adapted from a speech by Asquith in the House of Commons, reported in *Hansard*, 28 March 1912; **p.112**: W. L. Blease: from: 'The Emancipation of English Women' (Constable, 1910); **p.134**: adapted from an article in the *Daily Mail*, 21 May 1915; **p.147**: Winston Churchill: from *The Oxford Dictionary of Quotations* (Oxford University Press, 1979); **p.147**: Richard Toye: from *The Labour Party and the Planned Economy* (Boydell and Brewer, 2003); **p.152**: Lord Rothermere: adapted from an article in the *Daily Mirror*, 22 January 1934; **p.152**: Beatrice Webb: from *The Diary of Beatrice Webb*, Volume 4, 1924–1943, (Virago, 1986); **p.171**: A. J. P. Taylor: from *English History 1914–1945* (Oxford University Press, 1965); **p.172**: Travis L Crosby: from *The Unknown David Lloyd George: A Statesman in Conflict* (I. B. Tauris, 2014); **p.172**: T. Lynch: from: *Yorkshire's War* (Amberley, 2014); **p.174**: Sidney Webb: from *The Letters of Sidney and Beatrice Webb: Volume 3, Pilgrimage 1912–47* (Cambridge University Press, 1978); **p.178**: R. Skidelsky: from *Britain Since 1900 – A Success Story?* (Random House, 2015); **p.180**: J. Stevenson and C. Cook: from *The Slump: Britain in the Great Depression* (Routledge, 2013); **p.180**: Britain, 1929–1998, pp. 7–8., C. Rowe, 2004, Pearson Education Limited.; **p.181**: P. Sauvain: from *Key Themes of the Twentieth Century* (Stanley Thornes, 1996); **p.199**: J. Gardiner: from *The 30s: An Intimate History of Britain* (Harper Collins, 2011); **p.199**: From *The Long Shadow* by D. Reynolds, Simon and Schuster, 2013, p. 145.; **p.199**: P. Clarke: from *Hope and Glory, Britain 1900–1990* (Penguin, 2004); **p.205**: Winston Churchill: from a speech in the House of Commons, reported in *Hansard*, 5th Series, Vol. 361, 1940; **p.213**: Harold Macmillan: from a statement about 'Kim' Philby, reported in *Hansard*, Vol. 545, 7 November 1955; **p.214**: Peter Hennessy's lecture to the British Academy in February 2008, The British Academy Review, July 2008; **p.215**: Paul Addison: from *The Road to 1945* (Pimlico, 1994); **p.215**: © David Kynaston, 2008, 'Austerity Britain 1945-51', Bloomsbury Publishing Plc.; **p.217**: D. Healey: from *The Time of My Life* (Politico's Publishing Ltd, 2006); **p.222**: © Peter Taylor, 2000, 'Loyalists', Bloomsbury Publishing Plc.; **p.228**: Barbara Castle: from *Fighting all the way*, pan Books, 1994; **p.231**: © David Kynaston, 2008, 'Austerity Britain 1945-51', Bloomsbury Publishing Plc.; **p.233**: from the 'Peoples of the British Isles: A New History from 1870 to the Present' by T. Heyck and M. Veldman, Lyceum, 2015, p. 218; **p.242**: 'British Culture and the End of Empire' by S. Ward, Manchester University Press, 2001, p. 91.; **p.245**: Robert Pearce: from *Oxford Dictionary of National Biography* (Oxford University Press, 2004); **p.249**: 'Experimental Theatre in the 1960s', Arthur Marwick, Oct-94 *History Today*; **p.250**: From 'The Swingers Who Never Were' by Dominic Sandbrook, *New Statesman*, 21 March 2005; **p.250**: P. Clarke: from *Hope and Glory* (Penguin, 2000); **p.255**: C. Beckett and F. Beckett: from *Bevan* (Haus Publishing, 2004); **p.258**: Sir William Beveridge: from 'Social Insurance and Allied Services' (HMSO, 1942); **p.257**: S. Aiston: from Journal of Twentieth-Century British History (Cambridge University Press, 2004); **p.263** © David Kynaston, 2008, Austerity Britain 1945-51, Bloomsbury Publishing Plc.; **p.263**: D. Sandbrook: from *White Heat* (Abacus, 2006).

Every effort has been made to trace or contact all copyright holders, but if any have been inadvertently overlooked the Publishers will be pleased to make the necessary arrangements at the first opportunity.

Although every effort has been made to ensure that website addresses are correct at time of going to press, Hodder Education cannot be held responsible for the content of any website mentioned in this book. It is sometimes possible to find a relocated web page by typing in the address of the home page for a website in the URL window of your browser.

Hachette UK's policy is to use papers that are natural, renewable and recyclable products and made from wood grown in sustainable forests. The logging and manufacturing processes are expected to conform to the environmental regulations of the country of origin.

Orders: please contact Bookpoint Ltd, 130 Milton Park, Abingdon, Oxon OX14 4SB.
Telephone: +44 (0)1235 827720. Fax: +44 (0)1235 400454. Lines are open 9.00a.m.– 5.00p.m., Monday to Saturday, with a 24-hour message answering service. Visit our website at www.hoddereducation.co.uk

© Mike Byrne, Nick Shepley 2015
First published in 2015 by
Hodder Education,
An Hachette UK Company
Carmelite House
50 Victoria Embankment
London EC4Y 0DZ

Impression number	10 9 8 7 6 5 4 3 2
Year	2019 2018 2017 2016

Cover photo © duncan1890/iStockphoto

Illustrations by Integra Software Services and Barking Dog Art

Typeset in 10.5/12.5pt ITC Berkeley Oldstyle Std Book by Integra Software Services Pvt. Ltd., Pondicherry, India

Printed in Dubai

A catalogue record for this title is available from the British Library

ISBN 9781471837593

Contents

Part Two: The World Wars and their Legacies: Britain, 1914–64

Introduction

Arguably the most dynamic and fascinating period of British history began in the mid-nineteenth century and ended in the mid-twentieth. This textbook is written to support the modern British history component of AQA's A-level history breadth specification. It covers this fascinating century of change and conflict. It tells the story of the British people from the Industrial Revolution, through two world wars, economic crisis and economic boom, to the 'Swinging Sixties' and the Beatles. Few periods of British history have seen such rapid and dramatic change. Understanding this period will help you to make sense of British society today and Britain's changing place in world affairs. This book will help you to master these changes and to understand the various ways in which the past has been interpreted.

▲ Harold Wilson with the Beatles – (*l* to *r*) Paul McCartney, George Harrison, John Lennon and Ringo Starr – at a Show Business Awards luncheon in London in March 1964.

v

TO THE GREAT E'

LONDON DARTON

The key content

'Challenge and Transformation: Britain c1851–1964' is one of the breadth studies offered by AQA, and as such covers over a hundred years. The content is divided into two parts:

Part 1 (1851–1914) is studied by those taking the AS examination.

Parts 1 and 2 (1851–1964) are studied by those taking the full A-level examination.

Each part is subdivided into two sections.

PART 1: VICTORIAN AND EDWARDIAN BRITAIN, C1851–1914

This section covers the society, politics and economics of the Victorian and Edwardian periods from the height of the Industrial Revolution to the First World War. The focus is not just on the key personalities of the era but also on issues of breadth as highlighted in the Key Questions.

Reform and challenge, c1851–86

This section focuses on the society, economics and politics of the Victorian Age. Beginning at the height of the Industrial Revolution in 1851, it incorporates the politics of the two great political rivals, Gladstone and Disraeli. It also covers the condition of the poor in Victorian Britain, the need for social reform and the trade union movement. The question of Home Rule in Ireland also features as a main theme of challenge to the established political order.

Challenges to the status quo, c1886–1914

Despite Britain having experienced a 'golden age' of prosperity and world power during the mid-nineteenth century, the two decades after 1886 featured growing social conflict in Britain. A long economic downturn, increasingly militant trade unions, unrest in Ireland, a constitutional crisis between the 1906 Liberal Government and the House of Lords, and the growth of a suffragist movement all threatened to tear the country apart by 1914. Only the outbreak of the First World War seemed to put these social conflicts on hold. The focus of this chapter is on the social and economic forces that were shaping late Victorian and Edwardian Britain.

PART 2: THE WORLD WARS AND THEIR LEGACIES: BRITAIN, 1914–64

Between 1914 and 1945 Britain experienced conflict on an unprecedented scale. Two world wars placed immense burdens on the country's politics, economy and society. This part of the book examines wartime politics and society and the economic legacy of the conflicts. It examines the two inter-war economic depressions and the development of social reform after the Second World War.

The Great War and its impact, 1914–39

During the First World War, the charismatic and energetic Liberal politician David Lloyd George rose to power as the Government struggled to survive during the conflict. By the end of the war, his party was in disarray and a new electoral force, the Labour Party, had emerged. The inter-war period saw Labour and Conservative governments and after 1931, a coalition National Government. It also saw the development of extremist parties such as the British Union of Fascists. The period was one of economic crisis in the old industrial heartlands of Britain where shipbuilding, mining and other heavy industry went into decline. However, in some parts of Britain rising living standards and new industries brought affluence for many British people during the 1930s.

Transformation and change, 1939–64

The impact of the Second World War had even more pronounced changes on Britain. It resulted in a dramatic growth in the role of the state in the economy and society after 1945. A Labour government elected that year brought about sweeping social reforms, including the establishment of the National Health Service. A post-war political consensus between the Labour and Conservative parties developed, meaning that on economic and social policy there were broad areas of agreement. In the immediate aftermath of the war, Britain experienced nearly a decade of acute economic hardship, but in 1954 an economic boom began. This lasted until the early 1960s, but in 1964 it gradually began to diminish.

Key concepts

But the study of history does not only include narrative – interesting though the stories often are! There are four concepts which steer our thinking and our understanding of the past. These are important in your study. Consider:

● Change and continuity: To what extent did things change? What are the similarities and differences over time?
● Cause and consequence: What were the factors that led to change? How did the changes affect individuals and groups within society, as well as the country as a whole?

Consider when writing an essay:

● the extent you agree with a statement
● the validity of a statement
● the importance of a particular factor relating to a key question
● how much something changed or to what extent something was achieved.

In addition, you will be learning about different interpretations: how and why events have been portrayed in different ways over time by historians. In the first section of both the AS and A-level examination you will be tested on this skill with a selection of contrasting extracts.

The key questions

The specification lists six key questions around which the study is based. These are wide-ranging in scope and can be considered across the whole period. They reflect the broadly-based questions (usually covering 20–30 years) that will be set in the examination.

1 How did democracy and political organisations develop in Britain?

You will learn how voting rights were extended throughout the period and what effect this had on the Conservative and Liberal parties. You will also learn about the development of the Labour Party after the First World War and the growth of extremist parties between the two world wars. Additionally, you will also explore the nature of the post-1945 political consensus.

2 How important were ideas and ideologies?

You will learn about the various political ideas and ideologies (ways of thinking about how the world should be), which shaped the period. The beliefs of politicians, intellectuals, social reformers and civil servants had a profound effect on how British society developed. You will explore why some ideas became dominant and others declined.

3 How and with what effects did the economy develop?

Between 1851 and 1945 the British economy went through both rapid growth and gradual decline. You will learn about the factors that resulted in both processes and the results of economic transition for British politics and society. You will also learn about the differing economic ideas that politicians and economists believed in.

4 How and with what effects did society and social policy develop?

British society and the country's class system also developed throughout the period, from the rigid class structure of the Victorian era, to a more egalitarian age after the Second World War. You will examine how and why the class system developed and changed. This was also a period unprecedented in the level of social reform which took place, and you will examine the impact of social policy from Gladstone to the 1945 Labour Government.

5 How and why did Britain's relationship with Ireland change?

British relations with Ireland underwent a dramatic transformation. In 1851, Ireland was the oldest colony in the British Empire. By the end of the period of study, Ireland was an independent country, with Northern Ireland remaining part of the United Kingdom. You will examine the political debates over the issue of Home Rule for Ireland and the escalation of tensions leading to Ireland's War of Independence and Civil War.

6 How important was the role of key individuals and groups and how were they affected by developments?

This book also focuses on key individuals such as William Gladstone, David Lloyd George and Winston Churchill. It examines the role of organisations and political parties such as the Tariff Reform League, the Fabian Society and the Labour Party. You will evaluate the extent to which these individuals and groups were instrumental in bringing social, economic and political change to Britain. You will also examine the impact of these changes on key groups and individuals.

How this book is designed to help your studies

1 With the facts, concepts and key questions of the specification

At the beginning of each chapter the book flags up the elements of the specification and the key questions that are being covered.

Activities are provided helping you to create notes, and enabling you to consider the main areas of interpretation throughout the period.

The Look Again feature encourages you to look back and compare your learning with previous periods in the book, to make comparisons across time.

Key dates are listed throughout.

Key words and phrases are defined at the first relevant point in the text, and there is a full glossary on pages 274–76.

Chapter summaries and diagrams are provided to help consolidate your learning.

At the end of Part 1 and Part 2 there is a dedicated section reviewing the six key questions over the previous chapters.

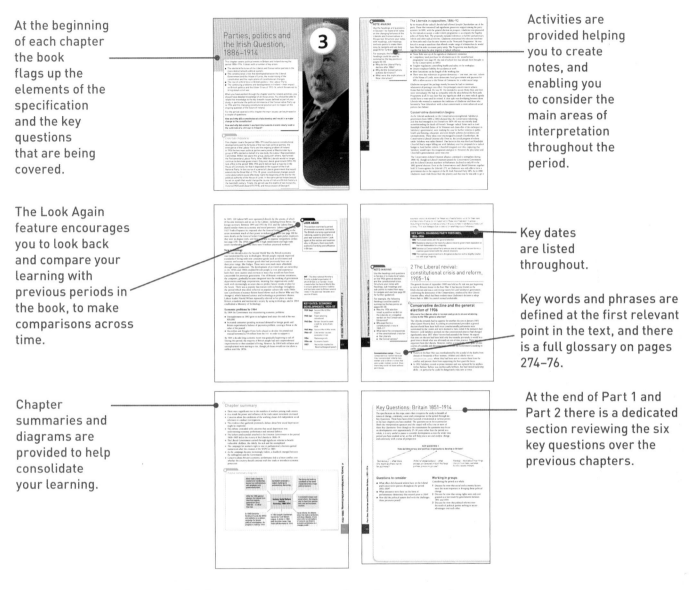

2 With the skills needed to answer examination questions

The book provides guidance in answering examination questions in the form of a separate 'skills' section at the end of each chapter.

Interpretation skills are developed through the analysis of extended pieces of writing by leading academics.

3 With the skills in reading, understanding and making notes from the book

Note-making

Good note-making is really important. Your notes are an essential revision resource. What is more, the process of making notes will help you understand and remember what you are reading.

How to make notes

Most note-making styles reflect the distinction between key points and supporting evidence. Below is advice on a variety of different note-making styles. Throughout each section in the book are note-making activities for you to carry out.

The important thing is that you understand your notes. Therefore, you don't have to write *everything* down, and you don't have to write in full sentences.

While making notes you can use abbreviations:

Full text	Abbreviation
First World War	FWW
Social reforms	Soc refs
Home Rule	HR
Labour Party	Lab Party

You can develop your own abbreviations. Usually it is only yourself who has to understand them!

You can use arrows instead of words:

Full text	Abbreviation
Increased	↑
Decreased	↓

You can use mathematical notation:

Equals	=
plus, and	+
Because	∵
Therefore	∴

Note-making styles

There are a large number of note-making styles. However you prefer to make notes, by hand or on a laptop or tablet, the principles are the same. You can find examples of three popular styles below. All of them have their strengths, it is a good idea to try them all and work out which style suits you.

Style 1: Bullet points

Bullet points can be a useful method of making notes because:

- they encourage you to write in note form, rather than in full sentences
- they help you to organise your ideas in a systematic fashion
- they are easy to skim read later
- you can show relative importance visually by indenting less important, or supporting points.

Usually it is easier to write notes with bullet points after you have skim-read a section or a paragraph first in order to get the overall sense in your head.

Style 2: The 1–2 methods

The 1–2 method is a variation on bullet points. The method is based on dividing your page into two columns: the first for the main point, the second for supporting detail. This allows you to see the structure of the information clearly. To do this, you can create a chart to complete, as follows:

Main point	Supporting detail

Style 3: Spider diagrams

Spider diagrams or mind maps can be a useful method of making notes because:

- they help you to categorise factors: each of the main branches coming from the centre should be a new category
- they help you see what is most important: often the most important factors will be close to the centre of the diagram
- they can help you see connections between different aspects of what you are studying. It is useful to draw lines between different parts of your diagram to show links
- they can also help you with essay planning: you can use them to quickly get down the main points and develop a clear structure in response to an essay question
- you can set out the spider diagram in any way that seems appropriate for the task, but usually, as with a spider's web, you would start with the title or central issue in the middle with connecting lines radiating outwards.

Politics, political parties and the Irish Question, 1851–86

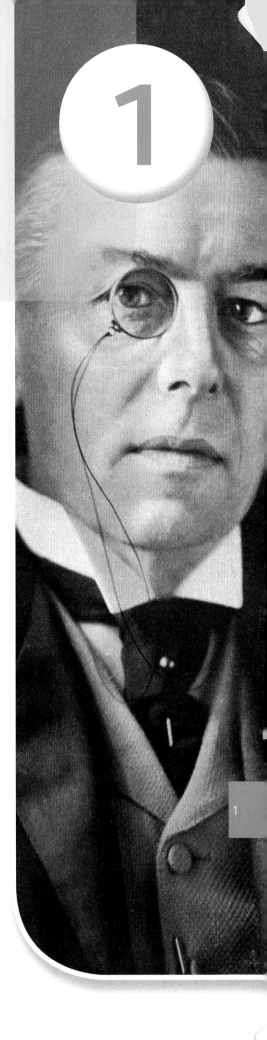

1

This chapter covers the political events in Britain and Ireland during the period 1851–86. It deals with a number of key areas:

- The political system and how the right to vote was extended to create a more recognisably democratic country.
- The way the political parties developed and adapted to these changes and the impact of two outstanding political leaders – Gladstone and Disraeli.
- The problems in Ireland, their impact on British politics and the policies adopted to deal with the 'Irish Question'.

When you have worked through the chapter and the related activities, you should have detailed knowledge of all those areas. You should be able to relate this knowledge to the key breadth issues defined as part of your study:

- How did democracy and political organisations develop in Britain?
- How important were ideas and ideologies?
- How and why did Britain's relationship with Ireland change?
- How important was the role of key individuals and groups and how were they affected by developments?

For the period covered in this chapter, the main issues can be summarised in the following questions:

Why was there opposition to the idea of extending the vote to more people and why in the end was this resistance overcome?

How and why did events in and attitudes and policies towards Ireland impact on the political system and begin to address the problems of Ireland?

The focus of these questions is on the development of tensions and the range of causal factors that contributed to that development.

CHAPTER OVERVIEW

In 1851 the two main political parties were the Tories (or Conservatives) who had dominated the system in the early years of the century, and the Whigs (or Liberals) who had emerged in the 1830s as the more dominant force. Both parties were in a state of transition. From 1851 to 1886 the Liberals would continue to dominate government. Only one Conservative government took office in that period with a majority in the House of Commons – there were three other Conservative governments of short duration which operated as 'minority governments'. The period was dominated by the emergence of two extraordinary politicians, the Liberal leader William Ewart Gladstone and the Conservative leader Benjamin Disraeli. These two men dominated their parties and had an immense impact on the way those parties developed. They also detested each other to a degree that is unusual in the entire political history of this country. Each of them was involved in bringing about political change that, while falling short of creating a democracy, set the country on the path to democracy. As they battled with problems and each other, a great issue that had been ever-present but only periodically in the forefront of politics, finally rose up to deliver its own impact and change the shape of British politics in ways that can still be traced down to the present day – the Irish Question.

1

1 The political system in the mid-nineteenth century

In order to understand the politics, social issues and economic policies of the period 1851–64 it is necessary to grasp clearly what conditions existed in all these areas in 1851 and some of the background factors which had shaped them. Therefore some of what follows necessarily relates to events before 1851, which cannot form the basis of any exam questions. However, it is essential to understanding the context of what follows.

In 1851 the United Kingdom, comprising England and Wales, Scotland and Ireland was a country of massive and complex contradictions. It had been undergoing political, social and economic change at an unprecedented rate for decades and would continue to do so in the decades to come. Constitutionally the United Kingdom was complex. England and Wales was a single legal and administrative country dating from the laws of 1536 and 1543 which are sometimes misleadingly referred to as 'Acts of Union'. In fact, they were simply the extension of English law and administration into Wales, which was already under English control. Scotland was very different. In 1706 and 1707 the English Parliament and the Scottish Parliaments passed, respectively and separately, Acts of Union that merged two sovereign independent nations into one – Great Britain. Ireland was already under British control when the Act of Union between Great Britain and Ireland was passed in 1800. There was an Irish Parliament which was abolished, but that parliament had always been subservient to the British Parliament at Westminster.

The House of Commons had MPs elected to it from all the constituent parts of the UK. However, some types of laws passed at the Westminster Parliament still needed to be passed separately for England and Wales, Scotland, and Ireland. So for example what is generally referred to as the Great Reform Act of 1832 (see page 5) was in fact three separate reform acts, each relating to a different part of the UK.

The role of the monarch in this system was changing. Up until 1832 it had been accepted that the prime minister was appointed by the monarch and that government policies were only carried forward with the approval of the king or queen. Queen Anne in 1709 was the last monarch to actually use the power of royal veto to reject a law. However, subsequent monarchs had used their influence to stop legislation they did not like in less obvious but just as effective ways. In 1834 William IV became the last monarch to actually sack a prime minister he disagreed with. He was quickly forced to reverse his decision. William IV died in 1837 and was replaced by his eighteen-year-old niece who became Queen Victoria. She would reign until 1901. Though she would often try to influence prime ministers and the policies they adopted she had to accept that real political power did not lie with her. The political system, while far from democratic, even after being reformed in 1832, was moving towards a situation in which political parties contested for power at general elections and these elections would solely determine the composition of the government and its policies.

Democratic – Democracy can be generally defined as a political system in which those considered to be adults have the right to vote for their political representatives and through them to have a significant influence over government policies. Beyond this general principle however there is no precise formula about the specific details of the political system and democratic systems vary in form around the world.

Comparing old and new money

Throughout this book there will be references to money using the old system of British currency. Before February 1971, Britain's system of money was not based on the decimal system. The £1 unit was made up of 20 shilling units. Each shilling unit was made up of 12 penny units. When the currency was decimalised the rate set was 1 new penny = 2.4 old pennies because 100 new pennies would make up a pound while 240 old pennies had previously made up a pound.

The road to democracy: the Parliamentary system in the mid-nineteenth century

How much progress had been made towards democracy in British politics by 1851?

In 1851 the right to vote was still restricted to a limited number of men. The right to vote (or 'franchise') was based on an Act passed in 1832 which has become known by the title 'The Great Reform Act', though historians are very divided as to whether the title 'Great' is really appropriate.

On the surface, Parliament in 1851 looked much the same as now with MPs elected to the House of Commons and peers, or Lords, sitting in the unelected House of Lords. However, in practice the situation was very different. MPs were elected for two different types of constituency – counties and boroughs. Generally speaking, county MPs represented rural areas while borough MPs represented urban areas. To qualify as a county MP a man had to show that he possessed property in some form valued at £600 – a sum which in today's terms would equate to around £700,000. Borough MPs needed to possess property to the value of £300. The difference marked the greater prestige accorded to county 'seats' in the House of Commons. These qualifications were abolished in 1858 as they were proving difficult to enforce and easy to evade.

Before 1832 anyone owning land in county areas valued at 40 shillings for rent (or £2) was entitled to vote for candidates in the county seats. In practice this meant men though in fact there was no law that prevented women from voting. By 1832 this was a relatively modest sum. In boroughs the right to vote was set out in the borough charter which was granted by the Crown and set out all the rights and privileges that residents in the borough enjoyed. The right to vote in boroughs varied a great deal; in some only members of the town council could vote, in some it was ratepayers and in others virtually all male inhabitants could vote. In 1832, as will be seen, a standard voting qualification was introduced for boroughs and several new qualifications were allowed in counties. Also in 1832 all qualifications (or 'franchises') were stated to be for men only. All counties returned two MPs to Parliament regardless of the size of the population. Most boroughs also returned two MPs though some smaller ones had been reduced to one MP under the 1832 Act.

Elections were very different, too. All voting was done in public and the votes cast recorded and published. Many elections were not even contested because running an election campaign could be expensive and in many constituencies the majority of voters would support candidates who either were, or were supported by, prominent local men whose influence could not be disregarded. Once elected many MPs went only rarely to the House of Commons and some almost never attended. MPs were not paid and attendance was entirely their choice.

Before 1832 the borough constituencies which dated from the Middle Ages had remained unchanged. As a result the growing industrial towns such as Manchester, Leeds and Merthyr Tydfil had no representation in the House of Commons. At the same time some boroughs which had originally been large and populous in medieval times had declined in population or in a few extreme cases even ceased to be populated at all. Such boroughs (popularly known as 'rotten boroughs') still retained the right to MPs who effectively bought the seats from the landowners.

NOTE-MAKING

Use the headings and questions in Section 1 to make brief notes on Britain's political system and the right to vote. Structure your notes with headings, sub-headings and sub-points to make them easy to navigate and use (see page x for further guidance).

For example, the following headings could be used to summarise the key points on pages 2–8.
- The voting system and who had the right to vote.
- The factors shaping the development of the Liberal and Conservative parties.
- The reasons why there was resistance to further reform after 1851.

Ratepayers – Rates are taxes payable to local authorities rather than the central or national government. Such taxes therefore varied locally. The only local rate that was universal was the Poor Rate which, under a law dating from 1601, had to be paid in order to support those who could not support themselves.

Rotten boroughs – Boroughs which had once been large and populous and which had declined in population, but which still retained the right to MPs. These MPs 'purchased' their seats from landowners.

The House of Lords

The House of Lords was also very different to today where it exists mainly to propose, revise and amend legislation and to sometimes delay it. In 1851 it had full power to reject or amend any legislation coming from the House of Commons, except that by custom it did not interfere with financial matters such as the annual Budget that gave the government its income. Peerages were hereditary, passing from father to son or the next male heir in the family. It is important to understand that not all men using titles had the right to sit in the House of Lords. For example, Lord Palmerston, an important figure in this chapter, held an Irish peerage. Only a limited number of Irish peers (28) were entitled to a seat in the Lords and they were elected for life by their fellow Irish peers. Lord Palmerston spent his entire career as an MP. Lord John Russell, another important figure in the chapter, was called Lord John as a courtesy. He was a younger son of the Duke of Bedford, and it was customary to accord the sons of dukes and marquises (the highest grades of peer), this courtesy. Lord John was therefore also an MP for most of his career, before eventually being created an earl.

Today we accept that all the leading government ministers are MPs not Lords. In 1851 the Government was made up of ministers who could be either in the House of Commons or the House of Lords, including the prime minister. The only exception was the chancellor of the exchequer who had to be an MP because of the Commons' special control of finance. However, in 1851 the chancellorship of the exchequer was not as important a government post as it has since become.

Parliament passed laws by a procedure which remains the same today. A proposed new law or a change to an existing law is known as a parliamentary bill until it has passed the stages of consideration in Parliament and received the Royal Assent. There are five stages for a bill to pass in order to become law. All five have to be carried out by both Houses of Parliament. In 1851, and until reform of the House of Lords in 1911 (see page 76), apart from finance bills the Lords had equal power over the process. The stages of a bill are:

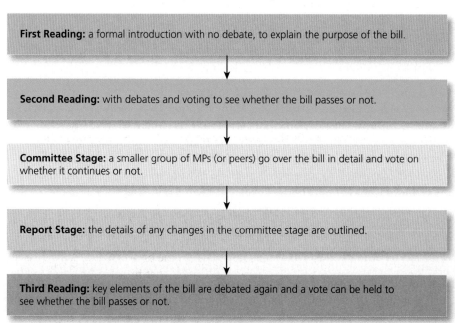

First Reading: a formal introduction with no debate, to explain the purpose of the bill.

Second Reading: with debates and voting to see whether the bill passes or not.

Committee Stage: a smaller group of MPs (or peers) go over the bill in detail and vote on whether it continues or not.

Report Stage: the details of any changes in the committee stage are outlined.

Third Reading: key elements of the bill are debated again and a vote can be held to see whether the bill passes or not.

All the legislation you will study in this book had to pass this process before becoming law. The time that a bill takes, then and now, can vary enormously from a few days to years.

The 'Great' Reform Act of 1832

The Reform Act (strictly speaking three separate Acts as explained in the chapter summary on page 29) was the basis of the political system during the period 1851–67, so its terms and implications are important to understand.

So why was the Reform Act important?

● Many 'rotten' and 'pocket' boroughs were abolished.
● Seats were given to the new towns and cities.
● A standard voting qualification – ownership or legal occupancy of property with an annual value of £10 – was introduced in the boroughs. The £10 qualification included the middle class but excluded the working class.
● Electoral registers were set up to list all qualified voters, promoting a need for party organisation to win elections.
● The changes helped preserve and strengthen the system of government by the elite classes.
● The House of Lords opposed the Reform Act and rejected two versions of it. This led the Government to threaten to flood the Lords with new pro-reform peers. The Lords were forced to back down, thus creating a precedent for any future conflict between the Commons and the Lords.
● After 1832 the House of Commons was clearly the more powerful partner in Parliament.

> **Pocket boroughs** – boroughs controlled by individual landowners (the borough being 'in their pocket'). They were also known as 'nomination boroughs' because the landowners effectively nominated the MPs.

The extent to which the Reform Act of 1832 can be seen as genuinely 'great' depends to a considerable extent on perspective. Credible estimates suggest that there were around 500,000 eligible voters prior to 1832 and that this rose to around 800,000 after the Act. If the assumption is that the Act ought to have delivered a high degree of democracy with at least adult male suffrage and secret voting, then clearly it was disappointingly limited. Radicals of the time certainly saw it that way. If, on the other hand, the emphasis is put on continuity and gradual progression, then the Act appears in a better light and can be argued to have been a great breakthrough, at least on the gradual path to democracy, paving the way for the next Reform Act in 1867.

Political parties and party realignment to 1868

How and why did both the Conservative and Liberal parties change in nature over the 1850s and 1860s?

During the 1850s and 1860s the Conservative Party (Tories) and the Liberal Party (Whigs) underwent significant changes. This was in part the result of changes brought about by the 1832 Reform Act but also by a major split in the Conservative Party.

The development of the Conservative Party to 1868

In 1833 the Conservative Party was still most widely known as the Tory Party and had just undergone a split which had taken some of its more liberal-minded and progressive members over to the Whigs. Those that remained were generally the more conservative-minded Tories some of whom were 'Ultra-Tories', meaning that they held extreme reactionary views about politics, economics and religion, and were determined at the very least to oppose any further reforms following the Great Reform Act of 1832 and Catholic Emancipation in 1829 – some 'Ultras' even hoped to repeal both measures. This was the initial cause of the Tory split as some Tories favoured Catholic Emancipation while others opposed

> **Catholic Emancipation** – MPs and peers have to take an oath of allegiance to the Crown before being allowed to enter Parliament. Before 1829 this oath was worded so that Roman Catholics could not say it without renouncing their faith. The 1829 Act removed these parts, making the oath one that all Christians could accept.

it. Many Tories distrusted their leaders Wellington and Sir Robert Peel for allowing Catholic Emancipation. Peel, who emerged as the leader by 1834, also accepted the Reform Act which he had originally opposed.

In the period 1834–41 Peel aimed to create a party capable of supporting a government. He consciously shifted the party towards a more moderate attitude. He began this process in what has become known as the Tamworth Manifesto of 1834. Broadly the manifesto dealt with:

- maintaining the idea that the monarch still retained genuine executive power in the constitution – in reality Peel knew perfectly well that the monarch's role had been changed by the 1832 Act
- confirmation that the Reform Act was to be regarded as irrevocable – to warn off those who thought that it might be repealed
- acceptance of the principle that moderate reform would be pursued where there was a clear case for change.

A general election was held in January 1835 and the Conservatives gained some seats but not enough to overturn the Whig majority and Peel resigned. However, he succeeded in persuading some leading Whigs, such as Sir James Graham and Lord Edward Stanley (later Lord Derby) to switch their allegiance to him. The Conservatives won further seats in the general election of 1837, which in accordance with the constitutional practice of the time was held on the death of William IV. In the next general election in 1841, with the country in the grip of a great financial and economic crisis, the Conservatives won with a substantial majority. Peel's governments between 1841 and 1846 brought in many reforms and set the country firmly on the road to economic free trade (see page 37). But Peel's policies upset many of his backbench MPs and when in 1845–46 he undertook to repeal the Corn Laws, which protected British agriculture from foreign competition, the Conservatives split. Almost all Conservative leaders apart from Lord Derby supported Peel, while most backbenchers, led by Benjamin Disraeli, opposed him. As a result the party was left with few recognisable men of stature. Peel himself died in 1850 after a riding accident.

Lord Derby led the Conservatives after Peel's resignation and his main contribution was to hold the party together after the disastrous split with Peel in 1846. Derby tried at various times between 1846 and 1859 to win back the 'Peelites' (Gladstone, Lord Aberdeen, Sir James Graham and others) who had been Cabinet ministers under Peel, but he failed. A significant barrier to their return (especially that of Gladstone, the leading Peelite) was the rise of Disraeli, who was never forgiven by the Peelites for making vicious and personal attacks on Peel during the Corn Law debates in 1846. Disraeli gradually emerged between 1846 and 1852 as the number two to Lord Derby. In Derby's minority government of 1852, formed due to a split in the Whig Government, Disraeli was made chancellor of the exchequer and Leader of the House of Commons. He repeated these roles in the further minority Derby Governments of 1858–59 and 1866–67, before taking over from Derby as party leader and prime minister in 1868.

The development of the Liberal Party to 1868

In 1830 the Whigs, after years of political opposition to the dominant Tory Party, finally came to power. The Whig leader Lord Grey was determined to end his long and largely powerless career by passing a major reform of the

> **Free trade** – An economic policy that allows imports and exports to enter and leave the country without imposing taxes or limitations on quantities.

political system – the Reform Act of 1832 was the result. By 1846 the Whigs were increasingly becoming known as Liberals. They were generally supported by independent radicals in Parliament and by the Peelites (the Conservatives who had continued to support Peel in 1846) who saw them as the best option for protecting Peel's policies. Lord John Russell had emerged as the Whig leader after the defeat in 1841 and he unified the party around the idea of repealing the Corn Laws in 1845 and supported Peel's policy when the Conservatives split over the issue.

The two leading figures in the party by 1851 were Russell and Lord Palmerston – Russell had the leading role as the longer-established figure in the Liberal ranks but Palmerston had a personally loyal following in the Commons. Russell and Palmerston had an uneasy relationship and clashed disastrously in 1851. Palmerston was removed by Russell as foreign secretary and then turned against Russell and brought his government down in February 1852. The Liberal split was repaired in late 1852 when Russell and Palmerston agreed to put their differences aside and serve under the Peelite Lord Aberdeen in a Liberal-Peelite coalition which William Ewart Gladstone, a passionate supporter of Peel, also agreed to join. This marked the start of a seven-year process by which the Peelites, by far the most important one being Gladstone, were gradually absorbed into the Liberal Party.

The Aberdeen Government was brought down by the disasters of the early stages of the Crimean War and in 1855 Palmerston became prime minister. Russell accepted his demotion in the national interest (although he did retire from politics for a while in the late 1850s) and from here on until Palmerston's death in 1865 he was effectively second in command, with Gladstone emerging alongside him. The tendency of the party to internal warfare was seen again in 1858 when dissent within the party led to a defeat in the Commons which brought Palmerston's government down. However, in 1859 the issue of Italian unification brought all shades of Liberal opinion together in agreement that Britain should support the cause of Italian unity. This led to the formal formation of the Liberal Party with Palmerston at its head. Gladstone, who disliked Palmerston personally and his foreign policies in particular, had been indecisive about his relations with the party, sometimes agreeing to serve with, and under, Palmerston, but then resigning. In 1859 he threw in his lot with the Liberals once and for all. Russell came out of retirement to join Palmerston's government.

Palmerston was essentially conservative on many issues and particularly on the issue of parliamentary reform (see page 8). So long as he was leader, Russell, who had long wanted to extend the vote beyond the 1832 limits, was unable to make any move. He did however eventually gain the support of Gladstone for reform – Gladstone having originally also opposed it. In 1861 Russell received an earldom and went to the Lords. When Palmerston died in 1865 the barrier to parliamentary reform was gone. Russell took over as prime minister and with Gladstone (now the Liberal leader in the Commons) agreed to propose a new reform bill to Parliament. They were defeated when a section of the Liberals, led by Robert Lowe, turned against them and voted against the bill. The resulting Conservative Government under Lord Derby put through its own Reform Act in 1867. When the general election of 1868 was held Gladstone was the acknowledged leader of the Liberals – Russell having gone into permanent retirement when his government fell in 1866.

Crimean War

The Crimean War (1854–56) saw Britain side with France in a war with Russia which was seen as threatening the Turkish Empire – Britain saw this as a Russian threat to India in the longer term. The war was fought in the Crimea region of Russia bordering the Black Sea and though Russia was eventually defeated, the war revealed the many inefficiencies of the British Army and the appalling lack of welfare for soldiers, particularly those wounded in action and struck down by disease. The infamous and disastrous charge of the Light Brigade is perhaps the best-known incident of the war.

Italian unification

At that time Italy was divided into separate kingdoms and states with a number of different rulers. The north-eastern part of Italy was under the control of the Austrian Empire. Between 1848 and 1871 Italy was unified into the single state that exists today. 1859 was the start of a particularly crucial period in this process.

Demand for and resistance to further parliamentary reform

Why was it 1867 before a further reform of Parliament took place?

As early as 1851 the Whig prime minister Lord John Russell suggested to his Cabinet that the Government look at proposing further parliamentary reform. He met strong resistance however from his colleagues and particularly from Lord Palmerston, the foreign secretary. As a result Russell shelved the idea but he remained convinced that the 1832 settlement could not be expected to last indefinitely. However, following the Whig Government's split in 1852 which caused Russell's resignation, it was Palmerston who gradually emerged as the party's leading figure, becoming prime minister during the Crimean War. As a result Russell did not become prime minister again until Palmerston died in 1865. While Palmerston lived, the Whigs, officially known as the Liberal Party from 1859, would not take on the issue of reforming parliament again.

Palmerston had been a Tory minister in the 1820s. He had originally opposed parliamentary reform but changed his mind in 1830 and agreed to join the Whig Government to pass a limited reform that would prevent revolution. Though he opted to stay with the Whigs after the Reform Act was passed, he never changed his basic conservative ideas.

- He took seriously the pledge that the Government gave in 1832 that the Reform Act was a 'final and irrevocable' solution to the crisis situation that had arisen over parliamentary reform.
- He was no democrat – he did not believe that the working classes were fit for participation in the political system.
- He realised that the terms of the 1832 Act had left the Whigs or Liberals as the dominant party in British politics. Political self-interest meant that changing the system might disturb that.

There were a number of factors working against the idea of further parliamentary reform before 1865 and Palmerston's opposition was only one of them.

- Although the Conservative Party could not form majority governments from 1846 to 1865, it remained numerically strong in the House of Commons and it opposed further reform.
- Therefore for reform to have a chance of success the Whigs, radicals and Peelites needed to be united behind the idea. However, at least 60–70 Whig MPs agreed with Palmerston. The Peelites were also opposed.
- The House of Lords was firmly against any further parliamentary reform so any attempt would have needed to be strong enough to force the measure on the Lords, as had been done in 1832.
- Even the radicals were divided over whether only better-off working-class men should get the vote or whether to aim for universal adult male suffrage.

Overall it can be argued that Palmerston may have been the single most important factor in preventing further parliamentary reform before 1865 simply because he held such political authority. A significant support for this interpretation is that once he died in 1865 his successor as prime minister, Russell, who had long been in favour of further reform and was now supported by Gladstone, introduced a new reform bill in 1866. This would have given the vote to some better-off working-class men. However, this bill was defeated when the anti-reform Liberals rebelled. This shows that, even without Palmerston on the scene, achieving further reform was not going to be easy. It is clear that up to 1865 the majority of MPs, and an overwhelming majority of peers, were against the idea of further parliamentary reform. Therefore the argument that Palmerston was simply at the head of this general opposition is also a perfectly sustainable interpretation.

KEY DATES: THE POLITICAL SYSTEM IN THE MID-NINETEENTH CENTURY

1832 Great Reform Act passed.

1837 Queen Victoria ascends the throne.

1841 Peel leads the Conservative Party to victory in the general election.

1846 Conservative Party splits.

1859 Official formation of the Liberal Party with Lord Palmerston as leader. Palmerston makes it clear he will not agree to further parliamentary reform.

1865 Palmerston dies.

1866 The Liberal Government tries to pass a parliamentary reform bill but is defeated.

2 Gladstone, Disraeli and the beginning of democratic politics

The 1850s and 1860s saw the rise to political dominance of the Liberal William Gladstone, and the Conservative Benjamin Disraeli. Neither of these men was a democrat in any meaningful sense of the word, yet the social and political forces that were developing around them and the political parties they led were such that democratic ideas began to force their way onto the political agenda.

Gladstone, Liberalism and the development of the Liberal Party

How important was Gladstone to the development of the Liberal Party in the period 1851–74?

Gladstonian Liberalism

Gladstone's impact on the development of the Liberal Party was immense. The political philosophy he brought to it and tried to impose on it has become known as 'Gladstonian Liberalism'. Historians argue about two things:

- how far Gladstone succeeded in shaping the party into what he wanted it to be
- how far his influence was negative rather than positive.

First, it is important to establish what exactly is meant by Gladstonian Liberalism. His political ideas were shaped by:

- his deep religious convictions – he could only justify his involvement in politics to himself if he could see that it served God's will in some way
- his idea that he had some kind of rapport with ordinary people
- his belief that 'missions' or great moral issues were good for society and politics
- his belief that government had to be conducted along moral lines.

His political philosophy can be summed up as follows:

- Good government meant minimum intervention from above and maximum freedom left to the individual.
- Good government was prudent in its spending and did not waste the taxpayer's money.
- Free trade was the only sound and moral economic system for a civilised country.
- Reform of abuses or out-of-date practices was best carried out by the individuals or the institutions involved on a voluntary basis. Only if voluntary action failed should government intervene to bring about a satisfactory reform.
- Unfair privileges which protected particular groups against competition were damaging not only to society and/or government but also, in the long run, to those who were unfairly protected – Gladstone mainly had in mind here the aristocracy.
- The Anglican Church was the most perfect form of worship revealed by God but other faiths and other Christian denominations must be respected and shown an example by the Anglican faith.

NOTE-MAKING

Use the headings and questions in Section 2 to make brief notes on Gladstone and Disraeli and their impact on their parties and Britain's political system. Structure your notes with headings, sub-headings and sub-points to make them easy to navigate and use (see page x for further guidance).

For example, the following headings could be used to summarise the key points on pages 9–16:
- How liberal was Gladstone in his ideas?
- What criticism of him was there in the Liberal Party?
- What impact did Disraeli have on the Conservative Party?

● Society was naturally hierarchical in nature and the traditional ruling classes were best fitted to hold the reins of government, but aristocracy and the wealthy elites had a duty not to put their own selfish interests before those of the wider community.

These views clearly illustrate that Gladstone was really very conservative in most of his ideas. There was also plenty of potential contradiction in his ideas: How far should intervention go if there was a case for it? What exactly was an abuse or an out-of-date practice? How far should individual freedom outweigh the wider public interest? All this worried Gladstone a great deal. The social reforms of Gladstone's first two governments, 1868–74 and 1880–85, are discussed in detail in Chapter 2. However, there is hardly a single piece of reform legislation passed by those governments which cannot be said to have offended the strict principles of Gladstonian Liberalism as well as having derived some influence from them. All the reforms carried out by his Governments caused Gladstone doubts because one way or another they all compromised his beliefs as well as conformed to them. For Gladstone, in every case it was the overall balance of the effect or the sheer

William Ewart Gladstone, 1809–98

Gladstone came from a wealthy business family based in Liverpool. He attended Eton and then Oxford, was a brilliant scholar and extremely religious. He hoped for a career in the Church of England but accepted his father's demand that he enter politics and advance the family's interests and status. As a young politician Gladstone was noted for his extreme Tory views on most issues. In the 1833 reformed parliament Gladstone sat as the member for Newark, a constituency under the control of the Duke of Newcastle who was a leading Tory. The Duke and Gladstone's father had agreed to share the election costs. Lord Macauley, a liberal-minded Whig politician and historian at the time characterised Gladstone as 'the rising hope of those stern unbending Tories'.

Gladstone's ultra-conservatism however began to moderate in the 1830s and 1840s under the influence of Sir Robert Peel. Peel saw Gladstone's great ability and gave him a junior government post in his 1834–35 administration. In 1841 when Peel returned to power he made Gladstone vice-president of the Board of Trade and two years later he was promoted to president. In 1845–46 Gladstone became Peel's colonial secretary and an important supporter in the fight to secure the repeal of the Corn Laws. Peel's resignation and the split in the Conservative Party appalled Gladstone and for a while he contemplated giving up politics altogether – an idea which he rejected, but which he considered again and again throughout his career.

In the 1850s, with Peel dead, Gladstone faced a choice to return to the recovering Conservative Party under Lord Derby or move towards the Whigs led first by Lord John Russell and then by Palmerston. Gladstone disliked Palmerston because he saw his aggressive style of foreign policy as immoral. Even worse, Palmerston's adulterous lifestyle and relationships with much younger women offended his strict religious principles. However, a return to the Conservatives was an even more offensive prospect. This would have meant that he would be working alongside Benjamin Disraeli who had now emerged from obscurity to a leading position alongside Lord Derby. Gladstone detested Disraeli for the leading role he had played in attacking and whipping up opposition to Gladstone's revered Peel in the 1840s. Gladstone therefore swallowed hard on his distrust and dislike of Palmerston and became, in some ways, the unlikeliest of Liberals.

necessity of change which was the final argument that made him throw his weight behind a measure or at least allow it to go ahead. This constant tension between Gladstone's principles and the practical needs of running a government and reforming the country created considerable problems within the Liberal Party. More traditional 'Whig' Liberals felt Gladstone was too radical at times. However, genuine radicals in the party took quite the opposite view.

Gladstone in the period 1874–80

In 1874 the Liberals were defeated in the general election. Gladstone took this as a sign that he could no longer play a useful role in politics and in 1875 he retired from the party leadership. However, although he stopped attending Parliament he did not resign his seat as an MP. In 1876, outraged by what he saw as Disraeli's immoral attitude to foreign policy, he became active in politics again. In 1880 he decided to contest the general election in a Scottish constituency, Midlothian, where there was a strong chance of overturning the existing Conservative MP. Gladstone, now in his seventies, turned the Midlothian campaign into a national crusade against Disraeli's government. The Midlothian campaign has sometimes been presented as a milestone in democratic politics, with Gladstone campaigning all over the country appealing to the widened, and secretly voting, electorate from 1867. In reality this is an exaggeration. It is true that the Liberal Party felt obliged to accept Gladstone back as leader but that was due more to the force of his personality than the nature of his campaign. Also, and a point generally ignored, Gladstone did not trust the democratic process to see him elected at Midlothian. He therefore also stood for election in Leeds, a totally safe Liberal seat which guaranteed his place in the Commons should the Midlothian campaign have failed. The Leeds seat was then passed to Gladstone's son Herbert who had failed in his attempt to win a seat in Middlesex. This is hardly a good example of the advancement of democracy.

Disraeli's foreign policy

In 1875 army units of the Islamic Turkish Empire slaughtered around 12,000 Christians in Bulgaria, which was then part of the Turkish Empire and had rebelled against Turkish rule – many women and children were among the dead. Disraeli believed good relations with the Turkish Empire was a vital British interest so he played down the seriousness of the atrocities. Gladstone condemned this as an immoral response.

Joseph Chamberlain and the radical challenge to Gladstone

What impact did Joseph Chamberlain have on the Liberal Party?

When Gladstone formed his government in 1880 he was forced to accept Chamberlain into the Cabinet because of his immense reputation among the radical Liberals and the sheer weight of his influence. Gladstone disliked Chamberlain and refused to offer him more than the presidency of the Board of Trade, a junior post which was not always accorded Cabinet-level status.

Chamberlain was appalled by Gladstone's indifferent attitude to social reform and his 'obsession' with Ireland. Chamberlain was not opposed to improving the state of Ireland but he did not see it as a separate issue: to him Ireland needed to be seen within the context of social problems across the whole UK. Nevertheless he supported Gladstone's Second Land Act of 1881 on the grounds that it brought Irish tenant farmers into closer alignment with the rest of the UK.

As President of the Board of Trade Chamberlain brought in an Electric Lighting Act which allowed town councils to establish electricity supplies and an Act to ensure fairer wages for seamen. He also passed an Act to control the safer shipment of grain and attempted to bring in legislation to regulate shipping to prevent insurance scams known as coffin ships, a problem that was becoming a national scandal at the time. In this last

Coffin ships – Ships that were basically unseaworthy and were sent to sea with the intention that they would sink and allow an insurance claim to be made.

Joseph Chamberlain, 1836–1914

Joseph Chamberlain was born in London in 1836, the son of a prosperous shoemaker and nonconformist by religion. As a nonconformist he could not go to public school or university so was educated at University College School in London, the premier school for nonconformist families at that time. He left aged sixteen. In 1854 at just eighteen he was sent to Birmingham to represent his father in a new venture, making metal screws, and from humble beginnings Chamberlain built a business empire on an international scale including significant connections in the USA – two-thirds of all metal screws made in the UK were made by Chamberlain's company. By his late thirties Chamberlain was a multi-millionaire by modern calculations. He retired from business affairs in 1874 to concentrate on politics.

He first entered local politics in Birmingham. As a town councillor of the city from 1869 and subsequently as mayor in 1873–75, he oversaw a massive programme of civic improvements which brought lighting, clean water supplies, gas supplies, slum clearance schemes, schools, drainage and sanitation to the rapidly expanding urban area. At the same time he projected himself as a national Liberal politician through the National Liberal Federation and in 1876 became an MP for Birmingham. By 1880 he was so prominent in the party that he was given a Cabinet post. Chamberlain died in 1914 having suffered a debilitating stroke in 1906.

measure however he was defeated by influential members of his own party who forced the Cabinet to withdraw the bill. He also pushed for further parliamentary reform. His aim was to secure universal adult male suffrage but he could not get Gladstone to agree to this. In the end, the 1884 Reform Act gave male householders the vote in counties, bringing them into line with the borough householder vote of 1867.

Chamberlain believed that the 1880–85 Government had become a lost opportunity for extensive social and political reform and was determined to re-establish the Liberal Party as the party of social progress and greater democracy, especially after the Conservative social reforms of 1874–80. He therefore published a radical programme of reforms which he intended should become the official Liberal manifesto. The programme offered:

- universal adult male suffrage
- salaries for MPs – paid by constituents
- equal-sized constituencies
- free primary education
- dis-establishment of the Church of England – to achieve religious equality
- graduated income tax with higher rates for the wealthy
- free land grants for agricultural labourers – waste and derelict land to be bought by local authorities under compulsory purchase powers
- more protection in civil law for trade unions
- a reformed local rates system with higher taxes for the wealthy

- a new system of local government including elected councils for the counties and a National Councils Scheme for Ireland with an elected central board in Dublin
- increased and compulsory powers for local authorities to develop slum clearance schemes.

Chamberlain summed up the programme as follows:

'The community as a whole, co-operating for the benefit of all, may do something … to make the life of all its citizens, and above all, the poorest of them, somewhat better, somewhat nobler, somewhat happier.'

Basically the radical programme proposed, as another leading radical ally of Chamberlain put it, 'the intervention of the state on behalf of the weak against the strong, in the interests of labour against capital, of want and suffering against luxury and ease'. Chamberlain, in another speech, sought to drive home the point in language which seemed to some to go too far:

'Private ownership has taken the place of these communal rights and this system has become so sanctioned by law and custom that it might be very difficult and perhaps impossible to reverse. But then I ask, what ransom will property pay for the security which it enjoys? What substitute will it find for the natural rights it has ceased to recognise?'

> Why would Chamberlain's ideas, as expressed in these quotations, have offended Gladstone?

By using the term 'ransom' Chamberlain seemed to be using the threat of social disorder as a weapon. He recognised this himself and in subsequent speeches substituted the word 'insurance' instead. However, the damage was done and critics accused Chamberlain of revolutionary socialist leanings. This was untrue. Chamberlain most certainly believed in the rights of private property and their extension as wide as possible. He was not a socialist and indeed conceived that the radical programme was a counter to socialism. Gladstone rejected the radical programme out of hand and it therefore became known as the 'unauthorised programme'.

Chamberlain's frustration with Gladstone grew in 1886 when Gladstone formed his third government with the specific aim of passing Irish Home Rule. Gladstone hoped that he might be able to exclude Chamberlain, but his senior colleagues insisted that Chamberlain must be offered something. Gladstone finally offered Chamberlain the post of President of the Local Government Board hoping that Chamberlain would reject this as too junior a post. Chamberlain saw through the ploy however and accepted, seeing that it offered scope for reform proposals.

Gladstone's decision on Home Rule for Ireland (see page 25) split the radicals of the party with some following Chamberlain and others remaining loyal to Gladstone. The National Liberal Federation (NLF), which Chamberlain had created, also stayed loyal to Gladstone. Chamberlain was forced into a rather unnatural alliance with the conservative Whig element of the Liberal Party which had also rebelled against Home Rule. These two elements then created the Liberal Unionist Association. To try to maintain a separate radical identity, Chamberlain also created a National Radical Union as a direct rival to the NLF. Though there were attempts to reconcile the rebels and the mainstream Liberal Party up to 1889, Gladstone's insistence on remaining as leader and Chamberlain's refusal to accept Irish Home Rule as Liberal policy made this impossible. As will be seen in Chapter 3, by the early 1890s the 'Liberal Unionists' were effectively the allies of the Conservatives.

Disraelian conservatism and 'Tory democracy'

How important was Disraeli in the development of the Conservative Party, 1851–80?

Disraeli's impact on the Conservative Party

In 1867, after he had masterminded the passage of the Second Reform Act (see pages 17–19), Disraeli made a comment that has become famous. 'Yes,' he said 'I had to educate our party'. The comment was specifically about the issue of political reform, however subsequently it has been used to discuss Disraeli's wider impact on the Conservative Party. The implication of the premise that Disraeli 'educated' the Conservative Party is that Disraeli was consciously schooling or training the party in new ideas; making Conservatives rethink their basic political principles and adopt (by implication) newer and better ones more suited to the times.

Benjamin Disraeli, 1804–81

Disraeli was the son of a well-known writer and literary critic, Isaac Disraeli. Though relatively wealthy, Isaac Disraeli did not possess the vast wealth of the Peels or the Gladstones and he had little connection with, or interest in, the political world. Consequently when his son turned his attention to politics there was little he could do to assist him.

Disraeli was sent to train for the law but eventually gave up the training. In a series of attempts to achieve independent wealth to support a political career he borrowed money to invest in a number of dubious business ventures. Before long Disraeli was hopelessly in debt. These debts stayed with him

well into middle age and his life was a long cycle of borrowing and repaying debts. Only his marriage to a wealthy widow and his eventual political fame helped him to escape his debts.

Disraeli unsuccessfully contested elections in 1832 and 1834 as an independent radical Tory. In 1837 he finally secured election for the two-seat constituency of Maidstone, in partnership with a Mr Wyndham-Lewis whose wife Disraeli had impressed. Disraeli later married Mrs Wyndham-Lewis after her husband died. From 1841–47 Disraeli represented Shrewsbury. In 1848, after two years of negotiation, he bought a country estate in Buckinghamshire with a loan from the immensely wealthy Conservative peer the Duke of Sutherland. He sat as MP for Buckinghamshire from then on until he took a peerage as Earl of Beaconsfield in 1876.

Disraeli became notorious in the 1830s for a string of relationships with married women, one of whom sensationally committed suicide when the affair ended. His financial dealings were suspect and his debts left him in perpetual fear of prosecution. He dressed outlandishly and wore his hair long and in artificially created ringlets – all much against the mood of the time. However, he began to carve out a reputation for himself as an effective backbench speaker, but when Peel formed his government in 1841 and reshuffled it in 1843 there was no place for Disraeli. Only the great clash with Peel in 1845–46 propelled him into a leadership role. Following the retirement of Lord Derby in 1868 Disraeli finally became leader of the party and prime minister. In 1874 he led the party to its first clear general election victory since 1841. In the 1880 general election he was defeated and he died in 1881.

To evaluate the validity of this view there needs to be some comment on what it was that Conservatives allegedly stood for, or against, prior to allegedly undergoing this treatment at Disraeli's hands. There is some substance to the idea that Conservatives in the 1850s and early 1860s had become rather passive in their politics. The two-thirds of the party which had split from Peel in 1846 certainly had little natural inclination for reforms. They had seen enough of that under Peel and had not liked what they had seen. There had never been any great enthusiasm among Conservatives, including Peel, for the idea of government directly intervening with legislation to deal with social problems. Those Conservatives who favoured social reform, and there were more than is sometimes realised, tended to the view that individual MPs had the responsibility to propose reforms to Parliament. There was also a strong resistance to the idea of extending the right to vote to wider classes. Given these factors there is some clear ground for the idea that Disraeli did seek to take the party in a new direction within the period stated. That, however, is not the same thing as claiming that he actually changed their basic views by a process of re-education.

In 1872, under pressure to show that he was still a viable leader, Disraeli embarked on a series of speeches. Two major public ones were made at Manchester and the Crystal Palace in London and others were at smaller party meetings. There is no doubt that this was a new direction. His audiences for these speeches were from the newly formed and still rather struggling National Union of Conservative and Constitutional Working Men's Associations. This had been formed in 1867 to promote the appeal of the Conservatives to the newly enfranchised working-class voters of the boroughs (see page 17). Disraeli's speeches attracted attention in the press, but it is much less certain how far his focus on social reform was enthusiastically embraced in the party. A further point is that although Disraeli raised dealing with social problems as an aim of the party, he failed to deliver any specific proposals for social reforms. Much of what he had to say was routine denunciation of Gladstone and the Liberal Government and only a very small part of each speech was devoted to the 'new direction'.

The details of the social reform policies introduced by Disraeli's Conservative Government 1874–80 are discussed in Chapter 2. The bulk of the reforms were carried out in 1875–76 under the initiative of Richard Cross, the home secretary, who used existing government reports by senior civil servants over the previous twenty years. It is well-known that Disraeli had absolutely no firm proposals to offer his Cabinet in 1874. He did 're-educate' his Cabinet on trade union reform, insisting on concessions to the unions over picketing in the face of some fairly firm reluctance on the part of his colleagues. He also supported Cross over interventionist social reform legislation, much of which was little to the taste of the majority of the Cabinet. Once the ideas in the government reports had been pillaged, however, the Disraelian cupboard was bare. In the 1880 election campaign it did not even occur to the Conservatives to claim the credit for their legislation.

Disraeli encouraged the reorganisation of the Conservative's Central Office though the actual work was carried out by Sir John Gorst. More elections were contested by Conservative candidates in 1874 than in 1868, perhaps as many as 50 more. Disraeli's biographer Robert Blake observed that 'in 1872 and 1873 Disraeli was able to do something that no Conservative leader had done since Peel; to present his Party as having not only a distinctive colour and style, but also a broad-based appeal'. Of course this very much refers to how the party was projected by Disraeli, and leaves open the question of how far he had really remodelled it.

To sum up, there is a strong case for saying that Disraeli took the Conservative Party in a new direction, even if it might legitimately be said that at times he was not entirely clear himself as to which particular direction that was! It is much less certain that he ever re-educated, or even seriously attempted to re-educate, the party as a whole. At times he put pressure directly on Cabinet colleagues or party officers for the acceptance of particular policies. He understood the need for some kind of party discipline within the parliamentary party and the need for effective and sustained opposition.

Source A Adapted from a speech by Disraeli in 1872. Quoted in *Gladstone, Disraeli and Later Victorian Politics* by Paul Adelman, Longman, 1974, pp. 88–89.

Gentlemen, I think that the Tory Party, or as I will venture to call it, the National party, has arrived at the conclusion that it is its first duty to maintain the power and prosperity of the country. There is another great object of the Tory Party – to maintain the institutions of the country because to them we ascribe the power and prosperity of the country. Another great object of the party and one not inferior to the upholding of our institutions, is the elevation of the condition of the people.

Source B Adapted from the memoirs of Richard Cross, home secretary in the Disraeli Government, 1874–80. Quoted in *Gladstone, Disraeli and Later Victorian Politics* by Paul Adelman, Longman, 1974, pp. 89–90.

When the Cabinet came to discuss the Queen's Speech, I was, I confess, disappointed at the want of originality shown by the Prime Minister. From all his speeches I had quite expected that his mind was full of legislative schemes, but such did not prove to be the case; on the contrary, he had to rely on the various suggestions of his colleagues, and as they themselves had only just come into office, there was some difficulty in framing the Queen's Speech.

> Read Sources A and B and answer the following questions:
> 1 What is Disraeli referring to when he speaks of the 'institutions of the country'?
> 2 Which of these two sources do you find more valuable in making an assessment of Disraeli's contribution to the Conservative Party and why?

Disraeli's final legacy to the Conservative Party

Disraeli died in April 1881. Though his health had been failing for some years he was remarkably active in the House of Lords during 1880 and between the election defeat and his death he wrote a number of papers and made several speeches in the House of Lords setting out what he saw as the priorities for the Conservative Party in the future. High on his list was the issue of the defence of the rights of property, which Gladstone, through his land reforms in Ireland, was seen to be threatening.

Echoing Peel's strategy back in the 1830s, Disraeli advocated the broadening of the party to attract dissident Liberals. He saw the potential for this in 1880 when more than 50 Liberal MPs voted against Gladstone's Irish Compensation Bill and it passed the Commons only on Irish votes. A leading Liberal peer, Lord Lansdowne, defected to the Conservatives on the issue. This foreshadowed the eventual split with the Liberal Unionists in 1886 over Irish Home Rule. At the same he emphasised the need to increase the party's appeal to working-class voters. After his death a group of more progressive conservatives set up the Primrose League, aimed at spreading conservative principles particularly among working-class men – the primrose was Disraeli's favourite flower. The Primrose League reached a peak of 1 million members by 1891 and though its popularity declined in the twentieth century it was not disbanded until 2004.

Finally, and of immense significance for the future, Disraeli laid great stress on the maintenance of the integrity of the House of Lords. He made a great deal of this in 1880, arguing that the Lords must exercise a restraining influence on radicalism while taking care to avoid an actual constitutional crisis which might call its constitutional position into question. Later, Disraeli's successor, Lord Salisbury, laid particular stress on this and it was central to his thinking in creating first an alliance and then a coalition government with the Liberal Unionists. However, Salisbury's caution in constitutional matters was not followed by his successors (see page 20).

Parliamentary reform and its impact

Why did the Conservatives pass a radical measure of parliamentary reform in 1867?

With Palmerston dead, the new prime minister Lord Russell (he had become an earl in 1861) and Gladstone, the leading Liberals in the Lords and Commons respectively, agreed to introduce a new reform bill (1866) to give the vote to a strictly limited number of working-class men in borough constituencies – overall about 400,000 new voters. This was opposed by the Conservatives and a minority of Liberals who stuck to the Palmerstonian line. As a result the Liberal Government was defeated and resigned. Lord Derby then formed a new minority Conservative Government. Officially the Conservatives opposed reform but the prospect of it in the Russell–Gladstone bill had raised expectations in the country. Demands for reform had been increasing for years and a Reform League founded in 1865 was holding meetings all over the country. Derby realised that to stand against reform completely was impossible.

At first Derby and Disraeli were inclined to play for time, promising to look at the issue later. Even before they met Parliament, however, it was clear this was not going to work, and both Derby and Disraeli had begun to moderate their opposition seeing that this might be a chance to win greater support for the Conservatives as a party of reform and end their permanent minority status. However, agreeing a proposal that satisfied the ministers in the Government proved impossible before Parliament met, without the risk of resignations. As a result Disraeli faced the House of Commons in February with no bill. Instead the Government announced it would bring forward resolutions on reform – a delaying tactic. However, during the debate on the resolutions Disraeli, apparently acting entirely on his own initiative, suddenly announced that a bill would be introduced immediately. Historians have debated as to whether this was panic on Disraeli's part, fearing a defeat, or a clever move to force the party to rally round a bill and keep the opposition divided.

Once committed, Disraeli came up rapidly with a bill that he hoped would unify the party and avoid resignations, but it ended up so complex that even Disraeli had little enthusiasm for it. Realising it would lead to the defeat of the Government and resignation, he and Derby agreed to introduce a more radical bill than the Liberal Government had proposed the previous year. This led to three resignations from the Government, but Derby and Disraeli rode out the storm. However, Disraeli's minority position in the Commons meant that he was constantly in danger of losing a vote. Consequently he adopted a flexible approach to amendments proposed in the House whenever he saw the possibility of defeat. As a result, the bill became gradually more and more radical in its terms until by the summer it passed the Commons it gave the vote to all male householders in the boroughs of England and Wales (Scotland and Ireland got their own Acts to bring them into line in 1868). Derby then piloted the bill safely through the Lords.

The terms of the Second Reform Act, 1867

The terms of the 1867 Act were far more radical than those envisaged by Russell and Gladstone in 1866. The main provisions were:

- In boroughs the vote was given to all male householders – owners and tenants alike. They had to have been resident in the borough for at least a year and paid their rates.
- Male lodgers who were not householders but paid £10 a year rent or more also had the vote.

- In counties all ratepayers who paid £12 a year or more received the vote and the copyholder and leaseholder qualifications were lowered to £5 a year.
- Over the previous 35 years since the 1832 Reform Act, the size of the electorate had risen due to population increase and increases in the value of property, from around 800,000 to 1.3 million. As a result of the 1867 Act it almost doubled to 2.5 million.

Seats were also redistributed:

- Those boroughs with a population of less than 10,000 now had one MP rather than two. This meant 45 seats could be redistributed.
- Twenty-five seats went to the counties.
- Fifteen went to boroughs that had not previously had an MP.
- One seat went to the University of London – Oxford and Cambridge universities had always had two MPs each.
- The four major cities of Manchester, Birmingham, Leeds and Liverpool were given a third seat – though voters could still only vote for two candidates.

The 1867 Reform Act applied only to England and Wales. As in 1832 separate Acts were needed for Scotland and Ireland. These were passed in 1868. The terms were the same for Scotland, but in Ireland borough voters were required to be £4 ratepayers.

Historical interpretations of the 1867 Reform Act

So how can the eventual radicalism of the Second Reform Act be explained? Several theories have been put forward. One version argued that Gladstone manipulated events in 1867 from the opposition benches. Clearly this interpretation relegates Disraeli to the background, but this theory is now largely discounted. Gladstone did not even attend some of the debates; he did not propose any of the key amendments and did not approve of the eventual terms. Another explanation is that pressure from outside Parliament forced Derby and Disraeli to concede radical demands. There is some evidence to support this idea. The Reform League headed by the ever-energetic John Bright was active. There were disturbances at Hyde Park following meetings to demand reform, but these were nowhere near as alarming or organised as the riots and radical threats that occurred at the time of the 1832 Reform Act.

The American historian Gertrude Himmelfarb presented 1867 as the triumph of Disraeli's own political ideas – Tory democracy – and that the Act was the result of political calculation on his part. However, it is clear that Disraeli did not plan the 1867 Act. There was no intention at the outset of the 1867 session even to introduce a bill. When the decision to propose a measure was taken there was total confusion in the Cabinet as to what to propose and many changes were made in the early stages. The final Act scarcely resembled the package that the Government had eventually settled upon.

A rather different but still convincing explanation is offered by Maurice Cowling. He argues that the explanation is primarily party political. The 1866 bill, he argued, would have been very damaging to the Conservatives because of the redistribution plans it contained. Derby, who had spent a lifetime in politics and who had been a member of the Whig government that brought in the 1832 Reform Act, saw this and described the bill in a letter as 'the extinction of the Conservative Party'. The exact details are complex but Robert Blake, the greatest historian of the Conservative Party, summed up his support for Cowling's view in this way:

'It is enough to say that the reduction in the borough franchise, together with the clause which added the borough leaseholders to the electorate in the surrounding county, was bound to involve Conservative losses.'

This leaves the 1867 Reform Act fundamentally as an attempt to protect the electoral future of the Conservative Party.

It is clear that Disraeli reacted to events in the 1867 session rather than leading them. His importance lay in his skill in managing a difficult position without a major defeat of the bill, which would have brought the Government down. Disraeli, of course, claimed to have 'educated' the party over parliamentary reform. The evidence is thin. It is true that he had floated the idea of a Conservative reform policy with his 'Fancy Franchises' bill in 1859, but it is equally clear that at the start of the 1867 session he had no idea that the eventual Act would be so advanced. Nor is it likely that he would have supported the eventual terms at the outset.

The reasons why the Conservative Government adopted reform in 1867 can be shown to be almost entirely strategic rather than principled. The historian John K. Walton points out that the 1867 Act removed many Liberal-supporting urban voters from the county constituencies and relocated them in boroughs, thus strengthening the hold of the Conservatives in the counties. Walton also points out that the number of county seats rose from 144 to 169 and that only minor changes were made to county voting qualifications as compared to the boroughs. Bruce Coleman argues that:

'The constituencies that the Conservatives most feared gained little from redistribution. London, which on size of the electorate, might have expected some 60 extra members, received only a handful. The established interests among which the Conservatives were so strongly represented had escaped relatively unscathed.'

The Ballot Act, 1872

The Second Reform Act had two results in terms of further reform. Giving the vote to all male householders in boroughs meant that the electorate more than doubled from around 1.1 million to 2.3 million. The vast majority of the new voters were working class. In most boroughs they were now the majority. It was therefore seen as a priority to extend and improve the working classes' education in the hope that this would insulate them against exploitation by revolutionaries. As the leading Liberal, Robert Lowe, a longstanding opponent of political reform, cynically observed, 'now we must educate our masters'. In 1870 the Gladstone Government introduced a major Education Reform Act (see page 49).

The first general election under the new voting arrangements came in 1868 and was won by the Liberals. Although this was a disappointment for the Conservatives who had hoped to reap the reward for the 1867 Act, it was in reality no more than a reaffirmation of the Liberal ascendancy that had existed since 1832. However, what became clear at the election was that new voters in both boroughs and counties could be vulnerable to pressure from employers or landlords to vote for their preferred candidates. There were many instances of complaints that tenants had been evicted or workers sacked for not voting the way they were supposed to. In 1867, as previously in 1832, the idea of voting taking place in secret had been rejected. Both Liberal and Conservative landlords and employers were guilty, but overall it seemed that Liberal candidates were more likely to lose out. Therefore there was a strong political argument for a Liberal government to act.

Private Member's Bill – A bill introduced by an ordinary MP rather than the government. In the nineteenth century this was much more common than today and sometimes governments could not stop such a bill passing even if they wished to, although more usually they were passed because the government agreed not to oppose them.

Gladstone did not approve of the idea personally. He held to the idealistic view that if a man was qualified to vote he ought to have the moral conviction to vote according to his conscience. Also many among the elite political classes still believed that the influence of the upper classes over the lower classes in matters that they were presumed not to understand, was legitimate. Even so the evidence of oppressive tactics and post-election retribution was too scandalous to ignore. Reluctantly therefore Gladstone agreed that voting in secret (or by 'ballot') was necessary. The 'ballot bill' was introduced to the House of Commons in 1870 but not by the Government. This was left to the Liberal MP Edward Aldam Leatham, whose sister was the wife of the leading radical John Bright. The bill was therefore a Private Member's Bill but it had support from the Conservatives as well as the Liberal Government. Its greatest impact would be felt in Ireland where it freed Catholic voters from pressure from Protestant landowners and employers – a result not entirely foreseen at the time.

The Ballot Act was not entirely aimed at landlords and employers using pressure to secure votes. It was also aimed at the bribery that was still evident in elections. It was still custom and practice for candidates to offer 'hospitality' in the form of food and drink – the latter in large quantities in some constituencies where the result might be close. Actual payment for votes was still not unknown. The Ballot Act checked these corrupt practices and they were virtually eliminated in 1883 by the Corrupt and Illegal Practices Prevention Act. This set strict limits on spending at elections, required detailed accounts of expenses and imposed heavy fines or prison sentences for violations.

Parliamentary reform, 1884–85

In 1884 Gladstone's government introduced a new (Third) Parliamentary Reform Act.

- It extended the vote to male householders in the counties on the same terms as had been given to borough householders by Disraeli in the 1867 Reform Act. Gladstone rejected Chamberlain's argument that universal adult male suffrage should be introduced.
- Additionally all men paying £10 a year in rent or holding land valued at £10 a year received the vote. Under these terms the total male electorate rose to 5.5 million.
- Gladstone also intended to tackle redistribution of seats but the terms were settled only after pressure from the Conservative leader Lord Salisbury who was determined to protect Conservative seats. A compromise was achieved without great difficulty. Salisbury agreed not to resist the extension of the right to vote in 1884 in return for Gladstone's agreement to the terms for redistribution to come in the following year.

The consequences of the Redistribution of Seats Act of 1885 were:

- a significant move to more equal-sized constituencies, the overwhelming majority of which elected a single MP
- boroughs with a population under 15,000 lost their MPs and were merged with their counties
- existing boroughs with a population of 15,000 to 50,000 were reduced to a single seat
- existing boroughs (23 in all) over 50,000 continued to have two seats
- larger towns and the counties were divided into single-member constituencies depending on their size.

KEY DATES: GLADSTONE, DISRAELI AND THE BEGINNING OF DEMOCRATIC POLITICS

1867 Second Reform Act passed

1868 Gladstone's first government

1872 Ballot Act introduces secret voting

1874 Disraeli's Conservative Party win general election

1880 Gladstone forms his second government following Liberals' election victory

1884 Third Reform Act

1885 Redistribution of Seats Act

▼ Figure 1 Governments from 1851–92.

Dates	Prime Minister	Party
1851–52	Lord John Russell	Whig
1852	Lord Derby	Conservative
1852–55	Lord Aberdeen	Whig/Peelite Coalition
1855–58	Lord Palmerston	Whig/Peelite Coalition
1858–59	Lord Derby	Conservative
1859–65	Lord Palmerston	Liberal
1865–66	Lord John Russell	Liberal
1866–68	Lord Derby	Conservative
1868	Benjamin Disraeli	Conservative
1868–74	W. E. Gladstone	Liberal
1874–80	Benjamin Disraeli	Conservative
1880–85	W. E. Gladstone	Liberal
1885–86	Lord Salisbury	Conservative
1886	W. E. Gladstone	Liberal
1886–92	Lord Salisbury	Conservative

WORKING TOGETHER

1 Make a list of the steps towards democracy covered in this chapter.

2 Create a mind map which summarises these steps towards democracy. Place each step in order of importance for the process, beginning with the most important at the centre top, then continuing clockwise round the page to the least important.

3 Now compare your mind map with a partner. How far are your mind maps the same? Discuss any discrepancies and justify your choices.

4 Review your list and revise your mind map if necessary.

3 The condition of Ireland and Anglo-Irish Relations, 1851–86

The relationship between Ireland and the British mainland has been a key theme in the history of the British Isles. Domination by mainland Britain has had a massive impact on the course of Irish history. Equally, however, events in and issues relating to Ireland have frequently had a major impact on British politics. In this section, after looking at the origins of the Irish Question, Irish affairs will be examined in two stages:

- the concept of Home Rule for Ireland and its implications for Britain
- the impact of Gladstone's policies towards Ireland.

In 1851 the relationship between Ireland and Great Britain was probably as bitter and tense as it had been at any time during the nineteenth century.

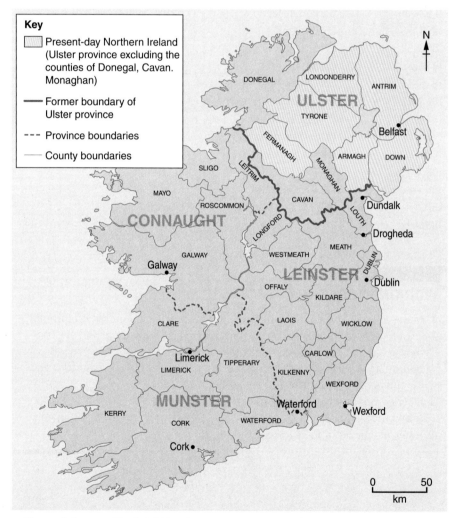

▲ **Figure 2** A map of Ireland showing provinces, counties and main towns and cities. This map shows the boundary of Ulster province established in 1921 by the Anglo-Irish Treaty.

The immediate history of the Irish Question over the course of the century thus far can be summarised as follows:

- In 1800 the Act of Union constitutionally united Ireland with the rest of Great Britain. This created a 'United Kingdom of Great Britain and Ireland'.
- Under the Act of Union, Ireland's separate parliament was abolished and 100 Irish MPs were elected directly to the House of Commons at Westminster, which increased to 105 under the 1832 Reform Act. A limited number of Irish peers were also admitted to the House of Lords.
- Although Ireland was a predominantly Roman Catholic country, the Anglican Church was established as the official state church in Ireland. This was a source of constant resentment until, in 1869, during Gladstone's first government, the Anglican Church was 'dis-established', giving it the same status as other churches in Ireland.
- In the period 1845–51 Ireland suffered from the potato blight which destroyed potato crops all over Europe. However, in Ireland the poverty-stricken peasantry depended very heavily and sometimes almost entirely on potatoes as their main source of food. As a result, around 1 million people in Ireland died of starvation and related diseases, while around 2 million emigrated. Yet all other food produce was unaffected. At the height of the famine, food in great quantities was leaving Ireland for export – it simply was not available to people who could not pay for it. Governments failed to take any effective action to combat this 'potato famine' and the anger it produced in Ireland passed down the generations.
- The north-eastern counties of Ireland comprising the province of Ulster were different from the rest of Ireland in that the majority of the population was not Roman Catholic. These Protestant-dominated (Anglican and Presbyterian) counties had been settled from Scotland and England in the sixteenth and seventeenth centuries. The landlord tenant arrangement in Ulster made them less vulnerable to the kind of poverty found in the rest of Ireland and the impact of the potato famine was felt far less. The major city of Belfast was established in the seventeenth century and rose in the nineteenth century to be the greatest industrial city of Ireland on a par with those of Britain. It had numerous industries but increasingly the shipbuilding industry took the lead. By the late nineteenth century Belfast's population was matching that of Dublin.
- The central social problem in Ireland was the depressed economic condition of the rural peasant farmers. They farmed land that was often owned by English landlords, many of whom lived permanently in England. Their impoverished Catholic tenants mostly had no security in their tenancy agreements and could be vulnerable to eviction. Farming methods were primitive and unproductive compared to England. Another factor was the impact of eighteenth-century laws imposed by Britain requiring Catholic estates to be sub-divided between all surviving sons when an owner died, rather than the system of the eldest inheriting the whole estate. These laws had long since been repealed but their effect was still felt in the small and uneconomic plots of land which many Catholics farmed.
- Gladstone went a long way towards solving the land problem with two Land Acts in 1870 and 1881 (see page 26), which, taken together, had the effect of giving tenants proper tenancy rights, protection from unfair rents and the right to sell on their tenancy as a business.

The idea of Home Rule and it implications

Why was Home Rule controversial as a solution to the problems of Ireland?

Home Rule for Ireland meant that the Act of Union of 1800 would be amended to allow for the creation of an Irish Parliament that would administer the internal affairs of Ireland separately from the rest of the UK. Under such an arrangement all matters of foreign policy, trade and national security would remain under the control of the Westminster Parliament and Ireland would still be a part of the UK. The idea arose from a campaign led by the great Irish nationalist leader Daniel O'Connell in the 1840s. O'Connell is one of the greatest figures of Irish history. His memory is preserved in the form of a great monument, which stands at the lower end of O'Connell Street in Dublin – one of the principal streets of the Irish capital. O'Connell had previously led the 1820s' campaign in Ireland to have the parliamentary oath amended so as to allow Roman Catholics to become MPs. The campaign provoked mass protests in Ireland and had led in part to the decision of the Tory Government of the Duke of Wellington to allow Catholic Emancipation in 1829. However, O'Connell's success was only due in part to the mass campaigning in Ireland. Crucially there was a majority of MPs in the House of Commons who were in favour of changing the oath. The Government therefore had no real choice but to give in.

The situation was very different when O'Connell decided to confront Peel's Conservative Government in the 1840s with a demand for the repeal of the Act of Union. The idea was completely unacceptable, not just to the Peel Government but to the Whig opposition as well, so this time there was not the slightest chance that O'Connell would succeed despite the mass demonstrations he planned in Ireland. Home Rule was, in effect, a watered-down version of this.

The problem from the British point of view was that Home Rule seemed to be nothing more than a useful platform on which to build the case for eventual separation and an independent Ireland. This was unthinkable. Economically, Ireland was seen as integral to the economy of the British Isles as a whole and thus could not be allowed to go its own way without causing disruption to the British economy. In imperial terms the independence of Ireland would have had (it was argued) disastrous effects on the unity of the empire as a whole. How could the empire be expected to remain intact if the United Kingdom itself could not do so? Most important of all was the strategic issue. Ireland lay on the other side of the British mainland from continental Europe. Great Britain could not afford to allow Irish independence as this might compromise security in the event of a war with a major continental power. Suppose Ireland decided to side with the continental power or was invaded and overrun? In those circumstances Britain would face the disruption of sea access to British ports from the Atlantic and the possibility of invasion from two sides. From a strategic point of view, Ireland's independence was out of the question. Home Rule, however, was never accepted as an objective by more extreme Irish nationalists for whom only complete independence and the setting up of a republic would suffice. This was the aim of the Fenians.

The term 'Fenian' derives from a semi-mythical Irish warrior group, the Fianna – there are references to them in medieval Irish literature. It was first used in America by a group of Irish republicans in the late 1840s, the era of the potato famine. The Fenians argued that Ireland had a right to independence from Britain and that it could only be achieved through force. Initially their activities were based in North America and involved attacks on Canada. Following the American Civil War they began to plan a revolt in Ireland itself. The revolt was postponed on several occasions but eventually went ahead in 1867. The rising in Ireland was accompanied by sabotage attempts in Britain aimed at disrupting the British response to the revolt.

The rising was not merely a failure, it was a complete fiasco. Many leaders were arrested and others fled to the USA. Three Fenians were executed in November 1867. They had attacked a police carriage in order to release two Fenian leaders being transported to prison. In the attack a police sergeant was killed. In the aftermath these Fenians were proclaimed martyrs, the so-called 'Manchester Martyrs'.

'Fenian' is often taken to include the Irish Republican Brotherhood (IRB), which was founded in Ireland in the late 1850s. In effect the Brotherhood was an Irish-based counterpart to the Fenians. However, while the Fenians could be an open organisation in the USA, the IRB was a secret society in Ireland, bound by oaths of secrecy and (supposedly) tight internal discipline. It had much the same ideas as the Fenians: independence and the creation of a democratic republic by the use of force. The actions of the Fenians were important in convincing Gladstone that Ireland must be the priority when he became prime minister for the first time in November 1868. However, one issue that neither Fenians nor Home Rulers ever really faced was the question of how Protestant-dominated Ulster could be accommodated in any nationalist agenda.

Gladstone's Irish policy, 1868–86

How successful was Gladstone in his attempts to solve the problems of Ireland?

Gladstone's approach to Ireland was based on his belief that the situation there was a moral reproach to the principles of enlightened government for which Britain was supposed to stand. To Gladstone, Britain's world mission was to provide an example to corrupt, repressive regimes elsewhere. Ireland, with its periodic mini-famines as well as the potato famine of 1845–51, its constant state of tension between landlords and tenants, religious bigotry and almost permanent suspension of civil liberties through Coercion Acts, made British pretensions to superior civilised government a mockery.

Coercion Acts – These Acts made it legal for individuals to be detained in prison without being charged and brought to trial for a specific offence.

When Gladstone finally took office as prime minister in November 1868, he was quoted as saying, 'My mission is to pacify Ireland'. He held to this objective for the rest of his political career. Gladstone's ideas on Ireland changed over time but at all stages he insisted that Ireland was a 'Liberal Crusade' that must be the main focus for the Liberal Party. Even when he retired in 1894 he still left the commitment hanging over the party for his successors. Not only that, but he was prepared to put the party through a disastrous split in 1886 over his obsession. In 1868 Gladstone believed the problem was essentially one of religion and landlord–tenant relations. He dismissed Home Rule, which was being demanded by some relatively moderate Irish MPs, as 'absurd'.

The problem of the Irish Anglican Church

The religious issue, Gladstone believed, could be solved by reforming the Anglican Church in Ireland and so appeasing and reconciling the majority Roman Catholic population. In 1869 he carried through this policy, not without opposition from within his own party as well as from the Conservatives, in the Irish Church Act. This disestablished the Anglican Church of Ireland, meaning that it was no longer the official state church in Ireland: it was no longer entitled to tax the population and its bishops no longer had a place in the House of Lords. In terms of British politics it was a radical thing to do. The opposition, especially in the House of Lords, compelled Gladstone to ask the Queen to use her influence to help it pass. She did this, but bitterly resented being drawn into the controversy. Roman Catholics in Ireland obviously approved of this but they were less grateful than Gladstone had supposed. To them the Irish Church had been such an unfair imposition on them that its removal seemed no more than the end of a great injustice, long overdue. The Act was to set the tone for much of Gladstone's future Irish policy – too little and too late for Ireland's liking – too much and too soon for Britain's. In any case, the Act did not come into effect until 1871 and by then Irish opinion had been soured by Gladstone's limited attempt to resolve the crisis in landlord–tenant relations.

The problem on the land

Gladstone saw the problems on the land as the result of too many mainly absentee landlords failing in their class duty to look after their tenants. The land issue he addressed with the 1870 Land Act. The Act was intended to address the problem of Irish tenants being vulnerable to unfair eviction from the land that supported them. Gladstone believed the Land Act would provide a stimulus for Irish landlords to mend their ways and take a more Christian attitude towards their tenants. He was no advocate of interference with the rights of property-owners unless it was absolutely necessary. The Act set up land tribunals which had the power to intervene in disputes over what was a fair rent. However, the wording of the Act meant that in reality tenants still had little protection against their landlords over rents. This became very apparent when bad economic times began to return in full force in the mid-1870s. As evictions increased a new nationalist organisation, The Irish Land League, began to organise tenant resistance to evictions and violence ensued.

When he returned to power in 1880 Gladstone was forced to accept that his Irish policies of 1868–74 had failed. Relations between tenants and landlords were worse than ever and the Irish Land League was organising rent strikes. Though officially not condoning violence it was also engaged in a campaign of terror against landlords. Since 1874 a new Irish Nationalist Party led by Charles Stewart Parnell seemed at times to be promoting not merely Home Rule but independence. In 1880 Gladstone was still rejecting the idea of Home Rule, and independence he always regarded as quite inconceivable, although he accepted that tougher action was needed to protect Irish tenant farmers from unreasonable landlords. At the same time he was determined to crack down on the 'sheer lawlessness' of the Land League. The crackdown came first. Gladstone introduced a new coercion bill aimed at curbing violence. This was to show Parliament that violence would not be tolerated and prepare the ground for a new, more radical Land Act.

In 1881 he produced a second Irish Land Act making significant concessions to tenant farmers. They were granted what became known as the three 'Fs':

- *Fixed* tenancies from which they could not be evicted so long as they paid their rent.
- *Freedom* to sell their tenancy to another if they chose.
- *Fair* rents through appeal to new land tribunals if the landowner tried to raise rents unfairly.

This Act gave much more protection to tenants and its overall effect was to greatly ease the tension on the land. Even the Land League realised this, though it continued to campaign on behalf of tenants with arrears of rent. However, land reform did not stem the political demand for Home Rule as the minimum constitutional reform for Ireland, which Gladstone persisted throughout in ignoring.

In 1882 he negotiated a deal with the Irish National Party leader and president of the Land League, Charles Stewart Parnell, to release Parnell from prison – where he had been sent under the coercion legislation. This was known as the Kilmainham Treaty. It was an informal, verbal agreement, named after Kilmainham Prison where he was being held. In return for his release Parnell agreed to use his influence to stop the ongoing violence of the Land League. Gladstone also agreed to pass a Rent Arrears Act for Ireland to help tenants who owed rents due to rent strikes organised by the Land League.

The Phoenix Park murders

For Gladstone all this was difficult as it seemed to be compromising with violence, but Parnell's influence in Ireland was so enormous that Gladstone saw he had to be brought onside somehow. Gladstone's policy had unforeseen consequences. The Irish secretary, W. E. Forster, angry at what he saw as giving in to Parnell, resigned. In his place Gladstone appointed Lord Frederick Cavendish, his nephew by marriage – he was married to a niece of Gladstone's wife. Gladstone loved Cavendish almost as a son and regarded him as his personal protégé. His promotion of Cavendish to such an important post was not well received initially, but this was soon forgotten due to a terrible event. On his first day in Dublin, Cavendish was walking through the city's famous Phoenix Park having a discussion with his top civil servant, a Roman Catholic Irishman named Thomas Burke. Burke had been targeted for assassination by an extreme nationalist fringe group of terrorists, the 'Invincibles'. The assassins had no idea who Cavendish was, but he attempted to protect Burke and soon the two men lay stabbed to death. The Phoenix Park murders made further cooperation with Parnell difficult for years to come.

Gladstone's 'U-turn' on Home Rule

Why did Gladstone change his mind over Home Rule for Ireland after opposing the idea so long?

In 1885 Gladstone's government was running into serious problems. Party morale was low and the Government could not be sure whether some Liberal MPs would attend debates or support government policies. Furthermore Parnell, impatient with the lack of progress for Ireland under Gladstone, began to oppose the Liberals in the Commons. In the summer of 1885 this situation led to a defeat over the Budget and Gladstone decided to resign. A general election could not be held until the winter because the new electoral registers needed after the 1884–85 Reform Acts were not ready. Salisbury therefore took over as prime minister of a minority Conservative government. Realising the potential of Parnell's new attitude he moved quickly to appease Irish opinion. The Coercion Acts were ended and the government set up a scheme (Ashbourne's Act, 1885) to provide government funding for loans to enable Irish tenants to buy the land they were renting from their landlords. The idea proved popular with some landlords who were fed up with continually falling rents.

Going into the election campaign Parnell was at a loss what to do. He did not really believe that there was any realistic hope of getting Home Rule from the Conservatives, but it was obvious that some constructive concessions might be achieved. The bizarre thing was that Gladstone had already concluded that Home Rule would have to be allowed for Ireland at the end of 1884 though he had no timescale in mind, nor did he think in terms of attempting it himself. Gladstone told only his wife, his sons and his friend Lord Granville, the foreign secretary. After months of further reflection Gladstone came to two momentous conclusions in September 1885: first, that Home Rule must be granted sooner rather than later; and second, that he should commit himself to the cause. Gladstone's high moral principles however meant he shrank from going public on the issue in case he was accused of bidding for the Irish vote. He was even less inclined to tell Parnell privately. On the contrary he said in a speech in November 1885 that it was essential that the result of the election should place in power 'a party totally independent of the Irish vote'. Parnell opted to support the Conservatives. On 21 November, two days before the elections began, he instructed all Irish voters in seats where the Irish National Party were not standing to vote Conservative. Not only that but he denounced Gladstone and the Liberals in aggressive terms. Across England, Wales and Scotland this is estimated to have caused the Liberals to lose between 25 and 40 seats. The results of the general election left the Liberals 86 seats ahead of the Conservatives. Parnell's Irish Party held exactly 86 seats with 18 others held by various independents. Into this confused and potentially explosive situation Gladstone's son, Herbert, chose to throw a detonator – in mid-December he revealed his father's conversion to the idea of Home Rule.

Salisbury was still prime minister and Gladstone seems to have believed that he might be prepared to take on Home Rule himself. However, though Salisbury accepted that Home Rule might theoretically be a valid argument, he had no intention of splitting the Conservatives on the issue. When he met Parliament in January, the Queen's Speech made it clear the Union would be preserved as it stood. A few days later it was announced that a new Irish Coercion Act would be introduced. The following day the Liberals introduced a motion critical of the Government's policies as outlined in the Queen's Speech. The Irish National Party abandoned the Conservatives and voted with the Liberals and the next day Lord Salisbury resigned.

Gladstone now formed a government (his third) with an obvious, but still formally unstated, intention to introduce a Home Rule Bill. Despite the enormity of the issue he refused to consult with anyone over the drafting of the bill. Its terms were finally revealed to his Cabinet colleagues late in March with the intention of introducing it early in April. It was accompanied by a new Land Purchase Bill which would further assist tenants to buy land with the aid of mortgages supplied through a massive government loan scheme requiring £120 million to be raised on government credit. Joseph Chamberlain and Sir George Trevelyan, the two leading radicals in the Government, resigned. Soon the semi-retired, but still hugely influential, veteran radical MP John Bright would signal his opposition. Some of the leading old Whig aristocrats had refused to serve in the first place. Gladstone had managed to rouse opposition from both the progressive and conservative wings of the party. He had brought about a split in the Liberal Party that would change the course of British politics forever. The details of Gladstone's attempts to bring about Home Rule for Ireland are covered in Chapter 3.

KEY DATES: THE IRISH QUESTION, 1851–86

1800 The Act of Union between Great Britain and Ireland is passed.

1845–51 The potato famine hits Ireland.

1869 The Irish Anglican Church is 'disestablished'.

1870 The First Irish Land Act gives Irish tenants limited rights.

1881 The Second Irish Land Act greatly extends tenant rights.

1886 Gladstone introduces a Home Rule Bill for Ireland, which fails to become law.

Chapter summary

- The political system was significantly changed by the 1832 Reform Act, which created a standard voting qualification in boroughs and extended the vote to the middle class.
- The Tory Party was modernised by Peel but then split into two parts due to his policies as prime minister in 1841–46, culminating in his decision to end the Corn Laws in 1846.
- The Liberal Party was formed in 1859 from the Whigs and the Conservative supporters of Peel, along with the radicals.
- The impact of two outstanding political leaders, Gladstone and Disraeli, greatly affected the way in which these two parties developed from 1868 to 1886.
- Further parliamentary reform which would allow working-class men to vote was delayed, in part due to the opposition of the Liberal leader Lord Palmerston.
- Working-class men who were householders in boroughs were finally allowed to vote by the 1867 Reform Act, which was passed by the Conservatives after the Liberals had split over the issue. All male householders were allowed to vote in 1884.
- Over the period 1867–85 the political system became more democratic through the extension of the vote to some working-class men, the adoption of secret voting and the redistribution of seats on a fairer basis over the country.
- The problems in Ireland caused Gladstone to prioritise that issue and begin attempts to 'pacify' Ireland when he became prime minister in 1868.
- The rise to prominence in the Liberal Party of the radical Birmingham MP Joseph Chamberlain created a challenge to the dominance of Gladstone's ideas.
- Gladstone's decision to give Ireland Home Rule split the Liberals in 1886.

Chapter summary diagram

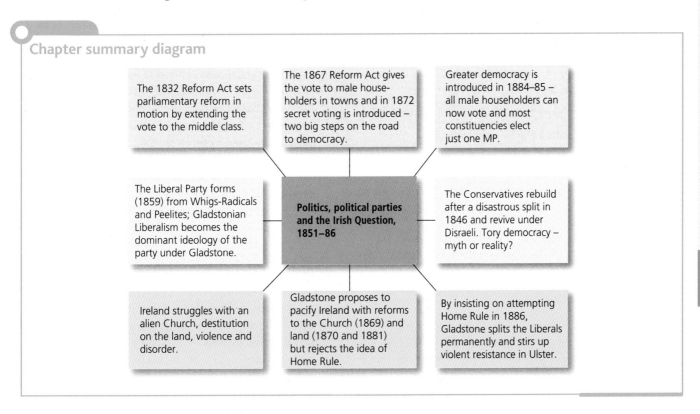

The 1832 Reform Act sets parliamentary reform in motion by extending the vote to the middle class.

The 1867 Reform Act gives the vote to male house-holders in towns and in 1872 secret voting is introduced – two big steps on the road to democracy.

Greater democracy is introduced in 1884–85 – all male householders can now vote and most constituencies elect just one MP.

The Liberal Party forms (1859) from Whigs-Radicals and Peelites; Gladstonian Liberalism becomes the dominant ideology of the party under Gladstone.

Politics, political parties and the Irish Question, 1851–86

The Conservatives rebuild after a disastrous split in 1846 and revive under Disraeli. Tory democracy – myth or reality?

Ireland struggles with an alien Church, destitution on the land, violence and disorder.

Gladstone proposes to pacify Ireland with reforms to the Church (1869) and land (1870 and 1881) but rejects the idea of Home Rule.

By insisting on attempting Home Rule in 1886, Gladstone splits the Liberals permanently and stirs up violent resistance in Ulster.

Working on essay technique: focus, structure and deploying detail

As well as learning the facts and understanding the history of the period you are studying, it is very important to develop skills in answering essay-style questions.

Essay focus

Whether you are taking the AS exam or the full A-level exam, Section B presents you with essay titles. Each question is marked out of 25.

AS examination	Full A-level examination
Section B – Answer ONE essay (from a choice of two).	Section B – Answer TWO essays (from a choice of three).

You may come across various question stems, but they all have the same basic requirement. They all require you to analyse and reach a conclusion, based on the evidence you provide.

For example: 'Assess the validity (of a quotation)', 'To what extent…', 'How successful…', 'How far…' etc.

The AS titles always give a quotation and then 'Explain why you agree or disagree with this view.' Almost inevitably, your answer will be a mixture of both. In essence, it is the same task as for the full A-level – just more basic wording.

> ### EXAMPLE
>
> Look at the following AS-level practice question:
>
> 'The Conservative Party did more than the Liberal Party to advance the cause of parliamentary reform in the period 1851 to 1885.'
>
> **Explain why you agree or disagree with this view.**
>
> **(25 marks)**
>
> This question requires you to compare the achievements of the Conservative Party with those of the Liberal Party specifically in relation to the issue of parliamentary reform. So there are two elements to the answer:
>
> - the achievements of the Conservatives
> - the achievements of the Liberals.

Each question will reflect, directly or indirectly, one of the breadth issues in your study. The questions will have a fairly broad focus.

Structuring your answer

A clear structure makes for a much more effective essay. In order to structure the question in the example effectively you should aim to have several paragraphs. In each of these paragraphs, try to deal with one factor. Remember to address the factor in the question.

It is a good idea to cover the factor in the question first, so that you don't run out of time and forget to do it. After you have covered that factor, then cover the others in what you think is their order of importance.

Remember that you also need a short but clear introduction that briefly explains your argument in relation to the question and a conclusion that provides a summary. This is a useful structure that can be applied to many questions.

Writing a focused introduction

It is vital that you maintain focus on the question from the beginning of your essay. One way to do this is to use the wording of the question to help write your argument. The first sentence in answer to the practice question, for example, could look like this:

> The view that the Conservatives did more than the Liberals to advance the cause of parliamentary reform in this period rests to a considerable extent on their having passed the 1867 Reform Act after the Liberals' own attempt had failed the previous year.

This opening sentence provides a clear focus on the demands of the question, recognising that the task is to compare the Conservatives with the Liberals. It provides a springboard for the clear essay plan suggested above. Remember, you must learn how to apply this approach to other questions you may encounter. You are not just learning how to respond to this question.

Focus throughout the essay

Structuring your essay well will help with focus throughout the essay, but you will also need to remember to maintain this throughout the piece. Here are some ideas that will help you to focus your answer.

- Use the wording of the question to help write your answer.
- Link any argument with a specific piece of evidence that supports it. This will ensure that the factual detail you include is relevantly presented.

For example, in answer to the question on page 30 you could begin your first main paragraph with:

> It can be argued that it was the Liberals rather than the Conservatives who did most to bring about parliamentary reform in this period because they raised the issue with a bill in 1866. Had it not been for this it is unlikely that the Conservatives would have considered such a policy. Even though the Liberals split and their bill failed, the very fact that they had tried made it impossible for the Conservatives to ignore the issue when they took over.

Summary

- Work out the main focus of the question.
- Plan the structure of your essay with a series of arguments focusing on the question, always staying with the stated focus.
- Use the words in the question to help formulate your answer.
- When you make an assertion always give it factual support – in other words do not simply make a claim without showing what evidence it is based on.
- Return to the primary focus of the question at the beginning of every paragraph.
- Make sure that your meaning is clear to the reader – to check this it is very helpful to have time at the end to read through your answer.

Deploying detail

As well as focus and structure your essay will be judged on the extent to which it includes accurate detail. Detailed essays are more comprehensive than essays which are vague or generalised.

There are several different kinds of evidence you could use that might be described as detail. This includes correct dates, names of relevant people, statistics and events. You can also make your essays more detailed by using the correct technical vocabulary. In this essay on parliamentary reform you could use words and phrases such as 'householder franchise' and 'universal adult male suffrage' that you have learnt while studying this subject.

ACTIVITY

Consider the following AS-level practice question:

'Gladstone's policies towards Ireland in the period 1868–86 were a complete failure.'

Explain why you agree or disagree with this view.

(25 marks)

1 Create your own brief essay plan for the answer, making a list of points you will make and setting out how these will fit into paragraphs.
2 Using your notes from this chapter, find evidence to support each of these points. It is best to use different types of detailed evidence, for example not just statistics or technical vocabulary, but also dates and specific people.
3 Write a short conclusion based on the plan you have produced.

Working on interpretation skills

Section A of the exam paper is different from Section B. Unlike Section B, it contains extracts from the work of historians. Significantly, this section tests different skills. In essence, Section A tests your ability to analyse different historical interpretations. Therefore, you must focus on the interpretations outlined in the extracts. The advice given in this chapter on interpretations is for both the AS and the A-level exams.

- For the **AS exam**, there are two extracts and you are asked which is the more convincing interpretation (25 marks).
- For the **A-level exam**, there are three extracts and you are asked how convincing the arguments are in relation to a specified topic (30 marks).

An interpretation is a particular view on a topic of history held by a particular author or authors. Interpretations of an event can vary, for example, depending on how much weight a historian gives to a particular factor and whether they largely ignore another factor.

The interpretations you will be given will often be from recent or fairly recent historians, and they may, of course, have been influenced by events in the period in which they were writing.

Interpretations and evidence

The extracts given in the exam will contain a mixture of interpretations and evidence. Aim to maintain a focus on the *interpretations* offered by the extracts rather than just the *information or evidence* mentioned in the extracts. Therefore, it is important to identify the interpretations.

- *Interpretations* are a specific kind of argument. They tend to make claims such as 'Disraeli was mainly concerned with securing power rather than genuinely concerned about the working classes'.
- *Information or evidence* tends to consist of specific details. For example: 'Gladstone's reforms were considered to be seriously limited by the radicals in the Liberal Party'.

Analysis of an interpretation

We start by looking at an individual extract and seeing how we can build up skills. This is the essential starting point for both the AS and the A-level style of question on interpretations.

The AS mark scheme shows a very clear progression of thought processes:

Level 5	Answers will display a good understanding of the interpretations given in the extracts. They will evaluate the extracts thoroughly in order to provide a well-substantiated judgement on which offers the more convincing interpretation. The response demonstrates a very good understanding of context. *21–25 marks*
Level 4	Answers will display a good understanding of the interpretations given in the extracts. There will be sufficient comment to provide a supported conclusion as to which offers the more convincing interpretation. However, not all comments will be well-substantiated, and judgements may be limited. The response demonstrates a good understanding of context. *16–20 marks*
Level 3	The answer will show a reasonable understanding of the interpretations given in the extracts. Comments as to which offers the more convincing interpretation will be partial and/or thinly supported. The response demonstrates an understanding of context. *11–15 marks*
Level 2	The answer will show some partial understanding of the interpretations given in the extracts. There will be some undeveloped comment in relation to the question. The response demonstrates some understanding of context. *6–10 marks*
Level 1	The answer will show a little understanding of the interpretations given in the extracts. There will be only unsupported, vague or generalist comment in relation to the question. The response demonstrates limited understanding of context. *1–5 marks*

Now study Extract A (on page 33) and answer the practice question below:

With reference to the extract [A] and your understanding of the historical context, how convincing do you find the extract in relation to Gladstone's impact as a political leader?

Extract A

Gladstone had begun life as the most reactionary of Tories and he never had much sympathy with democracy, equality, social improvement. Gladstone was a great 'popular' statesman because he became more and more convinced in the 'seventies and 'eighties of the 'selfishness' of the upper classes and the 'goodness' of the masses. By 1880 this had become a belief on his part that a special understanding existed between himself and the people. It was his passionate moralism that gave Gladstone his strength and weakness in politics. Everyone admits his dominating personality, his remarkable powers of work, his administrative gifts, his supreme oratorical powers both in the Commons and outside. But he was also a bad party leader and party manager, tactless and awkward with many of his colleagues, and neglecting vital issues both of policy and organisation in order to pursue, ruthlessly and relentlessly, his personal crusades.

Adapted from *Gladstone, Disraeli and Later Victorian Politics* by Paul Adelman, (Longman), 1974, pp. 6–7.

To help you answer this type of question you need to assess the interpretation in the extracts. You could carry out activities 1–5 below to help you do this, or devise your own method.

ACTIVITY

Questions on Extract A:

1 What is the interpretation of Gladstone's impact in Extract A? (Is the view of Gladstone's impact in this extract positive or negative overall?)

2 What evidence can you find in the extract to support the interpretation? (What topics are mentioned to support the interpretation?)

3 What do you know (that is, contextual knowledge) that supports the arguments in the extract?

4 What contextual knowledge do you have to contradict these claims?

5 Using your judgement, how convincing are the arguments/interpretations?

Look back at the mark scheme on page 32, and see how your answers might match up to the levels shown there.

In relation to Extract A's assertions about Gladstone's impact, you should be able to find arguments both to support and to contradict. Remember, you can apply this approach when responding to other, similar, questions.

Extract B

For a politician of Gladstone's energy, longevity, vision and administrative power his record is mixed. His greatest triumph was as Chancellor of the Exchequer. On parliamentary reform he was outmanoeuvred by Disraeli in 1866–67 and Salisbury in 1884–85. However, his cultivation of provincial Liberal support in the early 1860s, the masterly way in which he reunited the party after the debacle of the Second Reform Act, and the brilliant and innovative style of his Midlothian campaigns, reveal a political mind of extraordinary flexibility and penetration. Gladstone was completely at home in the world of 'high politics' and on the platform in the world of 'low politics'. No one had a better grasp of how these two worlds fitted together. Gladstone made mass politics into a crusade against sin. In doing so he imposed some shape and purpose on the unknowable and potentially threatening electorate enfranchised by the Second and Third Reform Acts. He was able, at his greatest, to turn the voters' attention away from their immediate material preoccupations and encourage them towards the pursuit of higher ideals.

Adapted from 'Gladstone: Politics as Crusade' by David Cooper, in *Years of Expansion: Britain 1815–1914*, ed. M Scott-Baumann (Hodder & Stoughton), 1995, pp. 293–95.

Comparing two interpretations

As part of the building up of skills, we move on to comparing two interpretations. This is the format of the AS question, but will also be useful in the process of gaining confidence for A-level students.

ACTIVITY

6 Consider the full AS-level practice question below:

With reference to Extracts A and B and your understanding of the historical context, which of these two extracts provides the more convincing interpretation of Gladstone's impact as a political leader between 1868 and 1886? (30 marks)

Follow the same five steps for Extract B as you did for Extract A, then compare the results of the two and come to a conclusion about which extract provides the most convincing interpretation.

Remember that the higher end of the mark scheme refers to 'supported conclusion' (Level 4) and 'well-substantiated conclusion' (Level 5). For Level 4 'supported conclusion' means finishing your answer with a judgement that is backed up with some accurate evidence drawn from the extract(s) and your knowledge. For Level 5 'well-substantiated conclusion' means finishing your answer with a judgement which is very well supported with evidence, and, where relevant, reaches a conclusion that reflects a wide variety of evidence.

Contextual knowledge should be used *only* to back up an argument. None of your knowledge should be 'free-standing' – in the question in Activity 6 (page 33), for example, there should not be a paragraph saying what you know about the topic, unrelated to the extracts (page 33). All your knowledge should be used in context. For each extract in turn:

- Explain the evidence in the extract, backed up with your own contextual knowledge. In this example, explain the evidence for the impact of Gladstone's leadership.
- Explain the points in the extract where you have evidence that contradicts the notion that Gladstone was a strong leader.

Then write a conclusion that reaches a judgement on which is more convincing as an interpretation.

Economy, society and social reform, 1851–86

2

This chapter covers the economic and social events that took place in Britain during the period 1851–86. It deals with a number of key areas:

- Economic developments in agriculture, trade and industry; economic ideas; how economic prosperity began to falter.
- The impact of changes in society and the problem of poverty.
- Social reform movements; government social policies and reforms; education reform and trade unions.

When you have worked through the chapter and the related activities, you should have detailed knowledge of all those areas. You should be able to relate this knowledge to the key breadth issues defined as part of your study:

- How and with what effects did the economy develop?
- How and with what effects did society and social policy develop?
- How important was the role of key individuals and groups and how were they affected by developments?
- How important were ideas and ideologies?

For the period covered in this chapter, the main issues can be covered by considering the following question:

What pressures and problems did social and economic change cause and what solutions did governments adopt?

CHAPTER OVERVIEW

This chapter covers the period 1851–86 focusing on social and economic developments, solutions that emerged, and the success and limitations of those solutions. In 1851 politics revolved around the Conservatives (Tories), the dominant party in the early years of the century, and the Liberals (Whigs) who had emerged from the 1830s as the more dominant force. Both parties understood the nature of the problems facing the country at a time of rapid and sustained social and economic change. Both were concerned that while responses were needed, the hierarchical economic and social structure should be maintained. As the political representatives, first and foremost of the economic and social elites, both parties subscribed to a philosophy known as 'political economy'. The key principle of this was that government should interfere to the least possible extent with economic matters, leaving producers to make their profits as best they could. However, the scale of social problems brought about by rapid industrialisation and urbanisation put severe pressure on these ideas. Between 1868 and 1885, three successive governments – two Liberal and one Conservative – introduced an extensive range of social reforms.

● NOTE-MAKING

Use the headings and questions in Section 1 to make brief notes on Britain's economy and the policy of free trade. Structure your notes with headings, sub-headings and sub-points to make them easy to navigate and use (see page x for further guidance).

For example, the following headings could be used to summarise the key points on pages 36–39:
● The impact of the industrial and agricultural revolutions
● The arguments for and against free trade.

1 The British economy, 1851–86

In 1851 Britain already dominated the world in terms of industrial production. Britain was in effect the 'workshop of the world' – as the other less industrially advanced nations, either by choice or because there was no other option, relied on Britain for the majority or in some cases all their industrial imports. British manufactured goods surpassed those of all other nations in quality and were either cheaper or in some cases the only products available. This made Britain the greatest economic power in the world, but it was not a situation that could be expected to last indefinitely.

Improvements in industry, trade and agriculture

Why was the economy expanding in the 1850s?

In the 1850s as trade increased, the British economy dominated the world to an unprecedented extent. It is estimated that by 1870 as much as 30 per cent of world trade was connected to Britain in some way. Britain had become the commercial capital of the world as well as the world's leading industrial power. The nation had undergone half a century of industrialisation and urbanisation on a revolutionary scale and at a pace then unprecedented in human history, becoming, in effect, the world's first industrial nation. This process is known as the Industrial Revolution. Over the first half of the nineteenth century coal production in Britain more than trebled. Imports of raw cotton went up more than tenfold in this period, fuelling a massive increase in the production of cotton products that far outstripped demand in Britain and fuelled in turn a massive export trade. From the 1830s railways began to spring up, linking important industrial and commercial centres. This in turn stimulated the engineering industry on an unprecedented scale. All these developments demanded massive increases in the use of machinery and new technologies. British agriculture also underwent a revolution. In the late 1840s machinery finally began to impact widely in the agricultural sector. The 1850s and 1860s would see a growth in investment in agriculture – rising and more varied production and farming profitability that has given rise to the expression, the 'golden age of British agriculture'. However, by the 1870s British farming was coming under pressure from world markets. By the 1880s the increased use of steam shipping and refrigeration was bringing cheap meat imports into Britain from Argentina, Australia and New Zealand. Cereals such as corn were arriving in increasing quantities from the USA, Canada and eastern Europe. For consumers these developments brought the blessing of cheaper and more varied food. For farmers it meant the challenge of increased competition.

Changing economic ideologies – free trade and protectionism

Why did free trade become the dominant economic policy between 1851 and 1865?

In the eighteenth century British governments pursued economic policy as a means of aggressively protecting the British economy from competition from other countries. This 'protectionism' involved taxes on imports, bans on the import of certain commodities and restrictions on trade and goods not transported in British ships. However, in 1776 a Scottish economist named Adam Smith (1723–90) published a highly influential book, *The Wealth of Nations*, which argued against this policy and insisted that national wealth would be best served if all such taxes and artificial barriers were removed. The first prime minister to take up the idea was William Pitt the Younger in the 1780s. However, war with France, covering most of the period 1793–1815, halted the process. Pitt died in 1806 but his influence lived on and in the 1820s Tory governments began to move back to his policies of 'freeing trade'. Among the strongest supporters of this was Sir Robert Peel and when he became prime minister with a strong majority in 1841 he moved quickly towards a free trade economic policy. Peel was facing a trade depression and a severe financial crisis which the previous Whig government had failed to cope with. He was therefore in a strong position to force through measures in the face of serious opposition from the agriculturalists who believed that British farming could not survive without protection from overseas competition. They argued that Britain would be vulnerable in wartime if British agriculture suffered the collapse they claimed was inevitable. They also maintained that the loss of employment in farming would bring about social unrest on a massive scale.

Peel reduced taxes on imports in 1842 and again in 1845 in order to make it cheaper to import raw materials, for example cotton, and therefore cheaper to produce industrial goods for export. In this way he hoped to increase profits and subsequently employment. If employment increased this would also have the effect of stabilising or increasing wages. He countered the arguments of the agriculturalists by pointing out that unemployment and low wages were already much in evidence in British farming and that competition would force farmers to farm more profitably by investing in more efficient forms of production. Peel also shifted the burden of taxation to the wealthier classes through the first ever use of income tax in peacetime: in his 1842 Budget only those with substantial incomes were taxed. His policy had the effect of reducing the cost of living for the lower classes through the reduction of indirect taxes such as tariffs and excise duties.

▲ Sir Robert Peel, Prime Minister 1834-35 and 1841-46. His flaming red hair and strong Protestant views earned him the nickname 'Orange Peel'.

In 1846 Peel's free trade policies finally split the Conservative Party when he took the step of ending the Corn Laws which protected British agriculture (see page 6). His protégé and admirer, Gladstone, saw himself as the defender of Peel's legacy and was determined not merely to protect the economic and financial reforms of 1841–46 but to extend free trade to the greatest degree possible. In his two terms as chancellor, 1852–55 and 1859–66, he systematically reduced taxes on imports and exports and on goods circulating within the country. He also oversaw a trade treaty with France in 1860. Known as the Cobden Treaty after Richard Cobden, a veteran free-trade campaigner, over the next twenty years it produced a tripling of trade with France. Overall exports rose fourfold over the course of the 1850s and 1860s. Although the majority of Conservative MPs had opposed Peel over the removal of the Corn Laws in 1846, his successor as leader, Lord Derby, officially abandoned agricultural protection as a party policy as early as 1851. By the 1860s free trade was unchallenged as the economic policy that best served Britain's interests.

The 'mid-Victorian boom' and the onset of depression

In the 1850s both British agriculture, industry and trade with overseas countries were booming. Agriculture became increasingly mechanised and profitable, though not as profitable as manufacturing. In 1857 the first steam-powered ploughs were introduced on farms. As agriculture mechanised surplus labour from the agricultural sector was being employed in industry, which was becoming increasingly specialised and mechanised. The expansion of railways, for example, led to increased demand for engine parts requiring very precise and standard components that could only be manufactured by skilled workers. The movement to the towns meant that by the time of the 1851 census over half of the population was living in urban areas. Those urban areas were showing the evidence of what the historian Asa Briggs referred to as 'an age of unprecedented prosperity'. New industrial buildings were springing up alongside new and impressive town halls. Massive ships filled the ports of London, Liverpool and Bristol. In 1858 the mighty ship the *Great Eastern* – designed by the famous mechanical and civil engineer Isambard Kingdom Brunel – was launched after four years in construction. At 18,915 tons it was the largest ship ever built and it would not be surpassed in scale until 1901.

The repeal of the Corn Laws was once seen as a key factor in agricultural prosperity in the 1850s and 1860s. However, that view has been generally discounted over time. The so-called mid-Victorian boom was across the whole economy not just the agricultural sector. As has been shown in the previous section, the repeal of the Corn Laws was only one part of Peel's strategy for reviving the British economy and dealing with the budget deficit left by the Whigs. Peel reduced taxes on imports and exports in 1842 and again in 1845. He also introduced income tax for the wealthier classes in 1842. These policies had already revived the economy before the Corn Law crisis arose. Consequently the repeal of the Corn Law, by the time it fully took effect in 1849, had only a small impact on food prices. Taxes had been reduced on all imports and on all internal sales of food by then. In addition the boom can be argued to have been due in part to Gladstone continuing Peel's policies still further in the 1850s. These policies were aimed at increasing industrial production as much as encouraging investment in agriculture. The historian Norman Gash took the view that the mid-Victorian boom was essentially driven by the growth of the industrial sector:

'Substantially the wealth of Britain consisted in its ability to make cheap cloth, iron, steel and machinery for the rest of the world and transport them to the customer in British ships. It was a unique position which could not last forever; but while it lasted Britain led the world economy.'

Another possible interpretation of the boom is that it was mainly the result of improved world trade conditions in the 1850s. As Britain was already the world's leading industrial power, the actions of British governments in promoting free trade simply helped rather than led the boom. They did encourage British farmers to invest in improving agriculture by using better methods, including more machinery and this in turn further stimulated industrial production. However, there were other factors which helped the boom take place.

- Agricultural prosperity rested not primarily on rising prices but on more efficient methods of production. Consequently for urban workers, already enjoying rising wages and sustained employment, the real price of food was actually falling and this meant that the working classes had more disposable income to spend on industrial products and better and more plentiful food, and this was also a stimulus to the economy.
- There was much more confidence in the financial system, which meant people with wealth became more inclined to invest it. In 1844, Peel had introduced reform of the banks in the form of the Bank Charter Act, improving their stability with new regulations that would underpin the British banking system until the Great War, 1914–18.
- Also in 1844 Peel introduced regulation of private companies in a Companies Act, which improved confidence that new companies were not frauds. The 1844 Act became a basis for updating the regulation of companies in all the following decades throughout the nineteenth and twentieth centuries.
- The expansion of the railway system and the improvement in telegraph communications also helped the infrastructure of the country to support economic expansion as goods could be transported quickly and cheaply all year round and information could be sent almost instantly.

All this means that interpretations vary as to what actually was the primary cause of the economic boom.

However, in the 1860s there was a sharp reminder that prosperity in Britain with its reliance on the imports of raw materials and access to export markets was vulnerable to events overseas. In the USA, after years of rising tension between northern and southern states over the issue of slavery, a civil war broke out which would last until 1865. The slave-owning southern states exported vast quantities of raw cotton to Britain to feed the production of cotton products for domestic use and export. The northern states used a blockade of southern ports as an economic weapon of war, thus creating a 'cotton famine' in the great cotton towns of Lancashire and southern Scotland. Tens of thousands of factory workers were thrown out of work or onto short-time working. In the winter of 1860–61 exceptionally severe weather led to a serious crisis in London as docks were forced to close, building projects were put on hold and supplies of material ran short, causing widespread unemployment and hardship.

Short-time working – When the amount of time worked in the week is reduced because there is not enough work available for a full week – it is an alternative to reducing the workforce and keeping those still employed on full time.

The London weather crisis, desperate though it was at the time, was purely the result of a particularly cruel winter, the end of which brought an end to the crisis. Even the 'cotton famine' crisis was a relatively short-term issue – as soon as the civil war ended supplies of cotton quickly resumed. However, in the 1870s new and more structural problems began to emerge. As technology in the form of steam ships and refrigeration allowed cheaper imports of food into the country, British agriculture began to feel the full impact of foreign competition. From around 1872, a series of short-term economic slumps followed by equally short-term recoveries set a pattern of boom and slump that would persist into the mid-1890s. This pattern, controversially known to some as the Great Depression, will be considered in detail in Chapter 4.

2 Society, class and the problem of poverty

Industrialisation and urbanisation changed British society at a pace that amazed and terrified contemporaries. By 1851 the ten-yearly census (the first was in 1800) showed that for the first time more British people lived in urban areas than in rural areas. Within the urban areas new and more complex class structures developed.

The social impact of industrialisation

Was class the most important divisive issue in British society in the 1850s?

In the new industrial towns the social elites consisted of factory owners, some of whom owned vast industrial enterprises employing thousands of workers, and professionals such as lawyers and bankers. Such men were generally regarded as a new middle class, though in terms of wealth some were soon rivalling the resources of the traditional landowning upper class. Some of the wealthiest, anxious to remove any lingering doubt as to their wealth and status, used their money to buy land and remove themselves physically and socially from their origins – the traditional option of those who made their money in towns and sought respectability in the country. However, increasingly many of these newly enriched elite urban citizens were remaining in their urban setting, seeking to civilise their surroundings and establish a social order that would replicate that of the rural hierarchies with themselves at the apex.

NOTE-MAKING

Use the headings and questions in Section 1 to make brief notes on Britain's society, class and the problem of poverty. Structure your notes with headings, sub-headings and sub-points to make them easy to navigate and use (see page x for further guidance).

For example, the following headings could be used to summarise the key points on pages 40–46:
- The social impact of industrialisation.
- Managing the challenge of poverty.

▲ Smoking factory chimneys in a nineteenth-century industrial town, from a wood engraving c.1880.

These elites faced a challenge from a new, mass working-class population that threatened to grow out of control numerically and socially. By 1851 around four-fifths of the lower classes worked in some form of industrial activity. Increasingly this activity was centred on major urban areas. Only mining remained as a large-scale industrial employer outside of direct linkage to urban areas and even here smaller urban developments were growing up as the demand for miners rose in proportion to the demand for coal. These working classes had much greater access to information and ideas than their rural counterparts. Though access to education was still restricted it was possible for working-class men, and to a lesser extent women, to learn to read and write and to improve their understanding of social and political issues. It was also easier to organise working-class activities, through for example trade unions, in urban areas. The realisation that towns had to be controlled and social order established, prompted middle-class social reformers to press for changes in how factories were regulated and who they could employ. Public health became an increasing concern in urban environments where diseases could escalate to epidemic proportions at terrifying speed.

Religious tensions

Not all social divisions were along class lines. A religious social divide also became increasingly apparent and confrontational over the course of the nineteenth century. This was the division between members of the Anglican Church and other Protestant churches that did not conform to its teachings. These nonconformists or dissenters were to be found in all classes in the urban areas and represented a force of people united by religion even if divided by class. Such churches, Methodist, Presbyterian, Unitarian, Baptist and others, did not agree with each other on all aspects of religious belief and practice, but they were united in their second-class status compared to those who accepted the Anglican version of Christianity. Not even the distrust felt by all Protestants towards Roman Catholicism could overcome these tensions between the established state Church and those who dissented from its teachings. By 1851, there remained many barriers to dissenters in British society. In 1851 a religious census was carried out covering all places of worship in existence in the country. It covered Anglican and nonconformist churches, Roman Catholic churches and synagogues. The census showed that total Anglican attendance was not much more than that of the various dissenting churches: 3,773,000 against 3,487,000. Dissenters were in a comfortable majority in many northern industrial towns like Sheffield, Leeds and Bradford, and formed a big majority in Wales.

Regional differences

While social and religious tensions were on the rise, regional differences were being steadily eroded. To be sure there were still differences in culture between the north and the south, or the West Country and Wales. Dialects in some regions seemed like a foreign language to visitors and in Wales of course there was a completely different (though not foreign) language widely spoken. Even so the general trend was towards greater integration and cohesion. The advent of the railways massively reduced travelling times and improved the accessibility of remoter regions to a large degree. Distances that had taken days to cover could now be covered in hours. The needs of railway timetables led to a standard time being adopted for the whole country for the first time. Goods could be moved as well as people. Diets that had been regionally based moved towards a more national diet as coastal produce found its way inland and vice versa. The invention of the telegraph system in the 1830s had spread by 1851 across the country, meaning that messages that had taken hours or days to send could now be transmitted in minutes. The great London newspapers – once so expensive to transport that they were available as an elite luxury – were now attracting a much wider readership.

Working-class reaction

In the 1830s and 1840s the pressures generated by industrialisation and urbanisation threatened to undermine social cohesion. The most obvious examples of this was the rise of trade union activity and the emergence of the movement known as the Chartists (see pages 45–46 for more on trade unions). Though the Chartist movement largely predates the period of this syllabus, an understanding of the movement and its aims is important to understanding later developments.

The Chartists

The Chartists took their name from a set of political demands in a document known as the 'People's Charter' written in 1836. This took the form of a parliamentary bill for working-class political rights that had been ignored in the Great Reform Act of 1832. The Chartists demanded the government pass a new Reform Act. In summary, these demands were that:

- all men have the right to vote at age 21
- property qualifications for MPs be abolished
- voting be done in secret
- every electoral constituency have roughly the same number of voters electing a single MP
- MPs be paid an annual salary of £500 (an enormous income at that time, equivalent today to over £560,000 per annum) so that they be free from corruption and so that working men could be elected
- general elections be held annually so that MPs were regularly held accountable by their constituents.

These demands had no prospect of being accepted by Parliament and the Chartists lacked the means or scale of support that would have been needed to force Parliament into acceptance. In any case the 'Six Points of the Charter', as they became known, were only the means to an end. At its heart Chartism was essentially a social and economic movement aimed at improving the material conditions of the working classes.

Chartism played a part in prompting the Conservative government of Sir Robert Peel to focus on economic and social changes in the period 1841–46. Chartism also had a long-term impact on the working classes themselves by putting particular emphasis on working-class education and personal responsibility, for example on alcohol abuse, and it also had a thriving women's movement. Though Chartism had declined by 1851 and was virtually extinct by the mid-1850s, its influence was still felt well into the future. Former Chartists were very active in the Reform League of 1865 which campaigned for a new Reform Act to give the vote to at least some, if not all, working-class men.

Managing the challenge of poverty

How cruel was the Victorian Poor Law?

In a rapidly increasing population the problem of poverty assumed greater and greater importance across the course of the nineteenth century. The 'Poor Law', the system for preventing those people who could not support themselves from dying of starvation or exposure, had been set down in an Act of 1601. In theory this was supposed to be a national system covering all of England and Wales – it predated the unions with Scotland and Ireland so never applied there. Under the system, central responsibility lay with the Privy Council, a largely symbolic institution today and even in the nineteenth century largely in disuse as an administrative force. In any case the power to administer the Poor Law on a day-to-day basis was delegated under the system to the individual parishes of England and Wales: the smallest local authority units linked to the Anglican Church – there were around 15,000 such parishes. As a result, over time different parishes developed different practices for dealing with the 'relief' of the poor. The only basic requirement under law was that every parish had to impose a tax to provide funds to support the poor. However, it is important to understand the term 'the poor' as it was then defined. This was taken to mean any person who could not support themselves to the minimum requirement to stay alive. Such a person was defined as a 'pauper'. A person might become a pauper because they were physically or mentally unfit to work, too young to do so, too old to do so, or because no work was available for them.

By the 1830s there were very great fears developing that the cost of poor relief was spiralling out of control. Some commentators argued that the Poor Law should be abolished for everyone who was able-bodied who should be forced to survive on market forces as best they could. The Whig government which came to power in 1830 addressed the issue in 1832 by setting up a Royal Commission to investigate and recommend a solution, the first ever such commission. The result was the Report of the Poor Law **Royal Commission** of 1834.

The Report of the Royal Commission

The Report concluded that relief could be safely offered to unemployed able-bodied men and women so long as the standard of living provided did not rise above that of the lowest class of independent labourer. It recommended that relief to the able-bodied be given only in **workhouses** to which they must apply for admission. Work would be expected in return for food and shelter. Workhouses would need to be 'well-regulated' and 'deterrent', with a strict regime to deter those who could work and with males and females in separate institutions – even married couples. The Report recommended that children and the old and/or infirm must be treated separately and differently to the able-bodied. Both needed shelter and in the case of children, education was needed. If able-bodied parents claimed relief then their children, whom they had failed to support, would be separated from them and sent to the appropriate institution. In order to ensure that these principles were applied universally, the Report recommended the setting up of a Poor Law Commission in London with the power to force parishes to join together as 'Poor Law Unions' to provide relief to those in need. The Government adopted these recommendations in the Poor Law Amendment Act of 1834, which set up the Commission and gave it powers to enforce its regulations. The new system of poor relief set up in 1834 is known to historians as the 'New Poor Law' or the 'Victorian Poor Law'.

Royal Commission – A formal public inquiry into a specific issue that is of major importance and usually an issue of controversy. It operates independently of the government that sets it up and once begun cannot be ended except by its own decision. The Commission must produce a report with findings, evidence and recommendations for a course of action, though the government can choose to ignore these if it wishes.

Workhouse – A place of refuge where paupers could receive food and shelter (known as 'relief') in return for doing work of some kind. The earliest reference we have to one comes in 1631. In 1723 Parliament passed an Act confirming that it was legal for parishes to demand that paupers enter a workhouse to get relief. By the 1770s there were 1,800 such workhouses, meaning roughly one in seven parishes had one.

By 1851 these recommendations had still not been fully implemented and they never were subsequently, up to the abolition of the Poor Law in 1929. Separate workhouses were rare, though segregation of the sexes, children and the aged/infirm was used inside many workhouses. The Poor Law Commission appointed paid inspectors to supervise the changes to be brought in based on the Report. Even after 1834, in some areas, especially towns, the able-bodied still got relief outside of workhouses. For temporary unemployment this was more practical and cost-effective than supporting the unemployed in workhouses. The cost of maintaining the poor remained with local rates as the central government still made no contribution to the actual relief costs. Workhouses were expensive to build and therefore even if they reduced expense in the long run it might take years to recover the initial cost. In fact it proved more expensive to provide relief inside workhouses in some areas. This was because factors such as food, heating, cleanliness, etc., were generally far better in well-run workhouses than anything the lowest paid could afford independently. Workhouse diets were dictated by the Poor Law Commission which issued instructions to workhouses showing what different meals should be served at different times of the day to the able-bodied, to children and to the sick and aged. The 'deterrent' aspect in these workhouses for the able-bodied relied on the severe discipline, loss of personal freedom and general humiliation of the individual.

During the 1850s and 1860s, with the economy booming and unemployment at minimal levels, workhouses began increasingly to cater mainly for the aged, sick and abandoned women and children with no means of support. Those who could be considered able-bodied were sometimes expected to work, though this was not universal in all workhouses. Indeed in common speech the term 'workhouse' generally gave way to the expression 'poor house'. As working-class diets began to improve in the 1850s the gap between them and workhouse diets began to close and reverse. In 1871 new dietary regulations were issued to all workhouses to bring them up to date with the higher standards.

Gladstone as chancellor of the exchequer

After Peel's fall in 1846 and his death in 1850 his free trade approach was taken up by the greatest of his political followers William Ewart Gladstone (see page 10). Gladstone was chancellor for two periods 1852–55 and 1859–65. During these periods his policies certainly coincided with rising prosperity and improved standards of living. The diet of the working classes improved considerably in the 1850s and 1860s. Unemployment was also much lower and the value of real wages rose. It is however a matter of interpretation as to how important Gladstone's policies were in bringing about these improvements. While Gladstone played a part, a general upturn in world trade and greater political stability in Europe were also important factors. It could also be argued that Peel had set the scene for improved living standards through his policies in 1841–46 during which he introduced income tax for the better-off classes and freed the lower classes from the burdens of indirect taxation on necessities such as food or fuel. It could then be argued that Gladstone was simply carrying on these Peelite policies to their logical conclusion.

Other reforms

However, Gladstone did introduce some new reforms that made a significant contribution. Perhaps the most important of these was the introduction of Post Office Savings Accounts in 1861. This enabled the General Post Office to provide simple savings accounts for ordinary workers to save money. Gladstone introduced this Act to encourage working-class families to save money for

Real wages – Defined as the value of goods or services that wages can actually buy. For example, if wages remain the same while food prices increase, their 'real' value has gone down. On the other hand if food prices fall the 'real' value of wages has risen.

their own security. Since essentially the government was acting as banker to investors it was also good for public finances. The Act set a maximum total deposit per account at £150 (today, in terms of income, you would need around £90,000 per annum to match the same figure for purchasing power so it was a significant amount). Depositors were allowed to deposit a maximum of £30 per year until they reached the maximum total. For this they received interest at a rate of 2.5 per cent per year. The Post Office Savings Bank (POSB) accounts were immediately taken up by working-class families. The success of the POSBs was important in convincing Gladstone that at least some working-class men were now fit to vote – something he had opposed previously. The scheme encouraged over 600,000 savers within two years to put money aside for emergencies and within five years total deposits had topped £8.2 million, a huge boost to public finances. In 1860, Gladstone also sponsored the Cobden Treaty with France, which resulted in British exports to France doubling. Since the British economy was very dependent on exports this was a further boost to living standards.

In his first period as chancellor Gladstone mainly concentrated on completing Peel's work but he did reduce the threshold on income tax from £150 to £100, so increasing the number of relatively wealthy taxpayers and enabling him to go further in reducing the cost of living. When he became chancellor again in 1859 there was a budget deficit due to the Crimean War but Gladstone refused to put up indirect taxes to deal with it and simply raised income tax until it was dealt with, in this way protecting living standards for the vast majority of people. While there can be different interpretations as to just how important Gladstone's reforms were, most people at the time had no doubt that they owed their improved diets and general standard of living to the 'People's William' as he became popularly known. Gladstone abolished stamp duties on newspapers in 1855, which made newspapers cheaper to buy and encouraged working-class literacy and awareness of events. The working classes were cleaner, more literate and more self-sufficient than ever before.

The Cooperative Movement and 'self-help'

Working-class self-help was also increasingly evident through non-profit-making cooperative schemes. The most influential were the Rochdale Pioneers who set up a co-operative scheme in 1844. This group of workers in Rochdale set up a shop to sell items that were normally too expensive for ordinary workers to buy – and the business expanded rapidly. The co-operative set up a model operating system known as the Rochdale Principles. These included: strictly limited returns for investors (that is, individuals would not get rich from profits); the reinvestment of surpluses into the business; democratic management; the promotion of education schemes for members and the public; being non-political and tolerant of all religions. In the 1850s and 1860s such schemes began to spread to a wide range of activities including schemes in major cities such as Leeds and Edinburgh for building good-quality affordable housing for workers. Taken together these initiatives played a key role in changing upper-class perceptions of the working classes. From having previously been seen as a dangerous and ignorant threat to social stability, the working classes were being transformed into the backbone of the country.

The emergence of trade unions

Trade unions certainly underwent a considerable period of development between 1815 and 1848 but the extent of their influence is questionable. In 1815 trade unions were still illegal. After the ban was lifted in 1824, underground unions came into the open and new ones were formed, but the process was

Cooperative schemes – These schemes involved the principle of working together rather than in competition and working to share in group rather than individual prosperity.

Cooperatives

Cooperatives were encouraged by those social reformers who raged against bad social conditions but distrusted any large-scale government intervention to deal with them. The best known, Samuel Smiles (1812–1904), wrote two highly influential books, *Self Help* (1859) and *Thrift* (1875), among many other writings which praised individual effort. In *Thrift*, Smiles approved of the Poor Law, calling it, *'one of the most valuable acts that has been placed on the statute-book in modern times'*. He also championed the Post Office Savings Banks introduced by Gladstone and the new insurance companies, such as the aptly-named Prudential Insurance Company (1848), and the non-profit-making Friendly Societies.

slow and there were many disappointments. By 1848 there were many more unions but many had failed. The extent to which they influenced economic and social change was limited, as was their role in popular protests. Nevertheless the unions of the period did start to organise labour and some tried to develop constructive social and economic initiatives in the form of schemes aimed at helping workers save to protect themselves from unemployment or setting up benefit funds. Most workers did not join trade unions in this period and many unions did not survive for very long and this obviously limited their impact. It was not really until the 1850s that unions started to become more influential.

In 1851 the Amalgamated Society of Engineers (ASE) was formed. Unlike the earlier unions, especially the schemes encouraged by Owen, this union was set up not to change society but to improve the pay and conditions of its members within the existing social and economic system. The ASE aimed to negotiate with employers on the basis of mutual interest rather than seek confrontation through strikes. The membership was already relatively well-paid by working-class standards and the union was able to charge relatively high membership subscriptions which allowed it to set up benefit schemes covering unemployment, sickness, death grants for widows and orphans and funeral expenses. Other better-off workers began to follow the ASE example and so developed what became known as New Model Unions – carpenters, shoemakers, tailors, cotton machinists and miners. In 1868 these unions met to form the Trade Union Congress (TUC), as an overall organisation to promote the interests of unions and help them avoid conflicts with employers and, perhaps more importantly, with each other.

It was not plain sailing however. The TUC was set up in part to combat problems that arose in the period 1866–67. A series of strikes in Sheffield caused concern when violence, intimidation and even some attempts at arson occurred. These became known as the Sheffield Outrages. In 1867, the Boilermakers' Society attempted to sue one of its branch treasurers who had stolen funds. Its case failed when the court ruled that its funds had no protection in civil law. Despite this and notwithstanding the fact that most unskilled workers were still not unionised, the momentum of trade unionism was maintained. The response of the Government to the problems of 1866–67 was not to crack down on unions but to set up a Royal Commission to look into the problems.

3 Social reform, 1851–86

By 1851 there had already been significant progress in terms of legislation to address specific social problems so it is important to understand something of this process in order to provide a context for later developments in the 1860s and 1870s. The 1830s saw rising concern about the widespread use of children working in the factories that increasingly dominated the textile industries, mainly cotton and wool manufactures. Evidence that children as young as five were working long hours and suffering injuries stirred the consciences of humanitarians and offended the beliefs of devout Christians. There was a strong factory reform movement agitating for textile factories to be regulated. In 1833 the Whig Government set up a Royal Commission to investigate, report on the situation and recommend legislation. The recommendations were immediately translated into the Factory Act of 1833. This landmark Act, which would affect the pattern of social legislation for decades, restricted the employment of children in textile factories.

NOTE-MAKING

Use the headings and questions in Section 3 to make brief notes on social reform legislation. Structure your notes with headings, sub-headings and sub-points to make them easy to navigate and use (see page x for further guidance).
- What was the impact of social reform movements?
- Which were the most effective policies of governments in addressing the social problems?
- Which were the least effective policies?

However, the really crucial part of the Act for the future was the requirement for inspections of factories to be carried out regularly. This meant the setting up of a professional factory inspectorate, acting under the authority of the Home Office, to carry out the inspections with the right to demand entry and the authority to act as a magistrate in case of violations. Under previous Acts there had been no effective supervision. The new inspectors were empowered to make and enforce rules and regulations on the detailed application of the Act. This was a momentous innovation. From now on all new social reform legislation came with the creation of an inspectorate to supervise it: the New Poor Law in 1834; prisons, 1836; police forces, 1839; education, 1840; mines, 1842; public health, 1848. By the 1860s all these inspectorates had expanded rapidly in number, for example only one education inspector was appointed in 1840 but by the late 1860s there were 70.

Public health issues were brought to the fore by a serious cholera epidemic in 1831–32 which killed thousands. In 1842 a government-ordered Sanitary Report was published, one of the great social documents of the nineteenth century. It recommended comprehensive, far-reaching and compulsory powers of public health regulation. In 1843 the prime minister Sir Robert Peel decided to set up a Royal Commission on the Health of Towns to look into the findings and recommendations. This reported in 1845, confirming the need for reform. It was left to the Whigs to take action after Peel resigned in the summer of 1846. The result was the Public Health Act of 1848. The Act set up a Central Board of Health with far-reaching powers to impose sanitary reforms on areas where the death rate rose above a set limit. In the 1850s and 1860s inspectors began to conduct investigations into, and to produce highly influential reports on, a wide range of public health issues covering endemic and epidemic diseases, dangerous working environments, social problems associated with child neglect and environmental pollution.

Endemic and epidemic diseases – Endemic diseases are those that are always present but not running out of control – in the 1850s measles and diphtheria would fit this category. An epidemic disease is one that is spreading rapidly such as cholera in 1831 and again in 1848–49.

Gladstone, Disraeli and social reform, 1868–85

To what extent were the social reforms in the period 1868–85 motivated by genuine concern for the working classes?

Gladstone became prime minister for the first time in December 1868 following the Liberals' victory in the general election in November. It was to be a government known to history as the 'Great Reforming Ministry'. Gladstone himself, having set up his Cabinet, claimed that it was a government of which his great mentor, Sir Robert Peel, 'would have been proud'. In terms of the sheer number of reforms passed and the scope of the different areas they covered, there can be no doubting the 'greatness' of the scale of the reforms. However, in terms of what was actually achieved and the extent to which these reforms directly improved life for large numbers of people, the picture is much less clear. Two areas of the reforms were dealt with in Chapter 1: Ireland (where Gladstone took personal charge) and the Ballot Act. In this chapter the focus will be on the social and administrative reforms which were introduced, their benefits and, perhaps as importantly, their limitations.

Gladstone has sometimes been presented as a champion of equality of opportunity for all classes. Before examining his reforms in detail it would be as well to consider this idea. Gladstone did not believe in equality of opportunity in anything like the modern sense of the expression. He did not believe all men were equal, except before God and the law of the land. He did not believe that everyone was entitled, as a basic human right, to vote, though he came to believe that all men (most definitely not women) could aspire to earn that right. He did not believe that everyone was entitled to the same educational opportunities. He did not believe that *all* privilege was wrong. To Gladstone therefore, equality of opportunity only meant giving wider access to elementary education and removing such privileges as he deemed to be harmful. The benefit of elementary education he saw as primarily to do with religious instruction and harmful privilege he defined as that which, when abused, harmed the moral superiority of the upper classes and undermined their social authority.

Gladstone's views on social reform were made clear in a speech in 1871 (Source A) in which he attacked radical social reformers who demanded more government intervention and warned against their ideas.

Source A Adapted from a speech made by Gladstone at Blackheath, London in 1871. Blackheath is in what was then Gladstone's constituency of Greenwich. From a report in *The Times*, 30 October 1871.

They are not your friends ... who teach you to look to the Legislature [Parliament] for the radical removal of the evils that afflict human life ... The social problems that confront us are many and formidable. Let the Government labour to its utmost, let the Legislature labour days and nights in your service; but ... whether the English father is to be the father of a happy family and the centre of a united home is a question which must depend mainly upon himself. Those who ... promise to the dwellers in towns that every one of them shall have a house and garden in free air, with ample space ... I have no doubt they are sincere ... but I will say they are deluded.

> How useful is Source A to an understanding of Gladstone's attitude to social reform?

In 1868 Gladstone's main priority was Ireland. He drafted the legislation to disestablish the Irish Church (1869) and reform land tenure (1870) personally (see pages 25–26). He was also much preoccupied with foreign affairs (which lie outside the scope of this book) and taken together these issues left him little time to focus on other matters. Therefore, for the most part, Gladstone left other major legislation to his colleagues.

Education

Education had been at the centre of a national debate throughout the 1860s. Three great Royal Commissions had been set up to look at concerns about the quality and extent of education in England and Wales, which was widely held to be falling behind that of other nations including Scotland for that matter, which had a separate school system. The Clarendon Commission 1861–64 looked at public schools and its report led eventually to the Public Schools Act, 1868. The Taunton Commission 1866–68 looked at the 782 endowed or grammar schools, which had originally been set up with endowment to provide free classical education for boys, along with a further 160 schools of various types. Its report led to the Endowed Schools Act of 1869. In both cases the Acts provided for the modernisation of the administrative structures of these schools so as to enable them to provide more modern and relevant education, and in the case of the endowed schools to allow girls to attend. However, the Acts were there to facilitate changes already occurring in the schools but hampered by out-of-date rules under which they had to be governed. The seven public schools involved – Charterhouse, Eton, Harrow, Rugby, Shrewsbury, Westminster and Winchester – served the children of the wealthiest classes. The endowed schools broadly speaking served the middle classes. Taken together these schools served around one-seventh of the population.

Working-class – elementary or popular – education was considered by the Newcastle Commission 1858–61, which looked at the range of schools run by the Anglican Church, the nonconformist churches and others. These were the National Schools run by the Anglican Church and the British and Foreign Schools run by the nonconformist churches such as the Methodists, Presbyterians or Baptists, which had been receiving government grants to assist them since 1833. They provided basic literacy, numeracy and religious education to as many working-class children as could afford the basic costs of attendance, usually up to the age of around eleven. Its report was critical of the availability of working-class education and its quality. The process of educational reform was carried on largely outside the arena of party politics. After years of debate the Public School Act was finally passed under Disraeli's Conservative Government in July 1868. Gladstone's government passed the Endowed Schools Act the following year but neither government had much to do with their contents, which were based on the reports of the Royal Commissions.

Education for the masses

The Elementary Education Act of 1870 was the work of W. E. Forster, a leading Liberal politician from Yorkshire who had made his fortune in the woollen cloth industry. It was based on the report of the Newcastle Commission. It was the most difficult of all the education reports to act on as it involved interference with schools run by the churches and involved the question of public finance for its cost implications. Gladstone supported it as it was less radical in tone than he had feared it might be, but only with many misgivings. The Act was mainly motivated by necessity. The Government was already spending large sums annually on education, but both the quality and sufficiency of provision across the country was patchy at best.

Forster aimed to bridge the gaps through new schools which would be set up by a new system of locally elected School Boards. The Act helped limit government spending on education by throwing some of the burden onto local rates. Both aims were broadly consistent with Gladstonian principles but Gladstone really believed that education was an individual or family responsibility and the idea that the Act might lead to some universal system of compulsory state education in the future appalled him. In any case, dealing with elementary education, which was directed primarily at the working classes, was a necessity because of the extension of the vote to some working-class men in boroughs in 1867. Better education of the working classes was therefore a priority if a 'civilised' political system was to be maintained.

▲ W. E. Forster, education reformer and creator of the 1870 Education Act.

Types of school

The Anglican Church ran elementary schools all over England and Wales known as 'National Schools', within which religious teaching followed the doctrine of the Anglican Church. Non-conformist churches ran schools known as 'British and Foreign Schools'. Since there were different beliefs in different churches, these schools taught religion based solely on scripture. Both types of school had received government grants since 1833.

Forster's proposals met opposition from nonconformist groups who objected to public money being available to Anglican Church schools. In the end their concerns were partly met by the adoption in the Act of the Cowper-Temple clause, named after the leading Liberal MP who devised it. This banned the teaching of religious education with any reference to particular beliefs of different Christian churches in the new Board Schools. Gladstone had grave reservations about this but swallowed his doubts in the interest of party unity. The Act was an important foundation on which to build a genuine national system of education for England and Wales.

Other social reform legislation

Education was generally recognised as a major public issue, vital for the economic future of the nation and social harmony. However, there were many other areas of public life where Liberal ministers believed that modernisation was overdue.

Civil service reform

Gladstone had long approved of the idea of open examinations to recruit the most able into the civil service rather than the practice of family connections securing posts. In 1853, he had commissioned his private secretary Sir Stafford Northcote and a senior civil servant Sir Charles Trevelyan, to investigate civil service reform. The result was the Northcote-Trevelyan Report of 1855 which recommended that recruitment to the civil service should be by open examination and promotion within, on a merit system. Little real progress was made however. As prime minister from 1868 Gladstone showed no sign of doing anything about it until prompted by Robert Lowe, the chancellor of the exchequer. The change was introduced in June 1870; no Act of Parliament was needed for this. The Foreign Office and the Home Office initially stayed out of the scheme but the latter joined in 1873 when Lowe himself went to the Home Office. There were two levels of entry examination, an upper grade aimed at the public school and university elites and a lower grade for clerks aimed at the middle class, so the new system was still firmly class-based and irrelevant to the working classes.

Women's rights

Prior to the Married Women's Property Act of 1870 all property and income of a married woman was legally her husband's. This applied to any property or funds she had held as a single person. The Act provided that any form of income earned by a wife was legally hers and furthermore that any investments made with the money earned were legally separate from her husband's assets. A wife was now allowed to keep any property she inherited from her next of kin as her own unless that property formed part of a trust. She could also inherit money up to £200. The Act made a married woman liable to maintain her children from the profits earned from her personal property, a liability which had previously only applied to the husband. It was a significant step in the campaign for women's rights but it was driven by women campaigners with male support in Parliament. The bill was originally introduced in 1868 during the Disraeli Government and took two years to pass into law.

University employment reform

The Universities Tests Act 1871 removed 'tests' for teaching posts at the universities which had effectively reserved them to Anglicans only. Gladstone hated the idea of removing Anglican privilege in the universities, and referred to having to do it as 'beyond odious'. He had voted against precisely the same measure in 1866. He agreed to do it in 1871 only because he was pressured by other liberals, particularly some leading liberal theologians (religious

Civil service – The paid advisors, officials and clerks who work in government departments to implement the policies of the government of the day.

academics), who insisted that it was essential. Typically however, once convinced that it must be done he forced it through a not very enthusiastic Parliament with all his authority.

Local government reform

The Local Government Board Act 1871 is a much neglected but important innovation. The Act set up a Local Government Board, to be headed by a Cabinet minister, which took over many functions previously dispersed across different departments. These included public health (previously under two different departments), the Poor Law, urban improvements, roads, drainage and sanitation, and pollution. The Act made a major contribution over the following decades to the better working of existing legislation and provided a structure for future legislation to be deployed effectively. This Act was the result of the report of a Royal Commission rather than a specific government policy.

Trade union reform

The Trade Union Act 1871 and the Criminal Law Amendment Act 1871 were passed on the same day. They met with very different receptions from trade unions. Trade unions caused Gladstone some agonies. Instinctively he disliked the idea of unions as they were contrary to the free market, they worked against individual effort and individual responsibility and they were too often associated with violence. The Trade Union Act was greeted with relief by the unions as it allowed for their recognition as legal bodies with rights in law to protect their property and funds. It also recognised the right to strike. However, the Criminal Law Amendment Act made any form of picketing illegal, so wide was the range of offences defined in the Act. Even peaceful picketing carried a risk so though strikes were legal it was virtually impossible to mount an effective one. Gladstone left the details to his home secretary, Henry Bruce, who tried to legislate as best he could in accordance with his principles, to protect union funds and encourage respectability, while at the same time clamping down on potential violence. He kept the legislation largely in line with the recommendations of a Royal Commission on Trade Unions set up by Lord Derby in 1867, which reported in 1869.

Public health

The Public Health Act 1872 was the result of the findings of a Royal Commission on Sanitary Laws set up by the government of Lord Derby in 1867. It was intended to deal with the chaotic system of public health at local level. The number of local boards of health totalled 721 by 1872. The Public Health Act 1848 had formed 419 of the local boards and the remaining 302 were created under a Local Government Act passed in 1858. The Public Health Act 1872 merged these local boards into Municipal Boroughs and Local Improvement Commissions where they shared the same district. Many of the areas covered by boards were very small and the whole system was complex and inefficient. There were still areas with no proper coverage. The Act was purely administrative and had little impact. It created no new powers for local authorities. It ignored the reports and recommendations of government civil servants who had been pressing for fundamental reform backed by government money since the 1850s. Gladstone had no interest in making this issue a concern of central government.

Alcohol abuse

The Licensing Act 1872 greatly offended Gladstone's principles of minimum intervention and individual freedom and responsibility, but he was persuaded that it was needed to combat obvious social problems such as alcohol-related violence and crime, child neglect and absenteeism. In any case the Liberal Party's nonconformist lobby, some of whom wanted a total ban on alcohol, would have accepted nothing less. The Act, which was the work of Home Secretary Henry Bruce, was much weaker than the Government originally intended because of opposition from brewers and distillers, many of whom were Liberal supporters. In the end the Act required that magistrates issue licences to public houses, which could be refused if it was felt there were too many in a particular area. Pubs had to close at midnight in towns and 11 p.m. in rural areas. Sharp practices such as adding salt to beer to increase consumer thirst were banned. It was still too much for many brewers and distillers, who switched their allegiance to the Conservatives. There were riots in working-class districts when the police attempted to enforce closing times. The Act is widely seen as a major cause of the Liberal defeat in the 1874 general election with Gladstone, on hearing the result, commenting that 'we have been borne down in a torrent of gin and beer'.

The legal system

The Supreme Court of Judicature Act 1873 was intended to reorganise the courts of England and Wales by establishing the High Court and the Court of Appeal. It was also originally intended to abolish the role of the House of Lords as the highest court of the judicial system. However, Gladstone's government fell in 1874 before the Act came into effect and Disraeli's Conservative Government suspended the Act. Gladstone's wish to abolish the judicial role of the House of Lords was due to concerns about the poor quality of its judges. Judges in the House of Lords secured their position by virtue of the fact that their fathers were peers and so individuals would automatically inherit seats in the upper house rather than securing their position through merit. Therefore, some of the best legal brains in the country could not sit as judges in the upper house simply because of their family background. However, Disraeli's Conservative Government passed Acts in 1874 and 1875 which retained the judicial role of the House of Lords and ensured the quality of judges there by way of the Appellate Jurisdiction Act of 1876 which introduced life peerages. Through the power of the Crown, the government could appoint any individual to be a peer and thus a judge in the House of Lords. These life peers (or Law Lords) would hold a peerage for their lifetime only. Thus leading lawyers could be appointed to adjudicate in the House of Lords by making them life peers.

The army

Army reforms were introduced over the whole period of the Gladstone Government, mainly in response to long deliberations resulting from the deficiencies in the army seen in the Crimean War (see page 7). Most contentiously the practice of officers purchasing their commissions was abolished and the selection and promotion of officers was to be on merit. There were numerous administrative changes including:

- the organising of regiments by county, and division of regiments into two battalions rotating on service at home and overseas
- the central offices were brought under the control of one authority – the War Office
- a standard and up-to-date rifle (the Martini-Henry breech-loader) was introduced
- attempts were made to popularise army service to make it less the last resort for criminals
- flogging in peacetime was abolished
- overseas service was reduced from twelve years to six.

These army reforms Gladstone left to Edward Cardwell, the secretary for war. He did not really favour the complete ending of commission purchase, which did not operate in all sections of the army anyway, since he felt that this was a useful avenue for aristocratic service to the nation. In the end, however, he agreed to it. There was considerable opposition to these changes in the House of Lords and the bill needed for the ending of commission purchase was defeated there. Gladstone and Cardwell deserve credit for standing firm on this and Gladstone threatened to use the Queen's power of Royal Warrant if necessary – on which the Lords gave up their opposition. Though much was achieved there was still a great deal left to do. Cardwell could not get rid of the totally inadequate commander-in-chief, the Duke of Cambridge, who was a cousin of the Queen, and many further changes were resisted by the Duke and other senior officers.

Conclusion

While the scope of the reforms introduced in 1868–74 was impressive, to many more radically minded Liberals the actual impact they had was very disappointing. Gladstone's reluctance to involve the government, and government finance, more extensively left them angry and frustrated. Historians too have become less enthusiastic. Sir Robert Ensor, writing in the 1930s, described the 1868–74 government as 'the greatest ministry of Queen Victoria's reign'. By the 1970s Paul Adelman questioned the effectiveness of the reforms, the overall abilities of the ministers, and stressed Gladstone's preoccupation with Ireland, arguing that he showed little real interest in other reforms. One of Gladstone's biographers, Richard Shannon (1999), has argued that Gladstone remained throughout his career an 'unreconstructed Peelite', with the resulting distrust of government-led social reform.

Disraeli and the Conservatives take over

Gladstone's failure to develop a more interventionist social policy opened the way for Disraeli to construct a new, socially aware identity for the Conservatives. In speeches in 1872 he mocked Gladstone's failures and pledged the Conservatives, if elected, to bring forward meaningful social reforms that would directly improve the material conditions of the working classes. It was in many respects an improbable role for the Conservatives. Though there had always been individual radical Tories involved in social reform movements, the party line had been that social reform should be a matter of parliamentary consensus promoted by individuals – Disraeli proposed to change all that. In order to gain support from party sceptics, Disraeli linked social reform to the preservation of the social order: 'The Palace', he argued, was not safe 'when the cottage is not happy'.

The reforms of 1874–80 stand as an impressive achievement for the Conservative Government. They covered a wide range of important issues: public health reform, factory legislation, housing, education, trade union law, food and drink regulations and environmental pollution. They drew contemporary recognition of their worth from sources not naturally inclined to support the Conservatives, for example, from trade union leaders. The most notable of these was Alexander Macdonald, a former miner who had gone into the mines aged eight but had risen to become a leader of the Miners' National Association. In 1879 he claimed that, 'The Conservative Party has done more for the working class in five years than the Liberals have done in fifty.' Macdonald was not only a trade union leader but also a Liberal MP and one of the first working-class men to enter the House of Commons so this testimony cannot be taken lightly.

> **KEY DATES: GLADSTONE'S REFORMS, 1868–74**
>
> **1870** The Elementary Education Act
> Civil service reform 1870 – did not require an Act of Parliament
> The Married Women's Property Act
> **1871** The Universities Tests Act
> The Local Government Board Act
> The Trade Union Act
> The Criminal Law Amendment Act
> **1872** The Public Health Act
> The Licensing Act
> **1873** The Supreme Court of Judicature Act

Macdonald's view was heavily influenced no doubt by the government's trade union legislation. There is one area where Disraeli's personal intervention was clear and decisive – trade union law. The Cabinet was reluctant to undo Gladstone's 1871 Act which had made picketing effectively illegal. Disraeli was firm about the need to amend the law and he had his way. The Conspiracy and Protection of Property Act 1875 effectively reversed Gladstone's Criminal Law Amendment Act by placing industrial disputes under civil law rather than criminal law. Trade unions could not now be prosecuted for actions that were legal for individuals, meaning that peaceful picketing became legal.

The social reforms of 1874–80

Apart from the legislation on trade unions, Disraeli's role was essentially to support the reforming zeal of those in the Cabinet such as Richard Cross, a barrister from a northern industrialist family, who to the surprise of many he appointed home secretary, and other reforming ministers such as George Sclater-Booth, his president of the Local Government Board. The source of the ideas behind the legislation was not Disraeli, nor his ministers for that matter. The bulk of the ideas for reform lie in government reports going back to the 1850s and 1860s, much of them at the direction of Sir John Simon who headed a department which investigated the causes of epidemic and industrial diseases. Simon's reports gave detailed recommendations for improving public health in a variety of ways. Cross used these as the Liberals had done to a lesser extent in 1868–74.

▲ Richard Cross, Disraeli's choice to spearhead reform 1874-80.

The Public Health Act 1875

This brought all existing public health legislation under one Act, simplified it and made more elements of it compulsory. So comprehensive was it that it remained the basis for public health administration until 1936.

The Employers and Workmen Act 1875

This placed employers and employees on an equal legal basis for the first time. Before this Act breaches of contract by an employer were matters of civil law where a fine might be imposed, while breaches by employees were matters of criminal law and could result in fines or imprisonment. Disraeli commented that, 'we have settled the long and vexatious contest between capital and labour' and claimed this would 'gain and retain for the Conservatives the lasting affection of the working classes'.

The Artisans' Dwellings Act 1875

This gave power to local authorities to compulsorily purchase slum housing and demolish it to rebuild more sanitary houses. In terms of interference with property rights it was a very significant move. It has been criticised retrospectively for being permissive rather than compulsory, meaning that it allowed local authorities to act rather than forcing them to. However, this ignores the fact that Parliament would never have passed a compulsory measure.

Sale of Food and Drugs Act 1875

This brought in much tougher laws covering the preparation of food and 'adulteration' – that is mixing food, drink or medicines with other substances to increase volume. The Act provided a heavy fine for violations. This addressed a national scandal at the time in which, for example, chalk or sawdust was sometimes added to flour, fresh blood was painted over unfit meat and salt was added to beer to increase consumption.

Factory Act 1874

This reduced the working day to ten hours from ten and a half hours. It also stated that children could not be employed until the age of ten, rather than eight, and full-time working was only allowed for fourteen-year-olds rather than from thirteen.

Factory and Workshops Act 1878

Until this Act the inspection of 'workshops' defined as factories where less than 50 people were employed was left to the local authorities. This Act placed them under government inspection, which was much more rigorous and regular.

Education Act 1876

Lord Sandon was Disraeli's head of the Education Department. He produced an Elementary Education Act in 1876, which is sometimes known as Sandon's Act. This placed a duty on parents to ensure that their children received elementary instruction in reading, writing and arithmetic. It also created school attendance committees, which could compel attendance, for districts where there were no school boards; and the Poor Law Guardians were given permission to help with the payment of school fees.

How much credit does Disraeli deserve?

Disraeli can be argued to have shown some awareness of social issues in his 1840s novels *Coningsby* and *Sybil*, but equally these can be seen as a rather belated cashing in on the so-called 'Condition of England' question which focused on the appalling plight of the working classes and dominated the late 1830s and early 1840s. Similarly, Disraeli's later references to the 'One Nation' appeal of conservatism did not produce any firm commitment to social reform until as late as his 1872 speeches. Even then his comments were vague generalisations rather than specific proposals. However, the fact remains that Disraeli was the first leading Conservative to identify interventionist social reform as a specific objective of government. The historian P. R. Ghosh claimed that Disraeli made social policy an 'accepted, uncontroversial part of the Conservative agenda' and sees a consistent theme of social awareness stretching through his career from the 1840s to 1880. However, others including Paul Smith and, very significantly, Disraeli's admirer, biographer and historian of the Conservative Party, Robert Blake, have played down the extent of Disraeli's commitment to social reforms and (with the exception of the trade union legislation) give him only limited personal credit for them. Smith, while accepting the value of the reforms of 1874–80, argues that they had nothing to do with Disraeli's political philosophy but were simply pragmatic and politically expedient. Blake argues that they were no different in substance to reforms that a Liberal government (minus Gladstone) might have brought in.

Gladstone's second government, 1880–85

The Liberals won the 1880 general election with a majority of 51 over the Conservatives and Irish National Party combined. Gladstone was no longer officially the leader of the party since his retirement in 1875. During the election campaign Gladstone would make no commitment about his intentions, though it was obvious that in the country at large he was still regarded as the leader whatever the official position. Officially the leadership was shared by Lord Hartington in the House of Commons (he was heir to the Dukedom of Devonshire, not in the House of Lords) and Lord Granville, the leader in the Lords. The Queen, who detested Gladstone, wanted Lord Hartington to accept the premiership but was prepared to accept Granville if necessary. However, the days when a monarch could insist on such things had gone and both Hartington and Granville realised that unless Gladstone was willing to serve under one of them he must be prime minister. Gladstone had formed the opinion over the years that his first government had been compromised because he had needed to make too many concessions. He was determined to have a freer hand this time. He therefore told his colleagues that he would not serve in a government unless he was prime minister and if this was not acceptable he would go to the backbenches. Hartington and Granville therefore told Queen Victoria she must send for Gladstone.

Gladstone had not campaigned on any domestic issues during the election other than to attack Disraeli's lax control of finance. He did not even mention Ireland despite the mounting problems there. Most of his attention was focused on Disraeli's foreign and imperial policy which Gladstone believed was immoral and aggressive. Gladstone originally only intended to remain prime minister for a strictly limited time – in fact only long enough to clear the financial mess, as he saw it, that Disraeli had created and restore foreign policy to moral virtue. Gladstone decided that only he could deal with the financial position and so took the office of chancellor of the exchequer himself. Once in office, however, issues of foreign and imperial policy proved harder to deal with than he had anticipated. He was also confronted with the need to address the Irish Question – a topic he had ignored during the election campaign and for which he had no plans – and the issue of parliamentary reform was also revived (see Chapter 1 for Gladstone's handling of these issues). Gladstone was forced to postpone any thought of early retirement.

Social reforms, 1880–85

Social issues had no place in Gladstone's thinking at all at this point. He constructed a Cabinet overwhelmingly made up of traditional 'Whig' aristocrats. He appointed the rising radical leader Joseph Chamberlain to be president of the Board of Trade but only reluctantly included him in the Cabinet. The ageing radical John Bright was also given a Cabinet post as chancellor of the Duchy of Lancaster – a role that carried no actual ministerial work. It was mainly down to Bright's insistence that Chamberlain received Cabinet status.

However, the social reform record of the second Gladstone Government, while not ranking as great in any sense, was not as poor as has sometimes been claimed. As president of the Board of Trade Chamberlain brought in a series of useful but low-profile measures:

- Seamen's Wages Act 1880, to ensure fairer wages for seamen
- Grain Cargoes Act 1880, to control the safer shipment of grain
- Electric Lighting Act 1882, which allowed town councils to establish electricity supplies.

He also attempted to bring in legislation to regulate shipping to prevent insurance scams known as coffin ships, where shipowners deliberately over-insured ships that were dubious in terms of sea-worthinesss – a problem that was becoming a national scandal at the time. However, he was defeated by influential members of his own party who forced the Cabinet to withdraw the bill.

The Government also brought in the following:

- An Employers' Liability Act, 1880, which gave protection to workers who had accidents caused by the negligence of managers, superintendents and foremen. Railway companies were also made liable if their employees were injured through the negligence of signalmen, drivers and pointsmen. However, the Act did not cover accidents caused by ordinary workers.
- An Education Act 1881, which made attendance at an elementary school compulsory for all children aged between five and ten – though since it did not make such schooling free it was not easy to enforce.
- A Married Women's Property Act 1882, which extended the 1870 Act to cover all forms of property. The Act also gave married women power to enter into contracts and responsibility for their debts. It was therefore a landmark in the history of women's rights.
- A Factory and Workshops Act 1883, which attempted to introduce protection for workers in the notoriously dangerous white lead industry – though according to the evidence of the American writer Jack London in his exposé of life in London's East End in 1902 (*The People of the Abyss*) the degree of protection afforded must have been very limited.

Social reform from 1851 to 1885 was carried forward as much by the efforts of campaign groups, individual social reformers, civil servants and individual MPs as by government initiative. Indeed, it is questionable how much success their joint pressure might have had on governments had it not been for the underlying reality of advancing democracy, which left them increasingly accountable to the expanding electorate.

> **KEY DATES: GLADSTONE'S REFORMS, 1880–85**
>
> **1880** Seamen's Wages Act
> **1880** Employers' Liability Act
> **1881** Education Act
> **1882** Married Women's Property Act
> **1883** Factory and Workshops Act

> **WORKING TOGETHER**
>
> 1 Make a list of what you think are the eight most important pieces of social legislation covered in this chapter.
> 2 Create a mind map which places them in order of importance, beginning with the most important at the centre top on your mind map, then continuing clockwise round the page to the least important. Add to each entry one key reason for its importance.
> 3 Now compare your original list with a partner. How far are the lists the same? Discuss any discrepancies.
> 4 Review your list and revise your mind map if necessary.

Chapter summary

- The impact of industrialisation and urbanisation produced a rapidly changing society in Britain over the course of the nineteenth century.
- Changes in industry and urbanisation brought about a change in ideas about how the economy should best function.
- Free trade became the accepted economic policy for both the Liberals and the Conservatives.
- The rising and more diverse social structure produced increasing social tensions.
- The problem of poverty became more serious and attracted more government attention.
- Economic prosperity led to rising living standards.
- Trade unions, once illegal, became increasingly integrated into national life.
- Both the Liberal and Conservative parties realised that the modernisation of Britain was urgently needed.
- Over the period 1868–80 a vast number of new social reforms were introduced by both parties.
- Though the scope of reform was wide, the effectiveness of some legislation has been questioned, as have the motives of the politicians who passed them.

Chapter summary diagram

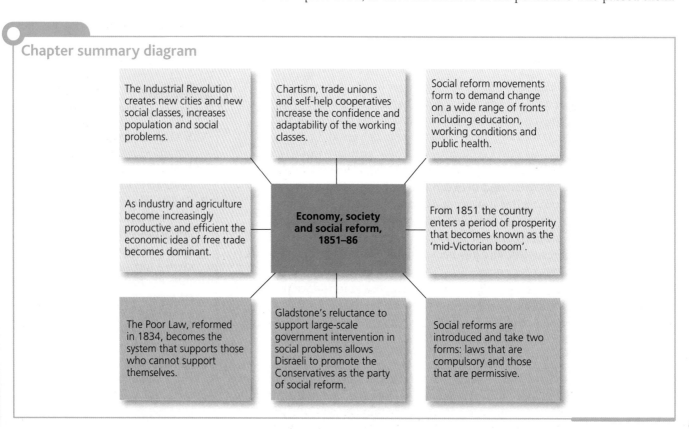

Working on interpretation skills: extended reading

To what extent did all classes share in the benefits of Britain's economic prosperity in the 1850s?

Emma Griffin discusses the extent to which different social classes benefited from the rising prosperity brought about by the industrial revolution.

In 1851 Britain was a nation in the midst of an industrial revolution. National wealth was growing and family incomes were rising. Large landowners and industrialists were profiting from the economic boom and many working people were also experiencing a standard of living that was higher than any earlier generations had known. Nonetheless, large 5
contrasts between wealth and poverty existed and there was little in the way of governmental policy aimed at reducing those contrasts.

Mid-nineteenth-century Britain was dominated by a small and very wealthy landed elite, who were able to make large profits from agriculture or mining. Next in wealth came the growing middle class. 10
Middle-class families earned their income through owning or working for shops, banks or business or through the provision of services such as medicine, law or education. Although they rarely enjoyed extreme wealth, they were still able to earn enough to employ servants and maintain a decent standard of living. Beneath the middle class was the working 15
class. Male workers tended to work with their hands for a living, though levels of skill, experience and pay varied widely between them. At one end there were the relatively well-paid skilled factory operatives or highly-trained craftsmen employing a few assistants. At the other were the poorly paid farmworkers and those who through ill-health or old age were 20
unable to perform sustained heavy labour.

Male workers were not the most poorly paid workers, however. Earnings were less again for women and children. Women tended to be concentrated in just a few sectors of the economy – needlework, laundry work, domestic service; all of them low-status and low-paid. Children 25
generally earned the lowest wages of all, and although age restrictions were in force in factories and mines, elsewhere in the economy there were no restrictions on the employment of children. Among these workers, very low pay and mistreatment were rife.

Material inequality was deeply entrenched in Victorian Britain and 30
accepted by many as the natural order of things. Furthermore, the exclusion of large sections of the population from the nation's political processes helped to maintain that inequality. Before the Great Reform Act of 1832, which gave the franchise to the urban middle class, landowners dominated both houses of Parliament and the laws of the land inevitably 35
reflected their interests. Through much of the early nineteenth century, the profits of great landowners were protected by the Corn Laws. This meant that bread was sometime more expensive than it needed to be, though it also helped protect employment in agriculture.

As well as studying the facts of an event in history, historians also use these facts in order to reach conclusions on, for example, why something happened. In other words, they have to interpret the facts in order to reach their conclusions. Often the evidence doesn't just point in one direction. There is scope for historians to reach different conclusions and produce different interpretations.

In this chapter, as well as Chapters 4, 6 and 8, there is one, longer interpretation to read, followed by some questions that are designed to help you build up your skills, as well as helping you to consolidate your knowledge of each chapter. The questions on this essay are on page 60.

Following the Reform Act, the nation's landowners were joined by [40] industrialists from the urban north of England and this led in due course to a reorientation of Parliament's interests. Peel's 1841–46 government lowered the cost of living for the working class by reducing or eliminating indirect taxes such as the Corn Laws which were abolished in 1846, which [45] lowered the price of bread much to the satisfaction of both the workers and their employers. To replace the lost income Parliament in 1842 settled upon an income tax. As the new law taxed incomes over £150 a year, it shifted the tax burden away from the less wealthy.

In the 1850s Gladstone continued to cut taxes and further reduced the [50] cost of living. Working-class diets improved and unemployment was virtually eliminated. However in 1851, the working classes remained excluded from the franchise. As a result, the laws of the land did little to protect and promote their interests. The government played no role in the provision of clean water, decent homes, or healthcare for those [55] who earned too little to buy these things for themselves. Workplaces were often highly dangerous, yet if a worker was seriously injured and unable to continue working, he or she received no compensation. Nor were families compensated for the loss of their loved ones in the workplace. Some of these improvements were introduced following the extension of the franchise to some working-class men in 1867; though [60] others – such as the minimum wage and equal pay – were delayed until the twentieth century.

One final factor which helped to maintain a very unequal share in wealth and poverty was the absence of an effective safety net for those who fell upon hard times. In 1851, there were no old-age pensions and no [65] unemployment benefits. The only statutory assistance for the poor came through the harsh and punitive Poor Law. In 1851, Britain celebrated its technical achievements and economic progress with the Great Exhibition. But it still had a long way to go in ensuring that every citizen received a decent share of the nation's wealth. [70]

Emma Griffin is a professor of Modern British History at the University of East Anglia.

ACTIVITY

Having read the essay, answer the following questions.

Comprehension

1 What does the author mean by the following phrases?
   a) 'the franchise' (line 34)
   b) 'indirect taxes' (line 44).

Evidence

2 Using paragraph 6, list the ways in which the author balances the evidence when discussing working-class living conditions in order to lead to her final conclusion at the end of paragraph 7.

Interpretation

3 Using your knowledge from your study of social reform, list evidence to support the author's conclusion (paragraph 6) that 'some improvements' followed the extension of the franchise in 1867.

Evaluation

4 How far do you agree with the author's view (paragraph 7) that the Poor Law was 'harsh and punitive'?

Working on essay technique: analysis

Analysis is a term that covers explanation and evaluation. In essence, analysis means breaking down something complex into smaller parts. This means that a clear structure which breaks down a complex question into a series of paragraphs is the first step towards writing an analytical essay.

Explanation

The purpose of explanation is to account for why something happened, or why something is true or false. An explanatory statement requires two parts: a **claim** and a **justification**.

EXAMPLE

Imagine you are answering the following A-level practice question:

'The improvement in the condition of the working classes in the period 1851–85 was mainly due to the efforts of Gladstone.' Assess the validity of this view. (25 marks)

You might want to argue for the validity of this view by pointing out that Gladstone was in office for a considerable part of the period as chancellor of the exchequer and as prime minister, presiding over many reforms. Once you have made this point, and supported it with relevant detail, you can then explain how this answers the question.

For example, you could conclude your paragraph like this:

Justification ——— Therefore Gladstone can be seen as having directly improved the condition ●——Claim
of the working classes because his policies **as Chancellor helped reduce**
their cost of living and the governments he led introduced policies aimed
at improving their living conditions.

Relationship

The first part of this sentence is the claim while the second part justifies the claim. 'Because' is a very important word to use when writing an explanation, as it shows the relationship between the claim and the justification.

Evaluation

The purpose of evaluation is to weigh up the evidence and reach a judgement. Evaluation, therefore, needs to consider the importance of two or more different factors, weigh them against each other, and then reach a judgement. Evaluation is a good skill to use throughout the essay as it will build towards the conclusion, which should reach a judgement which answers the question.

EXAMPLE

For example, using the same question on page 61, your evaluation points might include:

While Gladstone's time in office as prime minister resulted in many reforms it is arguable that the direct impact of these reforms was limited when compared to those of Disraeli's government in 1874–80.

Then some details for comparison:

However, it is also clear that many of the reforms across the whole period came not from the ideas of politicians like Gladstone and Disraeli but from the work of government civil servants such as...

And a possible conclusion:

Therefore it is not valid to conclude that the improvement in working-class conditions in this period was mainly due to Gladstone since it can clearly be shown that...

In this example the evaluation and judgement is helped by using a series of words that help to weigh up the importance of the factors. 'While' and 'however' are useful words as they can help contrast the importance of the different factors and 'therefore' leads to a firm judgement.

ACTIVITY

Again, consider the A-level practice question from the example on page 61.

Write a paragraph about comparing the reforms of 1868–74 with those of 1874–80. Make sure the paragraph:

- begins with a clear point that clearly focuses on the question
- develops the point with accurate details
- focuses on three specific areas such as education or public health for direct comparison rather than making general comparisons
- concludes with a brief judgement and a justification.

PRACTICE A-LEVEL QUESTION

'The social reforms of the period 1868-1885 were undertaken reluctantly and had limited impact.' Assess the validity of this view. (25 marks)

Plan an answer to this question, noting that the question requires a balance to be drawn between two separate issues: 'reluctance' and 'limited impact'.

Parties, politics and the Irish Question, 1886–1914

3

This chapter covers political events in Britain and Ireland during the period 1886–1914. It deals with a number of key areas:

- The electoral fortunes of the Liberal and Conservative parties in the more democratised political system.
- The constitutional crisis that developed between the Liberal Government and the House of Lords; the modernising of the constitution and the implications of constitutional changes.
- The rise of a third force in British politics – the Labour Party.
- The continuing problems and developments in Ireland – their impact on British politics and the Ulster Crisis of 1912–14, which threatened to bring about a civil war.

When you have worked through the chapter and the related activities, you should have detailed knowledge of all those areas. You should be able to relate this knowledge to the key breadth issues defined as part of your study, in particular the political dominance of the Conservative Party up to 1906 and the changing constitutional position and its impact on the ongoing question of the future of Ireland.

For the period covered in this chapter the main issues can be phrased in a couple of questions:

How and why did a constitutional crisis develop and result in a major change to the constitution?

How and why did events in and policies towards Ireland nearly lead to the outbreak of a civil war in Ireland?

CHAPTER OVERVIEW

This chapter covers the period 1886–1914 and focuses on constitutional developments and the fortunes of the two main political parties, the emergence of the Labour Party and the ongoing problem of Ireland. In 1906 the two main political parties were joined at Westminster by a group of MPs elected on behalf of a new body, the Labour Representation Committee. Within two years this group, along with others, had formed the Parliamentary Labour Party. After 1886 the Liberals would no longer continue to dominate government. Only one Liberal government (1892–95) took office in the period 1886–1906 and it did not have a majority in the House of Commons; for that it depended on the support of the Irish National Party. In the course of a period of Liberal government that would extend into the Great War of 1914–18, great constitutional changes would come about which would effectively mark the beginning of the end for the political authority of the House of Lords. In the same period Ireland would be set on a path that would change the course of Irish and British history in the twentieth century. Finally, the period saw the deaths of two monarchs, Victoria (1901) and Edward VII (1910), and the accession of George V.

1 Changing party fortunes, 1886–1906

The decline of the Liberal Party in the period 1886–1906 is very marked when compared to the previous period. From the official foundation of the Liberal Party formally using that name in 1859 to the middle of 1886, the Liberals were in office for the vast majority of the time. The only Conservative government in that period with an overall majority was Disraeli's Second Ministry of 1874–80. There were also two minority Conservative governments under Derby/Disraeli in 1866–68 and for a few months in the second half of 1885 under Salisbury. However, if we go back to 1830 and include the Whig and later Whig-Peelite governments, which were Liberal governments in all but name, the picture becomes even more complete. Between 1830 and 1859 there was only one Conservative government with a majority – that of Peel in 1841–46. All the other Conservative governments were short-term 'caretaker governments': Peel's 100 days in 1834–35; Derby's nine months in 1852 and Derby again in 1858–59.

The tendency of the Liberals to divisions however was a feature of the development of the Liberal Party over this period. In 1852 Derby's government only took office because of a major dispute between Russell and Palmerston. In 1858–59 the second Derby government came about in the same way. In 1866 Derby formed a third minority government following the Liberal split over parliamentary reform. However, each of these splits was repaired and the Liberal domination of the political system quickly resumed. Subsequently Gladstone's failed Irish Home Rule of 1886 split the party yet again and in the general election which followed the Conservatives, led by Lord Salisbury, won an overwhelming victory.

Liberal decline and Conservative ascendancy

To what extent was the success of the Conservatives in the period 1886–1905 the result of Liberal failures?

The split that occurred in 1886 over Gladstone's determination to press ahead with a Home Rule Bill for Ireland (see pages 27–28) was different to the divisions that had previously occurred in the party. All attempts to bring about reconciliation between Gladstone and the leaders of the Liberal Unionists – Joseph Chamberlain and Lord Hartington (soon to inherit his father's title as Duke of Devonshire) – failed. Though the Liberal Unionists seemed an odd group in the sense that they were made up of elements from the radical and conservative wings of the Liberal Party, their commitment to maintaining the Union was so great that it outweighed any differences. The Liberal Unionists therefore moved further and further into alliance with the Conservative Party. This meant that in the general election of 1892, although the Liberal Party won the largest number of seats (272) they faced a combined Conservative/Liberal Unionist opposition of 313 seats (268 Conservative and 45 Liberal Unionist). The Liberals were however pledged by Gladstone to introduce another Home Rule Bill for Ireland so they had the support of the Irish National Party, which had 81 seats. This gave the Liberals a working majority so long as they retained Irish support, but it was still a minority government that was not completely in control of its own destiny.

The Liberals in opposition, 1886–92

By no means all the radical Liberals had followed Joseph Chamberlain out of the party. Those that remained had significant grassroots support among the party activists. In 1891, with the general election in prospect, Gladstone was pressured by the radicals to accept a wider reform programme to accompany the flagship policy of Home Rule. The proposals included references to further parliamentary reform and other radical reforms. Gladstone announced this election manifesto in Newcastle and it has become known as the 'Newcastle Programme'. He was forced to accept a manifesto that offered a wider range of reforms than he would have liked in order to ensure party unity. The Programme was hastily put together but bore the clear imprint of radical influence:

- Home Rule was top of the agenda at Gladstone's insistence.
- Compulsory land purchase for allotments as in the 'unauthorised programme' (see page 13; the end of school fees had already been brought in by the Conservatives in 1891).
- Tougher regulations controlling health and safety in the workplace.
- Greater employer liability for accidents at work.
- More limitations on the length of the working day.
- There were also references to greater democracy – 'one man, one vote', reform of the House of Lords, more democratic local government and payment for MPs to allow access to the House of Commons for a wider social range.

Gladstone accepted the package mainly because he had no intention whatsoever of putting it into effect. His principal concern was to achieve Home Rule for Ireland. He was 82. He intended to secure Home Rule and then retire immediately. He had no sympathy with the ideas behind the Newcastle Programme at all. It was clear that any significant shift to a more radical agenda would have to wait until he retired. A clear split was developing between those Liberals who wanted to maintain the traditions of Gladstone and those who favoured a 'New Liberalism' with a clear commitment to more advanced social policies (see page 69).

Conservative domination begins

As the Liberals weakened, so the Conservatives strengthened. Salisbury's government from 1886 to 1892 showed that the Conservative reforming zeal that had emerged in the Disraeli era 1874–80 was not entirely dead, notwithstanding the death of Disraeli. Younger radical Tories such as Lord Randolph Churchill (father of Sir Winston and chancellor of the exchequer in Salisbury's government), were making the case for further reforms in public health and housing, education and even benefit schemes for sickness and unemployment. These ideas were encouraged by Joseph Chamberlain, the Conservative's Liberal Unionist ally. Even so, the actual progress of reform under Salisbury was rather limited. One factor in this was that Lord Randolph Churchill had a major falling out with Salisbury over his proposals for a radical budget to fund further reform. Churchill resigned over this, expecting that Salisbury would reject his resignation and give in. However the ploy failed and Churchill's governmental career was over.

The Conservative–Liberal Unionist alliance continued to strengthen during 1886–92, though no Liberal Unionists joined the Conservative Government and the Liberal Unionist numbers in Parliament declined to only 45 in the 1892 general election. Even so the Conservatives and Liberal Unionists together held 313 seats against the Liberals' 272, so Gladstone was only able to form a government due to the support of the 81 Irish National Party MPs. As in 1886 Gladstone made Irish Home Rule the priority and this time he was able to get it passed in the House of Commons, only to see it defeated in the House of Lords in 1893 (see page 83). Gladstone retired the following year, recognising that his Irish policy had no appeal in the country and was not seen by other leading Liberals to be as important as he had made it. He had also realised that the party was moving away from his vision of Liberal values.

Following Gladstone's retirement, Lord Rosebery took over as prime minister, but he resigned in June 1895 after the Government was defeated at the Committee Stage on an Army Bill. Rosebery unnecessarily chose to interpret this defeat as a vote of censure on the Government. Consequently the Queen, following the proper constitutional procedure, invited Lord Salisbury to form a new government. Salisbury agreed and formed a coalition government with the Liberal Unionists, offering them four cabinet posts. He then called a general election in July 1895 at which the Liberals were massively defeated. The party secured only 177 seats against 411 for the Conservative and Liberal Unionist alliance (71 of these were Liberal Unionists).

The Conservatives now had a majority of ten over all other parties including the Liberal Unionists, so in theory Salisbury could have reverted to a purely Conservative government. This however was not his intention. He wanted to keep the alliance firmly together and so continued the coalition government, which meant an overwhelming majority for his government. Joseph Chamberlain, at his own request, had become colonial secretary – Salisbury had wanted to make him chancellor of the exchequer or home secretary but Chamberlain now believed that the greatest challenge facing Britain was the maintenance and development of the British Empire. Salisbury, who wanted to concentrate exclusively on foreign affairs, had even suggested to the Liberal Unionist Duke of Devonshire (formerly Lord Hartington) that he be the prime minister, but Devonshire rejected this idea and became Lord President of the (Privy) Council – a prestigious but largely symbolic post.

The British Empire

From the 1870s until the turn of the century, Britain oversaw a massive expansion of the British Empire in both Africa and Asia. The details of that expansion are not the subject of the specification at which this book is aimed, but it is important to understand that the protection of the empire was, for economic and strategic reasons, immensely important to British governments and increasingly the subject of public approval and pride.

▲ Lord Salisbury, the intellectual powerhouse of late nineteenth century Conservatism.

Lord Salisbury – an assessment

Lord Salisbury was a strong and effective leader who struck a balance between traditional conservatism and moderate reforms. His strategy of cultivating the Liberal Unionists and including them in the 1895 coalition helped strengthen the Conservative Party's position. After his retirement in 1902 the strong position he had built up quickly began to crumble. Salisbury was also responsible for appointing Richard Middleton as the principal political agent of the Conservative Party in 1884, a post he held until his death in 1905. Middleton's sound organisational skills steered the Conservative Party's election campaigns across the constituencies – Lord Londonderry, a leading Conservative peer, credited Middleton specifically for the 1895 election victory. It is worth noting that he died in February 1905, nearly a year before the 1906 general election at which the Conservatives would suffer a massive defeat.

The khaki election, 1900

The formation of the coalition in 1895 effectively led to the eventual formal merging of the two parties in 1912. In 1900 when the next general election was held, some commentators were already referring to a 'Unionist' party rather than 'Conservatives' and 'Liberal Unionists', though the distinction between the two groups still remained at that time. Most political observers were predicting that the Liberals would win the next general election, but the outbreak of war in South Africa in 1899 led to a surge of patriotic feeling which shifted public opinion behind the Government. The Liberals, furthermore, were disastrously split (yet again), this time by the Boer War. Some Liberals supported the Government's policy but a smaller anti-war faction, in which Lloyd George was prominent, emerged, which was deeply critical of the war and this cost the Liberals support they were hoping to regain from 1895. As a result in the election of 1900, popularly known as the khaki election, Salisbury's government, still officially a coalition, won 402 seats (334 Conservative, 68 Liberal Unionist) against 183 Liberal seats, a very small increase for them. For the time being the Conservative, or Unionist, domination seemed secure.

> **Khaki election** – Khaki is a Hindustani word meaning 'soil-coloured' and used in English to describe the light yellow-brown colour of army uniforms.

The Liberal Party in 1902 was deeply divided and desperate to restore party unity. The Boer War had caused a deep and bitter clash within the party between Liberal imperialists, who patriotically supported the war, arguing that British interests in southern Africa had to be maintained, and a minority 'pro-Boer' group which opposed the war as an act of aggression against small states. In the late 1890s most well-informed political observers had expected the Liberals to win the next general election, but when it came in 1900 with Britain at war in South Africa, the voters supported the government of Lord Salisbury in a patriotic outpouring of imperial enthusiasm and angry rejection of the anti-war Liberals. The khaki election returned the Conservative–Liberal Unionist coalition with a huge majority:

● Four hundred and two MPs were elected who supported the government – 334 Conservatives and 68 Liberal Unionists.
● The Liberals secured 183 seats, a gain of only 6 over their disastrous showing in 1895 when they lost many supposedly safe seats.
● The Liberals could also expect the support of 77 Irish National Party MPs and two Labour Representation Committee MPs, but the government majority was immense and there was no immediate indication as to how the Liberals could recover their position.

The Boer War

This conflict was more commonly known as the South African War at the time. It began in October 1899 when forces of the republics of Transvaal and Orange Free State (OFS) attacked British territory in South Africa. Both were recognised by Britain as independent countries but both had agreed in 1884 to accept Britain's influence in the region by agreeing not to conduct relations with other countries without consulting Britain first. Transvaal was mainly inhabited by Dutch-speaking descendants of the original European settlers of southern Africa who had come from Holland. When the war began it went well at first for the 'Boers' (the Dutch word for 'farmer') as most of the people of Transvaal and the OFS were farmers. The British gradually wore down the Boers who conducted a mainly guerrilla campaign. By 1902 the Boer Republics were defeated and agreed to be taken into the British Empire. Later, in 1909, they became part of the Union of South Africa – the area known today as the Republic of South Africa. To counter Boer guerrilla tactics, the British resorted to a policy of putting non-combatants into large camps so they could not aid the Boer fighters. Due to inefficiency and poor hygiene, over 20,000 Boer women, children and elderly men died.

Liberal leadership problems

The Boer War was not the only issue dividing the party. The party leadership was also a very open question. Although the official leader of the Liberals was Sir Henry Campbell-Bannerman, a Scot with quite radical inclinations, his position was far from secure. He had succeeded Sir William Harcourt as the Liberal leader in the Commons only in 1898 when Harcourt gave up the role voluntarily, disillusioned with divisions in the party and the fact that Lord Rosebery had become prime minster rather than himself when Gladstone retired in 1894 (this had been partly due to Queen Victoria's influence in favour of Rosebery whom she liked, against Harcourt whom she did not). Nevertheless, though in his mid-seventies and apparently semi-retired, Harcourt did not give up his seat in the Commons. It was far from clear as to whether he might not want one last chance to be prime minister if the Liberals were re-elected, especially since the Queen died in January 1901 removing that particular obstacle. 'CB', as Campbell-Bannerman was generally known, was already in his mid-sixties and in poor health.

The former Liberal prime minister (1894–95) Lord Rosebery was more than ten years younger. However, Rosebery was an egotistical, arrogant individual, intellectually brilliant but petulant, pedantic and petty-minded. He was given to bouts of depression and introspection that made him a difficult leader to work with. Even so his social prominence, experience and intellectual gifts made him a hard figure to ignore and if the Liberals ever were in a position to form a government it was by no means certain that he would not gain significant support in the party if he were to press his claim.

There were also two rising stars of the Liberals in the Commons – Herbert Henry Asquith and Sir Edward Grey. Asquith was only 50, had already been home secretary (1892–95) and was a brilliant speaker, so could not be ruled out. Grey was younger still at 40 and the least experienced of all the leading Liberals, but he was a charismatic figure who had served as Lord Rosebery's second-in-command at the Foreign Office in 1892–94 and then in the same role to Lord Kimberley, who took over the Foreign Office in 1894–95 when Rosebery became prime minister.

Since both these men were peers, Grey was effectively the Government's leader in the House of Commons on foreign affairs and in that role he had impressed. He also had the prestige of a great family name – his great grandfather was a younger brother of the great Whig prime minister Lord Grey, who had passed the Reform Act of 1832. Apart from Lord Rosebery, all the leading Liberals had accepted 'CB' as leader by 1900, but this did not necessarily mean that he was automatically going to become prime minister if the Liberals won the next election. In fact, his acceptance as leader was partly related to his age and ill-health, the feeling being that he would soon either retire or die.

The Liberals and Labour

For the time being however the problem was how to restore the Liberals' electoral fortunes. It was pointless engaging in speculation over who should lead a future Liberal government unless there was some prospect of there being one. In any case, with so erratic a figure as Rosebery potentially in the frame it was hard to know what his intentions were. In the event, the Liberals were helped by the Government which encountered a whole series of problems that seriously undermined its unity and public image. In the meantime the Liberals had to take into account the new potential threat of the Labour Representation Committee (LRC), formed in 1900 by the TUC to encourage the election of working-class MPs to Parliament (see page 79). The LRC had fielded only fifteen candidates in 1900 and managed to get only two elected. However, the election had been called only a few months after the LRC had been set up. It was clear that it would contest many more seats whenever the next election came around. In many of those seats the Liberals would be either defending the seat or hoping to regain it from the Conservatives. If traditional Liberal voters were tempted to support the LRC the result could be disastrous for the Liberals. Splitting the Liberal or Labour vote in some marginal constituencies could see the Conservatives hold there too.

In 1903 Herbert Gladstone, the Liberal chief whip and son of the former leader, negotiated an agreement with Ramsay MacDonald, one of the LRC leaders. The Liberals agreed to withdraw candidates from 30 constituencies where it was clear that the LRC had a good chance of winning if there was no split vote. The LRC then decided to focus attention on only 50 seats where they had a maximum chance of success. The pact was informal and kept secret. For the time being the Liberals had to wait and hope that events would turn in their favour – they could scarcely have imagined, however, the extent to which that would actually happen.

New Liberalism

New Liberalism arose out of radical opposition within the Liberal Party to the direction that the party was taking in the 1880s. The radicals in the Liberal Party had always disliked the aristocratic nature of the leadership. By the 1880s most of the so-called Old Whigs who had been a major force in the formation of the Liberal Party were dead and the new generation of aristocrats in the party lacked real commitment to radical reform. Even Gladstone, who had been seen by many as the radicals' main hope in the 1860s, had married into the aristocracy and was clearly not a radical when it came to social reform. Gladstone basically believed that progress was achieved by self-improvement and individual effort. He was a man of immense personal wealth who gave generously to charitable causes, but did not believe that governments should intervene directly to help individuals by such methods as providing state pensions for the elderly or helping poorer families support their children. Gladstone's political philosophy emphasised the personal responsibility of the individual. The Gladstonian version of liberalism can be reviewed in detail in Chapter 1. These ideas were essentially very conservative, 'Peelite' principles. Gladstone became more liberal as he grew older on issues such as the right to vote and greater toleration of religious differences. He was even prepared to tolerate a degree of government intervention on social issues where the need was clearly not being met by individual efforts. However, on all these matters there was a limit to his liberalism. It never occurred to Gladstone, for example, that all men might have an inherent right to vote – he assumed that this right had to be earned by demonstrating virtues of education and civilised behaviour. He never accepted the idea that social reform should involve extensive government expenditure or offer the individual direct support that he believed they should gain by their own efforts.

KEY DATES: CHANGING PARTY FORTUNES, 1886–1906

1886 The Conservatives win the general election

1892 Gladstone returns at the head of a Liberal minority government dependent on the Irish Nationalists for a majority

1895 Salisbury's Conservative Party wins an overall majority of ten and forms a coalition government with the Liberal Unionists

1900 The coalition government wins the general election with a slightly smaller but still large majority

WORKING TOGETHER

Conservative dominance, 1886–1905 – a summary

The following list summarises the key reasons for conservative domination in this period:

- The Liberal split over Home Rule in 1886.
- The political skill of Lord Salisbury.
- Gladstone's persistence with Home Rule.
- Gladstone's refusal to pursue more radical social policies.
- Liberal divisions over the leadership post-Gladstone.
- Patriotic feelings over the Boer War.

Work in pairs to identify and justify the factor which you think was most important for conservative domination. In the case of the other factors explain why you think them of lesser importance. Present your findings to the class.

Using your knowledge of the context do you agree with Feuchtwanger's (Source A) or Behagg's (Source B) interpretation of New Liberalism?

These beliefs contrasted strongly with New Liberal principles which sought to put less emphasis on individual action and more stress on collective action, meaning that society as a whole, through government intervention, should take more responsibility for improving the conditions of poorer families. New Liberalism was therefore breaking into areas that were the stuff of nightmares for Gladstone. The following policy ideas were all being discussed as remedies for the social problems that were increasingly evident:

- pensions for the elderly
- state-funded sickness benefits for those suffering from illness or injury
- a national unemployment scheme
- direct payments to help working-class families support their children.

The adoption of similar schemes in Germany in the 1880s only served to increase the sense of urgency. In addition the so-called Socialist Revival of the 1880s (see page 78) saw various groups championing the cause of the working classes spring into existence. These groups insisted that working-class interests could never be properly advanced through the Liberal Party, with its connections to the upper classes and the world of business and commerce. To the New Liberals the emergence of groups that aimed to win over the increasing numbers of male working-class voters indicated that there was an urgent need to show that the Liberals could in fact offer a meaningful package of reform proposals to address working-class interests. Among the leading figures of the party to support this more radical approach was Sir Henry Campbell-Bannerman, Herbert Henry Asquith (widely seen by some as his logical successor as leader) and David Lloyd George, a backbench MP from Wales and an outstanding and inspirational orator, who was increasingly the hero of the radicals.

There is some debate among historians as to how radical or genuinely 'new' New Liberalism was in reality (see Sources A and B).

Source A From *Democracy and Empire: Britain 1865–1914* by Edgar Feuchtwanger, (Edward Arnold), 1986, pp. 276–77.

The New Liberalism was an off-shoot of a wider progressive movement away from individualism and towards collectivism. Little distinguished it from Fabian Socialism; Fabians came together with Liberals in groups such as the Rainbow Circle and in launching and writing for journals such as the *Progressive Review*. New Liberalism argued it was proper for the State to intervene to correct unequal distribution of income through old age pensions, and other social payments and through progressive taxation.

Source B From *Labour and Reform: Working-Class Movements 1815–1914* by Clive Behagg, (Hodder & Stoughton), 1991, p. 125.

The new Liberalism carried with it many of the social attitudes of the old Liberalism. There was the same insistence that the working class consisted of the undeserving as well the deserving poor. The proposed reforms were really aimed at the 'respectable' working class. Old age pensions for example were not intended for those who had failed to work for their own maintenance. Also to be excluded were those who had been in prison ... including those imprisoned as a result of involvement in strikes and political activity. This was designed as a control on working-class behaviour.

2 The Liberal revival: constitutional crisis and reform, 1905–14

The general election of September 1900 was held as the tide was just beginning to turn in Britain's favour in the Boer War. It has become known as the khaki election and was a convincing victory for Lord Salisbury's government, confirming the dominance of the Conservatives, reinforced by their Liberal-Unionist allies, which had been evident since Gladstone's decision to adopt Home Rule in 1886. Its control seemed unshakable.

Conservative decline and the general election of 1906

Why were the Liberals able to recover and go on to an overwhelming victory in the 1906 general election?

The Liberals certainly had no appetite for another election in January 1901 when Queen Victoria died. According to constitutional precedent a general election should have been held since constitutionally parliaments were summoned by the Crown and were deemed to have ended if the monarch died. However, Lord Salisbury pointed out that constitutional practice had changed significantly since 1837 when Victoria had ascended the throne. He argued that since an election had been held only four months previously it would be a good time to break what was obviously an out-of-date practice. There was no argument from the Liberals. However, within a remarkably short space of time a series of scandals and divisions began to erode the Government's standing in public opinion:

- Victory in the Boer War was overshadowed by the scandal of the deaths from disease of thousands of Boer women, children and elderly men in concentration camps where they had been sent to remove them from the conflict and prevent them from supporting the Boer guerrilla forces.
- In 1902 Salisbury retired as prime minister and was replaced by his nephew Arthur Balfour. Balfour was intellectually brilliant, but had limited leadership skills – in particular he could be dangerously indecisive at times.
- Despite a good deal of talk, the Government, with the exception of Joseph Chamberlain, failed to grasp the importance of social reform. Evidence was mounting concerning the condition of the working classes and the failure of Britain to match the kind of reforms covering old-age pensions and sickness benefits that already existed in Germany.
- A huge moral scandal arose in South Africa over the importation of Chinese workers for the mining industry. The terrible conditions endured by these workers gave rise to the term 'Chinese slavery', as the press and social reformers castigated the Government for allowing such a situation to arise and continue.
- A new Education Act in 1902 (see page 113) brought in much-needed improvements in the provision of secondary education, but in doing so it alienated nonconformists who, as traditional Liberal supporters, were confused and divided by the Boer War. They now reunited behind the Liberals, who they hoped would make amendments to the Act if elected.

NOTE-MAKING

Use the headings and questions in Section 2 to make brief notes on the 1906 general election and the constitutional crisis. Structure your notes with headings, sub-headings and sub-points to make them easy to navigate and use (see page x for further guidance).

For example, the following headings could be used to summarise the key points on pages 71–77.

- Was the 1906 election result a positive verdict on the Liberals or a negative verdict on the Conservatives (Unionists)?
- Why was there a constitutional crisis in 1909–11?
- What were the consequences of the constitutional crisis for:
  - the Liberals
  - the Conservatives?

Concentration camps – These camps were so-named because they 'concentrated' elderly men, women and children in areas that were under military control. Once there they could not leave without permission.

- Balfour's government failed to respond to the Taff Vale case (see page 80) by legislating to remove the threat of civil action against unions over strikes. Both the Liberals and (obviously) the LRC supported a change in law.

However, arguably more damaging than all of the above points was the fact that the Government and the party became seriously divided over economic and financial policy.

Chamberlain and tariff reform

In 1903 Joseph Chamberlain announced to the Cabinet that he believed that free trade should be abandoned. In its place he proposed a system of tariffs (taxes) on imports. He argued for 'general tariffs' to be imposed on all goods coming into the country, with 'preferential tariffs', or in some cases exemptions, to be applied to imports from the empire. Chamberlain had come to the conclusion that Britain had to maintain its status as a Great Power in the coming century, against the rise of large countries such as the USA, Germany and Russia. In order to do this he believed Britain had to develop the economic resources of the empire as a whole and bring about closer political links through the creation of a new imperial parliament that would meet regularly but in a different part of the empire each time. Chamberlain also now took the view that the scale of domestic social reform Britain needed could only be funded by the revenues that would flow from tariffs.

Chamberlain's ideas split the Cabinet. Typically Balfour refused to pronounce one way or the other, leaving a disastrous vacuum of authority. Unable to secure government unity behind his scheme, Chamberlain opted to resign as colonial secretary and set up a Tariff Reform League to carry out a national campaign. Some 30 or so Conservative MPs were so alarmed at Chamberlain's proposals that they broke away and joined the Liberals. Among them was a recently elected young MP named Winston Churchill. Chamberlain justified his plan by arguing that this was the only way that far-reaching social reforms could be funded and employment in Britain properly protected. However, the plan had the obvious drawback that food prices would have to rise. Both the Liberal Party and the LRC condemned the plan as detrimental to the interests of the great mass of the ordinary people of Britain.

Balfour's gamble

The next general election did not have to be held until September 1907 so there was time for the Government to look for a way to restore its position, but at the end of 1905 Balfour took a momentous decision. On the basis of an unexpectedly favourable by-election result he decided the Government should resign without calling a general election. It was not in itself unusual as a procedure – Rosebery had done exactly the same thing in 1895 – however Balfour might have reflected that that decision had not exactly turned out well for the Liberals! Balfour's aim was to force the Liberals either to refuse to take office or to do so and engage in a leadership struggle that would cripple them before an election could be held. It was a high-risk, too-clever strategy that misfired badly. The leading Liberals quickly agreed that Campbell-Bannerman should be prime minister and take office at once, calling for a general election in January 1906. In their electoral campaigns the Liberal Party and the LRC both focused on the need to maintain free trade and introduce new social reforms. The Conservative–Liberal Unionist alliance remained divided over free trade.

The result was a staggering election triumph for the Liberals on a totally unexpected scale. They won 400 seats. The Unionists were reduced to a mere 157, some two-thirds of whom were supporters of Chamberlain's tariff reform policy. Balfour himself lost his seat in Manchester and suffered the indignity of having to fight a by-election a month later to get back into the House of Commons. The by-election was hastily arranged for the City of London, a safe seat from which the elected MP stood down to make way for his leader. The overall result meant that the Liberals had a clear majority of 130 over all parties combined, but in practice, with the probable support of the Irish and Labour contingents, this would rise to over 350. The Unionist catastrophe was complete and could scarcely have been more humiliating.

The constitutional crisis, 1909–11

Why did the 1909 Budget lead to a constitutional crisis?

The Liberal Government that came to power in December 1905 with Sir Henry Campbell-Bannerman as prime minister was determined to bring forward a more radical policy of social reform, though somewhat like Disraeli's government in 1874 it had not formulated very specific plans. Nevertheless, following the general election victory, reforming legislation was not long forthcoming in 1906 (see page 115). In April 1908, Campbell-Bannerman was finally forced to resign due to illness which had dogged him for years – he died less than three weeks later. Asquith took over as prime minister and Lloyd George, who had built up a formidable reputation as president of the Board of Trade, was promoted to chancellor of the exchequer. He was replaced at the Board of Trade by Winston Churchill. Churchill was a former Conservative who had joined the Liberals in protest against the policy of tariff reform in 1903. He had since established himself as a radical reformer.

The new government was a shot in the arm for the principles of New Liberalism. Asquith was far more energetic and ambitious than Campbell-Bannerman. Lloyd George and Churchill were determined to use their new seniority to push for a much more ambitious programme of social reform.

▲ David Lloyd George, Welsh Radical and the only British Prime Minister so far for whom English was a second language.

Not only did they genuinely want more radical reforms, they also believed that it was a political necessity for the Liberals to show themselves capable of developing a truly progressive policy if the party was not to lose out in future elections to the Unionists and the Labour Party. Asquith had already been planning an ambitious Budget for 1909 in which he intended to raise taxes to fund social reform. In this way he aimed to destroy the anti-free-trade argument that only tariff reform could generate enough revenue to support social spending on a large scale. Now he handed the responsibility for completing the work and shaping the detailed plans to Lloyd George. There was however a complication. International tension had been building for some time and Britain had been involved in confrontations with Germany in 1898 over South Africa, and in 1905–06 over Morocco. The German Government was committed to an ambitious programme of naval expansion and a trading nation like Great Britain, with an empire reaching across the globe, could not afford to sacrifice naval supremacy. Thus increased spending on the navy was not optional and this, together with plans to fund social reform, meant a serious increase in government revenue was necessary. In his 1909 Budget, David Lloyd George planned to fund social and naval spending by increasing levels of personal taxation on the wealthier classes. There were two new strategies:

- A 'surtax' on higher incomes, on a graduated scale that taxed income of over £3,000 per annum at a higher rate and income over £5,000 per annum higher still.
- A tax on increasing property values when land was sold, and an annual tax on land value along with a tax on land leased for mining.
- In addition there was to be an increase in death duties, a tax on petrol and a new tax on car licences.

The response of the Unionist Party was immediately hostile. There was genuine resentment at the idea of the wealthier classes being deliberately targeted and anger at the intrusive nature of the land valuation proposals. However, behind that there was the realisation that if the Budget succeeded in generating sufficient revenue to fund both social reform and naval expansion, the case for tariff reform as the only means of funding for such government spending would be completely disproved.

The Budget rejected

Initially, neither Balfour nor Lord Lansdowne (the Unionist leader in the Lords) grasped the extent of the anger of the peers and the landowning classes they represented. They assumed that they would fight the Budget in the Commons and try to force concessions as best they could. However, as the Budget progressed in the Commons it became clear that the Government was in no mood to compromise. This raised the question of whether the House of Lords could find grounds to reject the Budget. The Lords had already rejected Liberal bills on education, the ending of plural voting and further restrictions on the sale and consumption of alcohol. However, none of these bills had any mass public appeal; the 1909 Budget was very different. It was constitutional practice that no 'money' bill should be interfered with in the Lords, but Lloyd George had included some clauses in the Budget which could be challenged as not strictly appropriate, such as a clause providing for the introduction of child allowances of £10 per year per child for less wealthy families.

In November 1909, after long debate, the Lords finally voted down the Budget. Asquith immediately called a general election for January 1910. The unnatural and unsustainable nature of the Liberal landslide of 1906 was revealed as, despite a popular campaign for the reforming Budget, the Unionists regained a lot of their lost support.

- The Liberals were reduced to 275 seats and the Unionists rose to 273.
- The Irish Nationalists held 82 seats and the Labour Party, fighting for the first time as such, won 40.
- The Liberals therefore had a substantial majority of support, even though technically it was a minority government.

The result meant the Lords had to allow the Budget through, but the nature of the political scene had now changed. Since 1906 the Liberals had set the Irish Home Rule question to one side – now the Irish Nationalists made it clear that their continued support for the Government was dependent on a new Home Rule Bill being introduced. Since such a bill could not pass the Lords' power of veto, it was clear that before any attempt was made the powers of the Lords would need to be restricted by a change in the constitution.

The origins of the resulting constitutional crisis, which was triggered by Lloyd George's Budget proposals, did not lie in the House of Lords' opposition to the principles of New Liberalism, for example, to the Government's social reforms. On the contrary, the Unionist leadership generally welcomed the introduction of old-age pensions and the reforms affecting children (see page 117–19). They even promised to improve upon them if returned to office. The real roots of the crisis lay in the political helplessness to which the Unionists were reduced in the House of Commons after the 1906 general election. With only 157 MPs, the Unionists were almost irrelevant in the lower house and it was not surprising that they began to consider how they might use their continued predominance in the House of Lords to try to redress the imbalance. At the height of the crisis over the Budget, Lloyd George made a speech in Newcastle (see Source C).

Source C David Lloyd George's speech at Newcastle, 9 October 1909. From *Great Lives Observed: Lloyd George* edited by Martin Gilbert, (Prentice-Hall), 1968, p. 37.

The question will be asked whether 500 men chosen accidentally from among the unemployed [meaning the peers] should override the judgement of millions of people who are engaged in the industry which makes the wealth of the country. Another question will be – who ordained that a few should have the land of Britain? Who made ten thousand people owners of the soil and the rest of us trespassers in the land of our birth? How is it that one man is engaged through life in grinding labour and another who does not toil receives more every hour, even whilst he slumbers, than his poor neighbour receives in a whole year of toil? The answers are charged with peril for the order of things the peers represent.

1 What evidence is there in Source C to suggest that Lloyd George deliberately intended to provoke the peers?

2 What other motives might he have had for expressing these views?

Unionist obstruction in Parliament, 1906–09

The Unionist leader Balfour had made a rather unwise comment in the heat of the 1906 election campaign, saying that 'the great Unionist Party should still control, whether in power or opposition, the destinies of this great Empire'. This was not intended as a commitment to blanket opposition to a future Liberal government. In fact it was aimed at the specific issue of Irish Home Rule. Balfour was only too aware that the power of the Lords needed to be used selectively and with caution if it was to be effective. Between 1906 and 1909, therefore, the bills chosen for obstruction by the Unionist peers were identified carefully, in the hope of extracting the maximum embarrassment for the Liberals while steering away from issues where the Government might secure popular support. The Lords rejected three major bills in the period 1906–08:

- An Education Bill in 1906 aimed at redressing some nonconformist grievances from the 1902 Education Act.
- A bill to end the plural voting rule that allowed men with property in different constituencies to vote in each of them.
- A Licensing Bill aimed at further restrictions on the sale and consumption of alcohol.

This hardly amounted to a wholesale wrecking of the Government's legislative programme. Significantly a trade union reform in 1906 was allowed to pass, even though this allowed trade unions protection from being sued by their employers over strikes. In addition, all of the social reforms detailed in Chapter 3 went through as they realised it would be counter-productive to reject reforms with wide popular appeal.

The House of Lords reformed, 1911

The Parliament Bill that the Government introduced in 1910 contained no surprises and provoked the greatest political crisis in Britain since 1831–32. It provided that:

- The Lords could not reject or amend financial legislation.
- There would be a limit of two rejections or amendments on other legislation in successive sessions within the life of a parliament.
- The maximum duration of a parliament (that is, the length of time between general elections) was reduced from seven to five years. This was actually a concession to the Lords since it reduced the time a government with a majority had to pass laws before facing a new election.

The bill was introduced in April 1910. It was clear that the Lords would not pass it unless forced to do so by the threat of a mass creation of new peers, such as had secured the passage of the Great Reform Act in 1832. However, in early May Edward VII died and Asquith refused to press the new King George V with the matter immediately. This left the way open for compromise talks between the Liberals and Unionists in the summer and autumn of 1910, which failed to produce a solution. Asquith therefore decided that another general election must be held and agreed with the King that if the Lords subsequently rejected the Parliament Bill a mass creation of peers willing to vote for it would follow. The general election in December 1910 produced virtually identical results as in January: Liberals 272, Unionists 272, Irish 84, Labour 42.

Even faced with the threat of a mass creation of new peers, there was still a die-hard attitude in the Lords that threatened to force the issue that far. Asquith, though prepared to force through the bill that way, did not really want to do so. Consequently negotiations dragged on into the summer of 1911 as leading Unionists tried to find a way to head off their angry backbench peers. Finally in August 1911 enough Lords gave up the fight by abstaining or agreeing to vote for the bill and the crisis ended with the Parliament Act voted through by 131 to 114. Robert Blake, in his history of the Conservative Party, laid the blame squarely on Balfour and the other leaders. The rejection of the 1909 Budget he called an 'insane decision' and an 'error that neither Disraeli nor Derby would have committed'.

The Conservative Party, 1906–14

Balfour's disastrous miscalculation at the end of 1905 left the Conservatives and Liberal Unionists in complete disarray. Not only had the Government suffered a massive defeat, they were still divided over the issue of tariff reform with some two-thirds of the Conservative–Liberal Unionist MPs supporting Chamberlain's view on the issue. Remarkably, Balfour's leadership continued.

In July 1906, Chamberlain suffered a stroke which ended his active political career – he eventually died of a heart attack in 1914. This weakened the 'Unionist Party', as it was increasingly being called, still further although it probably prevented a struggle between Balfour and Chamberlain over the leadership. Gradually, the 'Unionists' consolidated around Chamberlain's argument that only a policy of imperial economic development and a general tariff to protect the British economy could generate sufficient revenues to fund social reform. In 1910 there were two general elections sparked by the constitutional crisis that developed over the 1909 Budget (see page 74). Although the Unionists recovered to virtual parity with the Liberals in terms of seats, the support for the Liberal Government from the Irish Nationalists meant that the Liberals were still secure in power so long as they retained that support which could deliver over 80 MPs' votes. The great constitutional crisis of 1909–11 ended with the powers of the House of Lords being restricted by the Parliament Act of 1911. This finally weakened Balfour's position as leader.

In late 1911 Balfour resigned at last and was replaced by Andrew Bonar Law – not the most prominent figure in the party and a compromise between Walter Long and Austen Chamberlain (son of Joseph). Both wanted the leadership and support for them was evenly divided, so to avoid the danger of a long drawn-out struggle and subsequent bitter division Law was agreed on as the best option. He had been born in the colony of New Brunswick in 1858, which became part of Canada in 1867. Late in his life he would briefly be prime minister (1922–23) before a serious illness ended his career and not long after his life. In the meantime however his becoming leader carried a major implication. His family background was in Ulster and he identified strongly with the Ulster resistance to Home Rule. Law would prove eventually to be no makeshift leader but a really effective politician in the longer term. For the time being though, he had inherited a weak position in the Commons and he settled for underlining the Unionist support for tariff reform and opposition to Home Rule. Balfour remained an important figure in the party and would later be First Lord of the Admiralty and then foreign secretary in the wartime coalition governments.

Arthur Balfour

Balfour was Lord Salisbury's nephew. He become an MP in 1874. When Salisbury became prime minister in 1885 he gave Balfour the post of president of the Local Government Board and the following year made him Secretary for Scotland.In 1887 he promoted him to Chief Secretary for Ireland. Given the difficult situation in Ireland after the failure of Home Role in 1886, this was a very big promotion and caused a lot of adverse comment about Salisbury's decision. The popular slang phrase, 'Bob's your uncle', meaning something easy or straight forward to achieve or understand, is widely stated to have derived from this, since Salisbury's first name was Robert. There are however many other plausible explanations for the phrase. Later Balfour served as Leader of the House of Commons, effectively the deputy to the prime minister if the prime minister was in the Lords, and as First Lord of the Treasury - a post normally held by the prime minister. Balfour was to be the last non-prime minister to hold the post.

KEY DATES: CONSTITUTIONAL CRISIS AND REFORM, 1905–14

1902	Salisbury retires and is replaced as prime minister by his nephew Arthur Balfour
1905 Dec	Balfour resigns as prime minister but does not call for a general election
	The Liberals take over government with Campbell-Bannerman as prime minister; he calls an immediate general election for January
1906	The Liberals win the election with an overwhelming majority
1908	Campbell-Bannerman retires and is replaced as prime minister by Asquith. Lloyd George replaces Asquith at the Exchequer
1909	Lloyd George's 'People's Budget' provokes the House of Lords to break with accepted practice and reject it
1910 Jan	The Liberals hold a general election to confirm a mandate for their Budget. They lose their overall majority but secure a strong majority with Irish and Labour Party support
	The Liberals introduce a bill to reform Parliament by limiting the powers of the House of Lords
May	The death of Edward VII delays the progress of the crisis
Dec	Another general election confirms the Liberal Government's ability to pass the bill through the Commons
1911	The Parliament Act is finally passed in August

3 The rise of the Labour Movement and the emergence of the Labour Party, 1893–1914

NOTE-MAKING

Use the headings and questions in Section 3 to make brief notes on the Labour Movement and the Labour Party. Structure your notes with headings, sub-headings and sub-points to make them easy to navigate and use (see page x for further guidance).

For example, the following headings could be used to summarise the key points on pages 78–81.

● What factors led to the formation of the Labour Representation Committee?
● How important were the trade unions to the emergence of the Labour Party in 1906?
● Was the Labour Party making any real progress after 1906?

The term 'Labour Movement' is an umbrella expression which covers a range of different developments which are linked together by the general theme of helping the working classes of the country improve their living and working conditions and increase their ability to influence political decisions. The growth of trade unions was a major factor in this process. In the 1850s the development of New Model Unions such as the Amalgamated Society of Engineers (ASE) saw the highly skilled, better-paid working classes forming trade unions to protect and improve their standard of living (see pages 45–46). The focus of these unions was not so much on direct confrontation with employers, though that did happen from time to time. Generally these model unions saw strikes as counter-productive and a weapon of last resort. They charged relatively high subscriptions and used these to build up funds that could be deployed for welfare benefits for their members. Unemployment and sickness/injury benefit schemes resulted, along with death benefits, widows and orphans funds and medical benefits provision. These unions were as keen to protect themselves against other workers as to secure the best conditions from their employers. They represented an elite group of workers, which has sometimes been called the 'labour aristocracy'. Though some individuals within the New Model Unions were interested in politics as organisations, they were inclined to keep their distance from political action. To some radicals these unions were betrayers of the working class: they had come to terms with the capitalist system and were using it to benefit themselves to the exclusion of the wider working-class interest.

The socialist revival and the emergence of the Labour Representation Committee

To what extent was the socialist revival the main influence behind the emergence of the Labour Party?

In the 1880s a new wave of trade unionism began to embrace the lesser-skilled or unskilled lower-paid workers. This development, known as New Unionism (not to be confused with New Model Unionism which focused on higher-paid workers), brought into existence truly mass movement unions aiming to recruit huge numbers of workers, paying lower (affordable) subscriptions and focused much more on aggressive confrontation to secure better pay and conditions. Examples of these new unions were:

● the Dockers Union
● the National Union of Dock Labourers
● the Gasworkers' Union
● the National Sailors' and Firemen's Union.

The new trade unions enjoyed a close relationship with new political groups which were taking shape, inspired by socialist principles, which argued that private ownership of all forms of property should be abolished and property should be owned in common, by all of the people. The main socialist inspired groups were:

● **The Social Democratic Federation (1881)** – revolutionary group that believed in the forcible overthrow of the existing political, social and economic order. The SDF based its programme on the ideas of Karl Marx.

- **The Fabian Socialists (1884)** – largely upper-class intellectuals favouring a peaceful, democratic and gradual path to socialism. They took their name from a famous Roman general (Fabius) who favoured patient gradual strategies rather than spectacular but costly frontal attacks on his enemies. Many of the Fabians were writers and academics whose interest in politics was detached and analytical rather than practical or professional.
- **The Socialist League (1885)** – another slightly milder version of the SDF.
- **The Independent Labour Party (1893)** – trade-union-linked and with a strong nonconformist Christian tone, this group had the intention of breaking into the House of Commons by running candidates in promising constituencies.

In 1868 the Trade Union Congress (TUC) had been formed. This aimed to give more unity to trade unions, which often came into conflict with each other as much as with employers. By the 1890s problems in the economy were leading to increasing tensions between unions and employers. Even the leading New Model Union, the ASE, became militant and went on strike only to be forced back to work on the employers' terms.

Then in 1896 came a court case, *Lyons v. Wilkins*. This case, along with the rising influence of the inherently more militant New Unions, meant that the TUC became much more politically minded. In 1897 the TUC member unions voted to allow more central authority to the TUC to take a more militant line. In 1899 the TUC decided to push for a new initiative to ensure more working-class representation in the House of Commons. To do this it turned for advice to the existing political movements advocating working-class interests. The result was the formation of the Labour Representation Committee (LRC) in 1900.

The impact of the LRC was to bring together the trade unions, the Independent Labour Party (ILP), the Fabians and the Social Democratic Federation (SDF) in an alliance aimed at securing the election of MPs to directly represent the working class. From the start, the ILP was the dominant force in organising the strategy of the LRC, but the initiative was too late to have much impact on the general election of 1900. Only fifteen candidates were put up and of these only two were elected. However, the LRC was not discouraged: it aimed to prepare for the next election.

Lyons v. Wilkins

The case involved a strike by the Amalgamated Society of Leather Workers in which the union was taken to court by the firm of J. Lyons & Son, which complained that union pickets were intimidating workers who wished to continue working during the strike. Wilkins was the trade union official formally named in the action. Effectively the judgment upheld the right of workers to work, and suggested it was illegal to picket to prevent them from doing so. The defence counsel for the union appealed to Disraeli's 1875 Act, which permitted pickets 'attending in order to obtain or communicate information', but the judgment in *Lyons v. Wilkins* said there was no distinction between this, and 'watching and besetting', and encompassed both under 'persuasion' which it held to be illegal.

Karl Marx

Marx was a German-born philosopher who argued that a struggle between social classes for control of economic resources is the primary driving force in history. He argued that the emergence of a global socialist (or communist) society was an inevitable process and that it could be advanced more quickly by revolution against any existing ruling elite. Marx argued that the old agricultural elites of the pre-industrial age had already been overthrown by industrial capitalism and the next stage was for the industrial working class to overthrow the capitalist system in a revolution and establish control of economic resources. His ideas are contained in two main works, *The Communist Manifesto* (1848) and *Capital* (1867), in which he aimed to show that the capitalist system is forced to exploit labour in order to make profits and is doomed ultimately to fail. 'Capital' is defined as any form of wealth that can be used to invest in profit-making ventures. So capital might take the form of money, land, buildings, machinery, vehicles for transportation and so on. According to Marx, a worker's capital is his labour, skilled or unskilled.

Marx's ideas are highly controversial and some of his main assumptions can be disproved easily. Marx disliked trade unions, which he saw as conforming to capitalism and dividing workers rather than uniting them. He opposed parliamentary democracy and social reform legislation as attempts to buy off the workers and divert them from revolution. Many of his ideas are vague, especially those which relate to how society is to be administered after the overthrow of capitalism, thus Marxists do not agree about many issues and there are several different varieties of Marxism. Nevertheless, his ideas, and particularly the ways his ideas were subsequently interpreted, had great influence in the twentieth century.

The Taff Vale case and judgment, 1901

In 1900 the Amalgamated Society of Railway Servants (ASRS), the railwaymen's trade union, targeted the Taff Vale Railway Company which was refusing to recognise the union as the representative of its employees for negotiating pay and conditions. The union called a strike in August 1900 to force the company to back down. The Taff Vale Company reacted angrily. It regarded itself as a good employer – it had for example started a non-contributory pension scheme in 1893 for employees who had worked for the company for 25 years or more. The company initially got an injunction in the High Court against the strike but this was overturned on appeal by the union. In the course of this case however the issue of whether the union was liable in civil law for losses caused to the employer during the strike arose. In 1901 the employer sued the ASRS for losses and damages and finally won the case when it went to the House of Lords after conflicting verdicts in the lower courts. With damages set at £23,000 and legal costs close to £20,000 the union suffered a severe blow and the implications for unions undertaking strikes in the future were obvious.

The case became a driving influence for the LRC, which set itself the goal of securing a change in the law to make trade unions immune to being sued for losses resulting from strike action. Such a change, the LRC believed, could only be achieved if there was significant working-class representation in the House of Commons.

The fortunes of the Labour Party, 1906–14

In the 1906 general election the LRC secured 29 seats. In the January 1910 election, now formally constituted as the Labour Party, 40 Labour MPs were elected. In the December 1910 election Labour won 42. The number of candidates put forward in these elections fluctuated due to issues of cost, but overall the figures suggest a modest but clear progress in the party's fortunes.

This however is misleading. In 1906 the LRC formally changed its name to the Labour Party. In the House of Commons the 29 LRC candidates were joined by two independent Labour MPs and 21 trade-union-sponsored MPs who had previously sat as Liberals. This total of 52 was reduced in January 1910 to 40. It rose in December 1910 to 42 but then in a series of by-elections Labour lost seats, falling back to 36 by 1914. Purely in terms of parliamentary elections therefore the Labour Party was not showing signs that it could break through to displace the Liberals as the natural party of opposition to the Conservatives. It should be noted that in the 1910 election all the Labour MPs were elected in constituencies where the Liberals did not put up a candidate.

There were some positive indicators because the party did increasingly well in local government elections. It is also the case that some of the reforms introduced by the Liberal Government can be seen as concessions to Labour:

● The School Meals Act of 1906 was originally a backbench Labour MP's bill, which the Liberals agreed to take over.
● The Liberals also passed the Trades Disputes Act in 1906, which effectively reversed the Taff Vale verdict and freed trade unions from the fear of civil action over strikes.
● In 1909 a court case known as the *Osborne Judgment* held that it was illegal for trade unions to use members' subscriptions for political purposes, that is, to help fund the Labour Party. This was a severe blow to the party's finances. In 1913 the Liberal Government passed the Trade Union Act which reversed the *Osborne Judgment*.

- In 1911 the Liberals introduced payment to MPs of a salary of £400 a year, enabling working-class men to become MPs without needing outside support such as from patrons or trade unions.
- In 1912 the Government agreed to introduce a Minimum Wage Act for Mining to end the strikes that were crippling coal production (see page 104).

Interpretations vary as to the meaning of these concessions. It can be argued that the Liberal governments were only doing what they genuinely believed was the right thing by making concessions of this kind. Alternatively, it might be that the aim was to steal the Labour Party's thunder by heading off grievances, suggesting in effect that the Liberals saw the Labour Party as a genuine political rival. In the meantime the Labour Party had to adapt to its relationship with the trade unions as a period of hostile industrial relations ensued. At the end of 1910 a major dispute broke out in the south Wales coalfields which led to strikes and violent confrontations. In serious rioting in Tonypandy in 1911 a man was killed after a battle with the police. The army was called in by Winston Churchill, who was the Home Secretary in the Liberal Government. Sympathy strikes were mounted by the Seamen's Union and the railwaymen and dockers. In 1912 the mining strike went national and there were further strikes by dockers and transport workers. In 1914 the miners' union, the railwaymen and the National Transport Workers' Federation proposed the formation of a Triple Alliance to coordinate their action in the future. This seemed to some like a victory for a Marxist interpretation known as syndicalism, which argued that trade unions could, through a general strike, hasten the end of capitalism. In reality it was more about imposing more top-down control through the unions' leadership. Many of the strikes that had occurred had not been called with leadership approval but had developed locally and had been damaging. For example, the 1912 miners' strike had cost the railwaymen's union £94,000 in compensation for their members laid off during the strike.

For the Labour Party the rise of militancy among the unions was difficult to manage. It heightened differences between moderates and extremists in the party. The syndicalists condemned parliamentary democracy and the Labour Party as irrelevant. Labour leaders such as the future Labour prime minister Ramsay MacDonald tried to support the workers' position in the Commons while at the same time trying to arbitrate and find compromises behind the scenes.

Figure 1 Governments from 1886–1914

Dates	Prime Minister	Party
1886–92	Lord Salisbury	Conservative
1892–94	W. E. Gladstone	Liberal
1894–95	Lord Rosebery	Liberal
1895–1902	Lord Salisbury	Conservative/Liberal Unionist Coalition
1902–05	A.J. Balfour	Conservative/Liberal Unionist Coalition
1905–08	Sir H. Campbell-Bannerman	Liberal
1908–14	H. H. Asquith	Liberal

General strike – A situation in which all trade union workers go on strike to support a particular cause, regardless of whether they are directly involved in the dispute.

KEY DATES: THE LABOUR MOVEMENT AND LABOUR PARTY, 1893–1914

1893 Formation of the Independent Labour Party

1896 *Lyons v. Wilkins* case verdict restricts peaceful picketing

1900 Formation of the Labour Representation Committee – two LRC MPs are elected in the general election the same year

1901 The Taff Vale case verdict

1903 Electoral pact with the Liberals is agreed

1906 29 LRC-sponsored MPs are elected at the general election. The LRC formally changes its name to the Labour Party. Two independent Labour MPs and 21 trade-union-sponsored MPs join the Parliamentary Labour Party

1906 Trades Disputes Act

1909 *Osborne Judgment* threatens Labour Party funds

1910 January and December: general elections see 40 and 42 Labour MPs elected respectively

1913 Trade Union Act reverses *Osborne Judgment*

NOTE-MAKING

Use the headings and questions in Section 4 to make brief notes on the Irish Question. Structure your notes with headings, sub-headings and sub-points to make them easy to navigate and use (see page x for further guidance).

For example, the following headings could be used to summarise the key points on pages 82–88.

- What factors prevented Ireland from achieving Home Rule?
- How important was the revival of Irish nationalism?
- What was the impact of the third Home Rule crisis for:
  - British politics
  - Ireland?

4 The Irish Question

Chapter 1 gives the background to the Irish Question and Gladstone's attempts to deal with the problems of Ireland up to 1885. Up to this point no mainstream British politician of any stature had ever suggested that the solution to Ireland's problems lay in Home Rule. On the contrary, the assumption had been that from a British perspective Home Rule was a threat to the Union of Great Britain and Ireland and consequently out of the question.

Gladstone and the failure of Home Rule

To what extent was Gladstone's failure to achieve Irish Home Rule due to his own mistakes?

Gladstone's decision in 1885 to commit himself to achieving Home Rule for Ireland had profound consequences for British politics. In splitting the Liberal Party over the issue and then deciding, once defeated, to remain as leader and continue the fight, he created the Liberal Unionist Party which would ultimately move into a full alliance and eventual union with the Conservatives. This removed the radical leader Joseph Chamberlain, whom many had seen as a future Liberal prime minister, from the party and reinvented him as a minister in Conservative–Liberal Unionist coalition government. All this resulted from Gladstone's introduction of the first Home Rule Bill in April 1886.

Gladstone's proposal would have meant:

- A single Irish Assembly – Gladstone deliberately did not use the term 'Parliament' because he did not want to imply that the Union was being repealed and the old Irish Parliament of the eighteenth century being restored.
- All Irish MPs would be excluded from the Westminster Parliament.
- Britain would still retain control over issues of war, peace, national defence, treaties with other countries, trade and currency and, initially, the Royal Irish Constabulary.

The above points give a simplified sense of the complexity of Gladstone's proposals. The full terms seemed bizarre and convoluted, even to those who wanted Home Rule. Parnell said that the bill had 'great faults', but agreed to support it. Crucially Gladstone ruled out any concessions to the Protestants of Ulster who were opposed to being put under a Roman-Catholic-dominated assembly in Dublin. In June 1886 the bill was finally defeated by 341 votes to 311, with 93 Liberals voting against. In Ulster anti-Home Rule rioting gave way to wild celebrations. Gladstone called a general election for July 1886, hoping voters would endorse his vision of a pacified Ireland under Home Rule, but:

- the Conservatives won 317 seats to the Liberals' 191
- the rebel Liberals, campaigning as Liberal Unionists and supporting the Conservatives, won 77 seats
- the Irish National Party (INP) won 85 seats.

Home Rule was dead, at least for the time being, but Gladstone was not prepared to give up. His decision to remain as Liberal leader to make a further attempt in the future dramatically changed the course of British politics.

The Conservatives' strategy

The fact that the Liberals were committed to Home Rule meant that the Conservatives and the Liberal Unionists were obliged to cooperate in order to resist any interference with the Union that might end up becoming a step towards separation. Gladstone insisted that Home Rule was the way to strengthen the Union. Unionists – Conservative and Liberal – did not agree. However, simply disagreeing did not change the fact that Ireland could not simply be left without reform. Both Salisbury and Chamberlain accepted this.

Although Parnell and the INP eventually saw that Home Rule was never going to be on offer from the Conservatives, this did not mean that the Conservatives had no strategy. When Gladstone's second government fell in the summer of 1885, Salisbury took over as prime minister and moved quickly to appease Irish opinion. The Coercion Acts were ended and the Government set up a scheme (Ashbourne's Act, 1885) to provide government funding for loans to enable Irish tenants to buy the land they were renting from their landlords. The idea proved popular with some landlords who were fed up with continually falling rents.

The fall of Parnell

In 1891 Irish nationalism suffered a major setback when the INP split over a bitter dispute. Parnell's longstanding and adulterous relationship with Mrs Katherine O'Shea became public. The Irish Roman Catholic Church, which had previously supported Parnell despite his being an Anglican landowner, was outraged and turned against him. The party and the country split into pro- and anti-Parnell camps. The Liberal Party, conscious of the feelings of its important following among nonconformists, condemned Parnell as an adulterer. Gladstone commented that if Parnell remained as leader of the INP then his own leadership of the Liberals would be pointless since the policy of Home Rule would be impossible to sustain. Parnell, whose health had always been suspect, collapsed and died (he was only 45) under the strain. The bitterness of the dispute lived on after his death. It was not until 1900 that the party reunited with John Redmond, who had stood by Parnell in the crisis, as its leader.

Gladstone tries again for Home Rule

Despite these problems Gladstone attempted Home Rule again when he returned to power in 1892. In his revised Home Rule Bill of 1893 he made one important concession compared to 1886. He now agreed to allow 80 Irish MPs to sit at Westminster. The bill passed in the Commons by a majority of 30 because the INP held the balance of power and supported it. In the Lords however the bill was defeated by 419 votes to 41. The Lords' defiance risked a constitutional confrontation for refusing to pass a major bill already passed by the Commons. However, the Lords were confident that they could resist because:

- the Lords knew that there was little sympathy for the idea of Home Rule among the general public
- since the bill only passed because of the support of the INP, the Lords could claim that the interests of the United Kingdom were being threatened by a minority.

The defeat of the second Home Rule Bill did not result in Gladstone's immediate resignation, nor did he call for a general election since his Cabinet colleagues made it clear that they could not support such a move purely on the issue of Home Rule. However, he was increasingly out of step with his Liberal colleagues on more than just the Irish Question. Late in 1893 he was appalled to find that all his Cabinet colleagues agreed with an opposition motion to increase the size of the Royal Navy. Gladstone considered the additional cost a waste of public expenditure. He was also opposed to Sir William Harcourt's decision in the 1894 Budget to increase death duties, a proposal he called the most radical he had encountered in his entire political career. Gladstone resigned on 2 March 1894, convinced that the Liberal Party was moving in a direction he could neither control nor approve.

The nationalist revival

In these circumstances, it might be considered surprising that Ireland entered a relatively peaceful period. Many Irishmen had not really expected Home Rule to pass anyway and the improvement in the general condition of Ireland meant that many Irishmen felt that Home Rule could be left until there was better chance of success. However, this did not mean that Irish nationalism was a thing of the past.

National pride found expression in a great cultural revival that emphasised the importance of restoring the status of the Irish language, which had long been in decline. Irish sports began to flourish; Irish literature, dance and music recruited new enthusiasts. This movement was marked by the formation of organisations such as the Gaelic League, founded in 1893, and by the expansion of earlier groups such as the Gaelic Athletic Association (1884). Even so, despite the unthreatening tone of the cultural revival, nationalism of this kind could not be wholly divorced from a political context. The fundamental message of the revival was anti-British and encouraged a sense of distinct Irish consciousness. It required only a change in the political climate to harness this sense of a separate Irish identity to a political agenda.

Two new political groups emerged after 1900:

- A labour movement began to take shape, led by an able trade union leader named James Connolly. This was Marxist in outlook and argued for a violent class-based revolution to secure Irish independence as a means of then establishing a socialist state in Ireland.
- In 1905 a prominent Irish nationalist named Arthur Griffiths set up a new group called *Sinn Fein* (Ourselves Alone), modelled on similar movements for national independence in Europe.

There remained the extremist fringe of the Irish Republican Brotherhood (IRB), which still aimed at violent rebellion to secure independence. The IRB agreed with Connolly about the use of violence but was nationalist rather than Marxist in outlook. Griffiths completely ruled out violence as a means of gaining independence.

Concessions to nationalism

The alliance of Conservatives and Liberal Unionists, which formed the Unionist Government of 1895–1905, hoped to bury the issue of Home Rule once and for all. The Land Act of 1903, usually known as 'Wyndham's Act' after George Wyndham, the chief secretary for Ireland, substantially completed the transfer of land from landlords to tenants that had begun under Gladstone in the 1880s. This was the cornerstone of the Unionist strategy by which Ireland was to be pacified. The INP was in two minds about this process. On the one hand, they could hardly condemn the end of the hated absentee landlords; on the other, they recognised that with their passing they had lost one of their most potent political weapons. They consoled themselves with the thought that the Liberal Party remained pledged to the introduction of Home Rule and waited on events.

The impact of the constitutional crisis, 1909–11

The constitutional crisis of 1909–11 opened up the possibility of a new Home Rule Bill. The INP leader John Redmond pledged support for the Liberal Government providing it honoured its longstanding commitment to Home Rule. However, while the Liberals had a vast majority in the House of Commons they could focus on wider issues of social reform rather than open up the issue of Home Rule again. The official policy remained that Home Rule was the preferred solution. It was simply not the top priority as Gladstone had made it. However, in 1909 the British political scene began to change dramatically. The crisis over the 1909 Budget resulted in some momentous developments for Ireland. The general election at the beginning of 1910 saw the Liberals lose their overall majority in the House of Commons. From now on they were to be a minority government, with the Irish Nationalist MPs holding the balance of power. This was followed by the constitutional crisis and the Parliament Act of 1911, depriving the House of Lords of its indefinite veto over legislation.

These changes put Irish Home Rule back at the top of the political agenda. During the Budget crisis Redmond had opposed a Budget clause increasing whisky duty as it would have damaged Irish distilleries. The Government needed Irish support for the Budget which, added to the support of the Labour Party, would mean huge majorities and a clear mandate to take on any continued resistance in the House of Lords. In this crisis and the one that followed over the Parliament Act, Redmond based his support on the assurance that Irish Home Rule would be a priority once the curbing of the powers of the House of Lords had been achieved. He made it clear that the Irish would act to disrupt government policy if Home Rule remained on the shelf.

Redmond's threat of disruption was a bluff since there was no alternative government from which he could expect to obtain Home Rule. It was however a bluff that was not called. The Liberal commitment to Home Rule, though not as passionate as Gladstone's had been, was genuine. This was not to say, though, that any demands the INP presented would simply be met in full. Asquith, the prime minister, intended to introduce a limited Home Rule Bill that could not be credibly represented by Unionists as paving the way for eventual independence. This was an unrealistic strategy because the Unionists argued, with some justification, that any measure of Home Rule would stimulate further nationalist demands. Other leading Liberals, like Lloyd George and Winston Churchill, believed that a separate deal for Ulster would have to be devised in the end. Asquith knew they would face fanatical opposition within Ulster itself, along with strong resistance from the Unionist Party in Britain.

The Parliament Act, which was the key to overcoming opposition in the House of Lords, was in reality something of a mixed blessing. It ensured that a Home Rule Bill could be passed, but since the peers could reject the bill twice before being constitutionally compelled to accept it on the third occasion, it also meant that there would be a minimum period of two years before enactment, during which opponents could take up extreme positions.

Home Rule and the Ulster crisis, 1912–14

Was the third Home Rule Bill a reasonable and practical solution for Ireland's problems?

The third Home Rule Bill was introduced into the House of Commons in April 1912. The terms were:

- An Irish Parliament would be set up with an elected House of Commons and a nominated upper chamber called the Senate, with limited powers, especially restricted in financial affairs.
- Forty-two Irish MPs were still to sit at Westminster.
- Ulster was to be included in the new Home Rule Parliament.

It was a moderate proposal leaving considerable control of Irish affairs with the Westminster Parliament. It constituted a limited devolution of self-government. As such it was almost certain to be criticised by unionists and nationalists alike.

To John Redmond and the INP moderates it was barely acceptable and could only be sold to the more extreme INP members as a starting point for future progress.

To the Unionists it was entirely unacceptable for the same reason and because of the inclusion of Ulster. Bonar Law, the Unionist leader, was provoked into an extreme stance when, in July 1912, at a huge Unionist rally at Blenheim Palace, he observed that he could 'imagine no length of resistance to which Ulster can go, in which I should not be prepared to support them'. Asquith responded by calling Bonar Law's speech 'reckless' and 'a complete grammar of anarchy'.

In this bitter atmosphere the bill passed the Commons in January 1913. The verdict of the Commons was immediately reversed in the Lords by a massive rejection of the bill by 326 to 69. The whole process then had to be repeated, with totally predictable results. By August 1913 the bill had passed once more through the Commons, only to receive its routine rejection by the peers. A proposal for a constitutional conference in September 1913 foundered on the uncompromising positions taken by the opposing forces. The most that the Ulster leader, Sir Edward Carson, would accept was Home Rule excluding the whole of the nine counties of the Ulster Province. These included the counties of Cavan, Donegal and Monaghan (see map on page 22), all of which had Roman Catholic majority populations. These were impossible terms for Redmond and the most that Asquith would concede was a limited degree of independence for Ulster, within the Home Rule provisions. The scene was set for a new constitutional crisis.

Ulster prepares to resist

While attention had been focused on the fate of the Home Rule Bill at Westminster, events had been moving in Ireland itself. Ulster opinion had been hardening into die-hard resistance well before the introduction of the bill and in Sir Edward Carson it had found an able and articulate leader. In September 1912, Carson drew up a Solemn League and Covenant whose signatories pledged themselves to resist a Home Rule Parliament in Ireland should one ever be set up. Over 470,000 people signed this covenant – some using their own blood as ink. In January 1913 the Ulster Volunteer Force was set up and soon numbered 100,000 men. This provoked the setting up of a nationalist organisation, the Irish National Volunteers, a body pledged to support Home Rule. The creation of two groups with totally opposed objectives meant that the long-feared risk of civil war began to emerge as a real possibility.

In December 1913, Asquith's government resorted to a ban, by Royal Proclamation, on the importation of arms and ammunition into Ireland.

Neither of the two paramilitary forces was as yet properly armed, and the precaution seemed wise. At the same time Asquith was also preparing to extract more concessions from the Irish National Party, in the hope that the opposition in Parliament to Home Rule could at least be reduced. This could only be done by putting pressure on Redmond. He was persuaded, with great difficulty, to accept the exclusion of Ulster from Home Rule for a temporary period, initially set at three years, but almost immediately doubled to six. The concession compromised the whole concept of Ireland as a single unit and can be seen as the first clear move towards the idea of partition, but it was a risk Redmond felt he could take, because it seemed unlikely that Carson would accept temporary exclusion. Carson duly obliged by immediately rejecting the proposal.

> **Partition** – The splitting up of Ireland into two separate parts.

Mutiny in the army

In March 1914 the so-called Curragh Mutiny rocked the Government. The Government had long been concerned that, in the event of a confrontation with the Ulster Unionists, the enforcement of Home Rule would depend on the army. The army units in Ireland were largely controlled by officers of an Anglo-Irish Protestant background who were overwhelmingly Unionist in their sentiments. The main army base in Ireland was at Curragh in County Kildare, hence the name by which the incident became commonly known. In an attempt to lessen the risk of widespread resignations from the army in protest against Home Rule, the secretary of state for war, Jack Seely, approved instructions to General Sir Arthur Paget, the commander-in-chief in Ireland, that officers whose homes were actually in Ulster could be allowed a temporary leave from duty. There were rumours that the Government was about to order the arrest of the Ulster leaders (they had been considering this for some time), and Paget, in briefing his officers, was deliberately pessimistic, suggesting that Ulster would be 'in a blaze by Saturday'. As a result, 58 officers, including a brigadier-general, resigned. Action against the defectors was impossible because sympathy for them was widespread throughout the army. The Government was forced to conciliate the rebels and Seely even went so far as to suggest that force would not be used against the opponents of Home Rule. Although Seely was obliged to resign, the Government appeared weak and indecisive. The Ulster Volunteers began to arm themselves. In April, a series of landings of armaments took place along the Ulster coast. There was no interference from the authorities and the Ulster Volunteers were suddenly transformed into a formidable army. The Irish National Volunteers responded. In June, guns for the nationalists were landed near Dublin, but this time the authorities intervened. Three people were killed and nearly 40 injured. Although it was by no means as successful an effort as the Ulster landings, it still left considerable quantities of arms in the hands of the nationalist force.

The final stage of the crisis

Meanwhile, the Home Rule Bill was heading for its final passage. In May the Commons approved it for the third time. The usual rejection by the Lords followed but this time the Government had the option to force its passage into law by applying the Parliament Act. Asquith, Bonar Law and Carson had agreed by June to find some form of compromise but any agreement they made still needed to be accepted by or imposed on the Irish National Party. In late June, the Government proposed an amendment with the exclusion of the Ulster counties from the Home Rule Bill for a period of six years, with each county voting separately for its future. This idea had already been rejected by Carson, and the House of Lords amended the proposal to provide for the automatic exclusion of all nine Ulster counties on a permanent basis. This solution the Government could not accept.

> **WORKING TOGETHER**
> 1 Make a list of approximately ten points that you think are the most important reasons why Home Rule for Ireland had still not been implemented by the outbreak of war in 1914. Consider the actions of individuals as well as the events and situations that had an impact on the Irish Question. You will need to refer to Chapter 1 as well as this chapter.
> 2 Create a chronological flow chart using colour to indicate the importance of each reason. For example, use red for 'very important', blue for 'moderately important', brown for 'less important'. Add to each entry one key reason for your assessment of its degree of importance.
> 3 Now compare your original list with a partner's. How far are they the same? Discuss any discrepancies.
> 4 Review your list and revise your flow chart if necessary.

KEY DATES: THE IRISH QUESTION

1886 Gladstone introduces the first Home Rule Bill which splits the Liberal Party and fails to pass the House of Commons

1891 Death of Parnell

1892 Gladstone returns as prime minister of a minority Liberal government dependent on Irish National Party support

1893 Second Home Rule Bill passes the House of Commons but is rejected in the Lords

1894 Gladstone retires

1903 Wyndham's Act promotes even further land purchase opportunities for Irish tenants

1906 The Liberals return to government with a huge majority that allows them to ignore the Home Rule issue for the time being

1910 A general election over the Budget crisis deprives the Liberals of their overall majority and leaves them dependent on Irish National Party support for majorities

1911 The Parliament Act ends the ability of the House of Lords to permanently reject Home Rule

1912 The third Home Rule Bill produces a crisis in Ulster where the opposition to Home Rule is prepared to use force to resist it

1914 With Britain at war with Germany the Home Rule Act is passed but suspended for the duration of the war

Encouraged by King George V, the politicians convened a constitutional conference at Buckingham Palace on 21 July 1914:

- Asquith and Lloyd George represented the government.
- Redmond and John Dillon represented the INP.
- Bonar Law and Lord Lansdowne represented the Unionist Party.
- Carson and James Craig represented the Ulster Unionists.

The conference was intended to reach decisions in two stages:

- To debate the area of Ulster to be excluded. There were nine counties in the historic boundaries of the province of Ulster, but three of them, Cavan, Donegal and Monaghan, had Catholic majorities.
- To debate the terms of exclusion, whether they were to be temporary or permanent, and, if the former, then for how long.

In the event the discussions broke down at the first stage and the second stage was never even considered. After three days of deadlock, the conference was abandoned. Barely a week later Britain was at war with Germany. The crisis of war overtook the Irish Question at a crucial point. All sides in the constitutional conference realised that some kind of compromise was inevitable. Carson, in particular, was far more moderate in private than he was prepared to be in public. If the parties had been forced to continue the negotiations, a constitutional settlement would almost certainly have been reached. In the event, the war enabled all sides to agree to shelve the issue in a way that virtually guaranteed the renewal of the crisis at some later date. The Home Rule Act, officially known as the Government of Ireland Act 1914, was passed as an all-Ireland measure in September 1914 but its implementation was suspended for the duration of the war. This outcome was preferable to a civil war, but it only postponed the crisis for an unknowable length of time. It created the opportunity for extremists to strike for Irish independence during the Great War.

THE FIGHT FOR THE BANNER.

John Bull. "THIS TIRES ME. WHY CAN'T YOU CARRY IT BETWEEN YOU? NEITHER YOU CAN CARRY IT ALONE."

In this *Punch* cartoon Britain, as represented by 'John Bull' in the background, watches despairingly the struggle between John Redmond and Sir Edward Carson. ▶

Chapter summary

- Divisions over policy and leadership led to a decline in the electoral fortunes of the Liberal Party.
- At the same time the position of the Conservatives strengthened due in part to their alliance with the Liberal Unionists who had left the Liberal Party over Gladstone's Home Rule policy.
- After 1900 the Conservatives, or Unionists as they were now more commonly known, weakened due to a series of scandals, unpopular policies and the impact of the tariff reform debate.
- The Liberals resolved their leadership doubts and united around the defence of free trade.
- The emergence of New Liberalism and victory in the 1906 general election seemed to restore the political dominance that the Liberals had enjoyed prior to 1886.
- The emergence of the Labour Party challenged the position of the Liberals as the party of reform but an electoral pact agreement in 1903 led to Liberal–Labour cooperation and damaged the Unionists in the 1906 election.
- The decision of the House of Lords to reject the Budget of 1909 led to a constitutional crisis.
- The crisis resulted in the Parliament Act of 1911 which drastically reduced the powers of the House of Lords.
- With the Lords' powers of veto and amendment limited, Home Rule for Ireland became a genuine possibility for the first time.
- The Home Rule Bill of 1912 resulted in bitter resistance in Ulster and brought Ireland to the brink of civil war in 1914.

Chapter summary diagram

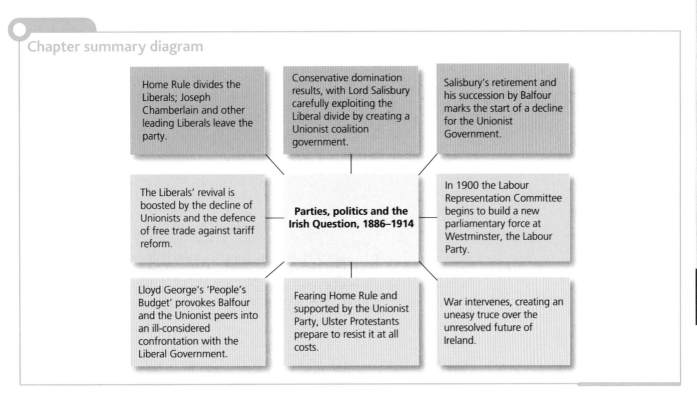

Home Rule divides the Liberals; Joseph Chamberlain and other leading Liberals leave the party.

Conservative domination results, with Lord Salisbury carefully exploiting the Liberal divide by creating a Unionist coalition government.

Salisbury's retirement and his succession by Balfour marks the start of a decline for the Unionist Government.

The Liberals' revival is boosted by the decline of Unionists and the defence of free trade against tariff reform.

Parties, politics and the Irish Question, 1886–1914

In 1900 the Labour Representation Committee begins to build a new parliamentary force at Westminster, the Labour Party.

Lloyd George's 'People's Budget' provokes Balfour and the Unionist peers into an ill-considered confrontation with the Liberal Government.

Fearing Home Rule and supported by the Unionist Party, Ulster Protestants prepare to resist it at all costs.

War intervenes, creating an uneasy truce over the unresolved future of Ireland.

Working on interpretation skills

The advice given here builds on the help given at the end of Chapter 1 (see page 32).

For the AQA A-level exam, Section A gives you three extracts, followed by a single question. The wording of the question will be something like this:

'Using your understanding of the historical context, assess how convincing the arguments in these three Extracts are in relation to...'

(30 marks)

The A-level mark scheme is very similar to the AS one on page 32.

Level 5	Shows a very good understanding of the interpretations put forward in all three extracts and combines this with a strong awareness of the historical context to analyse and evaluate the interpretations given in the extracts. Evaluation of the arguments will be well-supported and convincing. The response demonstrates a very good understanding of context. *25–30 marks*
Level 4	Shows a good understanding of the interpretations given in all three extracts and combines this with knowledge of the historical context to analyse and evaluate the interpretations given in the extracts. The evaluation of the arguments will be mostly well-supported, and convincing, but may have minor limitations of depth and breadth. The response demonstrates a good understanding of context. *19–24 marks*
Level 3	Provides some supported comment on the interpretations given in all three extracts and comments on the strength of these arguments in relation to their historic context. There is some analysis and evaluation but there may be an imbalance in the degree and depth of comments offered on the strength of the arguments. The response demonstrates an understanding of context. *13–18 marks*
Level 2	Provides some accurate comment on the interpretations given in at least two of the extracts, with reference to the historical context. The answer may contain some analysis, but there is little, if any, evaluation. Some of the comments on the strength of the arguments may contain some generalisation, inaccuracy or irrelevance. The response demonstrates some understanding of context. *7–12 marks*
Level 1	Either shows an accurate understanding of the interpretation given in one extract only or addresses two/three extracts, but in a generalist way, showing limited accurate understanding of the arguments they contain, although there may be some general awareness of the historical context. Any comments on the strength of the arguments are likely to be generalist and contain some inaccuracy and/or irrelevance. The response demonstrates limited understanding of context. *1–6 marks*

Notice that there is no reference in this mark scheme to *comparing* the extracts or reaching a judgement about which of the extracts is the most convincing.

Here is an A-level practice question (guidance on how to answer it is given on page 92).

Using your understanding of the historical context, assess how convincing the arguments in these three extracts (page 91) are in explaining the conflicts between the House of Commons and the House of Lords, 1884–1911.

(30 marks)

Extract A

The Liberal government's attempt to find a solution to the problem of poverty through tax reform brought to a head a long-maturing conflict between the Liberal Party and the House of Lords. During Gladstone's second ministry of 1880–85 the Conservatives in the House of Lords refused to allow the Franchise Bill of 1884 to become law unless it was accompanied by a parallel measure for the redistribution of seats. In 1893, the Liberals second Home Rule Bill was rejected by the Lords by an overwhelming majority. Other Liberal reforms were also obstructed or so amended that they had to be withdrawn. The Liberals for their part were by this time committed, under the terms of the Newcastle Programme of 1891 to the 'mending or ending' of the House of Lords. The quiescence [silence, inactivity] of the Lords between 1895 and 1905 when a Unionist government was in office, emphasized that the conflict between Lords and Commons was a party political as much as a constitutional one. Nor was the possibility of confrontation lessened by the landslide nature of the Liberal election victory in 1906. The new government's position in the House of Lords was fragile in the extreme. Only 88 of the 602 peers were formally committed to the Liberal Party.

Adapted from *The Edwardian Crisis: Britain 1901–1914*
by David Powell, (Macmillan), 1996, pp.39-42.

Extract B

The crucial test in the House of Lords took place in the last week of November 1909. During the debate a few Unionist peers pointed out that whatever the niceties of the constitutional argument, the House, by rejecting the budget, would be claiming the right to force an elected government to appeal to the country. Such a claim would fly in the face of a long-standing constitutional convention and could hardly be made to stick. These warning voices were not heeded and the House rejected the budget by 350 to 75 votes. This vote to all intents and purposes opened the election campaign. In a speech in the Albert Hall on 10 December Asquith set the keynote for the Liberal campaign: all the various Liberal reforms that had been thwarted by the House of Lords, would be pushed forward again. Since the Lords' veto was the great impediment, it must go: 'the will of the people, as deliberately expressed by their representatives, must within the limits of the lifetime of a single Parliament, be made effective.'

Adapted from *Democracy and Empire: Britain 1865–1914*
by E. J. Feuchtwanger, (Edward Arnold), 1986, p. 291.

Extract C

Balfour cannot be acquitted of blame for the consequences of the insane decision to reject the budget of 1909 in the Lords. Why did such a balanced man as Balfour see nothing objectionable in this use of the House of Lords? Deep in the subconscious mind of the party was a sense of prescriptive right to rule, inculcated by years of domination after 1886. This was an error that neither Derby nor Disraeli would have committed. The most revealing remark of all was made by Balfour just after he had lost his seat in Manchester in the January 1906 election. It was the duty of everyone, he said, to ensure that the Unionist Party should continue to control, whether in power or opposition, the destinies of Britain and the British Empire. If this proposition is taken literally it was a denial of parliamentary democracy. Indeed many Unionists behaved as if the verdict of 1906 was some freak aberration on the part of the electorate and that it was their duty through the House of Lords, to preserve the public from the consequences of its own folly till it came to its senses.

Adapted from *The Conservative Party from Peel to Churchill*
by Robert Blake, (Eyre & Spottiswoode), 1970, p. 190.

Possible answer

First, make sure that you have the focus of the question clear – in this case, explaining the introduction of social reforms. Then you can investigate the three extracts to see how convincing they are.

You need to analyse each of the three extracts in turn. A suggestion is to divide a large page to create a table similar to the one below or to devise a table of your own.

Extract	Extract's main arguments	Knowledge to corroborate	Knowledge to contradict or modify
A			
B			
C			

- In the first column list the extracts.
- In the second column list the main arguments each uses.
- In the third column list what you know that can corroborate the arguments.
- In the fourth column list what might contradict or modify the arguments. (NB 'Modify' – you might find that you partly agree, but with reservations.)
- You may find, of course, that some of your knowledge is relevant more than once.

Planning your answer – one approach
Decide how you could best set out a detailed plan for your answer:

- Briefly refer to the focus of the question.
- For each extract in turn set out the arguments, corroborating evidence, and contradictory evidence.
- Do this by treating each argument (or group of arguments) in turn.
- Make comparisons between the extracts if this is helpful. This is not required, but a relevant comparison may well show the extent of your understanding of each extract.
- An overall judgement on any one extract is not required, but it may be helpful to make a brief summary, or just reinforce what has been said already by emphasising which points in the extracts were the most convincing.

Remember that in the examination you are allowed an hour for this question. It is the planning stage that is vital in order to write a good answer. You should allow sufficient time to read the extracts and plan an answer. If you start writing too soon, it is likely that you will waste time trying to summarise the *content* of each extract. Do this in your planning stage – and then think how you will *use* the content to answer the question.

Then the actual writing!
- Think how you can write an answer, dealing with each extract in turn, but making cross-references or comparisons, if this is helpful, to reinforce a point.
- In addition, try to ensure your answer:
  - shows very good understanding of the extracts
  - uses knowledge to argue in support or to disagree
  - provides a clear argument which leads to a short interim conclusion about each extract, and which reaches a conclusion about the extracts as a whole.

Working on essay technique: arguments and counter-argument (balance)

Effective essays develop a good argument, and well-argued essays are much more likely to develop sustained analysis. As you know, your essays are judged on the extent to which they analyse. The mark scheme opposite is for the full A-level. It is virtually the same for AS level. Both stress the need to analyse and evaluate the key features related to the periods studied. It distinguishes between five different levels of analysis (as well as other relevant skills that are the ingredients of good essays).

The key feature of the highest level is sustained analysis: analysis that unites the whole of the essay. However levels 3–5 all refer to the importance of a balanced answer.

You can set up an argument in your introduction, but you should develop it throughout the essay. One way of doing this is to adopt an argument–counter-argument structure (see pages 94–95). A counter-argument is an argument that disagrees with the main argument of the essay. Setting up an argument and then challenging it with counter-arguments is the best way of evaluating the importance of the different factors that you discuss and balancing your essay. We will first look at techniques for developing sustained analysis and argument before looking at the counter-argument technique.

Level 5	Answers will display a very good understanding of the full demands of the question. They will be well-organised and effectively delivered. The supporting information will be well-selected, specific and precise. They will show a very good understanding of key features, issues and concepts. The answers will be fully analytical with a balanced argument and well-substantiated judgement. *21–25 marks*
Level 4	Answers will display a good understanding of the demands of the question. They will be well-organised and effectively communicated. There will be a range of clear and specific supporting information showing a good understanding of key features and issues, together with some conceptual awareness. The answers will be analytical in style with a range of direct comment relating to the question. The answers will be well-balanced with some judgement, which may, however, be only partially substantiated. *16–20 marks*
Level 3	Answers will show an understanding of the question and will supply a range of largely accurate information, which will show an awareness of some of the key issues and features, but may, however, be unspecific or lack precision of detail. The answers will be effectively organised and show adequate communication skills. There will be a good deal of comment in relation to the question and the answer will display some balance, but a number of statements may be inadequately supported and generalist. *11–15 marks*
Level 2	The answers will be descriptive or partial, showing some awareness of the question but a failure to grasp its full demands. There will be some attempt to convey material in an organised way, although communication skills may be limited. There will be some appropriate information showing understanding of some key features and/or issues, but the answer may be very limited in scope and/or contain inaccuracy and irrelevance. There will be some, but limited, comment in relation to the question and statements will, for the most part, be unsupported and generalist. *6–10 marks*
Level 1	The question has not been properly understood and the responses show limited organisational and communication skills. The information conveyed is irrelevant or extremely limited. There may be some unsupported, vague or generalist comment. *1–5 marks*

Argument and sustained analysis

At Level 4, essays will analyse the key issues discussed in the essay. They might for example have regular pieces of analysis at the end of each paragraph. While this analysis might be good it will occur as secondary to the factual detail discussed in the essay.

Level 5 answers will be analytical throughout. As well as the analysis of each factor discussed in the essay, there will be an overall analysis. This will run throughout the essay and can be achieved through developing a clear, relevant and coherent argument.

Effective arguments

Typically, essays examine a series of factors. A good way of achieving sustained analysis is to consider which factor is most important, as in the example below.

EXAMPLE

Consider the following A-level practice question:

'The failure to implement Home Rule for Ireland between 1886 and 1914 was primarily the result of the resistance in Ulster.' Assess the validity of this view. (25 marks)

Here is an example of an introduction which focuses on the question and sets out the key factors that the essay will develop. It alerts the marker to the fact that the question is being addressed from the outset and that a range of possible outcomes will be discussed.

Clear focus on the question

Points to other factors

There were three attempts to implement Home rule in this period in 1886, 1892–93 and 1912–14. In all three cases opposition in Ulster was clearly an important factor which affected the outcome. However, this does not mean that Ulster resistance was the primary factor in all of them or indeed in any of them. Though some of the factors involved in each Home Rule attempt remained the same – some changed with different circumstances. For example the first two Home Rule bills were the personal work of Gladstone. The third Home Rule bill came after his death. In both 1886 and 1892–93 the House of Lords remained an absolute veto over the proposals. In 1912–14 the Lords could only delay, not permanently prevent, Home Rule from being implemented. Clearly a number of different factors, some constant and some varying, played a part.

Recognises that you can't just cover named factor

Counter-argument

A counter-argument is essentially an alternative to the main argument of the essay. You may have decided that you agree with the assessment that Ulster resistance was the primary reason why Home Rule failed. Or you may have an alternative argument to offer – for example that different reasons were the primary cause on each separate occasion. Ultimately it is not important whether your argument agrees with the question or not. You should aim to set up an argument and then challenge it with counter-arguments. The best way to achieve this is to show the alternatives with each phase of your argument along with a judgment showing why it is less convincing. An example is given on page 95.

EXAMPLE

For example, suppose you have decided that resistance in Ulster *was* the primary factor in the failure: you could structure three paragraphs of discussion dealing with the three attempts to implement Home Rule. In each you would show the importance of the resistance in Ulster and look at alternative possibilities, showing why there is a case for their importance but also why you are rejecting them as the primary factor. The first paragraph dealing with 1886 could include some of the following ideas:

It was clear from the start of Gladstone's attempt in 1886 that attempting to force the bill on Ulster would result in violent resistance and that this would receive significant support in Britain. As Lord Randolph Churchill put it – 'Ulster will fight and Ulster will be right'.

It can of course be argued that Gladstone's decision to draft the bill entirely alone and with no consultation with any colleagues over any aspect of the proposals meant that a split in the Liberal Party was inevitable. It can also be argued that the veto held by the House of Lords would have proved decisive even had Gladstone managed to hold the party together in the Commons. However, in reality neither of these factors was as decisive as the Ulster issue. It would have been almost impossible for Gladstone to secure Liberal unity on Home Rule unless he had made major structural alterations to the proposals – that was precisely why he opted to go it alone. Furthermore, history had already shown (in 1832) that the Lords could be coerced into accepting legislation against their wishes if a majority in the House of Commons could be sustained. The fact was that Gladstone resolutely chose to ignore the Ulster resistance and the fact that it had a moral case in the eyes of many in Britain. It was this Ulster moral case that sustained the opposition within the Liberal Party and the Lords and ensured that Gladstone was defeated.

Now try to assemble the same structure for 1892–93 and 1912–14.

Your conclusion needs to be decisive and firm – here is an example of how to drive home your viewpoint:

Therefore, in conclusion, while Gladstone's mistakes, the opposition in the Lords and the general indifference or negativity of British public opinion all played a part in preventing Home Rule from being implemented, none of these emerges as the key primary factor. Resistance in Ulster on the other hand was the ever-present reality that stood in the way. Of all Gladstone's mistakes the greatest was to openly ridicule the Ulster opposition. By the later stages of the third Home Rule Bill Asquith's government had been forced to consider at least temporary separate status for Ulster and this concession in itself fatally undermined the idea of an all-Ireland settlement and opened the way to permanent Ulster exclusion. This U-turn had been forced on the government by the reality of Ulster resistance and the impossibility of coercing Ulster against its will. It was this reality that meant the 1914 Home Rule Act could be passed as a wartime necessity – but not implemented – also as a wartime necessity.

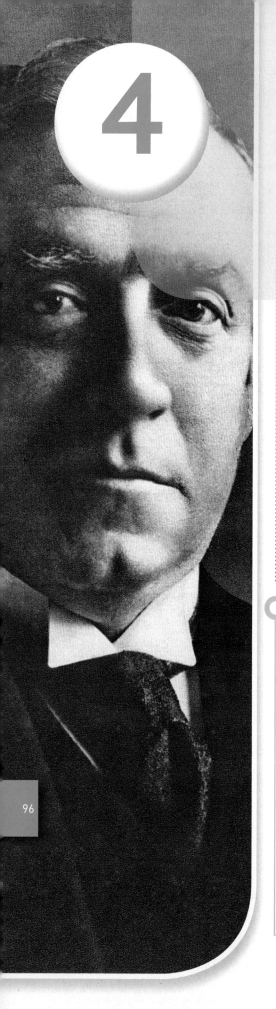

4

Society, social reform and the economy, 1886–1914

This chapter covers social and economic developments in Britain and Ireland during the period 1886–1914. It deals with a number of key areas:

- Economic performance and the issue of free trade or protection.
- The rise in the size, power and influence of the trade union movement.
- Concerns about the conditions of the working classes; the evidence and debate about how these might be improved.
- The social reforms undertaken by the Liberal governments from 1906–14 and their impact.
- The campaign of the right for women to vote in parliamentary elections.

When you have worked through the chapter and the related activities, you should have detailed knowledge of all those areas. You should be able to relate this knowledge to the key breadth issues defined as part of your study, in particular the nature and impact of social reforms, including why these were introduced and the extent to which they changed the lives of working-class people.

For the period covered in this chapter the main issues can be phrased as a question:

Why did social and economic reforms and the rights of women create such controversy and how successfully were these issues addressed?

CHAPTER SUMMARY

The period 1886–1914 saw significant changes in society. As a result, the policies put forward by the Conservatives, Liberals and Labour during this period had to be intelligible and attractive to the electorate – the majority of whom were now working-class men. Their standard of living in terms of the conditions in which they lived, what they had to eat, what security they had in their lives in terms of employment, health and safety were their main concerns. They might, in exceptional circumstances, be distracted by sentiment, such as when Queen Victoria celebrated her Golden and Diamond Jubilees (1887 and 1897); or patriotism, such as during the Boer War (1899–1902). However, such emotion was temporary. The ruling elites that still controlled the two main parties in the parliamentary system and the reins of government knew that they were engaged in a negotiation with the electorate for political power. The increased political awareness of the working class was apparent through the rise of trade unions, the rise of the Labour Party and the increasing agitation from women of all classes for full political equality. The need for reform was obvious – the means of providing it and the form that it should take was less so.

1 Economic conditions and controversy, 1886–1914

During the period 1850–1873 the British economy experienced a phase of rapid expansion that has been called the 'mid-Victorian boom' (see page 38). The economy grew, on average, by 3 per cent per year in those years. Railway construction increased from 6,000 miles of track in 1850 to 14,000 miles by 1875. Britain's staple industries, cotton and other textiles along with coal and shipbuilding, performed well, for example:

- The value of cotton cloth produced increased from £46 million in 1851 to £105 million in 1875.
- Coal production increased from 60 million tons in 1855 to 109 million tons by 1870.

From 1873, however, the British economy began to slow down. In 1872 unemployment stood at 1 per cent. By 1879 it had risen to 11.4 per cent and was still over 10 per cent in 1886.

Concerns about Britain's future as an economic Great Power gathered momentum in the 1890s. They were based on two considerations:

- First, there was the question of Britain's economic performance and the extent to which other nations were catching up with, or even overtaking, Britain as the leading manufacturing and commercial power.
- Second, there was the question of the condition of the working classes in Britain and the extent to which this was undermining Britain both economically and socially.

NOTE-MAKING

Use the headings and questions in Section 1 to make brief notes on the economy and the free trade versus protection issue. Structure your notes with headings, sub-headings and sub-points to make them easy to navigate and use (see page x for further guidance).

For example, the following headings could be used to summarise the key points on pages 97–102:
- What were the economic problems facing Britain in the period 1886–1914?
- What were the arguments for and against abandoning free trade?

Staple industries – Industries producing essential products for which there is a high and continuous demand and on which large-scale employment can be based.

The British economy in the late nineteenth and early twentieth centuries

To what extent was Britain a 'Great Power in decline' in the period 1886–1914?

Concern about the performance of the British economy stemmed from the 1870s. For nearly three decades before this the economy had been growing relatively consistently, but it was suddenly beset by a series of slumps interspersed with temporary revivals. The last of these slumps ended in 1896 and was followed by a steady, if slow, period of economic expansion up to 1914, with only one downturn in the period 1907–10. However, despite this 'recovery', the cycle of slumps over a 25-year period up to 1896 had been enough to undermine confidence in British economic strength, which had been taken for granted in the middle years of the century, a period which has been characterised as the 'mid-Victorian boom'. Economic historians disagree about the significance of the period after 1870. At one time it was customary to refer to the last quarter of the nineteenth century as the 'Great Depression'. More recently however, most economic historians have rejected this view, preferring to describe the period as one involving a 'retardation of growth'; that is to say, a slowing down of the earlier, rapid expansion of the economy, until a lower, more sustainable pattern of growth was reached in the 1890s.

Problems in industry and agriculture

In retrospect it is easy to see that fears about the strength of the British economy in this period were exaggerated. In fact, the economy was performing in a rather erratic way. For example, the period after 1870 was precisely when

Figure 1 Growth of industrial production, 1870–1913 (90 per annum).

Country	Growth rate
Belgium	2.5
France	2.1
Austria-Hungary	2.8
Denmark	3.4
Italy	2.7
Germany	4.1
Finland	4.1
Portugal	2.4
Russia	5.1
Netherlands	3.0
Spain	2.7
Switzerland	3.2
Norway	3.3
Sweden	4.4
United Kingdom	2.1

Britain was emerging as the world's leading shipbuilding nation, a status it was to maintain through many difficult periods until the Second World War. Output of iron and steel continued to increase, despite competition from Germany and the USA, and even the inefficient British coal industry continued to remain profitable in the years up to 1914, buoyed up by the consistently increasing world demand for coal. However, it is also true that Britain did not expand as rapidly as Germany or the USA in the newer industrial sectors, such as electrical engineering and chemical production.

The agricultural sector, however, faced a more difficult problem, in that cheap imports of cereals from the 1870s put pressure on British farmers and forced them to reduce their production. Even livestock farmers faced some competition as steamships with refrigerated cargo holds allowed cheap meat to be imported from abroad. The case for a 'Great Depression' in the agricultural sector is thus more convincing than that for industry, but even so the picture was not one of unrelieved gloom. Cheaper imports of cereals meant cheaper foodstuffs for livestock farmers and in some parts of the country, farm rents actually rose in this period as profits soared. Moreover, the availability of cheaper food meant that, across the nation as a whole, the value of wages was consistently rising in real terms, despite the effects of periodic slumps.

The most obvious, and most discussed aspect of economic performance, was the question of international trade. More specifically, there was the question of German imports and the size of the trade gap, which began to increase after 1870. Such gaps had, however, existed even in the 1850s and were always more than covered by the value of so-called 'invisible earnings' from insurance, shipping charges and banking services which brought increasingly vast profits into the British economy. London remained the commercial centre of the world and its dominance was unchallenged.

Nevertheless, having noted that much of the concern about British economic performance was exaggerated, it is important to realise that what people at the time believed to be the case is often more important to understanding the period than what subsequent historical research and deliberation reveal to have been the case.

Trade gap – A negative difference between the value of exports and the cost of imports.

Invisible earnings – So-called because they are purely paper transactions covering the fees charged for professional services rendered rather than actual products being sold.

The expansion of the service industries

A service industry is where services are provided to customers rather than goods being produced or raw materials extracted. There was a significant increase in the variety and scope of employment in service industries between 1886 and 1914. Service industries that expanded included:

- hotels and restaurants
- private domestic service
- transport and communication
- banking, finance and insurance
- public administration, education and health
- entertainment and recreation.

There was a significant increase in employment in hotels, restaurants and cafes, shops and offices, especially for women. About half of the total female workforce was in domestic service in the 1880s, but by 1900 this had fallen to about one-third, creating a shortage of domestic servants. The 'servant problem' got worse as more households could afford to employ a servant, but fewer women wanted to be one. Even so, domestic service remained an important part of the service sector of the economy.

The myth of the Great Depression?

In 1885 a Royal Commission was set up on the Depression of Trade and Industry by the prime minister Lord Salisbury. It reported in December 1886. Salisbury's main purpose was to deflect pressure from a Conservative Party group – the Fair Trade League. The Royal Commission amassed a vast amount of information and evidence to show that the effects of the slumps or depressions were severe. It was chaired by Lord Iddesleigh, formerly Sir Stafford Northcote, who had been Disraeli's chancellor of the exchequer in 1874–80 and was now Salisbury's foreign secretary. The report went into considerable detail on the problem of unemployment and the difficulties of the staple industries, such as cotton and coal, which relied heavily on export. It complained bitterly about the importation of fraudulent foreign goods purporting to be British in origin and demanded new, tougher laws. It complained about the negative effects of foreign tariffs and suggested retaliatory taxes of between 10 and 15 per cent against foreign imports other than from the empire. It seems clear from the Royal Commission's findings and other sources of the period that contemporaries thought Britain was facing a depression in trade and industry. In 1879 *The Economist* claimed that the year had been 'one of the most sunless and cheerless of the century'. In his 1884 speech supporting the Fair Trade League, Lord Randolph Churchill argued that Britain's trade was suffering from a 'mortal disease'.

Foreign competition

There is some evidence to support these views. Britain faced increasing competition in industrial production from the USA and Germany. Figure 2 shows how Britain's world lead in steel production had come to an end by the 1890s.

Figure 2 UK, US and German steel production as a percentage of world production, 1875–94.

	UK %	USA %	Germany %
1875–79	35.9	26.0	16.6
1880–84	32.7	28.4	17.7
1885–89	31.8	31.4	17.8
1890–94	24.6	33.7	21.4

Not only did Britain face competition in export markets, but the prices of industrial goods fell between 1873 and 1896. Between 1871 and 1896 the price of coal and textiles dropped by over 30 per cent. It would seem therefore that the term 'Great Depression' had some validity.

So was it a depression?

Although the rate of growth in the British economy did slow in the last quarter of the nineteenth century it is still difficult to describe what happened as a 'Great Depression', especially when a comparison is made with the later and better-known Great Depression of the 1930s (see page 175). In 1969, the historian S. B. Saul in his book *The Myth of the Great Depression* made this comparison and pointed out that although there was a serious lowering of business confidence, unemployment and problems in some industries, it would be wrong to state that the whole British economy was in depression. Saul also argued that the working classes did not suffer falling wages; instead it was profits that came under pressure. According to Saul:

'We are far from a full understanding of all the problems … this, at least is clear: the sooner the 'Great Depression' is banished from literature, the better.'

The Fair Trade League

This was a pressure group set up by Conservatives critical of the policy of free trade. The 'fair-traders' argued that the economic slumps that the country had begun experiencing in the early 1870s were the result of Britain facing protective barriers from other countries while permitting free access to British markets.

The statistics in Figure 2 show that Britain's percentage share of world steel production fell over a 20-year period. Why might this be misleading in terms of the health of the British steel industry?

The Marxist historian Eric Hobsbawm however is less sure:

'The years between 1873 and 1896 are known to economic historians … as the 'Great Depression'. The name is misleading. So far as the working people are concerned, it cannot compare with the cataclysms of the 1830s and 1840s, or the 1920s and 1930s. But if 'depression' indicates a pervasive – and for the generation since 1850 a new – state of mind of uneasiness and gloom about the prospects of the British economy, the word is accurate.'

In fact, throughout the period the economy continued to grow and in 1896 Britain was still one of the world's leading economic powers. Also while steel production and metal manufacturing generally faced increasingly serious competition from the USA and Germany, other industries continued to do well. For instance, during the 1880s coal output rose by 23.5 per cent and a lot of that increased production went for export. The 1886 Royal Commission had drawn attention to falling prices and the effect this was having on profits and investment, but it could equally be said that while falling prices were bad for businessmen they had the quite opposite effect for the working-class consumers. Falling prices for food and household industrial products during the period of the so-called Great Depression meant that in fact there was a significant rise in the value of real wages. Saul also pointed out that Britain was not the only economy to undergo a slow-down in economic growth – it was in fact a world trend. Both Germany and the USA faced similar problems and this was one of the reasons why both these countries introduced taxes on imported goods in the hope of countering their difficulties.

Therefore, although Britain did suffer some economic problems in the years 1873–96, these did not affect the whole economy and so far as industry was concerned the picture was mixed in terms of performance in different sectors. In agriculture though the situation was more severe, as it suffered from increased competition from overseas. This competition was felt in cereal crops such as wheat, but also increasingly in meat imported from Australia, New Zealand and Argentina.

How great are the differences in interpretation between Saul (page 99) and Hobsbawm?

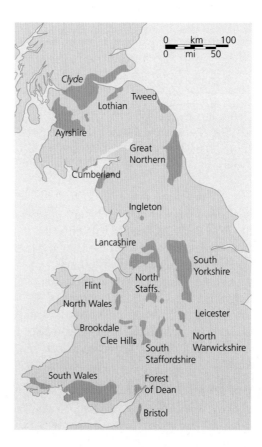

Figure 3 Selected British coalfields in the nineteenth century. Coal was the essential fuel of the Industrial Revolution and the discovery and exploitation of coal fields was vital to industrial expansion.

The cause was the technological development of steamships equipped with refrigeration which allowed meat to be kept fresh in transit over vast distances. There was also a rise domestically in 'market gardening' on small holdings and allotments in suburban areas which increased competition in the production of vegetables and fruits. The result was unemployment and underemployment in rural areas, leading to lower earnings and a further acceleration in population drift to urban areas, where of course the depression was having an effect in some, though not all, parts of industry.

Free trade or protection?

Why was the issue of ending free trade so controversial?

In 1879 Germany adopted a policy of imposing heavy taxes on imports of industrial products from abroad. The aim was to protect its own industrial production by making foreign imports more expensive for Germans to buy. Italy, a much less important economic trading partner for Britain, had already introduced tariffs in 1878. When France (1882) and the USA (1883) both introduced protective tariffs on imports the Fair Trade League in Britain began to gather some momentum. The conservative radical Lord Randolph Churchill associated himself with the aims of the League in a speech in 1884 but then changed his mind in 1887, after which the League gradually ran out of steam and remained simply a pressure group within the Conservative Party. Failing to make much impression on the Conservative Party let alone the country the League was disbanded in 1895.

For many years Joseph Chamberlain had been increasingly dubious about the wisdom of the UK's policy of free trade in a world that was increasingly turning to economic protection. Coming from a business background with interests overseas as well as in Britain, Chamberlain was not fundamentally anti-free trade in outlook. On the contrary, he hoped that international free trade could be restored. However, by 1900 he had come to the conclusion that British industry demanded protection in order to give it breathing space from the cheap imports of government-subsidised producers abroad. The money raised from import tariffs, he believed, could be used to fund social reforms, as well as to assist the modernisation of British industry. Such a policy was politically dangerous. Taxing imports meant a certain rise in food prices, since so much of the food consumed in Britain came from overseas. This in turn meant:

● it would be difficult to sell the idea to the working classes
● it would unite the Liberals in ferocious opposition
● it risked dividing the Unionists.

Whatever the risks, Chamberlain was not the man to shirk a challenge when convinced of the justice of his cause. As early as May 1902 he hinted at the idea of an imperial trading system in a speech in his political stronghold, Birmingham. The Government had just been forced to introduce a small tariff on imported corn to help pay for the costs of the Boer War and had been censured for doing so. In defending this tariff, Chamberlain hoped to undermine the credibility of free trade, which he saw as outdated. This speech occurred just before a colonial conference at which Chamberlain failed to convince the visiting prime ministers of the case for greater imperial integration. In the autumn of 1902 he left on a tour of South Africa that turned out to be a considerable success. Returning in early 1903 Chamberlain prepared himself for the launch of his great crusade. In May 1903, once more in Birmingham, he made a momentous speech that unquestionably changed the course of politics in the years up to the First World War. He declared himself in favour of a system of general tariffs on imports from foreign powers along with a system of lower tariffs, or in some cases exemptions, for imports from the empire. His ideas drew heavily on the arguments in the report of the 1885–86 Royal Commission. This speech initiated a debate that split the Unionists as a whole, with both the Conservatives and Liberal Unionists groups internally divided over their response.

Balfour attempted to preserve unity by adopting a fence-sitting strategy. On the one hand, he did not wish to break with Chamberlain and his supporters, who now included many mainstream Conservatives. On the other hand, he was personally unconvinced of the case for tariff reform. His main priority was to preserve the unity of the Unionist coalition. While Balfour was using all his political skills (which were not inconsiderable) to keep the Unionists together, the opposing groups were formalising their positions:

- Chamberlain headed a Tariff Reform League set up in 1903.
- The free trade unionists formed the Unionist Free Food League in the same year.
- Around 30 Unionists, including the young Winston Churchill, decided to defect to the Liberals.

The nation is not convinced

In September 1903, Chamberlain resigned from the Government in order to carry out a full-time campaign for tariff reform in the country at large, where it had failed to gain popular support. The trade unions were strongly in favour of free trade and there was no evidence to suggest that Chamberlain was converting the nation as a whole to his grand vision. Thus the Unionists remained divided, with no real prospect of resolving their differences, while the Liberals had a clear and united opposition to tariff reform that seemed to be in tune with public opinion.

'Through the Birmingham ▶
Looking-Glass'. *Westminster Gazette*, 6 October 1903. A contemporary view of Chamberlain's tariff reform campaign. The title is a reference to the popular sequel to Lewis Carroll's classic children's novel, *Alice in Wonderland*, which was called *Through the Looking-Glass and What Alice Did There*. In a fantasy world, Alice meets a comic and accident-prone character 'The White Knight'. 'Birmingham' is of course referring to Chamberlain's connection with that city, while the reference to Glasgow is because Chamberlain was due to make a major speech there.

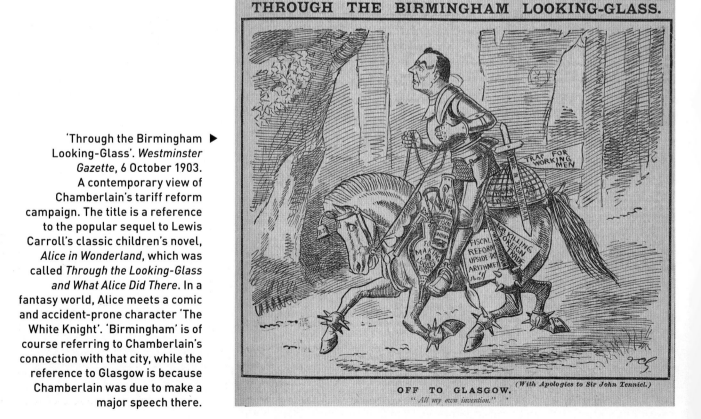

THROUGH THE BIRMINGHAM LOOKING-GLASS.

OFF TO GLASGOW. *(With Apologies to Sir John Tenniel.)*
"All my own invention."

After the 1906 general election the tariff reformers made up the majority of the much-reduced number (157) of Unionist MPs. They then suffered a huge blow in July 1906 when Chamberlain collapsed with a stroke and was effectively removed from active politics. Nevertheless, Chamberlain's ideas continued to gain ground within the party as it moved slowly but inevitably to a formal merger of the Conservatives and Liberal Unionists, eventually completed in 1912. By 1909 the Unionists had effectively been won over to tariff reform.

One of the key arguments of the tariff reformers that helped the process was that large-scale social reform could only be funded effectively through the money that would be raised through taxing imports. It was clear that the Liberals intended to fund social reforms through increased taxation targeted at the wealthier classes, while preserving free trade. The only feasible alternative was to argue that protective tariffs would fund social reform while protecting British employment and keeping up wages. Thus the Budget crisis of 1909 was in essence an extension of the free trade versus protectionism debate and both sides believed that their political fortunes were at stake in its outcome. The debate over free trade and protection rumbled on into and beyond the First World War. While the Liberals continued to command majorities in the House of Commons, free trade was untouchable. However, once war broke out in 1914 the economic and financial demands it brought began to undermine free trade, and in the difficult economic conditions of the post-war world the issue continued to focus debate and confrontation.

2 The impact of social change

The years up to the First World War saw the rise of a mass labour movement in Britain. Trade unionism spread to previously unorganised and unskilled workers – New Unionism – whose leaders showed greater militancy. The new mood was partly inspired by a revival in socialist activity. Britain's industrial and trading dominance was being challenged by the growing economic power of Germany and the USA. The profits from Britain's massive colonial empire partly reduced the economic impact of the decline in the staple industries of cotton, shipbuilding and mining.

The growth of the trade unions

To what extent was the expansion of the trade union movement the result of social and economic conditions rather than political ideology?

Between 1886 and 1914 trade unions grew at a faster rate than at any other time in their history. Membership figures stood at around 750,000 at the beginning of the period and increased to over 4.5 million in 1914. The effect of the First World War was to increase this figure to 6.5 million by 1918. New Unionism was boosted by the successes of a women match workers' strike at the Bryant and May factory in 1888 and then by the gas workers' and dockers' strikes in 1889. Trade unionism among unskilled, semi-skilled and even white-collar and professional workers spread rapidly. Convinced socialists such as John Burns and Tom Mann led the dockers in a struggle for fair pay and conditions that attracted worldwide attention. The resulting strike, which lasted five weeks, was in demand of a minimum of four hours work per day, which they failed to get, and a minimum wage of 6 pence an hour ($2\frac{1}{2}$p in modern terms), which they did get. Their success was due mainly to the financial support received from other trade unionists, including a £30,000 donation from Australia.

1 In what ways does the cartoon on page 102 present an unsympathetic view of the tariff reform campaign?
2 How would a supporter of tariff reform have countered the charges made in the cartoon?
3 How fully does the cartoon contribute to an understanding of the issues raised in the tariff reform campaign?

NOTE-MAKING

Use the headings and questions in the first part of Section 2 to make brief notes on the rise of the trade unions and the standard of living during this period. Structure your notes with headings, sub-headings and sub-points to make them easy to navigate and use (see page x for further guidance).

For example, the following headings could be used to summarise the key points on pages 103–06:
- The reasons why trade unions became more powerful in the period.
- The causes and consequences of poor living conditions.

In 1890 a huge May Day demonstration in favour of the eight-hour day surprised even its organisers by the scale of the turnout. However, much of the momentum that New Unionism had produced was lost in the 1890s as employers began to take a harder line. They were supported by two legal decisions. The case of *Lyons v. Wilkins* in 1896 set a precedent for outlawing even peaceful picketing and, in 1901, the Taff Vale judgment enabled the employer (the Taff Vale Railway Company) to sue the union (the Amalgamated Society of Railway Servants) for losses sustained during a strike (see page 80 for more details). These cases had the effect of curtailing the mood of trade union militancy which had affected even the older New Unions like the Amalgamated Society of Engineers. However, it also gave a stimulus to the TUC to forge ahead with the creation of the Labour Representation Committee (see page 79).

The years between 1910 and the outbreak of the First World War in 1914 saw a huge increase in trade union membership from 2.5 million to over 4 million. This was a trend that would continue strongly during the war and into the post-war period. The period from 1910 to 1914 was also marked by a wave of strikes. The increased militancy can be attributed to the following factors:

- From around 1900 the value of real wages was gradually falling owing to increases in the cost of living.
- From 1910 there was a fall in the level of unemployment which made many workers more willing to confront employers.
- Prices rose particularly steeply in 1911–12.
- The middle and upper classes were actually improving their position, leading to increased bitterness among the workers whose living standards had worsened.

Coal seams – Strata of coal underground that are large enough to be cut out and sent to the surface.

The first major confrontation came in the south Wales coalfield in the autumn of 1910. A dispute arose over payments for miners working difficult coal seams. Militancy had been on the increase in south Wales for a number of years and the general mood of bitterness soon resulted in a rash of strikes. It was not long before confrontations between strikers and the authorities produced violence. During rioting in Tonypandy, south Wales in 1911, a man died from injuries he had sustained in a fight with local police officers and many others suffered less serious injuries. The home secretary, Winston Churchill, felt that the seriousness of the situation required that army units be drafted in to support the local police. This decision elevated the Tonypandy riots to mythological status in working-class history. The wave of strikes went on for ten months before ending in defeat for the miners. This, however, was only the start of the unrest. In June 1911, the Seamen's Union went on strike and the dockers and railwaymen came out on strike in sympathy. Two months later, two strikers were shot dead by troops in Liverpool after a general riot broke out. In the same week, troops shot dead two men who were part of a crowd attacking a train at Llanelli.

In 1912, the first national pit strike began, lasting from February until April, with the miners demanding a national minimum wage. The Government responded to this with a compromise by passing the Minimum Wage Act for Mining, which set up local boards in colliery districts to fix minimum wages for miners working on difficult seams. In the same year there were also strikes at the London docks and among transport workers. In 1913 there were strikes in the metal-working industries of the Midlands and a major strike of transport workers in Dublin. The sheer numbers of people involved in these industrial disputes was unprecedented. From the late 1890s onwards, more and more unskilled workers had been drawn into trade unionism. In 1914 a so-called 'Triple Alliance' was formed between the Miners', the Railwaymen's and the Transport Workers'

Unions. These unions, covering three major industries, agreed to support each other if any one of them were to be involved in an industrial dispute. By 1910 around 17 per cent of workers were in trade unions, and the unrest encouraged the trend. By 1914 the figure had risen to 25 per cent. Perhaps the most remarkable feature of the period was the rise in female membership of trade unions. In 1904 there were 126,000 women trade union members. By 1913 there were 431,000, making up 10 per cent of all trade unionists.

Syndicalism

As industrial unrest became more confrontational the idea of trade unions as revolutionary organisations increased. In 1905 a French socialist, George Sorel, published a book entitled *Reflections on Violence*. In it he traced the actions of French trade unions, which were generally far more aggressive than their British counterparts, and argued that trade unionism should forget about trying to reform existing parliamentary systems and focus on creating an alternative revolutionary society governed on behalf of the workers by trade unions. Syndicalism, based on the French word for trade unions *'syndicats'*, developed from this idea. Syndicalists argued for class war and the violent overthrow of the capitalist system. The strategy would be to merge all trade unions into a single revolutionary organisation and use it to start a general strike of all workers in all industries to paralyse the country and destroy the parliamentary system of government.

In Britain the ideas were promoted through a magazine called *The Syndicalist* edited by Tom Mann, the organiser of the 1889 dock strike. He founded the Industrial Syndicalist Educational League in 1910 and organised a transport strike in Liverpool in 1911. In 1912 he was briefly imprisoned for publishing an article in *The Syndicalist* calling on the army not to fire on strikers, but the sentence was overturned after public protests. Other trade union leaders such as the dockers' leader Ben Tillett and the miners' leader A. J. Cook were also influenced by syndicalist ideas. More mainstream Labour leaders condemned syndicalism. Ramsay MacDonald, a Labour MP elected in 1906 and a future Labour prime minister, described syndicalism as 'the impatient, frenzied, thoughtless child of poverty, disappointment and irresponsibility'. George Barnes, a moderate trade union leader, Labour MP, and future government minister in the First World War, ridiculed syndicalism as 'fool's talk' and 'sheer madness'.

Urban growth and the standard of living of the working classes

While attempts to improve the urban environment in the late nineteenth century had some beneficial impact, the continued increase in the urban population meant that the living conditions of the working classes remained a serious concern. What helped focus greater political attention on the standard of living and general condition of the working classes was the publication of evidence in 'scientific' investigations into poverty that began to appear in the 1880s. Charles Booth, a shipping magnate, published details of his investigation into the London district of Tower Hamlets in 1887. He claimed that one-third of the population was living below the poverty line. Booth went on to conduct a series of investigations in London between 1891 and 1903. His work was paralleled by a study of poverty in York undertaken by Seebohm Rowntree, an industrialist turned sociological researcher, published in 1901. These investigations and others, similar if less well-known, were prompted partly by genuine humanitarian concerns and partly by violent demonstrations by unemployed men in the mid-1880s coinciding with one of the periodic economic slumps.

Poverty line – The level of income below which it is difficult to secure the basic necessities of life: shelter, food, clothing, etc.

These investigations were also intended to provide factual evidence about poverty, in contrast to the rather emotional and sensational accounts that were becoming common in the 1880s. Their chief value was to demonstrate that unemployment and poverty could not be viewed solely as the results of vice or laziness. Indeed, one result of Booth's findings was to show clearly that the chief factor in poverty was family size and that the number of children in a family was a more significant element in determining living standards than unemployment. The poor physical condition of many of the would-be recruits for the Boer War of 1899–1902 added fuel to the fires of publicity that scientific investigation had stoked. It added to the idea that poverty and degradation were turning the British lower classes into some kind of subspecies. Booth had written that the:

'lives of the poor lay hidden from view behind curtains on which were painted terrible pictures; starving children, suffering women, overworked men'

His (unrelated) namesake, William Booth, the founder of the Salvation Army, published a pamphlet in 1890 entitled **In Darkest England and the Way Out**, in which he portrayed the working-class districts as more distant than darkest Africa in terms of their remoteness from the experience of the upper and middle classes. This idea that the condition of the working classes posed some kind of nameless threat to civilised standards was to prove a potent force in promoting the acceptability of interventionist social reform such as that proposed by the New Liberals and the emerging Labour Party.

It was perhaps inevitable that people concerned with both the apparent economic decline of Britain and the supposed physical deterioration of the working classes should seek to establish some link between the two. The more extreme responses to the problem pressed for:

● sterilisation and selective breeding programmes
● bans on foreign immigration, as it was allegedly polluting the 'bloodstock' of the British race, contributing to unemployment and spreading disease. In 1905 an Aliens Act was introduced aimed at refusing entry to Britain to those immigrants thought to be incapable of supporting themselves, or carrying diseases.

3 Women's suffrage

One issue that the Liberals failed to resolve was the difficult matter of the claim of women to be able to vote in parliamentary elections.

The women's suffrage campaigns and the emergence of the suffragettes

Did the suffragettes help or hinder the campaign for women's political equality?

On the surface it appeared to be a fairly straightforward matter of basic logic and individual rights. During the second half of the nineteenth century women had made steady, if unspectacular, progress in legal and educational emancipation. The employment of women in clerical posts had expanded enormously and they had even made some inroads in the professions. An obvious target for similar progress was political rights. The campaign for women's suffrage began to gather momentum from the time of the Second Reform Act (1867). The anomaly that women living in boroughs could be householders but not voters while they might actually be employing men who were voters, was obvious from the start. John Stuart Mill, the great nineteenth-century philosopher and political theorist, who was an MP during the period 1866–68, urged the House of Commons to consider the illogicality of the situation but to no avail. Nevertheless, women did gain some significant political rights:

- In 1869 women gained the vote in town council elections in municipal boroughs.
- In 1870 they gained the right to be elected to the School Boards set up under the Education Act.
- From 1875 women could be elected to serve as Poor Law Guardians running the local workhouses.
- In 1889 they were included in the local government franchise, although they did not have the right to take office on the new county and county borough councils.

The first properly organised group to campaign nationally for the right of women to vote was the National Society for Women's Suffrage (NSWS) formed in 1868. It was an amalgamation of locally based groups that had developed during the 1860s. This group split in 1888 because some members wanted to affiliate to the Liberal Party while others wanted to be independent of party politics. However, in 1897 a new body was formed that was able to reunite the old NSWS members and bring in various other women's suffrage groups which had been springing up randomly. This new organisation was known as the National Union of Women's Suffrage Societies (NUWSS). By 1900 the NUWSS had some 400 branches all over the country and appeared to be a united and forceful pressure group. However, there was a new divisive issue waiting to bring further discord to their campaign.

There were two different approaches among those who believed that women had a right to vote. Some argued for the immediate inclusion of women in the franchise on exactly the same terms as men. Others wished to press for the right of all men and women over the age of 21 to vote. There was a danger in this second option from the women's point of view. This was the fear that it was so radical that it might lead to compromises, such as had happened with the gradual enfranchisement of men. If this happened one possible outcome might be that all men would get the vote but no women. Once that position had been established women arguably might find it even more difficult to secure the parliamentary vote. The difference of opinion led to a split within the ranks of the NUWSS. Emmeline Pankhurst, a widow whose husband had been a long-time Liberal campaigner for women's rights, formed a new movement called the Women's Social and Political Union (WSPU) in 1903. Pankhurst took the view that women should have immediate equality with men in the existing system of voting qualifications. Once this was achieved, attention could turn to campaigning for full democracy. Pankhurst had already broken her political connection with the Liberals in favour of the Independent Labour Party and later the Labour Representation Committee (LRC) which the ILP helped form in 1900 (see page 78). She believed it to be a better vehicle for her aims of economic and social equality for women. Now, assisted by her daughters, Christabel, Sylvia and Adela, she mobilised the WSPU to press the issue of female suffrage within the Labour Representation Committee.

The problem for the Pankhursts was that the LRC was itself divided over the issue. Most of the leaders were genuinely in favour of the basic idea of the right of women to vote. Some, such as the MP James Keir Hardie, a self-educated former shipyard worker who had started work at the age of seven and was elected to Parliament in 1900, were sympathetic to the demand for

NOTE-MAKING

Use the headings and questions in the second part of Section 3 to make brief notes on the campaign for women's political rights. Structure your notes with headings, sub-heading and sub-points to make them easy to navigate and use (see page x for further guidance).

For example, the following headings could be used to summarise the key points on pages 106–12.

- Why did the campaign for women's political rights become violent?
- How did the WSPU seek to promote the cause of votes for women?
- Was the Government or the Suffragettes most to blame for the stalemate that developed up to 1914?

immediate female suffrage on equal terms with men. However others, such as Philip Snowden, a former junior civil servant elected as an MP in 1906 and a future chancellor of the exchequer in the Labour governments of 1924 and 1929–31, preferred to wait for complete adult suffrage. Whichever view they took, the LRC leaders were also uncomfortably aware of the extent of hostility to female equality among working-class males, particularly within the trade unions where almost all the leaders opposed female equality in politics and in the workplace.

In 1905, Keir Hardie introduced a Private Member's Bill to extend the vote to women on the householder franchise that applied to men. This was the highpoint of WSPU/LRC collaboration and Emmeline Pankhurst worked with Keir Hardie to promote the bill. Its defeat was certain, however, and the lack of real enthusiasm for it within the LRC rank and file left the Pankhursts disappointed and disillusioned. Nevertheless the WSPU still helped Labour candidates in the 1906 general election campaign. However, this actually worsened relations as some Labour candidates rejected their help while others made it clear that they expected them to restrict their activities to making tea and passing around refreshments at meetings. Pankhurst became convinced that women must seize the initiative themselves and secure their own political destiny.

Liberal Party divisions

When the Liberals came to power in 1905, they were divided over female suffrage. Some, still following Gladstone's views, were opposed to it altogether while others, although sympathetic, were uncertain how best to proceed. For the Liberals the dilemma was that any kind of piecemeal or gradual enfranchisement of women based on property qualifications seemed most likely to benefit the Unionists. The results of granting full adult suffrage were difficult to assess, especially with the new Labour Party's ultimate political appeal still an unknown quantity. In the 1906 election, many Liberal candidates expressed their support for female suffrage, raising hopes among women campaigners that legislation might soon materialise. Yet these were false hopes. In reality the Liberal Government had no intention of risking political controversy over female suffrage. The most it would do was remove the obvious anomaly of the exclusion of women from sitting on local councils, by passing the Qualification of Women Act of 1907. This was naturally welcomed by the WSPU, but it hardly constituted a great leap forward, nor was it an acceptable commitment for the future. Frustrated by the lack of progress, the WSPU became more militant. Harassment of politicians at meetings, already employed during the 1906 campaign, was intensified. From such traditional tactics the WSPU graduated to:

- attacks on property: window smashing and arson
- the destruction of mail: pepper-filled letters were dispatched to politicians to provide a literally irritating reminder to the recipients of the women's displeasure with the lack of progress.

The more aggressive the WSPU became however, the harder any kind of concession became for the Government as it could not be seen to be giving in to violence. The more entrenched the Government's position became the more intense the anger of the women. The WSPU militants became known as 'suffragettes', a female-only term to distinguish them from the more moderate male and female 'suffragist' campaigners. Criminal proceedings resulted in imprisonments that led to hunger strikes, which eventually led the prison authorities to resort to force-feeding. It was an embarrassing state of affairs for any government, especially one calling itself 'Liberal', but, as with the constitutional crisis itself, neither side had a great deal of room for manoeuvre.

Deadlock

During the constitutional crisis of 1909–11 (see pages 73–77) both sides tried to extricate themselves from the deadlock. After the campaign leading up to the January 1910 general election, during which Liberal ministers had come in for some rough treatment at the hands of women activists, the WSPU called for a truce in the hope that the gesture would ease the tension. Parliament, rather than the Government, responded with a 'Conciliation Bill' drafted by an all-party committee. It proposed the enfranchisement of women on the basis of either a householder or occupation franchise, which would have meant in practice around 8 per cent of women getting the vote. The Government, though divided on the merits of the bill, initially agreed to allow time to debate it and it was introduced as a Private Members' Bill by a Labour MP, D. J. Shackleton. On its second reading it secured a majority of 110. The WSPU had welcomed the bill and had high hopes that it was the long-awaited breakthrough. However, the bill was dropped because the Government lacked real commitment to it and decided not to allow further parliamentary time for it. There were two factors in this:

- The Liberal prime minister Asquith, who was progressively minded on most issues, was not a supporter of female suffrage and had been deeply angered by the violence of the WSPU campaigns. To him, concessions amounted to giving in to fanatics.
- Other leading Liberals, like Lloyd George, were against it because they saw it as enfranchising the most conservative-minded sections of women and in the long run damaging to the Liberals' electoral chances.

It is only fair to point out that Sylvia Pankhurst, the most socialist-minded of the Pankhurst family, who was increasingly focusing on her work among the poor of East London, also doubted the wisdom of the bill for the second reason. Asquith's opposition was probably the decisive factor that ended the hopes for the Conciliation Bill in 1910. He made vague promises of a government bill to replace it but would not commit himself to a timetable. The loss of the Conciliation Bill temporarily ended the truce that had been declared by the WSPU. There was a mass demonstration and some violent episodes at the end of 1910 after which the truce was resumed in the hope of a fresh initiative.

The failure of compromise

In May 1911, a second Conciliation Bill, this time introduced by a Liberal MP, passed its second reading by 255 to 89. Lloyd George then announced that the Government had decided that further time would not be allowed for the bill that session. In November 1911, Asquith stated that the Government would introduce a suffrage bill next session providing for full manhood suffrage and would permit amendments to be moved that would extend the bill to include women's suffrage on the same basis as manhood suffrage. A third Conciliation Bill, introduced by a Conservative MP, failed to pass its second reading because the Government refused to support it.

The Government's manhood suffrage measure, called the Franchise and Registration Bill, appeared in June 1912 and passed its second reading. It was then shelved until January 1913. At this point the Speaker ruled that introducing amendments allowing a female franchise could not be allowed. Since there is no appeal against the rulings of the Speaker the Government had no alternative but to withdraw the measure. The Government therefore withdrew the bill and would not re-introduce it in an amended form.

All through these delays and evasions the WSPU became increasingly hostile in attitude and extreme in action. A bitter confrontation between it and the Government continued until the outbreak of the First World War, when the

Speaker of the House of Commons – The person who chairs Commons debates and is the final authority on rules of procedure.

Pankhursts changed tack by adopting a patriotic line and pressed for the full participation of women in the war effort. The failure to make progress on female suffrage, the deterioration of the campaign into terrorism and the dubious morality of the Government's tactics made this a grim and discreditable episode in political life before the First World War. The Government was reduced to illiberal expedients such as the Cat and Mouse Act of 1913 (see page 111), under which women on hunger strike were released and then rearrested, to try to control the situation.

The WSPU leaders became hunted refugees and Christabel Pankhurst fled to Paris to continue her direction of operations. The main blame for the situation, as it existed by 1914, must lie with Asquith as prime minister because he had passed over the chance to engineer some kind of compromise out of the Conciliation Bill in 1910. A lesser responsibility lies with the leadership of the WSPU for allowing their campaign to get so far out of hand that their actions began to blur the essential justice of their demands.

The campaign methods of the suffragettes and the Government's response

From the foundation of the WSPU in 1903 until the First World War, around a thousand suffragettes received prison sentences. Most of the early prosecutions were for public order offences such as disrupting public meetings, low-level damage to property and failures to pay the resulting fines. Christabel Pankhurst was first imprisoned in October 1905. While in prison suffragettes claimed to be political prisoners which would have entitled them to certain freedoms and rights not allowed to other prisoners, such as being allowed frequent visits and writing books or articles. However, the courts were inconsistent on this so initially some women were given the status of political prisoners while others were not. The WSPU campaigned to get all imprisoned suffragettes recognised as political prisoners, but this campaign was largely unsuccessful. The Home Office took the view that suffragettes becoming political prisoners would make them martyrs, and those initially granted the status were accused of abusing their freedom. As a result, ultimately very few women were granted the status.

The suffragettes answer to this was to stage hunger strikes while they were imprisoned. The first woman to refuse food was Marion Dunlop, a suffragette who was sentenced to a month in Holloway Prison for vandalism in July 1909. Dunlop refused food as a protest for being denied political prisoner status. After a 91-hour hunger strike, and with the risk of her becoming a martyr looming, Home Secretary Herbert Gladstone decided to release her on medical grounds. Her tactic was quickly taken up by other suffragettes and it became a common practice for suffragettes to refuse food in protest at not being designated political prisoners, with the result they would be released rather than risk their death.

The campaign intensifies

In the meantime the violent nature of the WSPU campaign was intensifying. The suffragettes turned to chaining themselves to railings, setting fire to mailbox contents, smashing windows and occasionally launching arson attacks and detonating bombs. In 1908 the Prime Minister's residence in Downing Street had its windows smashed. Extensive damage was done to golf courses, politicians were subjected to physical assaults, and churches were targeted because the Church of England was seen as opposed to the WSPU campaign. In February 1913 a house being built for Lloyd George in Surrey was bombed and extensively damaged, one of a number of such attacks on politicians' property.

As the suffragette demonstrations and aggressive action became more extreme, the Government was forced into a difficult position. Releasing any suffragette refusing food could not continue. In September 1909 a new strategy was introduced. Prisons began to force-feed suffragettes through a tube inserted into the nose or stomach. This had previously been used by doctors exclusively for patients in hospitals who were too unwell to eat or swallow food properly. For a healthy person who resisted the process force-feeding was hazardous and painful. Doctors were faced with the fact that force-feeding the women could result in damage to their circulatory, digestive and nervous systems as well as their mental health. Some suffragettes who were force-fed developed lung disorders such as pleurisy and pneumonia. Constance Lytton, the sister of a peer, used an alias when arrested to avoid preferential treatment and was force-fed before the prison authorities discovered her true identity and released her. She subsequently suffered a heart attack and a series of strokes that left her paralysed on her right side. The public reaction to force-feeding was generally sympathetic to the women suffering the ordeal.

Playing 'Cat and Mouse'

In April 1913 in the face of mounting criticism the home secretary Reginald McKenna passed the Prisoners' Temporary Discharge for Ill-Health Act – or Cat and Mouse Act as it became commonly known. The Act effectively turned hunger strikes into illnesses so that a suffragette would be temporarily released from prison when her health began to fail, only to be returned to prison when her health was restored. This allowed the Government to avoid blame resulting from death, or harm resulting from the self-starvation of the suffragettes. However, most women continued with their hunger strikes when they were brought back to prison. After this Act was introduced force-feeding as a general weapon was stopped and only women convicted of more serious crimes and considered likely to repeat them were force-fed.

Emily Wilding Davison

One suffragette named Emily Davison was severely injured after being trampled by the King's horse Anmer during the Derby race in June 1913, possibly in an attempt to throw a suffragette banner over the horse or jockey. Davison, a dedicated militant who had been in prison on nine separate occasions, died four days later. Herbert Jones the jockey survived with concussion after being dragged some distance while Anmer, despite performing a complete somersault, raced on rider less but apparently unperturbed to the finish line. The public response was immense. A memorial service in London saw tens of thousands of people lining the streets as Davison's coffin passed. There were, naturally, different opinions on her action. Some saw it as a courageous self-sacrifice, others as reckless endangerment of the jockey. Davison came from Northumberland and one immediate result was the setting up of the Northern Men's Federation for Women's Suffrage.

▲ Emily Davison is mortally injured by the King's horse

THE CAT AND MOUSE ACT

PASSED BY THE LIBERAL GOVERNMENT

THE LIBERAL CAT ELECTORS VOTE AGAINST HIM! KEEP THE LIBERAL OUT!

BUY AND READ 'THE SUFFRAGETTE' PRICE 1^d

▲ Suffragette poster condemning the Liberals' policy

In what ways do Sources A and B explain the differing attitudes to the right of women to vote in parliamentary elections?

As a response to the Cat and Mouse Act the WSPU set up a unit of women known as 'the Bodyguard'. Their role was to protect the leading suffragettes from assaults and arrest (or re-arrest after early release) by the police. For obvious reasons their identities were kept secret but the roles of some are known. The unit was commanded by a Canadian, Gertrude Harding, who had previously carried out attacks on public places, most notably on the Royal Botanical Gardens at Kew. The Bodyguard were trained in the martial art of Jujitsu by Edith Margaret Garrud, one of the first professional female instructors in martial arts in the Western world. Members of the Bodyguard were involved in a series of hand-to-hand combats with police who attempted to arrest suffragette leaders, and these received wide coverage in the press. Jujitsu is a martial art that relies in part on skill and technique to use an opponent's own force against them and the success that the unit members had in their confrontations with police offers led to the press giving them the title 'suffrajitsus'. The Bodyguard also used decoys and disguises and in some cases arranged escapes for detained leaders. They became skilled in the use of Indian clubs, widely used at the time for exercise, but deployed to good effect by the unit members to counter police truncheons.

Source A Adapted from a speech by Asquith in the House of Commons, reported in *Hansard*, 28 March 1912.

The natural distinction of sex, which differentiates the functions of men and women in many departments of human activity, ought to continue to be recognised in the sphere of Parliamentary representation. It is asked why should you deny to a woman of genius the vote, which you would give to her gardener? The answer is you are dealing, not with individuals, but with the masses. In my judgement the gain which might result through the admission of gifted and well-qualified women would be more than neutralised by the injurious consequences which would follow to the status and influence of women as a whole.

Source B Adapted from an article by W. L. Blease, a well-known male supporter of votes for women. From 'The Emancipation of English Women' by W. L. Blease, (Constable), 1910.

It is useless to talk about the equal worth of women, as long as men declare they are willing to admit women into everything except politics. In England, where politics is so important, disenfranchisement brands the disenfranchised with a permanent mark of inferiority. An adult who is unfit to take part in politics will inevitably be made to feel inferior in education, in professional and industrial employments, and in social relations.

4 Social reform, 1886–14

Despite the Liberal Unionist leader Joseph Chamberlain's radical views on social policy, the Conservative and later Unionist governments that he first supported and then joined, failed to get to grips with the social problems that were being identified during this period.

Social reform under the Conservatives–Unionists, 1886–1905

Why was reform under the Conservatives–Unionists so limited?

The only piece of legislation in the period 1886–1905 that made a fundamental change in a major area of social policy was an Education Act introduced in 1902. That apart, the only other notable reform was introduced in 1897 in the form of a Workmen's Compensation Act that enabled workers injured at work to claim compensation from their employers. Even this was limited in that it did not apply to some important categories of workers such as agricultural labourers, seamen and domestic servants. Chamberlain was committed to a much wider range of reforms to benefit the working classes and Salisbury was prepared to back him provided the reforms were not so radical as to be a serious threat to his party's unity. In particular, Chamberlain was keen to introduce a system of old-age pensions, but despite much discussion nothing materialised. Chamberlain's failure can be explained as follows:

- He was increasingly convinced that social reforms on the scale he envisaged could only be funded through strengthening economic ties with the empire and imposing taxes on imports. He therefore believed that his main task was to focus on the empire and to strengthen it politically and economically. It was for this reason that he had chosen to be colonial secretary in preference to the posts of home secretary or chancellor of the exchequer that Salisbury had offered him. Either of these offices would have made it much easier for Chamberlain to oversee social reform policies.
- Because Chamberlain was not in a government post that allowed him to focus directly on social reforms, the issues tended to be sidelined into committees in which those less enthusiastic about reform were able to delay things. For example, the question of old-age pensions was referred to a commission of enquiry that made no progress other than to consider the probable expense.
- In 1899 the Boer War began and the mounting cost of this conflict meant that the costs of social reforms became the overriding issue.
- By the time the Boer War ended, Chamberlain had become totally convinced that social reform was dependent on the creation of wealth through the development of the empire. This, he had come to believe, required an end to the policy of free trade, which had been adopted in the middle years of the century, and the reintroduction of protective tariffs. He left the Government in 1903 to campaign for this programme and without him the Unionists lost all focus on social reform.

The Education Act, 1902

One particularly relevant social issue was that of state education and the effectiveness of the system of elementary education that had been put into place during Gladstone's first administration in 1870. The idea that British education was inferior in many respects to that of other countries had long been taking shape. Attention was usually focused on the deficiencies of technical

---

NOTE-MAKING

Use the headings and questions in Section 4 to make brief notes on social reform. Structure your notes with headings, sub-headings and sub-points to make them easy to navigate and use (see page x for further guidance).

For example, the following headings could be used to summarise the key points on pages 113–23:
- The attempt to improve education opportunities for the working classes in 1902.
- Why were social reforms considered vital by 1906?
- Choose two reforms and explain why they, in particular, are important.
- How successful were the Liberal Government's attempts to improve social conditions?

and scientific education in England and Wales compared to that offered to the general population in Scotland, Germany or France. The Royal Commission on Education for the middle classes, the Taunton Commission 1866–68 (see page 48), had appointed a special sub-commission to examine the systems of education in Scotland and on the continent of Europe. The belief that national efficiency could be promoted, or, to put it another way, that national decline could be halted, by a reform of the education system was one of the reasons for the passing of a controversial Education Act by the Unionist Government in 1902.

The Duke of Devonshire, who was the Cabinet minister responsible for education, and Arthur Balfour, Salisbury's nephew and the Leader of the House of Commons, both favoured a fundamental reform of the education system. Both were impressed by the argument that an efficient and properly funded education system was essential for a modern state aiming to maintain its place in the world. In 1902, these two men took charge of the drafting of an Education Bill designed to bring about a substantial measure of reform. Lord Salisbury, a devout Anglican, was dubious about it because he foresaw objections from the Church of England's schools, but since he intended to retire from the premiership in the near future he did not oppose the idea. Joseph Chamberlain was also unenthusiastic, not because he undervalued education, quite the opposite, but because, as a nonconformist he anticipated the storm that would result from any attempt at government interference in the role played by the nonconformist churches in the provision of education, or from any attempt to fund Anglican schools from local rates. However, Chamberlain could not overrule Balfour who was the clear successor to Salisbury as prime minister.

The purpose of the 1902 Education Act was to provide a new structure for both elementary and secondary education under local authority control. The School Boards that had been set up under the 1870 Act had legal powers only in respect of elementary provision. However over the years, many more progressive Boards had ignored this and used the rates to provide secondary and adult education as well. The situation came to a head in 1901, when a court case was brought against the London School Board for doing this. The judge ruled against the Board. This judgment led to severe restrictions on School Board spending on technical, evening and adult classes, all of which could be argued to be contributing to the creation of a better educated population. At central level, responsibility for both elementary and secondary education had been assumed by a Board of Education, created in 1899 on the advice of a Royal Commission. Balfour and Devonshire therefore proposed to extend this principle to the local level.

The Education Act of 1902 was passed amid great controversy, as Salisbury and Chamberlain had foreseen. The Act swept away the old School Boards and created Local Education Authorities (LEAs) under the county and borough councils. These LEAs had responsibility for both elementary and secondary education and were also required to support the voluntary (Church) schools out of the rates. This latter provision caused the contention. Nonconformists were outraged by the idea of ratepayers' money being used to support Anglican schools. The Liberals, conscious of their traditional political support among nonconformists, fought the proposal every inch of the way in the House of Commons and a great national campaign of opposition began, in which the Welsh radical, David Lloyd George, himself a nonconformist, took a leading role.

Attempts at compromise failed completely. Joseph Chamberlain suggested avoiding using the rates altogether by increasing government grants, but the cost of the Boer War ruled out that idea. Another possibility was a clause introducing an 'adoptive principle', under which it would have been left to local authorities to decide whether or not to use the rates in this way. Balfour was against this on the grounds that it meant that the issue would always be a political one and lead to endless arguments at local level, as well as leaving some Anglican schools at the mercy of hostile local councils. A good many Tories sympathised with Balfour's position and the clause was removed.

The passing of the 1902 Education Act cost the Unionist Government dearly in political terms. There were over 70,000 prosecutions for non-payment of rates in the following year and in Wales, where nonconformity was strong, the opposition was bitter. The Liberals reaped the benefit of a great revival in nonconformity, which had been markedly on the decline. The issue also enabled the Liberals to mend the party split that had occurred over the Boer War (see page 68).

The Liberal Social Reforms, 1906–14

To what extent did the Liberal social reforms change the lives of working-class people in Britain?

The failure to develop a policy of social reform to meet the needs of the lower classes was one of the main reasons for the decline in the position of the Unionist Government by 1905. The Liberals were determined not to make the same mistake and after they formed a government in 1905 they started a programme of social reform. The reasons why social reform had become such an important issue were:

- the obvious inadequacy of the existing provision for the poor
- the growing interest in and studies into poverty by social reformers
- the concerns about national security raised by the Boer War.

In 1906 the main safety net provided by the state to protect people who lacked any means of support was the Poor Law, still based on the system introduced in 1834. The 1834 amendment had introduced the 'deterrent principle', which meant that people without any means of supporting themselves were discouraged from seeking aid unless there was absolutely no alternative. In order to achieve this, the workhouses, which were run on a strict regime of discipline, had been set up to accommodate anyone genuinely seeking support, but to deter those able-bodied men and women who were thought to be seeking help out of laziness, when really they were perfectly capable of working for a living (see pages 43–44 for more details).

The founders of this system had never intended to apply a harsh workhouse regime to defenceless people such as children, the sick and the elderly, or even those unemployed men and women who were honestly seeking work. However, over the course of the nineteenth century, the nature of workhouses had changed. From being originally intended as short-term deterrents for scroungers, they had become instead the primary refuge of the old, the sick, the disabled and abandoned women and their children. These people overwhelmingly made up the bulk of the workhouse population by the 1880s. Even so the deterrent principle was still applied, though in varying degrees of severity from place to place. The prison-like appearance and internal discipline of the workhouses made them an object of fear and shame for those most likely to end up in them. Many people routinely put up with severe deprivation rather than submit to entering a workhouse.

By the 1890s, the scandal of deprivation and the grimness of the workhouses had become significant political issues. Both of the main political parties were, in theory, committed to doing something about the situation. From the late 1860s onwards Conservative and Liberal governments both introduced legislation aimed at improving the state of public health and controlling the worst conditions in factories and agricultural work. These policies, however, did nothing to address the core problem of the working classes: inadequate or inconsistent incomes (especially in old age or infirmity) and a lack of access to medical treatment.

Investigations into social deprivation

From the 1880s onwards a series of investigations undertaken by social reformers anxious to force the government to take action, revealed the extent of the poverty that many people were enduring. In 1881 the publication of *Progress and Poverty* by an American, Henry George, sparked off the interest. Actual case studies of real families began to build up a picture of the standard of living of the poor. These studies showed conditions of overcrowding and substandard housing, malnutrition and ill-health, and caused the political debate to develop and intensify. Two investigations stand out as particularly influential. These were:

- Charles Booth's *Life and Labour of the People of London* – a massive study published over the period 1889–1903 in several volumes.
- Seebohm Rowntree's *Poverty, A Study of Town Life*, which appeared in 1901.

Booth argued that 30 per cent of the population of London fell below a poverty line income level of between 90 and 105 pence per week. Rowntree's study was based on York and painted a similar picture. Rowntree also applied a very tight set of guidelines for defining poverty so as to avoid any charge of exaggeration of his findings. The overall message of these investigations was that around one-third of the entire population was living in conditions which were dangerously deprived.

The influence of the Boer War

In itself this evidence might still have not been enough to produce a political response. However, the Boer War of 1899–1902 produced an unexpected impetus for social reform. Britain did not have a system of conscription so when additional troops were needed for the war the army had to rely on those men who were willing to volunteer. There was no shortage of recruits, but an alarming percentage of those who did apply were found to be unfit for military service through a variety of medical conditions.

The Boer War was a relatively small conflict against an enemy that did not pose any direct threat, so the high rate of rejection of volunteers did not affect the army too badly. However, it raised the question of what might happen if Britain faced a much larger conflict in Europe at some point in the future. The health of the nation therefore took on quite a different aspect when seen in that way and some people who might not have sympathised with social reform purely for its own sake became convinced of its necessity.

The Liberals in power

The Liberals took office in 1905 with a general commitment to the improvement of working-class conditions. However, though they were pledged to do this in general terms they took over the government with few really detailed proposals. This was partly due to the suddenness with which they came to power and the immediate need to call a general election. But it also stemmed from the divisions they had suffered in recent years and the potentially controversial nature of any new social reform legislation. So why was social reform a controversial subject?

Conscription – The compulsory drafting of men into the armed services.

- The enthusiasts for 'New Liberalism', such as David Lloyd George, wished to see the government intervening much more directly to help improve life for the lower classes. This meant introducing national schemes for unemployment benefits, sickness benefits, old-age pensions and even the introduction of child allowances, all of which would have to be paid for mainly out of the taxes imposed on the better-off.
- More traditional Liberals still clung to the idea of individual effort and enterprise as the means to self-improvement and argued that the country would be damaged if people became too dependent on the state.
- State intervention was to some people the road to socialism, which was seen as threatening the whole social and economic order.
- The supporters of tariff reform argued that significant social reform could be funded long-term only through protective tariffs on imports.

Therefore although the leading Liberals, like the new prime minister, Sir Henry Campbell-Bannerman, and his chancellor of the exchequer, Herbert Asquith, leaned towards intervention, they were only too aware of the need to move very cautiously in the interests of maintaining unity within the Liberal Party as a whole. The controversial nature of the question of how to go about improving the lives of the poorest sections of society meant that firm plans of action might have proved too divisive in the run-up to an election. However, when the Liberals won their great election victory in 1906 they were committed in principle to bringing in social reforms to benefit the lowest classes. Their attention centred on three areas:

- the condition of children in the poorest families
- the condition of elderly people with no means of independent support
- the problem of poverty resulting from sickness and unemployment.

Protecting vulnerable children

The least controversial of these areas was the question of the condition of working-class children. Children made up only the most directly vulnerable section of society, but were the only group that could not be held in any way to blame for their problems. Sickness could be seen as self-inflicted or feigned and unemployment as the result of sheer laziness. Even the elderly could be seen as poverty-stricken in old age because they had not saved during their working lives. None of these accusations could reasonably be levelled at children. Those who wanted reform on a wider scale saw the cause of suffering children as a powerful emotional starting point. Even so, some (including some Liberals) still believed that children were solely the concern of their parents or families and that any government intervention on their behalf would undermine individual freedom and individual responsibility. Despite such views, however, there was a general feeling that the pitiful condition of the poorest working-class children was nothing short of a national disgrace.

The first direct move to ease the suffering of deprived children came in 1906 with the passing of the Education (Provision of Meals) Act. The issue of undernourished children had increasingly been highlighted since the extension of local rate support to all schools in the 1890s and the creation of Local Education Authorities (LEAs) by the 1902 Education Act (see page 113). The problem was that children who were too hungry and physically weak could not benefit properly from education. Reports from local doctors and school inspectors were well documented by 1906. The result was a Private Member's Bill introduced by a Labour MP, which the Liberal Government took over and adopted as government policy. The 1906 Act enabled LEAs to provide school meals for 'needy' children by charging an additional rate of a halfpenny in the pound. However, the key word here was 'enabled'. The Act did not make it compulsory for LEAs to do this and many did not rush to take up their new power. By 1911 less than one-third of them were using additional rates to provide school meals and the Board of Education decided to take additional powers under which they could order such provision.

In 1907, the Liberal Government introduced a new Education Act, which made school medical inspections for children compulsory. Under this Act:

- at least three inspections had to take place during a child's school years
- these inspections were to be conducted in school and during school hours by a qualified doctor
- the first inspection had to be done as soon as possible after the child had started school.

Unlike the regulations covering the provision of school meals this legislation was compulsory from the start. This was because:

- compulsory elements in laws concerning public health matters had been used in all kinds of situations since the first Public Health Act of 1848, so compulsion on this kind of issue was not very controversial
- the recruitment of volunteers for the Boer War had produced a sense of urgency about improving the health of the young.

In 1908, the Children's Act introduced a variety of measures to deal with wider aspects of neglect and abuse. Juvenile courts and remand homes were set up to remove child offenders from the adult courts and prisons. Severe penalties were introduced for the ill-treatment of children, and also for selling them tobacco and alcohol in unsealed containers. Finally, in the Budget of 1909, Lloyd George introduced direct financial assistance for child welfare in the form of child allowances to be paid at a rate of £10 per year per child for the poorest families.

These measures to improve the welfare of children were the Liberal's principal achievement during their first two years in office. The Liberals failed in an attempt to introduce an eight-hour day for the mining industry. They did manage to ensure that the principle of workmen's compensation for injuries occurring in the workplace was extended to cover some 6 million workers, but overall, only the child welfare reforms prevented it from seeming a very unimpressive record. Even allowing for the progress in helping working-class children to obtain a better start in life, some of the more radical Liberals, such as Lloyd George, were less than satisfied.

Protection in old age

In April 1908, the prime minister Campbell-Bannerman was forced to resign through illness. Asquith was his natural successor and, in the Cabinet reshuffle that followed, Lloyd George, who had built up a formidable reputation at the Board of Trade, was promoted to the chancellorship of the exchequer. He was replaced at the Board of Trade by Winston Churchill. Churchill was a former Conservative who had joined the Liberals in protest against the policy of tariff reform in 1903. He had since established himself as a radical reformer. Lloyd George and Churchill were determined to use their new seniority to push for a much more ambitious programme of social reform. Not only did they genuinely want more radical reforms, they also believed that it was a political necessity for the Liberals to show themselves capable of developing a really progressive policy if the party was not to lose out in future elections to the Unionists and the Labour Party.

When the Liberals came to power in 1905 there was no provision for state pensions for the elderly. Old people were expected either to continue working to support themselves or to have saved enough in their working lives to maintain themselves in retirement. Failing either of these there was only the charity of their families or the workhouses provided under the feared and hated Poor Law. For most working-class people only the last two options really applied, as their incomes were too low for saving on a scale that would provide for old age, and their work was usually too physically demanding to be carried on in old age. The basic principle that some kind of financial support should be provided by the state for a dignified old age had been discussed since the 1880s, but the cost of providing such a system had deterred successive governments from taking on the issue. During the last phase of his time as chancellor of the exchequer, Asquith had been working on the idea of introducing a system of old-age pensions. His Budget proposals for 1908 contained provisions for financing the introduction of a scheme and Lloyd George inherited the responsibility for putting the finishing touches to the Budget and presenting it to the House of Commons. Lloyd George then took on the job of piloting an Old Age Pensions Bill into law. The provision that this made for the poorest of the elderly was relatively modest, especially when considered against the length of time it had taken to get any form of assistance provided. The first payments were finally made on 6 January 1909. The terms of the Act were:

- Pensions of 5s (25p) per week would be paid to those aged 70 or over who had annual incomes of £21 or less.
- For those with annual incomes over £21, a sliding scale of reduced payments would be made. Those with an annual income of £31 or over would receive no payment.

There were a number of categories of people excluded:

- those who had claimed poor relief in the previous year
- people who had been in prison in the previous ten years
- those who had failed to work regularly.

In practice these rules did not result in a great reduction in the number of claimants. The qualifying period for ex-convicts was eventually reduced to two years. By 1914, there were 970,000 claimants, costing the exchequer a total of £12 million a year. Though often criticised for the relatively high starting age (70 was a tougher milestone to achieve then than it has subsequently become), the system had a massive impact on the lives of its beneficiaries. The 'Lloyd George money', as it became widely known, released many from the threat of the workhouse or dependence on often hard-pressed relatives. A pensions system had been under discussion since the 1880s and the Liberals had made it a reality. Figure 4 shows the typical weekly living costs of an elderly person in 1908 (see page 2 for the comparison between old and new money).

Figure 4 Typical weekly living costs for one person in 1908. Published in the radical magazine, *The Woman Worker*.

	s.	d.
Rent	2	3
Paraffin (pint)	1	1/2
Coal	2	1/2
Tea	1	
Sugar	1	1/2
Potatoes	1	
Mutton	1	0
Flour	1	
Porter (a type of beer)	1	3/4
Pepper, salt and vinegar	1	1/2
Loaf of bread	2	1/2
Total:	4	51/4 (22p)

THE NEW YEAR'S GIFT.

A cartoon entitled 'The New ▶
Year's Gift' from *Punch* magazine,
recording the start of payments
of old-age pensions at the
beginning of 1909.

What interpretation is this
cartoon offering about the
introduction of old-age
pensions?

Protecting the sick and unemployed

Once the issue of old-age pensions had at last been tackled, Lloyd George
was determined to move on to the problem of the hardship caused by loss
of earnings due to unemployment and sickness. By the middle of 1908 this
was a serious issue because the general economic situation was becoming
difficult for lower income groups. Unemployment was rising and wages were
either stationary or falling. At the same time, inflation was reducing the
real value of wages by pushing up the cost of living. At the Board of Trade,
Churchill introduced an Act setting up labour exchanges in 1909. The aim of
these was to make it easier for the unemployed to get in touch with potential
employers by giving them access to information about work available in
each locality. Meanwhile, in 1908 Lloyd George went to Germany to study
the German system of social insurance at first hand, as a welfare system had
been in existence in Germany since the 1880s. By the autumn of 1908 a team
of civil servants were working on the principles of a scheme to introduce
unemployment and sickness insurance into Britain. Although work on the
schemes was well advanced by 1909, their eventual implementation was
delayed until the National Insurance Act of 1911. The first payments under the
new laws were not made until the summer of 1912 (for unemployment) and the
beginning of 1913 (for health). The delay was mainly because Lloyd George and
Churchill, who were the politicians in charge of the details, wanted to deal with
both sickness and unemployment at the same time. Unemployment insurance
was relatively uncontroversial and, on its own, could probably have been
introduced without any difficulty in 1909. Sickness benefits, however, were an
entirely different matter.

The controversy over sickness benefits was because friendly societies,
industrial insurance companies and doctors would all be affected by the
intervention of the government into this kind of benefit provision. Insurance
companies and friendly societies collected millions of pounds every year

120

▲ 'The Doctor'. This cartoon from *Punch* comments on the attitude of doctors to the National Insurance Act 1911.

1 Identify the politician depicted as a doctor and his colleague in the background.
2 What is the overall message conveyed in this cartoon?

in payments from lower middle-class and better-off working-class families, covering them for different benefits such as sick pay or doctors' visits. The poorest working-class families could not afford these policies and generally had no protection at all other than from charitable organisations. It took months of difficult negotiations for Lloyd George to work out and agree suitable safeguards and compromises. There was also opposition from the doctors' organisation, the British Medical Association, mainly due to the influence of the wealthier doctors who feared that the status of their profession would be lowered if they were paid by government. However, the adoption of a 'panel' system, which allowed insured patients to choose their own doctor from a panel of doctors under the control of a local health committee, proved very popular with the less well-off doctors, especially those in the inner cities. They realised that their incomes would rise considerably from this new source of patients.

National Insurance

The National Insurance Act of 1911 was in two separate parts. Part I dealt with health insurance and was the responsibility of the Treasury. Part II dealt with unemployment insurance and was the responsibility of the Board of Trade.

The health insurance system worked as follows:

● All workers earning less than £160 per year and aged between 16 and 60 were included – around 15 million in all.
● Weekly contributions were taken from the worker (4d), the employer (3d) and the government (2d). This encouraged Lloyd George to coin the slogan '9d, for 4d,' in his attempts to make the idea popular.

The resulting entitlement was:

● sickness benefit of 10s (50p) per week for thirteen weeks (7s 6d for women); 5s (25p) per week for a further thirteen weeks after that; later, the reduced benefit for the second thirteen-week period was abolished in favour of full benefit for 26 weeks
● a 30s (£1.50) maternity grant
● 5s (25p) a week disability benefit
● free medical treatment under a 'panel' doctor.

Non-working wives and children were not covered by the scheme, nor was hospital treatment, except for admission to a sanatorium, a kind of hospital especially for recovery from long-term debilitating conditions where the emphasis was placed on rest, cleanliness and good ventilation. This was mainly intended to benefit tuberculosis sufferers.

The unemployment insurance scheme was much less ambitious and covered far fewer workers. In all a total of 2.25 million were protected, mainly in construction and engineering trades, which were susceptible to fluctuating employment levels. The idea was to support workers out of work over a short period of time. It was not meant to tackle the problem of long-term unemployment.

The unemployment insurance scheme worked as follows:

● Weekly contributions were $2\frac{1}{2}$d (1p) each from workers, employers and the government.
● The insured workers were entitled to a payment of 7s (35p) per week benefit for up to a maximum of fifteen weeks.

Other Liberal reforms

Numerous other reforms were also undertaken by the Liberal governments and can be summarised as follows:

● A Trades Disputes Act in 1906 protected striking trade unions from being sued by employers – see also Chapter 3.
● A Workmen's Compensation Act in 1906 brought all categories of worker under the provisions for compensation for accidents at work and extended protection to cover injury to health.
● A Coal Mines Act in 1908 introduced a maximum eight-hour day for miners.
● A Trade Boards Act in 1909 set up boards to impose minimum wages in the so-called 'sweated trades' where low pay and long hours had long prevailed. Tailoring, box making, chain making and lace making were initially covered. The Act was widened to include more trades in 1913.
● A further Mines Act in 1911 laid down regulations for training, safety measures and accident procedures.

The emergence of a welfare society?

The effect of these social reforms meant a significant increase in government intervention. The state had now assumed an unprecedented degree of responsibility for individuals in the lower classes of society. A great expansion in the civil service was required to oversee its administration. The sums spent on the new benefits exceeded all official estimates. This welfare legislation entirely bypassed the operation of the Poor Law and, to a considerable degree, appeared to make the question of its reform irrelevant. The Unionist Government had set up a Royal Commission to examine the Poor Laws in 1905. By the time it reported in 1909 there was little political interest from any party in a major overhaul of the system. As a result the Poor Law largely fell into disuse until it was finally abolished in 1929. The overall impact of the Liberals' social reforms has often been criticised as 'too little, too late'. Marxist historians in particular dismiss them as limited concessions aimed at propping up the capitalist system. On the other hand they can be interpreted as the start of a welfare society, which would lead eventually to the creation after the Second World War of a welfare state (see page 253).

The reality for people at the time was that by 1912, when the National Insurance provisions began to take effect, a very considerable boost had been given to the incomes of the poorest families. The combined effect of child welfare support, old-age pensions, employment legislation, child allowances and National Insurance meant that a significant safety net had been established against poverty. Few poor families could fail to benefit from at least some aspect of this legislation. In particular, the relief to working-class budgets in respect of the support of elderly relatives, brought about by the Old Age Pensions Act, should not be underestimated. It is not clear how the Liberals could have done much more at the time, given the contemporary views on the limits of taxation and the fact that their philosophy was 'liberalism' (not 'socialism'), which still recognised a role for individual enterprise and personal responsibility.

KEY DATES: LIBERAL SOCIAL REFORMS

1906	Liberals win January general election; The Education (Provision of Meals) Act
1906–08	Legislation to help children from poorer families
1907	Education Act
1908	Children's Act
	Old Age Pensions Act
1909	Introduction of old-age pensions
1911	National Insurance Act

WORKING TOGETHER

1 Working in pairs, construct a table like the one below, to show the major social reforms of the Liberals.

Reform	Strength	Weaknesses

2 Compare your table with another pair and discuss any differences in conclusions.
3 Review the tables and then select the reform you consider to have been the most important, with a justification.
4 Then select the reform you consider to have been the most defective, with a justification.

Chapter summary

- There was a significant rise in the numbers of workers joining trade unions.
- As a result the power and influence of the trade union movement increased.
- Concerns about the conditions of the working classes led independent social reformers to conduct investigations.
- The evidence they gathered promoted a debate about how social deprivation might be improved.
- This debate coincided with concerns that social deprivation was undermining economic performance and national defence.
- The failures and scandals attached to the Unionist Government in the period 1900–05 led to the victory of the Liberals in 1906–14.
- The Liberal Government carried through significant reforms to benefit vulnerable children, the elderly, the sick and the unemployed.
- The campaign for women's right to vote in parliamentary elections gained momentum after the creation of the WSPU in 1903.
- As the campaign became increasingly violent, a deadlock emerged between the suffragettes and the Government.
- Concerns about Britain's economic performance led to a bitter conflict over whether the country should continue with free trade or introduce economic protection.

Chapter summary diagram

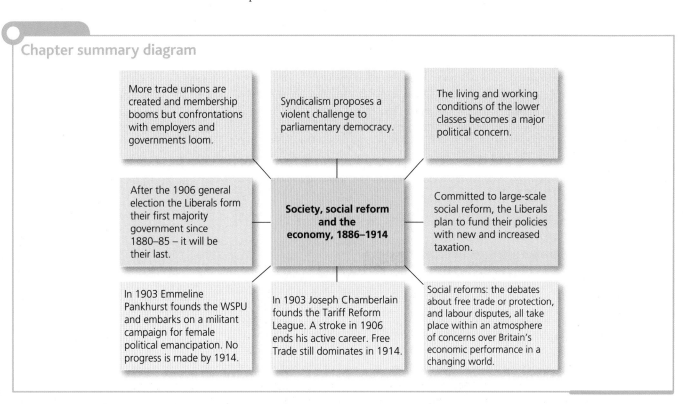

More trade unions are created and membership booms but confrontations with employers and governments loom.

Syndicalism proposes a violent challenge to parliamentary democracy.

The living and working conditions of the lower classes becomes a major political concern.

After the 1906 general election the Liberals form their first majority government since 1880–85 – it will be their last.

Society, social reform and the economy, 1886–1914

Committed to large-scale social reform, the Liberals plan to fund their policies with new and increased taxation.

In 1903 Emmeline Pankhurst founds the WSPU and embarks on a militant campaign for female political emancipation. No progress is made by 1914.

In 1903 Joseph Chamberlain founds the Tariff Reform League. A stroke in 1906 ends his active career. Free Trade still dominates in 1914.

Social reforms: the debates about free trade or protection, and labour disputes, all take place within an atmosphere of concerns over Britain's economic performance in a changing world.

Working on essay technique: evaluation and relative significance

Reaching a supported overall judgement is an important part of writing effective essays. One very important way to do this is by evaluating the relative significance of different factors, in the light of valid criteria. Relative significance means how important one factor is compared to another. This section examines how to evaluate and how to establish valid criteria.

The purpose of *evaluation* is to weigh up interpretations and evidence and then reach a judgement. This means that you need to consider the validity of at least two or (very often) more, different interpretations, weigh them against each other using evidence, and then reach a judgement. Evaluation like this is needed throughout your answer if it is to sustain an effective argument and support a balanced and substantiated conclusion.

EXAMPLE

Consider the following practice A-level question:

'British governments were mainly successful in dealing with the domestic challenges they faced in the period 1886–1914.' Assess the validity of this view. (25 marks)

In this example the evaluation is going to be based on identifying what the expression 'domestic challenges' is referring to. You will need to refer to both this chapter and Chapter 3 to do this. The concept you are applying to the evaluation is 'success'.

The arguments over the practice question above must be based on your own assessment of different ideas. Better essays will always reach a final judgement about success based on valid criteria.

It is up to you to come up with valid criteria. Criteria can be very simple and will depend on the exact wording of the question. For example, this question targets success and leaves the challenges unspecified, making the question very broad in scope. For this the following criteria might be used:

- **Duration:** which challenge was the most deeply entrenched for the longest amount of time?
- **Scale:** which challenge affected the most people?
- **Effectiveness:** which challenge was most decisively dealt with?
- **Difficulty:** which challenge was the most serious to face?

Think about the following when planning your answer to the question:

- How will you define success?
- Identify four key areas in which government policy either failed, succeeded or had mixed success.
- Support this by writing two or three sentences specific to the areas you have chosen.
- There were different governments in office during this period. Will you differentiate between them?
- Write an argument in around 70–100 words that summarises how far governments successfully met the challenges you discuss.
- Use words such as 'however', 'nonetheless', 'even so', 'alternatively' and 'on the other hand' to weigh up contrasting points.

A brief plan might take therefore take this form, or you could devise your own table:

Nature of challenge	Government in power	Degree of success	Degree of failure

---

ACTIVITY

Now consider the following AS and A-level practice questions which take different approaches to the same period. Apply the same techniques in attempting to write an answer to these questions.

AS-level practice question:

'The problem of Ireland was the most important problem facing British governments in the period 1886–1914.' Explain why you agree or disagree with this view. (25 marks)

A-level practice question:

To what extent were the Liberals a party in decline in the period 1886–1914? (25 marks)

Working on interpretations skills: extended reading

To what extent did Joseph Chamberlain have a negative impact on British politics?

Richard Toye assesses the contribution of Joseph Chamberlain's political career.

Joseph Chamberlain (1836–1914) was a forceful and creative statesman who had an important impact on British politics at three levels: the local, the national, and the imperial. His beginnings, as the son of a London shoemaker, were relatively humble, but he moved to Birmingham as a young man and became a successful industrialist. This was the city   5
that would become his life-time political base. As the grip of the landed aristocracy on government weakened in the late Nineteenth Century, Chamberlain was one of the new breed of businessmen-politicians, and had a modernising agenda to match. Chamberlain began his political career on the Radical wing of the Liberal Party, but by the end of it he had   10
moved into close cooperation with the Conservatives.

Chamberlain was a Unitarian – a type of Christian non-conformist – and this is an important key to his political impact. Nonconformists were hostile to the privileges of the Church of England, which tended to be associated with the Conservative Party. Many of them were to be found on the left of the   15
Liberal Party, which was an uneasy coalition held together by the forceful personality of its leader, W. E. Gladstone. Chamberlain was very interested in social reform and was one of the founders of the National Education League. But when Gladstone's government reacted to its demands by passing the Elementary Education Act (1870), the League was unhappy,   20
because the Church of England was still to be the main provider of schooling. Chamberlain led the so-called 'non-conformist revolt' against Gladstone, but the result of this was to help put the Conservatives into power.

Chamberlain's achievements as Mayor of Birmingham were more constructive. Although the Victorian era is often associated with the   25
doctrine of *laissez-faire* or minimal government, Chamberlain was a great believer in the power of the state. He became a pioneer of so-called 'municipal socialism', whereby local government took control of services and utilities out of the hands of private companies in the belief that they could be run more efficiently under public control. As well as taking over   30
the supply of gas and water, Chamberlain launched a programme of slum clearance, although the latter proved costly and politically contentious.

Chamberlain became an MP in 1876. The following year he established a new body, the National Liberal Federation, which had a positive impact on popular support for the Liberal Party. This caused some   35
suspicion from those who preferred the more traditional, elite ways of doing politics, but it contributed to the smashing Liberal victory at the general election of 1880. Chamberlain served as a cabinet minister for five years, and at the 1885 election promoted a set of Radical policies known as the 'Unauthorised Programme'. Over the following months,   40
the political situation became very confused, the end result being that – with Irish nationalist MPs holding the balance of power – Gladstone put

forward proposals for Home Rule (greater self-government) for Ireland. Chamberlain resigned from the Cabinet and fought hard against the plan, and Gladstone was heavily defeated.   45

Chamberlain and his fellow Liberal Unionists, as they were now known, were now in effective alliance with the Conservatives. He remained interested in social reform, but had only partial success in persuading the Tories to go along with his ideas. He joined the government in 1895, choosing the position of Colonial Secretary. That had not normally been   50
considered a very important role, but Chamberlain established himself as a key player, and took a controversial role in the events that led up to the Anglo-Boer War (1899–1902). At the 1900 election, his patriotic, imperial rhetoric helped ensure, yet again, the defeat of his former Liberal colleagues. Yet the tide was about to turn. In 1903, he announced   55
that he had become converted to the idea of trade protectionism (or tariff reform) which he saw as a way of halting Britain's relative economic decline. This departure from Britain's traditional free trade policy divided the Conservative and Unionist forces and revived the Liberals. In 1906 the Liberal Party won a landslide victory. A few months later, Chamberlain   60
suffered a severe stroke, which incapacitated him for the rest of his life. From the point of view of the Conservatives Chamberlain had contributed positively to the strength of Salisbury's government but the negative impact of his conversion to protectionism caused serious division and contributed to the 1906 defeat.   65

Joseph Chamberlain, then, can be seen as a charismatic and inventive figure, whose ever-present monocle and buttonhole-orchid helped turn him into a political celebrity. His dynamism led him to be admired, but also contributed to the fact that, at different times, he split both main parties. Gladstonian Liberals saw Chamberlain as a destructive and   70
negative influence but his ideas inspired other more radical Liberals such as Lloyd George. His reforming legacy can still be seen in Birmingham today, notably in the form of the university that he founded there. He was a flawed visionary, whose life and beliefs illustrate the complexities and contradictions of the Victorian era.   75

Professor Richard Toye, University of Exeter.

ACTIVITY

Having read the essay, answer the following questions.

Comprehension
1 What does the author mean by the following phrases?
   a) 'Radical wing of the Liberal Party' (line 10)
   b) 'Unauthorised Programme' (line 40)
   c) 'traditional free trade policy' (line 58).

Evidence
2 Using paragraph 5, list the ways in which the author balances the evidence when discussing Chamberlain's political impact.

Interpretation
3 Using your knowledge from your study of Joseph Chamberlain, list evidence to support the author's conclusion that Chamberlain was a 'flawed visionary'.

Evaluation
4 How far do you agree with the author's view that Chamberlain's tariff reform idea was the main factor in the Conservative defeat in 1906?

Key questions: Britain 1851–1914

The specification on this topic states that it requires the study in breadth of issues of change, continuity, cause and consequence in the period through six key questions. These have been either featured or mentioned at various points in the four chapters you have studied. The questions set in the examination (both the interpretation question and the essays) will reflect one or more of these key questions. Even though in the examination the questions may focus on developments over approximately 20–30 years rather than the period as a whole, it is very useful to pause to consider developments across the wider time period you have studied so far, as this will help you to see and analyse change and continuity with a sense of perspective.

KEY QUESTION 1
How did democracy and political organisations develop in Britain?

'Democracy' – what does this mean and how can it be achieved?

'Political organisations' – what groups are covered in this? Political parties, pressure groups?

'Develop' – think about how things changed over time, and what factors caused changes.

Questions to consider

- What effect did electoral reform have on the Liberal and Conservative parties throughout the period 1851–1914?
- What pressures were there on the form of parliamentary democracy that existed prior to 1914?
- How did the political system deal with the challenges these pressures posed?

Working in groups

Considering the period as a whole:

1 Discuss the view that social and economic factors were the most important in bringing about political change.
2 Discuss the view that voting rights were only ever granted as a last resort by governments between 1851 and 1914.
3 Discuss the view that political reforms were the result of political parties seeking to secure advantages over each other.

'How important' means you have to make a judgement on the significance of these ideas and ideology.

'Ideas and ideology' refers to beliefs – these could be political, economic or social.

Questions to consider

- Consider the importance of the following ideologies during this period:
  - Gladstonian Liberalism
  - New Liberalism
  - Socialism
  - Tory democracy
  - Tariff reform.
- Can it be argued that other factors beyond ideas and ideologies were the real forces creating historical change throughout the period?
- Who had most influence on the Conservative/Unionist and Liberal parties throughout the period 1851–1914?
- To what extent, if at all, did issues such as social reform or free trade impact on the outcome of elections?

Working in groups

Considering the period as a whole:
1 Discuss the effectiveness of Liberal ideas on social reform.
2 Examine the clash of ideas between Disraeli and Gladstone.
3 Discuss the effectiveness of Joseph Chamberlain as a political leader.
4 Discuss the increased activity of radical politics in the decade before the First World War and why this might have occurred.

· ·

'Effects' – how did changes in the economy affect the political and social situation?

'Economy' – what does this include? What different ideas were there about the economy at the time?

'Develop' suggests extending or increasing. How far can you relate it to the period 1851–1914?

Questions to consider

- What were the main economic developments in Britain in the mid to late nineteenth century? Why did they occur and what were their social and political effects?
- What were the main economic developments between 1880 and 1914?
- Did the economy always develop in ways that were beneficial to Britain? Were the benefits universally felt? Were there 'winners' and 'losers'?
- What impact did the gradual loss of economic competitiveness to other countries have on British politics between 1870 and 1914?

Working in groups

Considering the period as a whole:
1 Discuss the reasons for Britain's economic success at the height of the industrial revolution.
2 Discuss the state of the British economy in the period 1873–96.
3 Discuss the merits and shortcomings of free trade and protection after 1900.

When you are thinking about changes here, remember to treat social change and social policy change as two separate and distinct discussions.

What was the effect of the social policy changes that came into being?

Questions to consider

- How had British society changed between 1851 and 1914?
- How did the class system work on the eve of the war in 1914?
- Was there any kind of social mobility throughout the period?
- How did working-class organisations develop between 1851 and 1914?

Working in groups

Considering the period as a whole:
1 Discuss what factors encouraged change in British society.
2 Discuss what factors encouraged class conflict in British society.
3 Discuss why class identity became such a powerful issue by 1914.
4 How did social change affect politics, economics, society and culture?

What was the historical context to Britain's relationship with Ireland?

Were changes for the better or worse over the period?

Questions to consider

- Think of what Ireland's key problems were (land hunger for the peasants, absentee landlords, poverty).
- Think of key figures like Parnell, Gladstone, Chamberlain, Redmond and Carson – how did they affect the relationship between Britain and Ireland?
- Why did the Home Rule movement develop?
- How did the Irish parliamentary party manage to exert such power at Westminster?
- What is your overall assessment of the role of Unionism in the developing relationship between Britain and Ireland? Is it valid to see Unionism as mainly positive or mainly negative?
- Why was Ireland at the brink of civil war in 1914?

Working in groups

Considering the period as a whole:
1 How and with what success did British prime ministers attempt to 'solve' the Irish Question between 1851 and 1914?
2 Evaluate the contribution of Gladstone to resolving the Irish Question. How successful was he?
3 How far did Parnell advance the cause of Irish Home Rule?
4 What was the overall impact of terrorist attacks such as the Phoenix Park murders on relations between Britain and Ireland?

How do you measure importance? At the time? In retrospect?

Which individuals will you consider and why?

Which groups will you consider and why?

What is meant by developments? Did individuals and groups also affect developments?

Questions to consider

- Think of some of the key individuals, for example William Gladstone, Benjamin Disraeli, Lord Salisbury, Randolph Churchill, Joseph Chamberlain, Arthur Balfour, H. H. Asquith, Emmeline Pankhurst and David Lloyd George. Summarise their contributions to the government of Britain and/or to changes that took place in the period.
- Think of key groups, for example the Fabian Society, the Tariff Reform League, the trade union movement, the NUWSS and the WSPU and the Labour Party. What impact did groups have on the development of Britain throughout the period 1851–1914?
- How were key individuals affected by developments over which they had little control?
- To what extent did groups determine events? To what extent were they simply reacting to events?

Working in groups

Considering the period as a whole:

1 Compare the contributions of two British Liberal prime ministers of the period, Gladstone and Asquith. Prepare an argument explaining your view as to which of them made the more important contribution to constitutional and social reform.
2 Discuss which politician had the greatest influence and why. There are four prime ministers with lengthy spells in office: Gladstone, Disraeli, Salisbury and Asquith. Other politicians with a claim to have influenced events decisively could be Parnell, Chamberlain and Lloyd George.

Key Questions: Britain 1851–1914

5

The political impact of the First World War

This chapter covers the political developments that took place in Britain during the period 1914–39. It deals with the following areas:

● The impact of war on British parties and politics.
● The decline of the Liberal Party.
● Political developments in the inter-war years.
● The first two Labour governments.
● The condition of Ireland and Anglo-Irish relations.

When you have worked through the chapter and the related activities, you should have detailed knowledge of all those areas. You should be able to relate this knowledge to the key breadth issues defined as part of your study:

● What was the impact of war on British parties and politics between 1914 and 1939?
● How important were ideas and ideology, particularly in the emergence of radical political groups?
● How did the war affect Anglo-Irish relations?

The main development traced throughout this chapter can be phrased as a question:

How did the First World War shape British politics, 1914–39?

CHAPTER OVERVIEW

The First World War lasted for four years between 1914 and 1918, but the scale, intensity and destructiveness of the conflict transformed British politics during and after the fighting. The extension of the franchise in the Representation of the People Act in 1918 gave the vote to the majority of the population and this changed the shape of parliamentary politics throughout the inter-war years. In the immediate post-war period the political landscape changed as the Liberal Party went into decline and was replaced by the Labour Party as the main party of government and opposition. The development of mass democracy and the possibility of revolution in the immediate aftermath of the war focused the Conservative Party on the 'dangers of socialism'. An acrimonious atmosphere between the Conservatives and Labour existed throughout the 1920s. During the depression of the 1930s there was a growth in appeal to a minority of people in Britain of extreme political ideas such as fascism and communism. This chapter will explore how and why political attitudes, ideas and beliefs changed throughout the period. The final section of this chapter will focus on events in Ireland and examine how Ireland had established itself as an independent country by 1939.

1 The impact of war on British parties and politics

The First World War had a devastating impact on Britain's economy and society (see Chapter 6), and it transformed British politics. The ruling Liberal Party was placed under immense strain and divisions within the party developed as a result. A wartime coalition between the Liberals and Unionists was necessary from 1915 onwards and in 1916 Asquith was replaced by the most ambitious and driven politician of the day, David Lloyd George.

The Liberal Government in 1914

What kind of war leader was Asquith?

The Liberal Party that went to war in 1914 was no longer the reforming, powerful force it had been in 1906 when it won a landslide victory. It had been shaken by the prospect of civil war in Ireland and in 1910 had lost the overall majority that it had gained in 1906, though it was able to continue in government because it had the general support of both the Irish Nationalists and the Labour Party. The war appeared to offer the party an opportunity to become a unified and dynamic political force once more, but by 1918 it emerged even more divided and weakened. In large part the responsibility for this can be put down to its two wartime leaders, Herbert Asquith and, following him, David Lloyd George.

Here we will examine the political impact of the war, and in Chapter 6 we will turn to the economic and social factors.

NOTE-MAKING

Using a spider diagram (see page x), make notes on the main political challenges facing Asquith during the war.

◀ Herbert Henry Asquith, who served as Liberal prime minister from 1908 to 1916.

Gallipoli

By 1915 both sides were desperate to find a way to break the deadlock. Winston Churchill believed that an attack on Germany's new ally, the Ottoman Empire, presented the best chance of winning the war quickly. In April 1915, British, French, Indian, Newfoundland, Australian and New Zealand (ANZAC) troops landed in the Dardanelles Straits in the heart of the Ottoman Empire. It was the first seaborne landing of the war but ended in disaster as the Turks fought back with greater numbers than expected from entrenched positions on the cliff tops. Poor planning and shortages of supplies were blamed for the disaster, along with squabbles between Britain and France over their plans to seize Ottoman territory when the war ended. The allied armies were forced to withdraw in January 1916 after suffering 56,000 fatalities and 123,000 wounded.

134

What impression does Source A give you of Asquith's wartime government?

Running the war

Herbert Asquith has been described by many historians as a weak war leader. He was forced from office in 1916, but prior to that he was content for three men, Lord Kitchener, Winston Churchill and John 'Jackie' Fisher, to plan the war. Kitchener, though a Conservative politically, was appointed Secretary of War when the war began. Fisher as First Sea Lord was the highest-ranking officer of the Royal Navy. Churchill as First Lord of the Admiralty was the political head of the navy. None of these men had much faith in Asquith's potential as a war leader. Asquith increasingly appeared indecisive and remote and his critics within the Liberal Government and in opposition believed that he lacked the drive and energy to win the war.

The shell crisis

The devastating weapon of war that all sides used was artillery, heavy cannons which were now the main method for striking at the enemy from the trenches. Because the nature of the war was unexpected and artillery was used far more than was anticipated, a shortage of artillery shells became an acute problem for Britain.

In the first years of the war senior army officers such as the leader of the British Expeditionary Force (BEF), Sir John French, had an uneasy relationship with the civilian government. They believed that civilians had no understanding of military matters and should stay out of the running of the war. They were often supported by King George V who believed that the generals were being hampered by interfering politicians. Generals like French, in turn, believed they were answerable to the Crown, not to the prime minister.

Since late 1914, shortages in artillery shells had been a growing problem for the BEF, and by the spring of 1915 reports were being leaked to the press of shortages. Asquith publicly declared on 20 April, after assurances from Kitchener, that there were sufficient supplies of shells but by May French had leaked further reports to the *Times* newspaper. The *Times* ran a report blaming the Government for failing to supply troops, accusing them of complacently sacrificing lives. The *Daily Mail* criticised Kitchener and the scandal resulted in him losing significant power within the Cabinet. He lost control over munitions production and a new Ministry of Munitions was created, with David Lloyd George as its minister. Fisher resigned from the Government in 1915 as well, following one of the most disastrous episodes of the early phase of the war, the campaign at Gallipoli. Churchill was also forced to resign in disgrace, taking up command of a battalion on the Western Front during 1916.

Source A 'The Shells Scandal: Lord Kitchener's Tragic Blunder'. From an article in the *Daily Mail*, 21 May 1915.

The two things that have precipitated the Cabinet crisis are the quarrel between Lord Fisher and Mr Winston Churchill and the revelation of a serious shortage of high explosive shells. Of these the second question by far the more important of the two was forced upon public attention by the military correspondent of the *Times* in a striking dispatch from which was published recently. It was there stated specifically that 'the want of an unlimited supply of high explosives was a fatal bar to our success' in the attacks along the Frommelles-Richbourg line … It had brought to a head misgivings that had long been forming in the public mind as to our supplies of ammunition. Questions were immediately asked in the House of Commons but in view of the political situation were not pressed home.

The Coalition Government

Why did Asquith create a coalition in 1915?

The most significant effect of the shell crisis and Gallipoli was the creation of a coalition government (for more on the Ministry of Munitions, see chapter 6). Despite the fact that much criticism was directed at Asquith as a result of military failings, the resignation of Churchill and Fisher and the decline in Kitchener's role meant that the majority of blame was directed towards them. Andrew Bonar Law, the leader of the Unionists, was invited, along with his party, to join a coalition with the Liberals to win the war. The Labour Party was also invited to join and a Cabinet post was given to the Labour leader Arthur Henderson. The Liberal Party held on to the key ministerial posts and Bonar Law was given the role of Colonial Secretary. Churchill was effectively demoted to Chancellor of the Duchy of Lancaster and he resigned in November 1915. He took a commission in the army and served at the front for several months before returning to the Government in July 1917 as minister of munitions. Asquith was interested in holding his government together more than he was interested in genuinely sharing power with the Unionists.

The downfall of Asquith and the rise of Lloyd George

By 1916, Asquith came under increasing pressure to introduce compulsory military service, or conscription (see pages 162–63). He was opposed to this measure, viewing it as unnecessary and an extension of state control in the lives of the population, which was at odds with liberal thinking (for more on the conscription debate, see page 162). Asquith eventually relented and reluctantly allowed conscription to become law. His coalition partners, the Unionists and Lloyd George, had used public opinion to pressure him into it and as a result he appeared weak.

In June 1916 Kitchener was drowned when his ship was sunk by a German floating mine en route to Russia. This resulted in Lloyd George being made secretary of state for war. Asquith had been reluctant to give such a key job to Lloyd George but was pressured into offering him the role by Bonar Law and Lloyd George himself. This was more evidence that Asquith was becoming a weakened figure in the Cabinet, unable to assert himself. Three events in 1916 left the Unionists and critics within the Liberal Party convinced that Asquith could not win the war:

- the naval battle of Jutland
- the disastrous offensive by the British at the Somme
- the nationalist uprising in Dublin (see page 154).

The failure to secure a breakthrough on land or sea meant that there was no prospect of an end to the war in 1916. In addition to this, Asquith, who was suspicious of Lloyd George's growing status and popularity as the new secretary of state for war, attempted to reduce the powers that Lloyd George had. The newspaper owner Lord Northcliffe, a close friend of Lloyd George, used his newspapers to campaign for the management of the war to be handed over exclusively to the Secretary of State for War. Asquith agreed reluctantly to the formation of a small War Cabinet consisting of three members suggested by

NOTE-MAKING

Create a table with two sections showing the Liberal Government in 1914 and the Coalition Government a year later. Put the key political figures from the Liberal Government and the Coalition Government in each section, along with the events and developments that occurred. Underneath, write down how far the events of the war had brought about political change by 1915.

Lloyd George, but refused to agree to Lloyd George to be its chairman and demanded to chair it personally, feeling that he was being publicly undermined by Lloyd George. Matters came to a head on 5 December 1916 when Lloyd George resigned. Asquith also resigned, believing that no new government could form without him and that he would be able come back on his own terms. The gamble failed. Two days later, Lloyd George, with the support of the Unionists, the Labour Party and a minority of his own Liberal Party became the prime minister in a new coalition. Asquith became leader of what was now the Liberal opposition, but found opposing Lloyd George difficult because it appeared he was criticising the war effort.

Lloyd George and the generals

Once Lloyd George had established himself as prime minister and head of a smaller War Cabinet, he found himself at odds with the British army's generals whom he suspected were incompetent and out of touch. He had already clashed with Field Marshal Haig at the start of the Somme campaign in 1916 by asking why the army was still using cavalry tactics when the Germans were defending their trenches with barbed wire and machine guns. In his memoirs of the war, published in 1933, Lloyd George was critical of the generals, creating a lasting impression in British historiographies of the war that they had sacrificed countless thousands of fighting men. The reality was that while some of the generals were lacking in skill, others were innovators in tactics and technology and contributed to the winning of the war.

Lloyd George was widely seen as an effective and talented war leader, though his decision to replace Asquith had split the Liberal Party and left Lloyd George reliant on the Unionists. He was skilled in delegating important tasks to civil servants and business leaders who were able to effectively cooperate and achieve results. One example of this was the establishment of a new Ministry of Shipping, run by shipping magnate Sir Joseph Maclay. Maclay was not a political insider and was neither an MP nor a member of the Lords, but his knowledge of the industry helped to bring all British merchant shipping under the control of the Government. This meant that ships could be allocated to the most important routes to bring supplies back to Britain using routes that were most heavily defended from German U-boats.

By 1917 Lloyd George was keen to switch tactics once again, away from the Western Front towards focusing on defeating the Ottoman Empire. Generals like Haig believed that the Middle Eastern front was a 'sideshow', but Lloyd George thought that if territories such as Palestine could be liberated from the Ottomans it would provide a powerful boost in morale to the British people.

Interpretations of Lloyd George as wartime prime minister

The first chronicler of Lloyd George's wartime exploits was Lloyd George himself. In his memoirs, he presented Asquith as weak and ineffectual and generals such as Haig as incompetent. For much of the twentieth century Lloyd George's view of the war shaped Britain's shared memory of the conflict. Only as Britain reflected on the war's fiftieth anniversary in 1964 did new interpretations of the conflict emerge, but they had to compete with histories about the Second World War for a place in the public's attention. In 1961 the historian and later Conservative MP Alan Clark reiterated Lloyd George's views on the generals in a book entitled *The Donkeys*. The title of the book was taken from a statement attributed to a German general who referred to the British soldiers as 'lions led by donkeys'. Clark later admitted that he had invented

WORKING TOGETHER

1 Create a mind map which summarises the role of David Lloyd George as prime minister. Compare your mind map to the views expressed about Lloyd George both by himself and historians. Do you agree with their judgements?

2 Now compare your mind map with a partner's. Explain to each other the reasons for your view of Lloyd George.

the phrase. Historian A. J. P. Taylor, in 1969, accused all of Europe's political leaders, including Lloyd George, of 'blundering into the war', but conceded that Lloyd George had a powerful radicalising effect on government when he came to power in 1916:

'Lloyd George was the nearest thing England has known to a Napoleon, a supreme ruler maintaining himself by individual achievement.'

He argued that Lloyd George was an energising figure, as close to being a 'dictator' that Britain has experienced. This, in Taylor's eyes, was a necessary development. Taylor believed that only a quasi-dictatorial figure was capable of winning the war, and he contrasted Lloyd George with the distant and seemingly disinterested Asquith, whose war record was far less impressive.

The decline of the Liberals

Which party was the real winner in the 1918 election?

In 1918 Lloyd George was feted by the British public as 'the man who won the war'. However, within four years he was forced from office in disgrace and his party was finished as a significant force in British politics.

The coupon election and Lloyd George's government

By 1918 Lloyd George had effectively split the Liberal Party. The election of 1918 was fought between the ruling Liberal–Conservative coalition and the Asquith Liberals and Labour Party, which withdrew from the coalition a month before the election. Figure 1 shows the outcome.

Figure 1 General election results, 1918.

Party	Votes (millions)	Share of the vote (%)	Seats	Increase in seats since December 1910
Coalition Liberal	1.4	12.6	127	0*
Conservative	4.14	38.5	332	+60
Labour	2.25	20.8	57	+15
Liberal	1.39	13.1	36	-235
Other	1.61	14.9	105	

* This was the coalition's first election so while it appears as if they had not lost seats, the Liberals overall had experienced huge losses.

Source: House of Commons Library, UK Election Statistics: 1918–2012

The election was called the coupon election because Lloyd George and Bonar Law issued 'coupons' or letters of endorsement signed by both of them to Liberal and Unionist candidates who they knew would continue to support the coalition government. It was a way of ensuring that enough Lloyd George-supporting Liberals were elected so that his continuation as prime minister was tenable. Without the 'coupon' the Liberals would almost certainly have been totally decimated at the polls. Bonar Law and the Unionists wanted to retain Lloyd George as prime minister and this required a respectable number of his own MPs to support him. Lloyd George pledged to create a 'fit country for heroes to live in'; other ministers from the wartime government campaigned on anti-German policies such as placing the Kaiser on trial or extracting punishing reparations from Germany. Lloyd George tried to avoid discussing these topics,

KEY DATES: THE IMPACT OF WAR ON BRITISH PARTIES AND POLITICS

1914 Aug	Britain declares war on Germany
1915 May	Shell crisis Creation of Coalition Government
1916 June	Kitchener drowned, Lloyd George becomes secretary of state for war
1916 Dec	Lloyd George replaces Asquith as prime minister
1918 Mar	Representation of the People Act
1918 Dec	The Coupon Election

NOTE-MAKING

Pages 137–40 focus on the reasons for the decline of the Liberal Party after the First World War. Using a spider diagram (see page x), make notes on these reasons.

The Chanak crisis

By 1922 Turkey had made peace with all its neighbours except Greece. It was at war with the Greeks between 1919 and 1922. Lloyd George supported Greece, but initially Churchill, Lord Birkenhead and Lord Curzon (the foreign secretary) favoured a deal with the Turks, so the Cabinet was divided. In the end Lloyd George got his way and Churchill and Birkenhead agreed to support him. Curzon remained opposed – he detested Lloyd George's continuous interference in foreign policy. Britain had a military presence in the Dardanelles at the port of Chanak and when the Turkish army advanced on the military outpost Lloyd George ordered the British commander to resist, even though this would risk war. The general in question, Sir Charles Harington, refused the order and instead negotiated with his Turkish opposite number, preventing the outbreak of war.

knowing that they would be difficult to enforce. Instead he used his reputation as a pre-war social reformer (see page 74) to win votes.

- 150 Liberals who had pledged to support the coalition were given a letter of support from Lloyd George and Bonar Law which allowed them to run without a Unionist candidate to oppose them.
- 364 Unionists received the letter and were not opposed by Liberals supporting Lloyd George and the coalition – though Asquith Liberals did of course stand.
- Some Labour candidates who still supported the coalition also got the letter – though the Labour Party, having already pulled out of the government officially, rejected the idea.
- The term 'coupon' was used by Asquith to mock the arrangement, likening it to the rationing system.

The outcome of the election was a disaster for the non-coalition Liberals who lost 235 seats, and resulted in a landslide victory for the coalition. It also resulted in a growth in seats for the Labour Party to 57 seats, meaning that by 1918 they were a small but growing force in British politics.

The downfall of Lloyd George, 1922

The news in June 1922 that Lloyd George had been involved in a scandal selling knighthoods and peerages was deeply shocking. In the past titles had been sold by government ministers to their supporters in industry for large donations, but it was done in a discreet and largely unnoticed fashion. Lloyd George's trade in titles was run from a private office he established, and knowledge of the operation was widespread. During his six years as prime minister (1916–22) he sold 1,500 knighthoods and nearly 100 peerages.

Several titles were freely given away to Fleet Street newspaper magnates so that they would turn a blind eye and not report the practice. When the 1922 honours list was announced there were several names on it who had criminal convictions for fraud and the press finally published the story. Lloyd George himself called the honours system corrupt, but the scandal did immense damage to his credibility. Plans to go to war with Turkey (the Chanak crisis), which sought to revise the terms of the peace treaty they had been forced to sign in 1920, further dented his credibility.

On 19 October 1922, a meeting of Conservative MPs was held at the Carlton Club, the Conservative Party's most important private members club. It was called by the Conservative Party leader, Sir Austen Chamberlain, to rally backbench support for continuing the coalition at the next election. This turned out to be a miscalculation, with the meeting turning into a backbench revolt. Stanley Baldwin (president of the Board of Trade) spoke against continuing support for the coalition, but he was still only a rising figure not a decisive force. Bonar Law, previously a supporter of the coalition, had changed his mind and came out of retirement to support Baldwin. This was crucial as he was a credible prime minister whereas Baldwin was not. The backbenchers voted overwhelmingly to end the coalition at the next general election. As a result, Chamberlain and the other leaders immediately resigned from the coalition government. This forced Lloyd George to resign and call a general election for November 1922. The Conservatives won 344 seats, Labour 142, Asquith's Liberals 62 and Lloyd George's Liberals 53. The election was a disaster for the Liberals, who were now a divided party with a dwindling support base among both middle-class voters who gravitated towards the Conservatives and working-class voters who supported Labour.

Interpretations: the strange death of Liberal England

In 1935 the journalist and historian, George Dangerfield, attempted to explain why the Liberal Party had dwindled away in the decade after the end of the First World War. In his book, *The Strange Death of Liberal England*, he argued that there was something quite unexpected about the decline of Liberalism in the post-war years considering the party's dominance between 1906 and 1914. Dangerfield argued that there were four main challenges to Liberalism in the years after 1906, which dealt the party blows that it was unable to recover from. These were:

- the challenge of the Lords to the People's Budget (see pages 74–75)
- the challenge of the radical syndicalist trade union movement and the threat of a general strike (see pages 80–81)
- the challenge of the women's suffrage movement (see pages 106–12)
- the threat of civil war in Ireland following the passing of the third Home Rule Bill (see pages 86–88).

These threats to Liberalism were suppressed by the start of the war and the far greater external threat posed by Germany, but they had damaged the Liberals' reputation as a credible party of government by 1918.

The Wilson thesis

In 1966, historian Trevor Wilson put forward a different explanation. He argued that the decline of the Liberals happened between 1914 and 1935. In his book, *The Decline of the Liberal Party 1914–35*, he argued that the war had been an insurmountable challenge for the party. He referred to the war metaphorically as the bus that ran down the 'ailing old man' of the Liberal Party. The Liberals, divided between Whig and radical factions, were far less suited to cope with the challenge of the war than the more overtly patriotic Conservative Party or the class-conscious Labour Party. Liberal beliefs, such as free trade and civil liberties, were threatened by the war, and the division of the party in 1916 over the issue of conscription adds strength to Wilson's claims. Historian Kenneth O. Morgan broadly agrees with Wilson, in that he claims that 1916 and the downfall of Asquith was the beginning of the end for the Liberals.

The McKibbin thesis

In 2010, historian Ross McKibbin argued that the real cause of the decline of the Liberal Party was the growth of support for Labour. In his book, *Parties and the People, England 1914–1951*, he claims that Labour's rise was inevitable due to the development of the trade union movement and a mass working-class electorate. He believed that the war hastened the development of Labour and also caused the existing political system to break under its strain, providing Labour with an opportunity to seize the Liberals' mantle as the party of social reform at the end of the conflict. McKibbin stated in 1990 that the rise of the Labour Party predated 1914 and was underway throughout the life of the Liberal Government, which Labour had allied itself to.

The position of the Conservatives

In the inter-war years, the decline of the Liberal Party and the rise of the Labour Party were important factors in shaping the Conservatives. After the Representation of the People Act in 1918 (see page 141), the party looked to the many millions of newly enfranchised women voters as a potential source of electoral support.

Middle- and lower-middle class women who were concerned about the cost of living voted Conservative in the elections of the next two decades, enabling the party to dominate British politics throughout the era, whether in coalitions or as governments in their own right.

The rise of the Labour Party (see page 141–42), and the growth of the state during the war presented new challenges to the Conservatives and shaped the philosophy of Conservatism. The party became increasingly hostile to socialism and regarded the development of the Labour Party and the creation of a socialist state in the USSR as part of a combined threat to individual freedoms and the right to property. The fact that the Labour Party's leadership was equally opposed to Soviet communism was often ignored by the Conservatives.

The general election, 1923

Following the end of Lloyd George's coalition, the governments of the 1920s were led by the Labour and Conservative parties. Lloyd George had always believed in free trade and had opposed tariffs. When he fell from office in 1922 he was replaced by the Conservative leader Andrew Bonar Law, who was forced to resign due to ill-health in May 1923. So many leading Conservatives had refused to serve under Bonar Law that the Government was mockingly referred to as the 'second eleven'. His resignation weakened it still further. He was succeeded by Stanley Baldwin, the only possible successor as so many leading Conservatives were still refusing to serve. The foreign secretary, Lord Curzon, was superior to Baldwin in terms of status, experience and ability but he was also disliked for his arrogance and he was a peer, a big disability now in the new democratised political system after the war. Baldwin and other members of the Conservative Party sought an election victory that would give them a mandate to impose tariffs on imports and protect industry. To secure an electoral mandate for this Baldwin decided on a general election which was held in December 1923. The strategy failed. The Conservatives won 258 seats; Labour 191; the Liberals, enjoying a fragile reunification, 158. Since both Labour and the Liberals supported free trade, Baldwin resigned and paved the way for the creation of the first Labour government.

2 Political developments in the inter-war years

In the decade after 1918 many of the political certainties that seemed to have existed before 1914 rapidly disappeared. The Liberal Party, since 1906 the most dominant force in British politics, went into decline and was replaced by the Labour Party as the main political force for social reform. These changes, in turn, influenced the Conservatives, who now saw the threat of 'socialism' from Labour as the main challenge to its middle-class supporters. The most significant factor deciding the fortunes of the political parties was the rapid expansion in the franchise that took place as a result of the 1918 Representation of the People Act. Millions of new voters were able to participate in the political process for the first time in December 1918 when the first post-war general election took place.

Electoral reform

Why did the Government introduce electoral reform during the war before the outcome was certain?

One of the most significant consequences of the First World War was a fourth reform act, more widely known as the Representation of the People Act (to remind yourself of the first three Acts see Chapter 1). As with the previous extensions of the franchise, the 1918 Representation of the People Act was seen as a vital measure to preserve the stability of society during the immense strain of the war.

LOOK AGAIN

Look back at the section you have just read and examine how far the political parties had developed since 1914. What was the effect of the First World War on the party system during and after the conflict?

140

NOTE-MAKING

Using a spider diagram (see page x), make notes on the main reasons for electoral reform in 1918.

The Representation of the People Act, 1918

In March 1918, the Coalition Government passed an Act reforming the electoral system in Britain, giving all men over the age of 21 the vote and, for the first time, enfranchising some women. Women over the age of 30 who were local ratepayers owning or renting property, or married to a man who was, or who were graduates voting in a university constituency now had the vote. The size of the electorate almost tripled from 8 million to just over 21 million voters by the end of the year. The outcome of the war was by no means decided in March 1918, but the issue of the right to vote had been under discussion since 1915. According to the 1911 Parliament Act, which stated that a general election had to be held at least every five years, an election was due in December 1915. There was general agreement that it should be postponed, but Parliament was not prepared to allow an indefinite continuation – even a year was rejected. The date was set for September 1916 and then extended progressively to April 1917, November 1917, July 1918 and finally January 1919, by which time the war was over and the election had been held. There was wide agreement that whenever the election came any man who had served in the armed forces could not be denied the vote. There was also a much wider acceptance of the principle of women having a right to vote; even Asquith, a bitter opponent of the idea before the war, had changed his mind on this.

The Coalition Government was also concerned that the war had led to an upsurge in radicalism both at home and abroad, and the extension of the franchise was an important way of steering large sections of the population away from revolutionary thinking, which was becoming apparent in other countries:

- In 1917 two revolutions in Russia had seen the overthrow of the autocratic tsar and the fall of the replacement provisional government. By 1918 a communist Bolshevik government was in charge and it had a significant number of admirers in Britain's trade union movement.
- During 1917 and 1918 the USA fought alongside Britain and France as an associate power (an ally but not committed to the same war aims). President Woodrow Wilson began to articulate the USA's war aims and frequently referred to the importance of establishing fully representative democracies in Europe and beyond in the post-war era. Wilson and his ideas were popular with many people in Britain.
- In 1917 sections of the French army had mutinied and in 1918 it looked as if British and dominion regiments might follow suit. Introducing the vote for returning servicemen was one way to prevent revolutionary ideas spreading through the ranks.

Autocratic – Where absolute power is concentrated in the hands of one leader and they can rule without a constitution or parliament. In Russia, the Tsar had allowed a parliament, the Duma, to exist but it had little power and the Tsar was free to ignore and dissolve it at will.

The development of the Labour Party

Why did the Labour Party become a major political force after the end of the First World War?

The Labour Party was already an electoral force by 1910. During the First World War senior Labour politicians such as Arthur Henderson served in Asquith's Cabinet and then alongside Lloyd George. This gave the party a sense of confidence that it could form a government and use the civil service to create far-reaching social reform in the post-war era. The party was divided between members who were genuinely socialist in their outlook and who saw capitalism as an 'evil' to be defeated, and a majority of the party's leadership who wanted a 'gradualist' approach to social change. In 1918 Sidney Webb, one of the original Fabians (see page 79) and now a leading figure in the party, drafted 'Labour and the New Social Order', a clear party programme with a strongly socialist tone. It was the basis for a new constitution for the Labour Party. The fourth clause of the constitution promised extensive state control of the economy 'to secure for the workers by hand and by brain the full fruits of their industry'. Clause Four became a difficult and divisive issue within the party in the following decades, but it was not changed until 1995.

Ramsay MacDonald's first Labour government

Britain's first Labour government came to power in 1924, led by Ramsay MacDonald. It was a minority government and not even the biggest party, but its election alarmed many of the Conservative-supporting newspapers like the *Daily Mail* and *The Times*. Despite claims in the press to the contrary, the party was committed to parliamentary democracy and went to great lengths to demonstrate how moderate it was. However, Labour's opponents in the Conservative Party and the media compared the new government to the Bolshevik regime in the USSR and claimed that there might be Soviet sympathisers in the Cabinet.

National Executive Committee of the Labour Party – The governing body of the party that ensures that the party's constitution is upheld.

MacDonald and his government experienced strained relations with the National Executive Committee of the Labour Party. The prime minister was forced to make tough economic choices that affected the poorest voters and had to manage the threat of industrial action. As prime minister he had to compromise, but the party was critical of him for not being more radical. Because he was the head of a minority government, any attempt to introduce a more radical programme would have resulted in a withdrawal of Liberal support and the collapse of the government. The government lasted for nine months, too short a time to introduce much legislation.

MacDonald had become prime minister on the issue of free trade because Labour had more seats than the Liberals and both parties rejected Baldwin's solution of protection to combat unemployment. However, when MacDonald became prime minister he found that making significant improvements to the economy was almost impossible. He focused for much of his first term on foreign policy matters. He blamed his inability to bring about new measures to combat the problem of unemployment on the complex nature of government, stating that:

'what seems to be a simple thing … becomes a complex, and exceedingly difficult, and laborious and almost heartbreaking thing'.

MacDonald lacked a parliamentary majority so bringing about major economic measures to deal with unemployment was not an option for him. Both he and his chancellor of the exchequer were opposed to borrowing and raising taxation to help revive the economy or create jobs. He tried to present Labour as a moderate party, one that was 'fit to rule', not a party of radical socialist ideas. He wanted the other two political parties, the largely Conservative-supporting press and Britain's upper and middle classes to feel that they had nothing to fear from a Labour administration. Between 1921 and 1924 unemployment had declined from 12 per cent of the adult working population to 6.5 per cent, but started to climb again throughout MacDonald's year in office and rose to 8 per cent in 1925.

One positive side-effect of the inability to bring unemployment down was the dramatic fall in inflation from 15 per cent in 1920 to just under 1 per cent in 1924. This was not the result of economic strategy however. Inflation fell because spending had collapsed due to unemployment.

Measures that were passed included:

- Housing (Financial Provisions) Act 1924, which increased the amount of money available to local authorities to build homes for low-income workers.
- Welfare legislation that improved access to education and healthcare (see pages 193–96).

Government collapse

MacDonald's government collapsed in the autumn of 1924 following a motion of no-confidence which MacDonald only narrowly won. The motion against the Government was called over the decision of the attorney-general, Sir Patrick Hastings, to drop charges of incitement to mutiny against a socialist newspaper, the *Worker's Weekly*. The newspaper had published an article by the journalist John Ross Campbell which broke the law by demanding that soldiers:

'Refuse to shoot down your fellow workers! Refuse to fight for profits! Turn your weapons on your oppressors!'

On 6 August, under pressure from backbench Labour MPs, the prosecution against Campbell was withdrawn and MacDonald was accused by both the Liberal and Conservative parties of having secret communist sympathies. The case coincided with his attempts to normalise relations between Britain and the Soviet Union. A second motion was passed against the Government, calling for an enquiry into the withdrawal of charges against Campbell. MacDonald was forced to resign and call an election.

Ramsay MacDonald, 1866–1937

Ramsay MacDonald led three governments between 1924 and 1935. He was born in Lossiemouth in north-east Scotland in 1866 and as a young man moved to Bristol and London where he became involved in radical socialist politics. He was elected to Parliament in 1906 and was on the left wing (more socialist in his views) of the Labour Party until the end of the First World War. Throughout the war MacDonald was a pacifist, but he visited France and witnessed the fighting first hand. He moved away from the radical left of the party after 1918 and became very suspicious of communism after the Russian Revolution. When he became prime minister in 1924 he was the first ever working-class leader of Britain.

The general election, October 1924

Labour's election campaign was marred by the publication of a damaging story in the *Daily Mail*. The Conservative-supporting newspaper claimed that a letter from the Russian communist revolutionary, Gregori Zinoviev, to the British Communist Party had been discovered. The letter, a forgery, appeared to be an incitement to revolution, telling British communists to prepare to overthrow the government. The staunchly anti-socialist *Daily Mail* hoped it would dissuade people from voting for Labour or any other left-wing parties. The *Mail* and other Conservative-supporting newspapers exaggerated the threat of communism. The newspapers implied that 'class war' was possible in Britain and that the Labour Party was encouraging it.

Although its vote didn't collapse, Labour lost the election and the Conservative Party, under Stanley Baldwin, won a landslide victory. It had a majority of 223. This election was a pivotal moment for the Liberal Party as a declining force in British politics; it saw a 12 per cent decline in its share of the vote and a loss of 118 seats, leaving them only 40. The Conservatives were the clear beneficiaries, taking seats from both the Liberal and Labour parties. First-time Labour voters who were disappointed with Ramsay MacDonald switched to the Conservatives, as did Liberal voters who had lost faith in the ability of the Liberal Party to revive itself.

1 Study Figure 2. What does the change in seats indicate about the popularity of:
● the Conservatives
● the Liberals
● the Labour Party?
2 What might account for the changing fortunes of the parties?

Figure 2 General election results, October 1924.

Party	Votes (millions)	Share of the vote (%)	Seats	Increase in seats since December 1918
Conservative	7.85	47.2	412	+154
Liberal	2.93	17.6	40	-118
Labour	5.49	33.0	151	-40
Other	0.37	2.2	12	+4

Source: House of Commons Library, UK Election Statistics: 1918–2012

Baldwin's second government, 1924–29

The government formed by Baldwin presented itself as an alternative to the Labour Party and the 'threat' of socialism in Britain. However, Prime Minister Stanley Baldwin was a moderate within the party and wanted to be seen by the country as a centre-ground politician who could appeal to all social classes.

Baldwin believed that the language of 'class war' that had developed during the MacDonald government was damaging to Britain. He discouraged Conservative MPs from smearing Labour members as agents of the USSR.

Reforms to Labour's funding

Despite Baldwin's appeals to his party for harmonious coexistence with the Labour Party, many Conservative MPs still believed that Labour's relationship with the trade unions was the party's weakness. In 1925 a Private Member's Bill to prevent the Labour Party from receiving a political levy (donation) from the trade unions which, if passed, would have financially crippled it, was opposed by Baldwin in the House of Commons and subsequently failed. He was more concerned with political stability than political conflict between the parties.

Baldwin's conciliatory approach could not be sustained in the long run. Following the General Strike (see pages 170–71) he yielded to pressure to introduce laws reducing Labour's funding from the unions. In 1927 an amendment to the Trade Disputes Act 1906 meant that the political levy on union members could no longer be automatically deducted from their union membership and passed to the Labour Party; instead members had to agree to pay it. Over one-third chose to opt out, causing the Labour Party's finances to decrease by 35 per cent.

In March 1929 Baldwin held a general election. Although the Conservatives won the largest share of the popular vote, for the first time Labour gained the largest share of seats in the House of Commons (see Figure 3). In order to form a government and have an overall majority, Ramsay MacDonald had to rely on the attitude of Lloyd George who, following the death of Asquith in February 1928, was the unchallenged leader of the Liberal Party. The Liberals had run an energetic and well-organised campaign with by far the most detailed plans to deal with unemployment, but their decline was further underlined by their gaining only nineteen seats overall. Lloyd George declared that the Liberals would support the Labour Government, claiming that it would be basically endorsing Liberal policy anyway; the official Labour policy was to make no arrangements with the Liberals. Of course, since the Labour Party had the largest number of seats it did not actually need Liberal support, Liberal neutrality would be enough.

Figure 3 General election results, 1929.

Party	Votes (millions)	Share of the vote (%)	Seats	Increase in seats from 1924
Conservative	8.66	38.2	260	-152
Liberal	5.31	23.4	59	+19
Labour	8.37	37.0	287	+136
Other	0.31	1.4	9	-3

Source: House of Commons Library, UK Election Statistics: 1918–2012

MacDonald's second Labour government, 1929–31

In 1929 the Labour Party secured its second electoral success, forming a minority government that relied on Lloyd George's Liberal Party for co-operation. Many members of the Labour movement put their hopes in MacDonald's government, believing that it would bring about major social reform in housing, health and social welfare. The defeat of the General Strike in 1926 (see pages 170–71) had left many trade unionists hoping that the Labour Party, not the union movement, could improve the living conditions of working-class people. MacDonald had ambitious plans for social reform, but his partnership with the Liberals (which was not a coalition, but an agreement on how the parties would vote together) resulted in many reforms being watered down. Some social reform was possible:

- The 1930 Housing Act cleared 750,000 slum houses and replaced them with modern homes by 1939.
- The Coal Mines Act 1930 attempted to ensure better pay for miners and more efficient pits, but the weakness of the legislation meant that mine owners could ignore it.

MacDonald amended the Unemployment Insurance Act, giving the government powers to create public works schemes to alleviate unemployment. It was funded with £25 million of government money. However, the onset of depression in 1929 was far more significant in limiting Labour's plans for social reform than the influence of the Liberal Party. (For more on the effect of the Great Depression, see Chapter 6.)

The formation of the National Government, August 1931

By 1931 the Labour Government came under intense pressure from international banks to limit the amount that was spent on social welfare. These banks had significant power over Britain as they held large reserves of the British pound due to the amount of debt Britain had accrued by borrowing from the USA to finance the First World War. The reserves were normally in the form of bonds (a government-issued IOU) which had been exchanged for cash during the war when the war government was desperate for funds. The bonds were redeemable at a later date but could also fluctuate in value, depending on whether the currency they were issued in (the pound) continued to be valuable or not.

Banks that owned British debt could lose millions at a stroke if the value of the pound went down and so did not want to see economic policies introduced that might cause that to happen. A high-spending government would either have to tax or borrow, both of which would reduce the pound's value and cause the Gold Standard (see pages 169–70) to be re-adjusted.

During the summer of 1931 rumours circulated that the forthcoming Budget would be unbalanced – meaning that the Government had plans to spend more than it could afford, leading to an increase in borrowing. This caused banks in the USA to engage in panic-selling of the pound, exchanging it for other currencies, and the pound slumped in value. In order to reassure financiers that their investments were safe the Government proposed spending cuts, the main measure being the introduction of a 10 per cent cut in unemployment assistance. This would keep the value of the pound stable, but cause hardship for many of Britain's poorest. The threat of this cut split the Labour Party and the Government resigned on 24 August 1931. MacDonald formed a National Government with the Conservative Party immediately after the Labour Government had stepped down. The reaction of the Labour Party was immediate – MacDonald and his two senior colleagues, Philip Snowden and J. H. Thomas, were expelled from the party and Arthur Henderson took over as leader.

MacDonald called an election in October 1931, though whether it was his idea or that of Neville Chamberlain or Philip Snowden is unclear. Bizarrely it was agreed that each party in the National Government would put forward its own programme with a covering declaration by the prime minister. MacDonald came up with the idea of asking the electorate for a 'Doctor's Mandate', in effect an open authority for the National Government to do whatever it could agree on to deal with the crisis.

The National Government won the election by a huge majority but it was the Conservatives within it who won the vast majority of seats. MacDonald continued as prime minister, though only as a figurehead. The Labour Party's share of the vote slumped as many voters believed it was putting its own interests and those of the unions before the national interest.

The National Government implemented the spending cuts which had caused the previous government's downfall. The most dramatic result was a mutiny in the Royal Navy at the naval base of Invergordon. However, this was, in reality, a low-key affair. All armed services cuts were supposed to be strictly limited to 10 per cent – the 'mutiny' occurred because of mistakes in the way the cuts for able seamen were applied, resulting in cuts ranging from 13.5 per cent to 25 per cent in some cases. The admiralty hastily revised its figures following a carefully staged refusal by 12,000 men to 'fall in for work', which was accompanied by a moderately worded request for a review and expressions of loyalty to the Crown, and the 10 per cent maximum was properly applied.

National Government – A coalition of political parties that places national interest above party politics. Britain saw a series of National Governments between 1931 and 1945, which were largely dominated by the Conservatives.

The Government then announced that *all* public service workers would be on 10 per cent cuts – teachers had been on 15 per cent!

In addition to the spending cuts the National Government was able to introduce a limited number of tariffs. During the election the Labour, Conservative and Liberal members of the government avoided the issue of tariffs, fearing that the Labour opposition would gain votes from free trade supporters. The majority of Conservative voters and MPs had shifted their support to tariffs by 1932. This led to the resignation of Philip Snowden who had been chancellor of the exchequer up to the November 1931 election, after which he was given a peerage and became Lord Privy Seal – Neville Chamberlain replaced him at the exchequer. Herbert Samuel, the Liberal home secretary, also resigned from the Government in protest.

MacDonald steps down

MacDonald remained prime minister of the National Government until 1935 but from 1933 onwards it was clear that his health was failing and the stresses of dealing with the Great Depression were taking their toll. Stanley Baldwin held the office of Lord President of the Council until 1935 and the two men swapped roles when MacDonald stepped down. In Baldwin's manifesto he pledged new houses, jobs and government help for the most economically deprived parts of the country. He also pledged to improve Britain's defences, although there was little desire among the public for rearmament. However, in January 1936, when King George V died, a constitutional crisis began that was to dominate political events in 1936.

The abdication crisis

In 1936 Britain had three kings in one year, George V, Edward VIII and George VI. George V died on 20 January 1936 and his eldest son Edward VIII inherited the crown.

Edward was a handsome monarch whose glamorous playboy lifestyle as heir to the throne had made him popular with the public. His many affairs with married women were known about by the government but the details were hidden from the general public by self-censoring newspapers. Public attitudes towards sexual morality in the 1930s were very conservative and an heir to the throne behaving in such a manner would have brought the monarchy into disrepute. In the months after his coronation rumours circulated about a relationship with an American divorcee, Wallis Simpson. In November 1936, Edward informed Baldwin of his intention to marry her and Baldwin replied that the marriage would be seen by many in Britain as morally unacceptable. Edward was unswayed. It was unprecedented for a British monarch to disregard the advice of a prime minister on the issue of marriage or succession and his rejection of Baldwin's views on the planned marriage made a constitutional crisis between the King and the Government likely. The British Cabinet and the Dominions rejected even a morganatic marriage and presented him with three choices: abandon his marriage plans, marry and risk a constitutional crisis with the government, or abdicate. He chose the final option on 11 December 1936, making way for his brother, George VI.

Source B Winston Churchill, referring to Ramsay MacDonald, 28 January 1931 in the House of Commons. From *The Oxford Dictionary of Quotations*, (Oxford University Press), 1979, p. 149.

I remember, when I was a child, being taken to the celebrated Barnum's circus, which contained an exhibition of freaks and monstrosities, but the exhibit ... which I most wished to see was the one described as 'The Boneless Wonder'. My parents judged that the spectacle would be too revolting and demoralising for my youthful eyes, and I have waited 50 years to see the Boneless Wonder sitting on the Treasury Bench.

Source C From *The Labour Party and the Planned Economy* by Richard Toye, (Boydell and Brewer), 2003, p. 45.

The government was still committed to the twin pillars of orthodoxy, the gold standard and the ideal of the balanced budget; and the difficulties this caused were compounded by the delay and equivocation of ministers. Moreover, having accepted precepts that were economically conservative, the cabinet as a whole lacked the stomach to follow them through.

1 What can you learn about Ramsay MacDonald's government from Sources B and C?

2 Is it valid to call MacDonald 'boneless' (Source B)?

Morganatic marriage – A royal wedding where the husband or wife marrying into the royal family does not take on the title of king or queen, but instead has the lesser title of duke or duchess. It ensures that the non-royal can never become monarch if the royal dies, and, crucially, that children of the marriage are excluded from the line of succession.

▲ Edward VIII and Wallis Simpson – the king's relationship with a twice divorced socialite almost sparked a constitutional crisis.

Some historians have speculated that Edward's sympathies towards Nazi Germany might have persuaded the Government to force his abdication, using the issue of Wallis Simpson as an excuse. But this is unlikely for the following reasons:

- Edward's private comments about Hitler as a bulwark against communism were no more controversial than those held by many members of the British ruling class.
- His first visit to Nazi Germany took place in 1937, *after* the crisis, when Edward was the Duke of Windsor.
- There were some suspicions that Mrs Simpson might be a security risk, owing to her friendship with the German ambassador to Britain, Joachim von Ribbentrop. However, this was rarely mentioned by the Cabinet when discussing the issue.
- The main voice against the appeasement of Nazi Germany, Winston Churchill, was a staunch supporter of the King and even proposed forming a King's Party in the House of Commons.

Working together

Select one of the topics below to research. Your research question is: 'To what extent was this event a significant political development in Britain between the wars?'

- The fall of Lloyd George
- The formation of the National Government
- The abdication crisis

List five research questions for the topic you have chosen. These should be essential questions that you need to answer in order to understand the importance of the event. You can use this textbook and ideas from the Further research section on pages 268–73 to help

you. Otherwise, using a library or the internet can help you to find important information.

Once you have gathered your research, create a presentation for your partner, showing the extent to which the event you have chosen was important or significant.

Here are some good examples of research questions you might want to use (focusing on the abdication crisis question):

- What effect did the crisis have on the British public?
- How did attitudes towards the monarchy and politicians change as a result of the crisis?
- What was the effect on relationships between the government, monarchy and the Church?

The emergence of radical political groups

Why did a small minority in Britain embrace fascist and communist ideas in the 1930s?

Throughout the 1930s there was in increase in support for extreme ideas on both the far left and far right. Communist and fascist parties saw an increase in their membership as more people became convinced that liberal democracy no longer had the answers to the economic crisis. Neither fascist nor communist parties had any electoral success throughout the decade. However, because of the rise to power of Hitler and Mussolini and the events in Stalinist Russia, both ideologies were widely discussed and written about.

There was a profusion of books about fascism and communism and public meetings to discuss the apparent virtues and threats of both systems. In the case of the USSR, 'friendship' societies were established with the help of the Soviet Union to project a positive image of the communist 'experiment'.

The appeal of fascism and the BUF

One charismatic and forceful Labour MP, Sir Oswald Mosley, was inspired by the seemingly dynamic economic policies of Mussolini's Italy. Since 1922, a fascist one-party state had established itself in Italy under the charismatic dictator, Benito Mussolini.

Mosley was a former Conservative MP who had defected to the Labour Party. He was a member of the 1929 Labour Government, though not in the Cabinet, and resigned in protest at the failure of the Government to pursue the radical policies he believed were needed to deal with unemployment. He put these forward in the 'Mosley Memorandum' in 1930 arguing for:

- tariffs to protect the home market
- import restrictions
- imperial preference
- public control of the banking system
- government direction of industry
- the use of credit to promote economic expansion.

There was a lot of rank-and-file support for his programme and it was only narrowly defeated at the party conference in October 1930. Some leading Labour figures such as Aneurin Bevan and the miners' leader A. J. Cook supported Mosley's plan. Even some of the younger Conservative MPs expressed a degree of support for Mosley's ideas. Eventually he was expelled from the party when he announced the formation of the New Party, though he actually resigned on 28 February 1931. The historian A. J. P. Taylor argued that Mosley was the only man to rise to the challenge in 1930 and claimed his ideas were an 'astonishing achievement', evidence of a talent that would be wasted through impatience and arrogance that drove him towards fascism.

In 1932 Mosley drew all the fascist-style organisations in Britain together with the New Party to form the British Union of Fascists (BUF). The party's impact on the political system overall would prove to be negligible, but it briefly presented a challenge to law and order. The National Government passed the Public Order Act in 1936, banning groups from wearing uniforms and requiring permission for marches and demonstrations.

NOTE-MAKING

In this section you will be focusing on the political parties that emerged in the 1920s and 1930s. Structure your notes on:
- their ideas
- the limits of their appeal/impact
- the response of mainstream political parties to them.

Imperial preference – A policy of tariffs that favoured imports from the empire into Britain over other trading nations like the USA.

▲ Oswald Mosley addressing a fascist audience in the 1930s.

Mosley never became a threat to the National Government and his movement began to decline after 1936. However, Mosley's BUF demonstrated that there were significant numbers of people (the movement had 50,000 members at its height) who did not believe the existing political system of parliamentary democracy was capable of working at the height of the depression.

The appeal of communism and the 'fellow travellers' movement

The Communist Party of Great Britain (CPGB), founded in 1920, remained a small organisation throughout the Great Depression with no more than 3,200 members in 1929 at the height of the economic crisis. The party had a mixture of working- and middle-class members and while many of the major trade unions were affiliated to the Labour Party and therefore had no ties with the CPGB, some smaller unions such as the Boilermakers' Union and the Sign and Display Union (a signwriters' union based in the East End of London) supported the party.

Far more influential were a generation of thinkers, writers and public intellectuals who, while not being Communist Party members, expressed sympathy for communism. They were called 'fellow travellers' and they particularly admired Stalin's Soviet Union. Few of them advocated a communist revolution in Britain, but most believed that the massive level of state intervention brought about by Stalin to modernise Russia could also be used to lift Britain out of the Great Depression.

The Webbs and 'Soviet communism'

Sidney and Beatrice Webb were two of the most influential figures on the political left in Britain in the first half of the twentieth century. In the early part of their careers and marriage they had been social researchers and economic theorists (Beatrice Webb was a cousin of Charles Booth, see page 105), and they were supporters of the co-operative movement and the trade unions. They were founder members of the Fabian Society, and helped to establish the London School of Economics and the left-wing periodical, *The New Statesman*.

In 1932 the couple, now in their seventies, travelled to the Soviet Union to examine the country's rapid industrialisation and published a book, *Soviet Communism: A New Civilisation*, in 1934. In it they praised Stalin's economic policy and denied that Stalin was a dictator. When presented with evidence from British journalist Gareth Jones that a famine in the Ukraine, caused by Stalin, had killed 5 million people, Sidney Webb dismissed it as a rumour.

The Webbs believed that Stalin represented the only credible opposition to Hitler, and were devastated by the 1939 Nazi–Soviet Pact. The pact saw the Soviet Union that they admired so much form an alliance with Nazi Germany, which the Webbs viewed as a barbaric society. This decision left them with a deep sense of despair.

Support for the Spanish Republic

By 1936 it was becoming clear to much of the British public that peace in Europe was unlikely to last. In Germany, Hitler had begun to re-arm in defiance of the Treaty of Versailles. In Spain, a group of nationalist generals led an insurrection against the Spanish Republic, aided by both Hitler and Mussolini. Two and a half thousand volunteers from Britain travelled to Spain to fight in defence of the Republic. The British Battalion of the International Brigade was organised by the Communist Party of Great Britain, and the volunteers were effectively breaking the law by making the journey through France and across the Pyrenees to Spain. In 1936, the British Government agreed on a non-intervention policy.

The fate of the Spanish Republic was widely debated in Britain. Much of the centre-ground of British political opinion saw the war as an attack on democracy by the forces of fascism. There was a limited degree of support for the generals among the general public from anti-communists in Britain who equated the Spanish Republic with Stalinism.

The socialist writer George Orwell travelled to Spain to fight for the Republic and was nearly killed by a sniper's bullet. On return to Britain he wrote a book about his experiences entitled *Homage to Catalonia*. The Conservative Duchess of Atholl published a weekly magazine with 100,000 readers entitled *Searchlight on Spain*. The number of readers reflected the high degree of public engagement with the conflict and the vast majority of readers supported the Republic.

'Spain shops' opened across Britain, stocked with goods and foodstuffs that supporters of the Republic could purchase and then send to Spain. One source of support for the Spanish Republic was the trade union movement. In some of the poorest parts of the country, such as the mining towns of the south Wales valleys, money was raised for the Republic. By 1939 the TUC had raised over £2 million for the cause.

Read Sources D and E and answer the following questions.

1 How far do these views differ from the ideas of Britain's democratic politicians?

2 What factors (political, economic, social) already covered in this chapter might explain the appeal of these more extreme ideas?

Source D From the *Daily Mirror*, 22 January 1934, by newspaper magnate Lord Rothermere.

Timid alarmists all this week have been whimpering that the rapid growth in numbers of the British Blackshirts is preparing the way for a system of rulership by means of steel whips and concentration camps.

Very few of these panic-mongers have any personal knowledge of the countries that are already under Blackshirt [fascist] government. The notion that a permanent reign of terror exists there has been evolved entirely from their own morbid imaginations, fed by sensational propaganda from opponents of the party now in power.

As a purely British organisation, the Blackshirts will respect those principles of tolerance which are traditional in British politics. They have no prejudice either of class or race. Their recruits are drawn from all social grades and every political party.

Young men may join the British Union of Fascists by writing to the Headquarters, King's Road, Chelsea, London, S.W.

Source E *The Diary of Beatrice Webb, Volume 4, 1924–1943*, (Virago), 1986, pp. 279–84. This diary entry was written in early 1932 before the Webbs visited the Soviet Union.

What attracts us in Soviet Russia, and it is useless to deny that we are prejudiced in its favour, is that its constitution, on the one hand, bears out *our* Constitution for a Socialist Commonwealth ... Sidney and I are immersed in Soviet literature of all types and kinds – official reports and travellers' tales, of both which there are many, a few novels, more memoirs. At present we cannot make our way to any settled estimate of success or failure, whither success or failure be partial or on a colossal and catastrophic scale. The experiment is so stupendous, alike in area, in numbers involved, in variety, in speed, in intensity, in technological change and necessary alteration in human behaviour and human motive, that one's good mood alternates between the wildest hopes and gloomiest fears. All I know is that I *wish* Russian Communism to succeed, a wish which tends to distort one's judgement.

British politics on the eve of the Second World War

Despite the attractions of extremist ideas, both fascism and communism remained marginal political causes and after the outbreak of the Second World War fascism became even less acceptable. The issues that had divided popular opinion throughout the second half of the 1930s, re-armament and appeasement, were less divisive from late 1938 onwards when it became increasingly clear to most onlookers that war was unavoidable. Therefore, external events had a politically unifying impact on Britain and ensured that in September 1939 there was a widespread consensus across the country that Britain's declaration of war was necessary.

By the end of the decade, the National Government with its Conservative majority was still in power, but the opposition Labour Party was no longer in disarray. Under the leadership of Clement Attlee after 1935, the party began to recover electorally in national and local elections, even though they were unable to form a government. In 1935 Attlee's Labour Party won 102 extra constituencies to give them 154 seats in parliament, making Labour a serious parliamentary force once more. Attlee led the Labour Party in opposition to the policy of re-armament, instead arguing that supporting international law and the League of Nations would ensure peace. By 1937, however, the League of Nations appeared to have failed and the Labour Party voted to support the government's re-armament policy. The Liberal Party supported the government but by 1939 they had just 21 seats in the House of Commons, making them a marginal force in British politics. The Conservative Party continued to be the dominant party throughout the inter-war years, ruling directly for most of the 1920s and comprising the majority of National Government MPs throughout the 1930s. This was due to a number of factors:

- the tendency of newly enfranchised female voters to vote Conservative
- the support of the Party's traditional middle-class voters
- the Party's encouragement of home ownership
- the belief of many working- and lower middle-class people that the Party reflected their aspirations and hopes for social advancement.

Figure 4 Governments from 1914–39.

Dates	Prime Minister	Party
1910–15	Herbert Asquith	Liberal
1915–16	Herbert Asquith	Coalition
1916–18	David Lloyd George	Coalition
1918–22	David Lloyd George	Coalition
1922–23	Andrew Bonar Law	Conservative
1923–24	Stanley Baldwin	Conservative
1924	Ramsay MacDonald	Labour
1924–29	Stanley Baldwin	Conservative
1929–31	Ramsay MacDonald	Labour
1931–35	Ramsay MacDonald	National Government
1935–37	Stanley Baldwin	National Government
1937–40	Neville Chamberlain	National Government

KEY DATES: POLITICAL DEVELOPMENTS IN THE INTER-WAR YEARS

1922 Oct Lloyd George resigns as prime minister

1923 May Bonar Law steps down due to ill-health

May 1923–Jan 1924 First Baldwin ministry

Jan 1924–Nov 1924 First MacDonald ministry

Nov 1924–June 1929 Second Baldwin ministry

1931 Aug Establishment of National Government

1935 June Baldwin replaces MacDonald

1937 May Neville Chamberlain takes power

1939 Sept Outbreak of Second World War

LOOK AGAIN

In this section we have seen how politics changed during the inter-war years. What was the effect of economic crises on the support for different political parties throughout the inter-war period?

WORKING TOGETHER

1 What were the main political developments between 1918 and 1939? Work in pairs to break down the inter-war period into two sections, 1918–29 and 1929–39, on two separate sheets of paper. Discuss the following points and make notes on both periods:

   a) Who were the most significant political figures in the 1920s and 1930s?

   b) Which politicians had the most success in dealing with Britain's problems in the 1920s and 1930s?

   c) Which political ideas and ideologies succeeded and which failed in the 1920s and 1930s?

2 Working with a partner, compare the notes you have made on this section. Add anything that you have missed and check anything that you have disagreed on.

3 The condition of Ireland and Anglo-Irish relations

Between 1914 and 1939 the question of Ireland led to rebellion, war, independence and civil war. The struggle by the Liberal and coalition governments to hold the union together was matched by the struggle of Irish nationalists to create an independent country. This section explores developments in Ireland throughout the period.

NOTE-MAKING

This section focuses on the events of the Easter Rising. Using a spider diagram (see page x), make notes on these events and their consequences.

The Easter Rising

How well did the British handle the Easter Rising in 1916?

The outbreak of war in 1914 temporarily defused the growing crisis in Ireland over the issue of Home Rule (see pages 85–88). Home Rule was suspended for the duration of the war and men from both Catholic and Protestant communities across Ireland volunteered to fight in the British army. In the north the Ulster Volunteer Force formed the 36th Ulster Division of Kitchener's 'New Army', and Catholics joined the 16th Irish Division of the Army at the urging of John Redmond, the leader of the Irish Parliamentary Party and successor to Charles Stewart Parnell. The plight of Belgium, a small Catholic nation, overrun by Germany, motivated many Irish Catholics to join the army, though nationalists equated Belgium's situation to that of Ireland itself, another Catholic country occupied by its Protestant neighbour.

In addition to the Ulster Volunteers there was another armed militia group, the Catholic Irish Volunteers, which contained members of the Irish Republican Brotherhood. In 1913 the organisation had nearly 200,000 members, though at the outbreak of war the majority of them joined the British army. Redmond's call for the Irish Volunteers to fight split the movement. He believed the war would be short and would be fought to secure the rights of small nations such as Belgium or Serbia. He believed that the peace conference at the end of the war would be the opportunity to confirm Home Rule in Ireland once and for all. The remaining Irish Volunteers who refused to fight were not disarmed by the British government and many spoke openly about using the war as an opportunity for rebellion. One Irish nationalist, Sir Roger Casement, sought German help to force the British out of Ireland.

Sir Roger Casement

Casement was the son of a wealthy Anglo-Irish family and worked as a diplomat for the British government. He was an Irish patriot who wanted independence for Ireland from Britain. Casement believed that the First World War presented the Irish with the best opportunity to overthrow the British, and in 1914 he met with a German diplomat in America, who agreed to sell arms to him to enable a rebellion in Ireland which would divert British troops from the Western Front. While Casement was in Germany he met with Irish prisoners of war who had fought for Britain and tried to persuade them to fight for a free Ireland, but with limited success. Casement tried to return to Ireland in a German U-Boat, but both he and the shipment of arms that was being taken to Ireland on a surface vessel were intercepted by the British. Now a planned uprising, meant to begin in Easter 1916, would start without sufficient weapons. Casement tried to persuade the British to allow him to appeal to the rebels to call off the revolt and save their own lives. The British refused and Casement was tried and executed in 1916.

Germany had originally promised to support an uprising of the Irish volunteers on Easter Sunday 1916 by landing troops in Ireland, but the plan was unrealistic and the promise was half-hearted. The majority of the Irish volunteers failed to join the rebellion on Easter Sunday, but the following day a small group of revolutionaries in Dublin acted. They seized the city's post office and proclaimed the Irish Republic, starting a week of fighting that saw 450 Irish civilians and 100 British soldiers killed. Eventually the British sailed a warship up the River Liffey to crush the uprising, forcing the new government of the Republic of Ireland to surrender. The majority of the population did not support the rebellion and its associations with German help, especially as so many of their relatives were fighting on the Western Front. The goodwill that the British briefly experienced from the majority of the Irish quickly evaporated when executions began.

Fourteen men were executed effectively for treason in time of war, though not all were main leaders. Another rebel, not a leader, and actually not even involved in the rising, was executed for shooting dead a police officer while trying to resist arrest during a police round-up of possible suspects. In all, 90 death sentences were passed but the remaining 75 were commuted to imprisonment.

Following the rising 3,500 people were arrested and 1,480 people were held at internment camps in England and Wales, many of whom had nothing to do with the uprising. Many of these internees became dedicated revolutionaries and the camps provided an environment for republicans from across Ireland to organise together.

Asquith visited Dublin and believed Home Rule would help to prevent a further uprising, but was too indecisive to pursue the policy. Lloyd George, still Asquith's secretary of state for war, argued for immediate Home Rule with the six counties of Ulster remaining in the United Kingdom.

The 1918 general election and the declaration of independence

In the coupon election held in December 1918, the third largest party was Sinn Fein (see page 84). It was a non-violent party formed in 1906 and played no part in the Easter Rising but as there was a lack of awareness in the British press about the instigators of the rising, who were actually quite diverse, they called it the Sinn Fein Rebellion for want of a better headline. This led to some Sinn Fein members who had had nothing to do with the rebellion being arrested. After the rebellion many more extreme nationalists began joining Sinn Fein and this changed its political complexion by the time of the 1918 general election. The party won 73 out of Ireland's 105 seats and believed it had a mandate to declare independence. In January 1919 an Irish parliament (Dáil) and republic was declared at Mansion House in Dublin. In January the Irish Volunteers re-formed as the Irish Republican Army, led by Michael Collins and declared war on the British without the consent of the new Dáil. The new IRA was well-equipped due to two main factors:

● money from Irish Americans in Boston, New York, New Jersey and Philadelphia
● the easy availability of arms and explosives from Europe in the aftermath of the First World War (guns were often stolen from British army supply depots).

Michael Collins

Michael Collins was born in 1890 in County Cork to a prominent republican family. As a young man he lived in London and New York but in both cities was closely connected to the republican movement and was a member of the Irish Republican Brotherhood. He was a skilled organiser and was involved in military training for the Easter Rising. He was interned by the British in a prison camp in Frongoch in Wales after the rising, which enabled him to connect to other republican groups and plan the next uprising in 1918. Collins was assassinated in 1922 following the outcome of the Irish War of Independence. He helped negotiate the treaty that ended the war, but this involved losing the six counties of Northern Ireland. His killers were anti-treaty members of the IRA.

The Anglo-Irish War

The civil service in Ireland was technically still answerable to the British government but often the loyalty of senior civil servants was questionable. Collins had spies in the police and civil service and was forewarned of arrests. The IRA used guerrilla tactics against the British. it had no more than 3,000 to 5,000 active members at any one time, but their attacks were highly effective.

Members of the IRA:

- dressed as civilians so they could not be identified
- ambushed army and police patrols
- assassinated civil servants and police officers.

The British had 50,000 soldiers and 10,000 members of the Royal Irish Police. They supported these forces with an auxiliary force called the Royal Irish Constabulary Reserve Force, established by Winston Churchill in 1920. They were nicknamed the Black and Tans due to their uniforms and were made up of former soldiers, many of whom were traumatised by war and unable to re-adjust to civilian life. The men of the Black and Tans responded to IRA guerrilla attacks with savage violence, often perpetrated against civilians. The execution of prisoners, torture, reprisal killings and the burning of houses were all frequent tactics among the auxiliaries. Senior politicians and public figures in Britain and across the empire were horrified by their actions and many questioned whether Britain had a right to rule in Ireland.

The Government of Ireland Act

In 1920, Lloyd George proposed the Government of Ireland Act, which would create two Home Rule parliaments, one in Belfast for Ulster and one in Dublin for the rest of Ireland. A reduced number of MPs would be able to sit in the Westminster Parliament and there would be a Council of Ireland that would preserve unity across the country. The Act achieved significant successes in ending the war:

- In the south Sinn Fein proclaimed a second Dáil.
- In the north, Ulster Unionists felt protected from the possibility of being ruled from Dublin and established a Parliament for Ulster.
- Both sides refused to recognise the Council of Ireland.

The Sinn Fein president of the Irish Republic Éamon de Valera agreed to negotiate with the British to bring the war to an end. One major factor in encouraging him to negotiate was the growing weakness of the IRA. Collins conceded in 1921 as negotiations began, that the organisation only had three weeks of arms and supplies left. In July 1921 a truce was signed and the fighting ended three days later.

The Anglo-Irish Treaty

Sinn Fein wanted an independent republic for the entire country, including Ulster, but instead, Lloyd George offered dominion status for 26 counties, not including the six counties of Ulster that had Protestant majorities. This meant that Ireland's Dáil would still swear an oath of allegiance to the British Crown, an idea that was intolerable to Sinn Fein. Lloyd George was anxious to hold the union of Britain and Ireland together because he was supported in coalition government by the Unionist Party, who he feared would abandon him if the union ended. Sinn Fein was presented with the possibility of further warfare from Britain unless it agreed to the peace terms. Lloyd George was not too concerned about whether Northern Ireland remained autonomous as long as a treaty could be signed that would keep both Sinn Fein and the Unionists happy.

Guerrilla tactics – Fighting using ambushes, bombs and snipers. Guerrilla soldiers do not wear uniforms and often hide among the civilian population.

Dominion status – A self-ruling part of the British Empire, such as Australia or Canada.

He hinted to Sinn Fein that a future Northern Ireland might be made so small and weak that it would have little choice than to accept economic and political control from Dublin. On 6 December 1921 the Anglo-Irish Treaty was signed and an Irish Free State was agreed, which did not include the six northern counties of Ulster. The treaty gave the Irish Free State dominion status within the British Empire, ensuring that a British monarch would still be head of state and the British government would appoint a governor-general.

The Irish Civil War

Both the British Government and the Dáil voted for the Anglo-Irish Agreement but de Valera opposed it, believing that no Irish Republic could exist without the six counties. The Irish Free State was officially recognised in December 1922, but its existence did not stop the outbreak of further war in Ireland. The IRA divided into pro- and anti-treaty factions and fought a civil war that lasted until April 1923. One of the pro-treaty leaders who was assassinated during the war was Michael Collins.

▲ An illustration of the assassination of Michael Collins by anti-treaty members of the IRA in 1922.

Ireland on the eve of war

The civil war had left lingering animosities on both the pro- and anti-treaty sides in Ireland and the anti-treaty Sinn Fein members would not sit in the Dáil, meaning that a new pro-treaty party Cumann na nGaedhael (Society of Gaels) ruled Ireland for the next five years. The party was led by William Cosgrave who was Ireland's first president of the Executive Council (the equivalent of prime minister in the Irish Free State) between 1922 and 1932. De Valera realised that boycotting a role in government was pointless and it simply meant that he and his supporters were excluded from power. He formed a new party called Fianna Fail (Warriors of Destiny), and in 1927 entered the Dáil, even though the party was obliged to swear an oath of loyalty to the British Crown. In 1932, Fianna Fail, the anti-treaty party, won the general election, signifying a shift in public opinion towards full independence. The Irish economy was dependent throughout the 1920s on Britain and Cosgrave tried not to provoke Britain in any way. When de Valera became president of the Executive Council he took a different approach and abolished all debts from Irish farmers to British landowners, resulting in British retaliation. The British Government imposed trade sanctions on Ireland, placing a 20 per cent tax on agricultural imports to Britain, a move that devastated the Irish economy which was predominantly based on food exports.

In 1936 de Valera informed Edward VIII that he intended to create a new constitution for Ireland which would abolish the office of governor-general and claim a right to rule over the six counties of Northern Ireland. De Valera's constitution was deeply religious and gave the Catholic Church a 'special place' in Irish life, which made Northern Irish Protestants even more hostile to the south. In 1937 De Valera's new constitution was ratified and the role of president of the Executive Council was replaced with the new title of Taoiseach (prime minister). In the same year the Irish Free State was simply renamed Ireland. By 1939 the trade war with Britain ended and a new Anglo-Irish trade agreement was established, which gave Britain access once more to Ireland's three 'Treaty Ports', where British warships could be based. This was of crucial importance on the eve of the war, a conflict in which de Valera insisted Ireland should remain neutral. A minority of members of the Dáil argued that support for Germany might help the cause of reunification, but de Valera was not convinced.

WORKING TOGETHER

1 Create a mind map which summarises the reasons for Irish independence by 1937. Place these reasons in rank order, beginning with the most important at twelve o'clock on your mind map, moving clockwise to the least important.

2 Now compare your order with a partner. Explain to each other the reasons for your decisions.

KEY DATES: THE CONDITION OF IRELAND AND ANGLO-IRISH RELATIONS

1916 April The Easter Rising begins

1919 January Sinn Fein declares Ireland independent

Jan 1919–July 1921 Irish War of Independence

1921 Dec Anglo-Irish Treaty signed

June 1922–May 1923 Irish Civil War

1932 Feb Fianna Fail win the Irish general election

1932–1939 Trade war with Britain.

Chapter summary

- The First World War was a challenge for all the political parties but it caused the Liberal Party lasting damage, as it went into terminal decline after the war.
- Lloyd George emerged as a national hero by 1918, having led the country to victory, but he was involved in a corruption scandal in 1922 and his Conservative coalition partners forced him to call an election in which the Liberals were defeated.
- The Labour Party formed its first, short-lived government in 1924.
- In 1929 MacDonald formed a second Labour government which was soon overwhelmed by the Great Depression.
- Between 1931 and 1936 a fascist movement developed in Britain, led by Oswald Mosley, who formed the British Union of Fascists.
- During the 1930s the much smaller Communist Party of Great Britain, along with non-communist intellectuals on the left, admired the USSR and visited the country frequently.
- In 1936 the new king, Edward VIII, abdicated in favour of his brother, George VI, to marry the American divorcee Wallis Simpson.
- In 1916 a rebellion in Ireland was mishandled by the British, who decided to execute the ring leaders. By 1921 the British had lost most of Ireland after a bloody war of independence.
- Ireland endured a civil war after independence and Éamon de Valera, the leader of the new Irish Free State, had an uneasy and antagonistic relationship with Britain up to 1939.

CHAPTER SUMMARY DIAGRAM

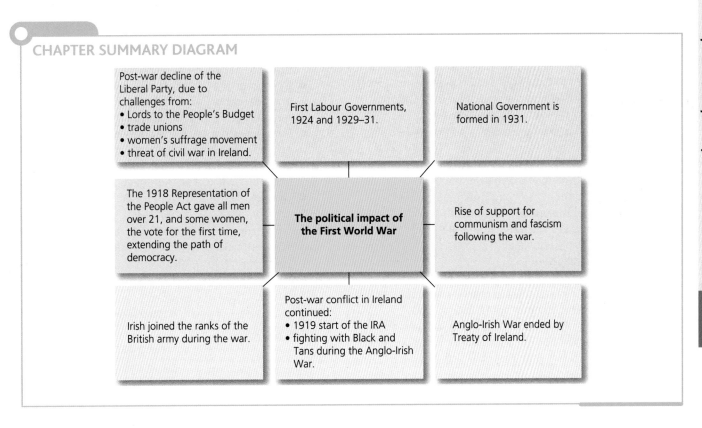

Working on essay technique: essay writing

Remember the skills that you built up in Chapters 1–4 on essay writing. The main headings were:

- **Focus and structure:** Be sure what the question is on and plan what the paragraphs should be about.
- **Focused introduction to the essay:** Be sure that the introductory sentence relates directly to the focus of the question and that each paragraph highlights the structure of the answer.
- **Deploying detail:** Make sure that you show detailed knowledge – but only as part of an explanation being made in relation to the question. No knowledge should be 'free-standing'.

- **Explanatory analysis:** Think of the wording of an answer in order to strengthen the analysis.
- **Argument and counter-argument:** Think of how arguments can be compared as part of a balancing act in order to give contrasting views.
- **Resolution:** Think how best to 'resolve' contradictory arguments.
- **Relative significance and evaluation:** Think how best to reach a judgement when trying to assess the relative importance of various factors, and possibly their inter-relationship.

ACTIVITY

Consider the following A-level practice question:

'The inter-war years, 1918–39, were a period of relative political stability.' Assess the validity of this view. **(25 marks)**

One of the most useful words in an essay question that enable you to develop an argument is 'relative' or 'relatively'. Relative means 'in relation to' or 'compared to', showing that you are not expected to look at the topic in isolation. This question asks you to make a judgement about how valid you think this statement is.

1 At the top of a large sheet of paper, write out the question.

2 On the left-hand side of the paper jot down the main topic areas that you might cover in an answer, under the broad headings:
   - The extension of the franchise
   - Changes to the party political system
   - Strikes and unrest
   - Extremist politics

3 On the right-hand side of the paper transform these ideas into a basic plan for an answer. Think of the structure. In outline, what evidence is there that the inter-war period was a time of political stability? What evidence is there that it was unstable? What overall picture seems to emerge?

4 Now look at the list of essay-writing skills above. See how they fit into your plan. Some, such as an introduction, will be there automatically. Consider the following:
   - Introduction: Is it simple or could it be complex? Does it do more than introduce? Does it highlight the structure of the answer?
   - Where can you add specific details to your plan so that you show a range of knowledge?
   - Does your plan successfully feature analysis and evaluation? Are you sure it will not lead to a narrative or descriptive approach?
   - It does not matter if you come down strongly on one side of the argument, as long as the argument comes through clearly and you show an awareness that there is another side.
   - Can you reach a judgement which 'resolves' any conflicting arguments?

5 Can you add precise details and/or quotations into this structure to provide evidence to support your arguments?

6 Has your answer shown an awareness of different interpretations?

7 Now write an answer to the essay using the notes you have made.

The economic and social impact of the War, 1914–39

6

In the previous chapter we saw how British politics was forever changed by the impact of the First World War. In this chapter we will look more closely at how the war directly affected the British people. Society was placed under immense strain by four years of total war and the economy was fundamentally weakened by the pressures of the conflict. Throughout the inter-war years, the memory of the war shaped British society and culture and left the British divided when the threat of a second conflict loomed towards the end of the 1930s. This section will address:

- The economic impact of the war.
- The effect of the conflict on industrial relations.
- The government's responses to social problems and the growth of state welfare.
- The development of a mass media during the 1920s and 1930s.
- How life changed for women during and after the war.
- How life changed for working-class people during and after the war.

The main breadth issues covered in this chapter are:

- How and with what effects did the economy develop?
- How and with what effects did society and social policy develop?
- How important was the role of key individuals and groups and how were they affected by developments?

The focus of this chapter can therefore be summed up by the following question:

How did Britain change socially and economically between 1914 and 1939?

CHAPTER OVERVIEW

The First World War had a profound economic impact on Britain during and after the conflict. In this chapter we will explore the growth of government intervention in the economy during the war. We will also explore the causes of the immediate post-war boom and slump and its effects on British society. This chapter will also examine the economic policies of Labour and Conservative governments throughout the period and the effect of the Great Depression on the National Government from 1931 onwards. The depression did not affect all British regions equally and some parts of the country such as south Wales and the north-east of England experienced far more severe economic hardship and poverty than others. From 1934, however, an economic recovery had begun, and in the south-east and the Midlands new light industries provided goods for a buoyant consumer economy. An expansion in house building and the development of better healthcare and mass popular culture led to many people having a far better standard of living at the end of the 1930s.

1 Economic developments, 1914–39

The economy of Great Britain underwent a profound transformation during and after the First World War. Not only did the war disrupt the British economy but it also led to the expansion of the state into areas of economic activity in which it had previously never involved itself. In the inter-war years mass unemployment became a constant feature of economic life in Britain. It was a phenomenon that had not been experienced on a mass scale before and by 1933 it had reached heights of 3 million. While there was a significant economic recovery in the second half of the 1920s, parts of Britain dependent on older heavy industries remained stricken by poverty and deprivation.

NOTE-MAKING

The Government intervened in the economy and the lives of British civilians throughout the war. Make notes on the growth of state power (DORA, for example) and the aspects of life in Britain that were affected by it.

Increased state role in wartime

Why did the state have such a dramatically increased role in the life of ordinary citizens after 1914?

Before the First World War, both parties agreed that the state should generally have as limited a role as possible in the lives of individuals. This was the philosophy of liberalism (see pages 6–7) and the idea of a limited state had broad appeal across all social classes. After 1916, however, there was a widespread public desire for compulsory military service and a widespread acceptance that only radical state intervention in the economy could win the war. This represented a huge shift in attitudes among ordinary British people and the political classes, one which was not reversed by the end of hostilities.

Ministry of Munitions

David Lloyd George, the chancellor of the exchequer, was made the minister of munitions. He was appointed to the role because of his skills as an organiser and the belief that he would be able to negotiate with the management and unions. The task of organising wartime production was taken away from the War Ministry and placed in Lloyd George's hands because of the immensely bureaucratic nature of the ministry. Time and energy were frequently wasted at the War Office on paperwork instead of making sure that enough supplies were being produced. By the time Lloyd George left the exchequer, Britain was already spending far more than it could afford and Lloyd George had accepted that he would not be able to balance the budget. At the Ministry of Munitions, he was interested only in maximising the supply of weapons and equipment and his main problem was not the budget but the trade unions. In the half decade before 1914 (see pages 103–05) industrial militancy had been at its height and even though union militancy had ended as a result of the outbreak of war, Lloyd George knew it could be easily reignited.

Conscription

By 1916, the British army had 2.3 million men at its disposal as a result of voluntary enlistment. It had so many soldiers that it was unable to equip and train all of them to be battle ready and had to gradually build up its forces on the Western Front. The fact that no breakthrough had been achieved since 1914 led to pressure from both the general public and popular press to build up forces for new measures to achieve a final victory. The *Daily Mail* ran editorials claiming that thousands of young men were avoiding military service and conscription was essential. Asquith was opposed to conscription; as a traditional Liberal he was reluctant to expand the reach of the state further into the lives of individuals and believed conscription was not only unnecessary but could not be justified. Instead he saw it as an attack on civil liberties and freedoms. Lloyd George saw it as a useful issue which with to build support among the public, and backed conscription along with the Unionists in the Cabinet.

Other pro-conscription politicians and journalists pointed out that even though the army was over 2 million strong, the rate of voluntary recruitment had significantly decreased from the high point of 100,000 per month in early 1915. The Government had already introduced measures to increase the numbers of volunteers in 1915:

● In May the upper age limit of soldiers was increased from 38 to 40.
● In July the National Registration Act was passed, by which a nationwide census of employment uncovered that 3.4 million men were in non-essential trades and could be eligible to fight if conscription were needed.
● In October the Derby Scheme was introduced. Asquith asked Lord Derby, Kitchener's director-general of recruiting, to create a compromise between the pro- and anti-conscription lobbies. Men aged between 18 and 40 were asked to join the army voluntarily or to 'attest' to join up if conscription was later introduced.

The Derby Scheme saw 2,185,000 'attest' in order to defer military service and only 215,000 men enlist. The 'attested' men were allowed to return to civilian jobs and were given an arm band indicating their pledge to fight at a later date, which was supposed to prevent them from being accused of cowardice. Public attitudes shifted towards conscription as a result of the scheme as there was widespread anger that so many men were seen to be avoiding enlistment. Asquith was left with little choice but to introduce conscription the following year.

The Military Service Act

Conscription was introduced in January 1916 with the Military Service Act. Thirty Liberal members of the Coalition Government voted against the Act and Liberal home secretary Sir John Simon resigned. The Act ruled that:

● All men aged between 18 and 41 were eligible for military service and could be conscripted.
● Seventy new army divisions could be raised.
● Local tribunals would be established at which conscientious objectors could apply for exemption from military service. Most applications were rejected, but 10,000 agreed to do civilian work instead.

However, the Act did not raise the large numbers of men expected. When enlistment was voluntary, men in reserved trades like engineering and mining often had to be rejected by the army when they volunteered to sign up. When conscription began, over three-quarters of a million men found ways to prove they were in reserved trades. In the first half of 1916 conscription resulted in 40,000 men joining the army per month, less than the 100,000 a month at the height of voluntary recruitment.

The Defence of the Realm Act (DORA)

On 8 August 1914 the Defence of the Realm Act (DORA) was passed through Parliament without any parliamentary debate. Thereafter it was amended several times to increase its scope. It gave the government far-reaching powers to suppress anti-war dissent – publishing anything that might directly or indirectly benefit the enemy was a criminal offence. However, the deliberate ambiguity of the Act's wording meant that this could outlaw virtually anything, including anti-war literature or news reports from the front line. The creation of the War Office Press Bureau meant that reports from the army could be censored by the government first before being released to the press.

DORA also gave the government the power to requisition land and property if it was deemed necessary for the war effort. A range of peacetime activities was also banned in the interests of national security. Fearing the possibility of German espionage and even an invasion (though this was highly unlikely to have been a serious plan by the German army) activities such as binocular usage and kite flying were banned. Purchasing alcohol was also heavily restricted as the Government did not want to have drunken or hungover workers at dangerous munitions factories. In 1915 an amendment to DORA required that alcoholic drinks like beer were diluted to make them less intoxicating and pub opening hours were restricted from 12 noon to 3 p.m. and 6.30 p.m. to 9.30 p.m.

Rationing

In 1918, during the last few months of the war, compulsory rationing on most basic foodstuffs was introduced. It had begun on a limited scale the year before due to Germany's U-Boat campaign but by the summer of 1918 was nationwide. Rationing policy had an important social element to it. Lloyd George's government made sure that everyone had a limited ration of food, which prevented extreme shortages in poorer areas that would be likely to cause strikes and unrest. Despite the Government's fears, the British accepted rationing without protest and the Government created the Consumers' Council to represent them. The council was designed to make rationing more acceptable to the public, but it was also the first official organisation that campaigned for consumers' rights to the government. In the inter-war era, the concept of consumer rights became more established as a result of the council, which insisted that in post-war policies concerning food, pharmaceuticals, transport and other key areas of consumption, the customer be given protection against unfair price rises and other unethical practices.

Problems with the staple industries and mines

What impact did the war have on Britain's heavy industries?

During the war, most of Britain's heavy industry, coal mines and railways came under government control. They were not nationalised and remained privately owned, but their output was directed by the state. The Government also managed industrial relations during the war, making compromises with the union movement to prevent strikes. At the end of the war, Britain's staple heavy industries were plunged into economic crisis and declined throughout the 1920s and 1930s, leading to high levels of unemployment in the regions that were most dependent on them.

Britain's 'staples'

The British Industrial Revolution had been based on four main industries: cotton manufacturing, shipbuilding, steel manufacturing and coal mining. Between them these industries employed millions of British workers on the eve of the First World War and had been key to economic success in the previous century.

By the eve of the war:

- The cotton industry generated profits of £50 million per year and 7,000 million yards of cotton were exported worldwide in 1913.

U-Boats – German submarines that attacked British shipping during the First and Second World Wars.

- The coal industry employed 1.1 million miners and other workers, and produced 290 million tonnes of coal a year.
- 975,000 tonnes of shipping was built and launched in Britain in 1913. Half of all merchant shipping worldwide sailed under a British flag.
- 6.5 million tonnes of steel were produced in 1910.

However, the war accelerated problems within the staple industries that had been developing for decades. Under-investment in new manufacturing processes meant that even before the war, British industry was slipping behind and losing market share to the USA and Germany. New industries in rival countries like Germany, such as the chemical industry (making dyes, fertilisers and pharmaceuticals), developed at a faster pace than their British counterparts and were more successful in capturing world markets. British chemical companies like ICI struggled to compete with German firms like Bayer and Hoechst. In the USA new industrial giants such as US Steel and Standard Oil began to dominate world markets, providing tough competition for British firms. The decline in profitability of British industry coincided with a rise in union power before the war (see page 81).

Industrial relations during the war

The many hundreds of thousands of skilled workers leaving to fight were replaced in the factories by women and unskilled male workers. This process was called dilution of labour, and the unions tolerated it on the understanding that they would operate the policy, allocating jobs to the new influx of non-skilled workers. Traditionally, unions had been vehemently opposed to accepting non-skilled workers into factories reserved for skilled, unionised men because it was thought to be a ploy by employers to bring down wages overall. However, they agreed to cooperate on three conditions:

- After the war, the returning soldiers got their jobs back.
- Factory profits were to be limited in exchange for limits on union rights.
- War production would be directed in part by the unions through local joint committees of unions, management and the government.

The final proposal was rejected, but the agreement between Lloyd George and the unions helped to keep strike action to manageable levels during the war. It was agreed in March 1915 between Lloyd George and the Unions after a meeting at the Treasury; the final deal was referred to as the 'Treasury Agreement'. Lloyd George's role in social reform before the war and his anti-Lords rhetoric during the constitutional crisis over the People's Budget made him popular with the unions. The adoption of dilution by the unions was a crucial moment in the history of the British trade union movement. It represented the first time that unions were able to participate in governance and cooperate with the government instead of challenging it. For Lloyd George there was an even greater significance: he called the agreement with the unions the 'Great Charter for labour' and was able to claim that he had made a landmark agreement with the people to win the war. A year later he would challenge Asquith for power and the agreement over dilution would give him widespread credibility.

Wartime strikes

Before the start of conscription in 1916 (see page 162), keeping skilled workers in their jobs was difficult. One-fifth of all skilled workers by 1915 had decided to enlist, even though between them the Admiralty and the War Office handed out nearly half a million exemptions to workers in essential industries. A shortage of skilled workers meant that by 1915 employers were not allowed

NOTE-MAKING

As you work through this section, use the headings to make brief notes on it. Set these notes out clearly using main headings, sub-headings and sub-points. For example:

Main heading: The problems with the staple industries and the mines

Sub-heading 1: The effect of the war

Sub-heading 2: The trade unions

Sub-heading 3: Government policy

When you have completed your notes on the first few pages, review the process and then devise your own sub-headings for the remainder of the section, using the headings and questions in the text to help you.

As you make your notes, consider the questions:
- What effect did the war have on Britain's traditional 'staple' industries?
- Why did Britain experience over a decade of industrial conflict between 1914 and 1926?
- What was the effect of government policy on British industry?

to 'poach' an employee from another factory with the offer of higher wages. New regulations under DORA that year meant that a munitions worker could not be taken on by an employer within six weeks of leaving his job without a legally required 'leaving certificate'. This often tied workers to workplaces, bosses they disliked and wages they resented, and was often viewed as a type of conscription, introduced long before conscription into the army existed. The policy was abandoned in 1917 following strikes in the workplace and 'go-slows'.

The improvement of wages and working conditions went some way to reducing industrial action, but the Government was also armed with legislation to prevent strike action and in 1915 strikes and resistance to dilution in the armaments industry became a criminal offence. However, Lloyd George was aware that direct confrontation with the unions could result in mass strikes and so in many instances he was conciliatory instead of confrontational. When miners in south Wales went on strike in 1915 he met their demands for a 'closed shop'.

Even though Lloyd George conducted a skilled policy of industrial relations, the days lost to strikes grew throughout the war. For example, in 1917 there were 48 strikes across Britain which involved over 200,000 workers and, by 1918, the relationship that the Government had with the workers was deteriorating.

Strikes and possible revolution in 1919

Following the armistice, there was an enormous wave of unrest across the country as not only workers, but soldiers and even the police went on strike as resentments and perceived injustices that had developed during the war were unleashed at the end of the conflict.

- As factories took on large numbers of men, the numbers of strikes declined. This shows that new jobs, many of which were well-paid following the immediate post-war strikes and unrest, satisfied unionised British workers.
- In 1919 there were 32 million days lost to strikes but the following year, at the height of the boom, the figure had fallen to 25 million.
- A year later, as unemployment soared and the workers who were in jobs saw their wages slump, strikes grew once more, reaching 84 million days lost.

Most of the strikers' grievances were over repressed wages, inflation and rationing, but a minority of strikers expressed more political and ideological grievances. The Government was able to contain the strikes by offering concessions. This suggests that while the *perception* may have existed that Britain was close to a revolution, in reality there was not much chance of one occurring.

Mutiny

Strikes by soldiers stationed in France and Britain were classed as mutiny at the end of the war. Many of the soldiers who disobeyed orders had been trade union members in peacetime and a small minority were inspired by the events of the Russian Revolution in 1917, which had begun with soldiers mutinying against their officers. In 1918 at Pirbright in Essex, soldiers refused to obey orders for three days, going on strike to protest against living conditions and pay. In November soldiers at Shoreham marched out of their camp in protest against brutal treatment by senior officers, leading to the Government offering mass demobilisation. Each week following the walk-out 1,000 soldiers were released from service. In France during January 1919, 20,000 British troops mutinied, demanding quicker demobilisation, better food, accommodation and weekend leave, which led to a wave of mutinies in British bases in Folkstone,

Go-slows – Workers deliberately being as unproductive as possible as a form of protest.

Closed shop – The practice among trade unions of preventing any non-unionised worker from having a job in a factory or workplace dominated by the union.

Demobilisation – The return of conscripted soldiers to civilian life at the end of the war.

Southampton, Felixstowe and twenty other camps. Troops refused to embark onto ships heading to France and Russia. Troops at Felixstowe created a soldiers' union. Only through speeded-up demobilisation and better conditions did the union and army strike activity dissipate, though throughout 1919 Lloyd George feared that the country was close to a Bolshevik revolution.

'Hands off Russia!'

Allied intervention against the Bolsheviks had started during the war because the new Bolshevik government had negotiated a separate peace with Germany in April 1918. The Bolsheviks' opponents were promising to continue the war and there were already British troops in Russia anyway to protect British-supplied munitions from the German advance. However, Lloyd George was quite clear that intervention to put down the Bolshevik revolution should end once the war was over, though Churchill and others argued for it to continue. Sympathy for the Bolsheviks was strong among some elements of the trade union movement and a 'Hands off Russia' campaign began. In May 1920 a confrontation occurred over the *Jolly George*, a ship which was intended to send munitions to Poland which was at war with Bolshevik Russia. There was some sympathy at government level with the Poles for their long years of oppression by tsarist Russia, but it was not shared by the London dockers or the Labour Movement more generally. Poland was a new state created out of the fall of the Russian, German, and Austrian empires. It had originally been carved up between them in the 1790s. Poland believed it was entitled to more of its old territory than it had received in 1919, hence its conflict with the Bolsheviks. However, despite initial successes, the war went badly for Poland at first and there were fears that the Bolshevik army would overrun Poland completely. The unions organised Councils of Action to oppose British intervention on the Polish side. Intervention by Britain and the other allied powers would have been inevitable however, had the Poles not rescued them from it by inflicting a comprehensive defeat on the Bolsheviks and winning the war.

Red Clydeside

In 1919 the biggest incidence of union unrest was at Clydeside, in Glasgow. The Clyde workers had actively protested against the First World War in 1914 and a May Day protest in 1918 demanding an end to the war drew crowds of tens of thousands.

In response to growing unemployment in the struggling shipbuilding industry, the Glasgow Trades Council proposed to reduce the working week from 54 hours to 40. This was intended to give surplus hours to unemployed men, many of whom were ex-servicemen.

Some unions, such as the Amalgamated Society of Engineers, opposed the reduction of working hours and pay that would affect their members. Matters came to a head on 31 January 1919 when 90,000 demonstrators filled George Square demanding the 40-hour week, raising the socialist red flag. At a time when governments across the Western world were very nervous about the possibility of revolution breaking out, the raising of the flag was an incendiary act. It is unclear if the police acted first, but by the end of the day, pitch battles had taken place between protesters and police, with tanks and soldiers being quickly transported to Glasgow from across Scotland and from England in order to put down any organised revolutionary violence. The scale of the violence and the potential for greater bloodshed from the army shocked union leaders who called on protesters to halt the rioting. The 40-hour week was never obtained by the workers and the Government offered them no concessions.

The Russian Revolution

In February 1917 the Russian Tsar (emperor) Nicholas II abdicated and was replaced by a provisional government. In October that year a radical socialist party, the Bolsheviks, seized power and proclaimed Russia a workers' state. This acted as an inspiration to many socialists, trade unionists and radicalised workers and soldiers across Europe in the revolution's immediate aftermath.

The miners' strike, 1921

In 1921 the Miners' Federation of Great Britain (MFGB) was the largest trade union, with over 900,000 members. Wartime state control of the coal mines had been popular with the miners because it gave them higher wages and a seven-hour day, conditions that could not possibly be maintained under normal market conditions, that is, without government subsidies.

Once the government's control of mines ended in March 1921, and they were returned to private ownership, wages decreased and hours lengthened. The problem was the collapse of the export trade in coal due to over-production globally, hence there was a glut of coal in Britain and prices fell dramatically. This was one reason why the Government refused to nationalise the industry permanently as the cost of subsidies was becoming too much. The owners reduced wages because they could not afford to maintain the subsidised wartime pay and conditions: mines that were economically viable to operate under wartime conditions were impossible to operate without huge losses in the new post-war situation.

The MFGB, the National Transport Workers' Federation (NTWF) representing dock workers, and the National Union of Railwaymen (NUR) had negotiated with one another previously. They had discussed the possibility of united strike action to protect wages if a post-war economic slump occurred. A miners' strike could easily be broken by the importing of foreign coal, but if dock workers refused to unload it and rail workers refused to move it across the country the strike could be potentially crippling and might quickly become a general strike.

When union leaders refused to accept pay cuts mine owners locked out their workers on 1 April and the Government used the Emergency Powers Act to send troops to south Wales in anticipation of unrest and violence.

Black Friday

The miners' attempts to strike in 1921 were sabotaged by the other two branches of the 'triple alliance' abandoning their cause. On Friday 15 April (referred to in the Labour Movement as 'Black Friday'), the NUR and the NTWF both decided not to strike in solidarity with the miners. The miners' leaders had made a crucial error in asking for support from the other unions but refusing to allow them to be part of the negotiations. This made members reluctant to strike and union leaders wary of the potential consequences of involving their members. The miners walked out between 15 April and 28 June, but were eventually forced to return to work, realising they could not defeat the mine owners. The miners were forced to accept pay cuts that left their wages 20 per cent lower than in 1914.

Black Friday left the miners with a lasting sense of anger and resentment towards the rest of the union movement. They hoped that the election of a Labour government might change their fortunes.

Locked out – The practice by employers of locking the factory gates and keeping workers out of their jobs until they agree to accept lower wages.

Emergency Powers Act – A piece of post-war legislation that gave the government similar powers to DORA. It enabled the government to use force to restore order, particularly with regard to industrial disputes.

The Gold Standard

Before the war the value of the pound had been decided by a fixed exchange rate, the Gold Standard. This was intended to ensure that the pound remained a strong currency, acceptable around the world, and made it attractive for foreign countries to deposit funds with the Bank of England. The Gold Standard was suspended in 1919 for six years so the Government had to decide in 1925 whether to continue the suspension with a new Act. Alternatively, it could allow it to run out and return to the pre-war system or replace the system with a new one but still linked to Gold. In the end the third option was chosen. The pre-war system was a 'specie' system, which meant that actual gold coinage was in circulation and holders of paper money had the right to exchange it for gold coins (or specie). At the start of the war the Government maintained the system but appealed to all citizens to patriotically refrain from exchanging paper money for specie and this appeal worked. Once the war was over the suspension was put in place.

The new system in 1925 was a Gold Bullion Exchange system which removed actual gold coins from circulation. This was announced by Chancellor of the Exchequer Winston Churchill in the 1925 Budget and enacted by the British Gold Standard Act 1925. Almost all reputable economists supported this action as the only way to stabilise the currency. Only John Maynard Keynes (a leading economist) opposed it and then mainly on the grounds that the exchange rate against the dollar 1:4.85 was too high – which is generally agreed to have been a correct view. The Treasury more or less demanded the return to Gold. So did Montague Norman, the governor of the Bank of England. Churchill took the widest advice he could and the Cabinet endorsed the return.

The exchange rate in 1925 was £1 to US $4.85 (Keynes believed that the value of the pound was fixed 10 per cent too high). In order to make the pound nearly five times as attractive to foreign investors, interest rates had to be kept high. This meant that foreign investors were attracted to Britain and put their money in British banks, but it also meant that the cost of borrowing money was equally high. As a result businesses found it more difficult to borrow money in order to expand and take on new workers, which added to Britain's problems with unemployment.

Many businesses wanted to come off the Gold Standard to make their exports cheaper so they could sell their products across the world, and so they could compete with the cheaper imports flooding into the country. The higher costs of British exports were offset by employers by reducing workers' wages or moving workers on to short-hours contracts, which meant that for many people paid employment often resulted in almost as much financial hardship as unemployment. On the other hand essential food imports and raw materials were made cheaper by the return to Gold – there were complaints from exporters that the real export problem was the old-style products for which demand was falling. In any case the prime issue for the return to Gold was the standing of the City of London as the leading financial centre. The main difficulty, which was key to the 1929–30 financial crisis, was the transition of Britain from a substantial net creditor, pre-war, to that of debtor, which meant that the system was dependent on foreign deposits which could be withdrawn. In the short term the move almost certainly brought more gains than losses but, as Keynes pointed out, it was deflationary in effect. The 1929 crisis was deflationary and so was accentuated, though not caused by, the return to Gold, which almost all countries capable of doing it adopted.

Short-hours contracts – A contract that does not guarantee fixed hours each week, meaning that workers' wages are never secure.

Net creditor – A country or an institution that lends more money than it borrows.

In September 1931 the Bank of England was forced to concede that it could no longer keep the pound in the Gold Standard. Interest rates were already at 8 per cent and would have to dramatically increase in order to prop up the value of the pound. That month a decision was taken to withdraw the pound from the Gold Standard, which effectively caused its devaluation. Many other countries came off Gold at the same time – in 1933 the USA devalued the dollar and the pound went higher than even the pre-war level. Coming off the Gold Standard enabled the Bank of England to reduce interest rates, an antidote to deflation, but the same was true of other countries.

The General Strike, 1926

Why was there a general strike in 1926?

The problems of the coal industry were mounting after 1919 because there was no demand internationally for British coal. By 1925 over 100 mining concerns had gone bankrupt. Wages were cut three times in that period and the seven-hour day was effectively abandoned. Seventy-three per cent of coal produced was done so at a loss. The industry was grossly inefficient with only 14 per cent of coal being mechanically cut, and the switch to oil ships further reduced demand. The response of the owners was to cut miners' pay, resulting in a strike by the MFGB, led by a popular and radical union organiser, Arthur Cook. His slogan 'Not a minute on the day nor a penny off the pay', had great resonance with the miners who had no sympathy with the mine owners' predicament.

The Government, fearing a general strike, established a Royal Commission under Sir Herbert Samuel into miners' conditions and offered a subsidy to the mine owners that would maintain miners' pay until 1 May 1926. The mine owners, knowing that the subsidy was coming to an end, told the miners they would have to accept pay cuts and threatened a lock-out unless they agreed. In March 1926 a government enquiry, the Samuel Commission, recommended a 13.5 per cent pay cut for the miners with the withdrawal of the subsidy. On 1 May 1926, 1 million miners across Britain were locked out of their workplaces for refusing to accept the new lower wages. The TUC announced that a general strike would begin on 3 May, knowing that abandoning the miners again would be catastrophic for trade union unity.

The Conservatives, particularly the chancellor of the exchequer, Winston Churchill, who had previously been quite sympathetic to the plight of the miners, saw the threat of a general strike as a plan to overthrow the state. However, the TUC were desperate for it not to be seen in this light; the majority of its leadership was far from revolutionary and distanced itself from radicals like Cook.

Government response to the strike

The Government, knowing the strike was coming, was far better organised than the TUC, publishing its own propaganda paper, *The British Gazette*, and using the new BBC to broadcast radio messages in support of the government position. The Labour Party distanced itself from the strikers and the TUC only authorised unions who could claim to have common interests with the miners to strike – miners, railwaymen, dockers, iron, steel, transport workers and printers.

An anti-union group of volunteers, the Organisation for the Maintenance of Supplies, was founded to do the work that the strikers refused to do. Its members manned buses, trains and telephone exchanges during the strike. The strike collapsed when it transpired that the 1906 Trades Disputes Act, which gave unions legal immunity from damages claims for loss of profits from businesses, would not apply. Union members began to return to work and the TUC appealed to the Government not to victimise the strikers. Baldwin told the unions he could not guarantee the rights of workers who returned to work and many were singled out as troublemakers. Miners' wages were slashed and the industry lost 30 per cent of its jobs; the strike had been a catastrophic failure for the miners. A new Trades Disputes Act in 1927 prevented sympathetic strikes and mass picketing. It also prevented civil service unions from joining the TUC and prevented them from striking on political grounds. It had a damaging effect on the Labour Party's finances, as the political levy that was once paid from union members' subscriptions to the Labour Party became optional for union members. They had to consciously choose to pay the levy, instead of it being an automatic deduction from their union dues. Miners, railway men and others who had been involved in the strike found it very difficult to find employment as employees shared names of 'trouble makers'. The union movement interpreted these changes as an act of 'revenge' by the government.

Sympathetic strikes – Strike action by a union that has no direct involvement in an industrial dispute, in solidarity with workers from unions who are on official strike.

Mass picketing – The use of hundreds or thousands of union members to prevent workers from entering a factory or business that is the subject of an industrial dispute.

▲ Police protection for volunteer bus drivers during the General Strike, 1926.

Interpretations: the role of the State during the First World War

ACTIVITY

Life in Britain was dramatically changed by the experience of the First World War. One of the most important features of this change was the dramatic expansion of the role and power of the state. This question challenges you to consider how far and in what ways the role of the state changed.

Sources A–C give different interpretations of the impact of the First World War on Britain.

1 In what way do Sources A and B agree and disagree?
2 In what way do Sources B and C agree and disagree?
3 Using material from the sources and your own knowledge, to what extent did the First World War change the role of the state?

Source A From *English History 1914–1945* by A. J. P. Taylor, (Oxford University Press), 1965, pp. 1–2.

Until 1914 a sensible, law-abiding Englishman could pass through life and hardly notice the existence of the state, beyond the post office and the policeman. He could live where he liked and as he liked. He had no official number or identity card. He could travel abroad or leave his country for ever without a passport or any sort of official permission. He could exchange his money for any other currency without restriction or limit ... All this was changed by the impact of the Great War. The mass of people became, for the first time, active citizens. Their lives were shaped by orders from above; they were required to serve the state instead of pursuing exclusively their own affairs. Five million men entered the armed forces, many of them (though a minority) under compulsion. The Englishman's food was limited and its quality changed, by government order.

Source B From *The Unknown David Lloyd George: A Statesman in Conflict* by Travis L. Crosby, (I. B. Tauris), 2014, p. 198.

Lloyd George made his plea for labour organisations to suspend their rules to allow women and unskilled workers to supplement skilled labour in war production – in other words, to allow 'dilution' of the workforce. Unity of the home front by all workers could produce enough munitions so that 'the incessant hammer of British guns' would crack the German steel barrier. Then, in his best oratorical style, Lloyd George concluded: 'you will hear the cheers of the British infantry as they march through their shattered entrenchments to victory, and in that hour the engineers will know with a thrill that the workshops of Britain have won a lasting triumph for the righteousness that exalteth a nation'.

Source C From *Yorkshire's War* by T. Lynch, (Amberley), 2014, p. 62.

The military authorities could arrest any persons they pleased and, after a court martial, inflict any sentence on them short of death. In addition, the military authorities were allowed to demand the wheel or part of the output of any factory or workshop they required. They were also allowed to take any land they needed. This, in effect, made the civil administration of the country entirely subservient to the military administration.

Post-war boom and depression

Why was there a boom and depression between 1918 and 1921?

The end of the war in 1918 was followed by a short-lived economic boom in Britain that ended in a recession in 1920.

Because of wartime restrictions and rationing, both individuals and businesses had been unable to spend and had accumulated considerable savings in cash and bonds. There was a high degree of demand within the economy and throughout 1919 consumers and businesses spent their savings. Individuals bought luxury items that had been rationed during the war such as coffee, soap, clothes and cigarettes.

There was a huge speculative boom as businesses issued new shares for traders, investors and other businesses to buy and more money poured into the London stock market than at any other time previously in British history. The total amount of new shares issued dramatically increased from £65 million to £384 million in 1920. Investors were keen to buy British shipyards, cotton mills and coal mines, but these were all poor investment choices. The monopoly that Britain had over these industries had vanished during the war and Britain now had new competitors in the USA, Japan and South America. In addition to this, these industries had become outdated and had received little investment during the war years, making them uncompetitive. In the case of shipping, there was an assumption by investors that global trade would quickly resume to pre-1914 levels and merchant ships would be in demand. Not only did this resumption of trade not happen as quickly as desired, but by 1919 there was a global surplus of ships. The British were slow to adapt their merchant fleets to oil away from steam-powered shipping that used coal. Ships from competitor nations that could adapt to oil were much more desirable.

British wartime industries still in the process of returning to civilian usage could not keep up with the level of demand. Goods in short supply became excessively expensive and as a result demand declined and the boom came to an end.

Recession, 1920–21

The recession that followed was one of the most severe slumps experienced by Britain prior to 1929. There had been periodic economic downturns in the previous century, but none had produced levels of unemployment on the scale of the 1920 slump. Unemployment levels rapidly increased to 12 per cent of the working adult population.

By 1921 2 million workers were unemployed and areas of the country like south Wales and Tyneside were deeply depressed as old industries like coal and shipbuilding collapsed. The crisis in the coal industry led to a wave of strikes. The cost of living had increased by 25 per cent between 1918 and 1920 and wages stagnated, meaning that unions were far more likely to strike to secure higher living standards for their members.

The recession was caused by a range of factors:

- **Deflation:** The Government cut spending by 75 per cent between 1918 and 1920. In addition, in order to return the value of the pound to its pre-war levels, the Bank of England raised the interest rate to 7 per cent. This meant that it suddenly became very expensive to borrow money. These two factors drained available money for spending from the economy.
- **Loss of export trade:** The global economy had been transformed by the war. It was no longer dominated by Britain and there were several new

NOTE-MAKING

In Chapter 5 you will have made notes on the political aftermath of the First World War. This section relates to the immediate economic fall-out from the war and should follow a similar structure. Focus on making notes on the boom and the recession, looking at long-term and short-term causes of the economic crisis, the attempts to deal with the crisis and its impact on living standards.

Speculative boom – An economic boom based on the stock market, often unstable and short-lived.

manufacturing and financial competitors who had taken up Britain's share of world markets for manufactured goods. British companies were forced to compete for business with foreign rivals who had taken advantage of the disruption to British trade during the war.

- **Underinvestment:** British industry suffered from long-term underinvestment and by the 1920s this had begun to cause serious problems. Many British firms were family run and as they passed from generation to generation their new owners neglected to spend money on new equipment and expertise.

- **Industrial relations:** In order to prevent a general strike in 1919 Lloyd George had offered British workers in the main industries (coal, rail, docks) generous pay rises and working hours. The workers, many of them former soldiers, refused to lose these conditions when times became tough. The creation of an eight-hour working day (48-hour week) resulted in a 13 per cent decrease in working hours, but no increase in productivity during the hours worked. Wage rates also stayed high due to Lloyd George's deal with the workers, meaning that products remained expensive and uncompetitive.

Source D Letter to R. J. Herron from Sidney Webb, a founding member of the Labour Party, discussing the apparent economic boom in 1920. From *The Letters of Sidney and Beatrice Webb: Volume 3, Pilgrimage 1912–47*, (Cambridge University Press), 1978, p. 137.

The General election, for which we must immediately prepare, will be one of supreme importance to every household. We are living in critical times. The present prosperity is largely fictitious. We have a cabinet that is intellectually bankrupt, and unable to find any effective or consistent policy … Meanwhile the cost of living continues to rise; the shortage of houses becomes week by week actually greater and more acute, and the misery of overcrowding more widespread. We have failed to reinstate in employment many thousands of the men who fought in our defence. Moreover, there are signs of short time [a reduction in working hours to reduce wage costs], workmen are being turned off in various industries, and I hear ominous threats of coming reductions in wages. The reason why practically nothing is being done by the Government to avert these evils, is that the Cabinet Ministers are seriously divided among themselves, about both home and foreign affairs, whilst the majority of the members of the House of Commons refuse to allow any interference with capitalist profit making.

1 What, according to Source D, is the evidence that the economy is in trouble?
2 Compare Source D to the information you have read throughout this section so far. How far is Sidney Webb's analysis supported by other evidence?

Attempts to solve economic problems, 1921–24

Lloyd George believed that there was little choice but to wait for the economy to improve on its own. He was anxious to appease middle-class voters who were experiencing financial hardship after 1920, many of whom wanted to see tax cuts and less government spending. He advocated a policy of spending cuts known as retrenchment. He did not want to alarm the middle classes with excessive spending and high taxes. Newspapers like *The Times* and the *Daily Mail* portrayed politicians who suggested greater spending as 'socialists'.

The Geddes Axe

In 1921 Lloyd George appointed Sir Eric Geddes to implement spending cuts. High taxes were blamed on excessive spending and Lloyd George believed tax cuts would revive the economy. The Anti-Waste League, a campaign group set up by the newspaper magnate Lord Rothermere, had won several seats from the Government in by-elections in 1921 so there was political pressure to reduce spending. Geddes recommended £87 million of cuts in the 1922–23 Budget. Most of these came from the military budget, but health, welfare and housing spending was reduced from £205.8 million in 1920–21 to £182.1 million in 1922–23.

The Great Depression and economic realignment

Why did Britain experience an economic crisis, 1929–34?

Between 1929 and 1934 Britain experienced an economic depression that afflicted most of the economies of the world throughout the decade. Britain's 'Great Depression' was shorter than that of the USA's, which lingered on until the end of the decade. It was also less pronounced than America's depression and that of many European nations, with the size of the economy shrinking by 5 per cent between 1929 and 1931. In the three years after 1931 the economy began to grow again and by 1934 had returned to 1929 employment levels. However, the depression represented a serious economic and political crisis in Britain, because at its height in 1931 some 3 million people were unemployed. This section will explore the impact of the depression on Britain's society and politics throughout the decade.

Long-term causes of the Great Depression

The causes of the Great Depression are varied and complex but one of the simplest ways for history students to explore the origins of the crisis is to divide them into long-term and short-term factors. Long-term factors might be described as 'structural' weaknesses in the British economy, which suggests that the fundamental way in which it operated had flaws that were exposed. Below are the main long-term structural problems that were facing Britain.

Lost markets

Prior to the First World War Britain was the world's largest exporting nation, but during the war it was unable to export to much of Europe and Asia. Many countries that had once bought British goods were either enemy powers or were occupied by them. America and Japan both took the opportunity to sell their products into countries once dominated by British imports such as China and the Ottoman Empire. Britain exported very little during the war as its domestic industries were turned over to war production. Even in British colonies like India, imports after the war had declined, the war years had led to India and the dominions rapidly expanding their industries, and in 1919 the British colonial government in India even put up import tariffs to keep out British goods and protect new Indian industries. The loss of world markets in manufactured goods led to the British economy being fundamentally weakened in the 1920s.

Debt

In 1914 Britain was the world's largest creditor nation and British banks dominated the global financial system. By 1918 Britain was the world's biggest debtor: the war had cost Britain £3.25 billion. Much of this had been raised by issuing war bonds to the public, but much had come from the USA. In 1916, American president Woodrow Wilson allowed US banks for the first time to lend money to Britain. The British believed that debts between the allies would hamper economic recovery across Europe at the end of the war and wrote off monies owed by Belgium, France and other allied nations, but America wanted the full amount loaned to Britain. The debts that Britain had incurred (amounting to 136 per cent of the country's entire annual economic output in 1919) and the damage to its trade left it greatly weakened. Government spending during the war had increased far beyond the ability of taxpayers alone to finance it, and borrowing was the only other realistic option.

> **War bond** – A war bond is essentially an IOU or a 'promise to pay' from the government. Governments that have to raise large sums of money to pay for armaments offer bonds to the public on the promise they when they are repaid they will have increased in value.

The world economy

With America as the number one trading power in the world and also the number one creditor, the international economy was unbalanced. America became highly protectionist (for more on protectionism and tariffs, see pages 101–02) during the 1920s and this made it difficult for Britain to sell her products into the USA and raise enough revenue to repay its war debts. By 1929 the unprecedented wealth of America meant that the world economy was too reliant on the USA and when it was plunged into economic crisis in 1929 (see page 177), there was a disproportionate effect on Britain and the countries that bought British goods.

Britain's 'staples'

Britain's four main industries, shipbuilding, coal, steel and cotton, were all in decline by the end of the First World War, as were the regions that were dependent on them. They faced major challenges because:

● there had been a lack of investment in new technology and skills over several decades
● new international competition in North and South America, Europe and Asia meant that demand for Britain's 'staples' declined over time
● the decline in these industries, once major employers, meant that after 1920 unemployment consistently stayed above 1 million.

Short-term causes of the Great Depression

While Britain had economic problems that had been developing over several decades, more short-term problems had also developed in the half decade before 1929. When the British economy faced major shocks in the form of economic crashes, the long-term structural weaknesses within the economy were revealed. Finally, the economic 'medicine' prescribed by the Labour Government from 1929–31 resulted in a dramatic growth in unemployment and poverty.

The Gold Standard

The Government's decision in 1925 to return Britain to the Gold Standard (see pages 169–70) left British goods far too expensive. The Gold Standard fixed the value of the pound at its 1914 level, whereas other economies such as France devalued their currencies and saw exports grow throughout the 1920s. Between 1925 and 1929, the high pound had a disproportionately greater impact on Britain's staple industries, contributing to industrial decline.

The Hatry Crash

Throughout the 1920s, Britain's stock market had been buoyant. Large sums of money that had been saved throughout the war due to a lack of consumer goods to purchase were available in 1918 to invest. Entrepreneurs like Clarence Hatry, a man who made his wealth buying and selling shares in companies, were able to amass vast fortunes on the stock market. The Bank of England and Labour and Conservative governments throughout the decade encouraged a practice called 'consolidation', where businessmen like Hatry were able to buy up businesses in related industries and merge them together into giant conglomerates. There is little evidence that this resulted in any greater efficiency or economic output, but it did lead to a growth in financial speculation throughout the decade. Previously, investing in the stock market had been the preserve of the wealthy, but after the First World War increasing numbers of small investors bought shares. Many people now felt more comfortable buying investments after purchasing wartime bonds.

In September 1929, Hatry was caught attempting to raise money for a merger of his iron and steel businesses into one large conglomerate, United Steel, using fraudulent loan certificates. When the scam was uncovered, the value of shares in Hatry's businesses collapsed overnight, depriving thousands of small investors of the savings they had invested. More significantly, the stock market no longer appeared to many investors to be a safe place to make money. The decline in confidence in the stock market meant that millions of pounds in investment dried up.

The Wall Street Crash

A month later a second stock market crash happened in the USA and had far more serious consequences than the Hatry Crash. When the chancellor of the exchequer, Phillip Snowden, stated publicly in the aftermath of the Hatry Crash that America's stock market on Wall Street was involved in an 'orgy of speculation', his words and the Hatry case in general were reported in America, a contributory factor in sparking a panic among investors. The subsequent collapse in share prices plunged America into depression and combined with the long-term problems in the global economy to spark a worldwide economic depression. Britain's exports declined by 50 per cent. They were worth one-third of its Gross National Product (GNP) and the collapse in trade was catastrophic for several key industries: coal, dock work, cotton, iron and steel, and shipbuilding. In addition to these industries, the shops and markets where miners, dock and mill workers spent their wages were also seriously affected. Unemployment that stood at 1 million in 1929 leapt to 2.5 million in 1930. The increase in unemployment put additional pressures on the Government, tax revenue declined, but the number of people applying for financial assistance rapidly increased. In 1931 the British economy shrank by nearly 5 per cent, but despite these problems the Government's main priority was keeping the pound in the Gold Standard system and supporting its value through spending cuts and high interest rates.

The growth of unemployment, 1929–32

By 1932 unemployment had hit an all-time high of 3 million. Much of the worst of the unemployment was concentrated in areas that were traditionally dependent on Britain's 'staple' industries (see pages 164–65). South Wales, the north of England, Scotland and Northern Ireland all suffered far higher rates of unemployment than the south-east of England and the Midlands. The most impoverished part of Britain was south Wales, where in some mining communities in the Welsh valleys, such as Dowlais, Tredegar and Ebbw Vale, unemployment reached 80 per cent. In these communities, hunger combined with despair and boredom, leading many former miners to leave and seek work in England. There was an exodus of impoverished Welsh families from south Wales to booming manufacturing and light industry towns in the south-east of England such as Reading, Slough and Croydon.

Former coal mining areas were not the only ones affected by depression. The collapse in the British shipbuilding industry caused mass unemployment on Tyneside in the north-east and in the shipyards of the Clyde in Scotland. The Harland and Wolff shipyard in Belfast that had built the *Titanic* slumped and only re-armament in the second part of the decade revived its fortunes. In the north-west of England the cotton and textiles industry in Manchester and Lancashire also shed tens of thousands of jobs.

The Labour Government's response

Britain's huge debts, along with her rising level of unemployment, led to a debate within the new Labour Government. The chancellor of the exchequer, Philip Snowden, believed that unemployment relief should come from taxing the wealthy and from corporate profits. However, as these profits slumped, and private, wealthy individuals with money were anxious to protect or conceal it, the cost of providing for the unemployed became unsustainable.

The economist John Maynard Keynes suggested government spending on public works such as new roads to provide jobs for unemployed men, but Snowden refused. He knew that the bankers in New York and London had little patience for further spending, as the value of British government bonds they had purchased during the war would decrease.

Source E From *Britain Since 1900 – A Success Story?* by R. Skidelsky, (Random House), 2015, p. 205.

MacDonald formed his second minority Labour government in 1929 just before the Great Depression hit. The economic slump raised the numbers of insured unemployed to over 20 per cent between 1930 and it was still nearly 12 per cent when war broke out in 1939. The world depression can plausibly be regarded as a delayed effect of the war. The war had disorganised world trading patterns. It had created large imbalances between the primary producing and manufacturing sectors of the world economy ... On top of this, and partly as a consequence, Britain had lost the trading and financial clout to stabilise the system as it had before 1914.

1 What does the author of Source E suggest were the long-term economic consequences of the First World War?

2 Using this source and your own knowledge, assess the view that the First World War was the most significant cause of the Great Depression.

The start of economic recovery

The depression did not last as long in Britain as it did in other countries such as America. Economic growth averaged 4 per cent a year between 1934 and 1937 as the decision to remove Britain from the Gold Standard in 1931 enabled the following economic measures:

- A cut in interest rates: borrowing for businesses and individuals became cheaper, which enabled more spending and job creation. It also made it less attractive to save money, so people investing their wealth bought property instead. This fuelled a housing boom in the south-east and the Midlands in the second part of the decade. The cut in rates was referred to as a 'Cheap Money' policy.
- The Government was able to allow a degree of inflation by the end of the decade. Instead of trying to prevent inflation completely (therefore protecting the value of the pound and its place in the Gold Standard), the National Government stimulated spending, which had the consequence of letting prices rise slightly. For example, the Government spent money on road building, which in turn stimulated the car industry (see page 179).
- The devaluation of the pound made British exports cheaper and more competitive.
- Banks became more willing to spend again.

Falling unemployment

Unemployment fell from 17 per cent of the working population in 1932 to 12.9 per cent in 1934 and 8.5 per cent in 1937. These were still very high levels compared to the decade before the First World War, indicating that unemployment, even in a period of recovery, was a constant feature of the inter-war years. The recovery featured long-term structural unemployment as the problem of persistent long-term unemployment in depressed areas like Wales and the north-east remained unsolved.

Special Areas Act, 1934

The Conservative, Labour and Liberal parties were predominantly *laissez-faire* in their attitude toward the economy, meaning that they believed that market forces would eventually lift the economy out of depression. Before 1934, the National Government was resistant to intervening directly to alleviate the impact of the depression, fearing that adding to government debt would harm the economy further. By 1934, however, it was clear that even though the depression was lifting in affluent parts of the country such as the south-east of England, mass unemployment continued to be experienced in the south Wales valleys, Tyneside and southern Scotland. The Special Areas Act 1934 saw direct state intervention for the first time to address the problem of unemployment in the hardest hit or 'special' areas. As a result of the Act:

- Two commissioners, one for Scotland and one for England and Wales, were appointed.
- They had £2 million to allocate to local authorities.
- This money could be spent on job creation schemes and developing public services.
- The money would not be invested in private companies, because the Government did not want to appear to be subsidising businesses during the depression.
- Further funds were allocated in 1936 (£3 million) and 1937 (£3.5 million).

In 1937 the Special Areas Amendment Act gave tax breaks to businesses that chose to set up in the special areas.

Economic realignment

While the global economic crisis had a huge impact on the British economy during the 1930s, so did a longer-term, less visible process – technological change. A better educated workforce and more investment going into research and development saw the development of new light industries based on chemicals, electronics, manufacturing and engineering. This, along with the arrival of multinational companies like the Ford automobile company in Britain meant that while heavy industry (coal, steel, ship building) declined, other new light industries flourished. These included:

- The car industry: concentrated around the Midlands and Oxford. In 1918 there were nearly 200 car manufacturers in Britain but ten years later, just over a quarter of those firms remained. Many had gone bust during the post-war slump and others had been bought by larger car companies. Most cars produced in the 1920s were prohibitively expensive, the Rover 10/25 cost £250 in 1929 (approximately £11,000 today) and was far beyond anything a working-class family could afford. Within five years, however, car prices had fallen considerably. An Austin Seven (a small family car) cost £125 and the Morris Minor SV was the first £100 car, going into production in 1931. Cars at these prices were affordable for middle-class motorists and if working-class families wanted to purchase one, there were numerous secondhand car sellers who would sell at anywhere between £40 and £70 on average. Some working-class families formed syndicates where they shared the cost and usage of the car.
- The chemical industry: one of Britain's largest companies, Imperial Chemical Industries (ICI), was formed in 1926 from several smaller firms. Brunner Mond, Nobel Industries, United Alkali and British Dyestuffs combined in order to match the strength of European and American chemical conglomerates. The company made dyes, explosives, fertilisers, pesticides, metals and paints. In 1926 it had 33,000 employees and by the eve of

the Second World War it was heavily involved in Britain's re-armament programme. ICI research during the 1930s resulted in the invention of polythene, Perspex and plastic.

- Consumer goods: low interest rates and easier access to mortgages led to a rapid extension in home ownership during the 1930s. This, combined with an extension in council house ownership, created new demand for furniture, carpets, curtains and wallpaper. Most new homes had running water, gas and mains electricity, creating new demand for electrical goods such as cookers, fridges, wireless radios and electric lights. Not only was there a growth in new manufacturers to provide these products, but also retailers such as Currys who sold them to a newly affluent market.
- The development of mass advertising in this period in newspapers and magazines and also on roadside billboards helped to develop new markets for products and create a new advertising industry.

The three sources below and on page 181 give different interpretations on the Great Depression in Britain during the 1930s. You should begin by reading each one and listing the main points made and the evidence used to support them. Then answer the following questions:

1 In what way do Sources F and G agree and disagree?
2 In what way do Sources G and H agree and disagree?
3 Using material from the sources and your own knowledge, state to what extent Britain was in economic crisis throughout the decade.

Interpretations: Britain and the Great Depression

To what extent was Britain in economic crisis during the 1930s?

There is a range of opinion over the impact of the Great Depression on Britain. Some historians argue that the Labour Government and the National Government were unable or unwilling to effectively intervene. Other historians argue that the depression was in fact not as long or as severe in Britain as it was in other countries.

Source F From *The Slump: Britain in the Great Depression* by J. Stevenson and C. Cook, (Routledge), 2013, p. 68.

From the collapse of the post-war boom in 1921 until the first year of the Second World War, Great Britain suffered unemployment on an unprecedented scale, with never less than a million people out of work. Depression during the 1920s gave way to the slump which followed the Wall Street Crash of 1929. Britain's worst years were experienced in the aftermath of the financial and political crisis of August 1931. From 1931 until 1935, the number of unemployed never fell below 2 million people and in the winter of 1932–33 reached its highest point at just under 3 million. Moreover, as the official figures were based upon insured workers they excluded categories such as the self-employed, agricultural workers, and married workers who did not sign on for the dole. As a result the total unemployed was almost certainly higher than official figures suggest.

Source G From *Britain, 1929–1998* by C. Rowe, (Heinemann), 2004, pp. 7–8.

These regional differences represent not so much conflicting opinions as conflicting truths; it is a matter of fact, not opinion, that some areas endured misery while other parts of Britain lived in much more comfortable circumstances. What historians have disagreed about is the overall performance of the British economy in the 1930s whether it was overall a time of economic failure and decline, except for a few pockets of affluence, or a time of economic success, except for some areas of special hardship ... The gulf between the old industrial England and the new suburban England has sometimes been characterised as the 'North-South Divide' but this is too simplistic. There were plenty of examples of the depressed 'North' in the south-east of England; and many pockets of the affluent 'South' in parts of the North and the Midlands.

Source H From *Key Themes of the Twentieth Century* by P. Sauvain, (Stanley Thornes), 1996, p. 50.

In the end, recovery came when people began to spend more money on products made in Britain, such as electrical goods. Twelve times as many people were using electricity in 1938 compared with 1920. Buying a car boosted the coal and steel industries as well as the growing motor industry.

Three million new houses were built in the 1930s, most of them in the Midlands and the South-East where light industry was booming, rather than in the heavy industrial districts in the North. The housing boom reduced unemployment in the brick, glass and timber industries as well as in the building trade. It also brought an increase in demand to the light industries themselves, since new house-owners were more likely to buy carpets, paint, light fittings, furniture, domestic appliances and electrical goods. At the same time people in employment were having much smaller families while their wages were increasing. This meant their living standards were rising. Successive governments also improved the country's social services.

KEY DATES: ECONOMIC DEVELOPMENTS, 1919–39	
1919–20	Short economic boom
1920–21	Economic recession
1921 Aug	Sir Eric Geddes appointed to cut government expenditure
1925 May	The Gold Standard Act is passed, returning Britain to a fixed exchange rate system
1929 Oct	The Wall Street Crash
1929–34	The Great Depression
1934–39	Economic recovery

WORKING TOGETHER

From what we have seen so far in this chapter, it is too simplistic to say that all of Britain suffered from an economic crisis throughout the decade. Instead, economic problems varied by region and over time. Below are a number of suggested explanations as to why the depression impacted on Britain in the way that it did.

Divide into pairs or small groups and allocate one factor per group. Each pair/group should research and develop its explanation/factor using this textbook and other resources such as the internet, and report back to the rest of the class.
- The long-term causes of the depression.
- The causes of regional decline.
- The reasons for recovery.
- The actions of the government.
- International factors in the depression.

LOOK AGAIN

In this section we have explored the changes to the British economy from 1914 to 1939. Look back at this section and evaluate why the war had such a huge impact on the British economy. Would Britain have experienced economic problems even if she had stayed out of the war?

2 Social developments, 1914–39

War, boom and depression not only had an impact on Britain's politics and its economy but also profoundly changed British society in the quarter-century between the start of the First World War and the start of the second. Not only did life and work opportunities for Britain's women change but, despite economic crisis in the first part of the decade, the 1930s were an era of rising living standards for most of the population. In the wealthier parts of the country this meant that there was greater leisure time, access to new forms of sports, culture and entertainment and more scope for holidays and car travel. However, even in the poverty-stricken 'special areas', unemployed men and women and their families were able to visit the cinema or sporting events in greater numbers than ever before. The beginnings of 'teenage' culture (though the term was not used at the time) can be seen in the 1930s with young people spending money on clothes, records and enjoying themselves at dances and on day trips. Consumer electrical goods filled the homes of middle-class families throughout the decade, owing to the greater number of homes that were electrified, many being built in new suburban housing estates. These consumers were being supplied by new supermarket chains such as Marks and Spencer and Sainsbury's and the advertising and public relations industries helped to create growing consumer demand for new products.

Changes in the role of women during and after the war

What effect did the war have on women's roles and responsibilities in Britain?

By the mid-1920s, it appeared as if many of the demands of the women's suffrage movement (see pages 106–12) made before the war had been met. The extension of the franchise, the development of new educational and career opportunities and the election of female MPs to Parliament had all begun to change the role of women in British society. However, the war had involved hardships and sacrifices for many British women and in the inter-war decades it was predominantly wealthy middle- and upper-class women who benefited from the new rights and freedoms. Poverty, poor health and hard working conditions were still a fact of life for many working-class women.

Women's work

At the start of the war there had been a large female industrial workforce 5.7 million strong. There were 200,000 women employed in the metals and chemicals industries that were essential to the war effort. By 1918 there were over 1 million in these two fields alone. In Britain's main cordite (explosives) factory at Gretna, 11,000 women worked to create explosives. Women also took roles in public life that had always been the preserve of men, such as working on the railways and trams.

Few women who took jobs in factories were union members and fewer still were encouraged by their male colleagues to join. Many were used to being paid not by the hour or day but by piece work, meaning that their wages were dependent on a high work rate. Many male workers were suspicious of this and believed that the arrival of women in the workplace would result in piece-work rates being applied to all workers.

Piece work – The practice of paying a worker for every item they create, not on an hourly rate. This can result in lower wages but conversely piece work helped improve the standard of living in agriculture in the 1930s. It was often used in industry as a temporary incentive to increase productivity on big orders without needing to take on extra workers who did not have the skills needed. This could increase earnings substantially while such an order was being filled.

▲ Women workers packing fuse heads in the Coventry Ordnance Works during the First World War.

By 1915, partly as a result of Lloyd George's compromises with the trade union movement, hundreds of thousands of female workers had entered munitions factories. In engineering works where cannons, machine guns, tanks and other machinery were made, 800,000 women found work. Thousands of women had also worked as auxiliaries, drivers, telephonists, signallers and nurses on the Western Front. In 1914, 40,000 women travelled with the British army to France as nurses as part of the Voluntary Aid Detachment, living in the same conditions as the fighting men. The following year the Women's Hospital Corps was established and two years later in 1917 the Women's Auxiliary Army Corps which divided women's roles into four services: cookery, clerical, mechanical and miscellaneous.

In 1914, the WSPU and the NUWSS (see page 107) suspended their campaigns for women's suffrage. The WSPU, which was controlled by Christabel Pankhurst from Paris, adopted an overtly patriotic and nationalistic stance, publishing a new newspaper in 1915 entitled *Britannia*. In large part they were motivated by the belief that a victory for Britain was a victory for civilised values and democracy and the hope that cooperation in the war effort would result in female suffrage when the war ended.

Franchise

In March 1918 the Representation of the People Act enfranchised women over the age of 30 if they were ratepayers or married to ratepayers occupying premises valued at £5 a year. Female graduates voting in a university election were also included. This meant some of the poorest women over 30 were still excluded. Female voters, however, now comprised 43 per cent of the electorate (8.4 million voters) in the December election that year. In the same Act, all men were enfranchised at the age of 21 and men aged between 19 and 21 who had seen active service in the war also got the vote. Had women been granted the same rights they would have made up the majority of the electorate due to the high losses of men during the war and the Government feared this might delay the legislation in Parliament. Britain's women did not receive the vote on the same terms as men until the Representation of the People Act 1928.

Employment opportunities

The lives of working-class women in Britain in the aftermath of the First World War were often extremely hard. Average life expectancy for women in Britain was 60 in 1921 but high incidences of death in childbirth (a working-class woman would on average have six pregnancies and produce four children) and a greater susceptibility among young working-class women to tuberculosis meant that average life expectancy for poorer women was 54.

The First World War had enabled many women to make considerable gains in the workplace due to the need for the entire civilian population to be mobilised for war work. The decade after the war saw many of the gains that women had made overturned as a result of the harsh economic realities Britain faced after 1918. Wartime employment was only required as long as the conflict continued. In addition the return of fighting men from the First World War forced out of the workplace many women who had acquired and often enjoyed well-paid skilled work. Consequently the numbers of employed women returned to 1914 levels when the war ended (approximately 5.7 million). The return of men to the workplace and the home seemed to herald a return to the traditional ideas about gender that had existed before the war and the struggle for female suffrage. When women did work they returned to their traditional occupations such as service or clerical work.

In the first three decades of the twentieth century, working in service as a maid, cook or cleaner was the largest source of employment for working-class women. In 1918, 1.25 million women were 'in service'. The work was unpopular and most women who experienced it were keen to find other employment if possible. However, opportunities were limited because of lower levels of education for women, and also because of prevailing ideas about what was 'women's work'.

In the 1920s there were clear gender roles in employment. Employers hired women for factory work or service if they were working class, or clerical work if they were educated (often this meant that the artisan working class or the lower middle class filled these roles). Clerical work was the biggest growth area for female employment in the 1920s with over 1 million employed as typists or clerks by 1921 and a further 300,000 ten years later.

From 1911 onwards specialist domestic schools were established to teach women the essential housework skills to equip them for their future role as homemakers. This very narrow type of education limited the economic opportunities of much of the female population. The only other opportunities for working-class women to earn a living was through sweated labour in the new light manufacturing that had developed after the war. Much of the work available was poorly paid and as unemployment benefit for women was set at

Light manufacturing – The industrial production of consumer goods such as furniture, radios and bicycles.

a lower rate than for men, there was no incentive for employers to offer better rates of pay. Two-thirds of all work done by working-class women was done from home, a system known as 'domestic outwork'. Baking, brewing, sewing and piece work was combined with household tasks and caring for children.

Middle-class women

For middle-class women between the wars there was some gradual improvement in opportunities for education, advancement and a career, particularly in fields such as education, law, science and the civil service. This change was a result of the Sex Disqualification (Removal) Act 1919, preventing the barring from a career in law or the civil service on the basis of gender. The Act gave women greater opportunities when applying for work in these fields and there is some evidence to suggest that male attitudes were gradually starting to change as well.

Ivy Williams, the first woman to be called to the English Bar in 1922 had first qualified as a lawyer twenty years earlier, when the Law Journal described her ambitions as 'futile'. In 1922 however, the journal had changed its editorial opinion and called her appointment as a barrister, 'one of the most memorable days in the long annals of the legal profession'.

The condition of the working classes during the 1930s

Why were some regions of Britain more poverty-stricken than others after 1929?

During the economic depression that began in 1929, it was the British working classes who were disproportionately affected, especially those in poorer areas dependent on declining industries. In this section we will explore how life for the working classes changed throughout the decade and how it varied across the country.

Regional divisions

While initially most of the country saw large increases in unemployment, the problem of long-term unemployment was regionalised. This meant that areas such as the south-east and the Midlands saw unemployment decline again by the early to mid-1930s, and other parts of Britain saw joblessness linger on until the eve of the Second World War. For parts of the country heavily reliant on outdated industries and struggling to compete (see Figure 1, page 186), the 1930s was a decade of crisis.

During the decade, very little was done to alleviate the long-term structural economic problems of these regions, even though many were designated 'special areas' under the Special Areas Act 1934 (see page 179).

In the south-east of England light manufacturing was accompanied by a housing boom and thousands of new jobs were created in the construction industries. In the south-east, Midlands and Oxfordshire a new car industry developed, with companies such as Morris, Austin and Ford creating new jobs. This demonstrated that the regions of Britain that were able to diversify and adapt did not suffer high levels of poverty and hardship.

WORK TOGETHER

There is an immense amount written online and offline about the changing employment and educational opportunities for women in the inter-war years. In pairs focus on one of the following topic areas:
- Women's wartime work.
- Life for working-class women between the wars.
- Growing educational opportunities for women between the wars.

Make notes on your topic area and then use these to explain the experience of women in inter-war Britain to another group in the class.

English Bar – The legal profession in England and Wales.

NOTE-MAKING

One easy way to understand how poverty and deprivation in Britain were different from region to region is to create a map. Draw an outline of the British Isles and annotate it with any regional differences in levels of poverty outlined in this section and from your own research. It is worth plotting the industrial heartlands from Figure 1 (page 186) so you can identify links between traditional heavy industries and the areas most affected by the Great Depression.

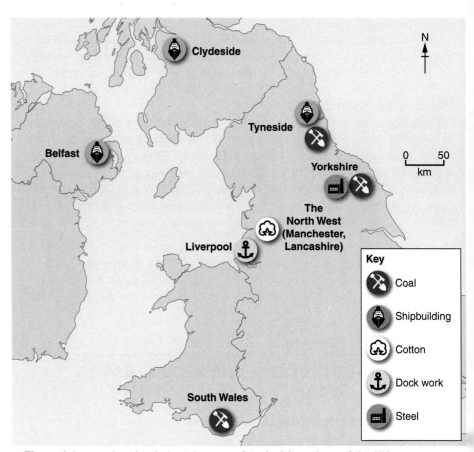

▲ **Figure 1** A map showing industries associated with regions of the UK.

Changing attitudes in the 1920s and 1930s

The experience of mass unemployment in the 1920s and 1930s had a profound effect on attitudes and beliefs in the inter-war years and beyond. Unemployment on such a scale (reaching 2.5 million by 1933) had never been seen in Britain before and for much of the rest of the twentieth century tackling it was seen by both political parties, the trade unions and the British people as the primary goal of the economy. Politicians of both parties, including future prime ministers Clement Attlee and Harold Macmillan, believed that the state had a much larger role to play in the alleviation of poverty and the management of the economy. Intellectuals such as Sidney and Beatrice Webb of the Fabian Society (see page 150) believed that the Great Depression was proof that free-market capitalism was redundant and irrational. They argued that an economy free of state control would only produce short booms followed by long slumps. Instead, the type of state intervention witnessed during the First World War would be necessary in future to create a planned economy that served society's needs.

In the most economically deprived parts of Britain a small minority of the long-term unemployed abandoned their trust in both political parties and gravitated towards the political extremes of fascism or communism (see pages 149–51). However, in many instances, political apathy and despair were the products of long-term unemployment. Jobless men were forced to contend not only with poverty but with endless days of boredom and meaninglessness spent in working men's clubs, cinemas, allotments and libraries. The sense of pride that many men had in their ability to provide for their families was lost and unemployment ceased to be a temporary phenomenon for many, becoming instead a way of life.

The 'Hungry Thirties'

In November 1931, the National Government instituted a family 'means test' for the payment of unemployment benefit after claimants had received 26 weeks of assistance. Thereafter claimants were required to register at a local labour exchange before any new benefits could be authorised. The local Public Assistance Committee would investigate the claimant's circumstances to make sure they were not trying to abuse the system.

The means test was the most controversial measure introduced by the Government during the depression and resulted in an outcry from the Labour Party, the trade union movement and hundreds of thousands of unemployed families.

The means test disqualified 'short-time workers': men who worked occasional days in collieries or shipyards but were dependent on welfare payments the rest of the time. The reforms therefore affected the most deprived parts of the country such as Tyneside and south Wales, where most workers worked reduced hours.

All forms of household income were taken into account when assessing what rate of relief a claimant was entitled to, which forced some children of working age to leave the family home. Many low-income families, however, relied on the earnings of all the adults in the family living under one roof, sharing what wages or benefits they had in order to survive. Unemployed parents with adult children who had jobs would lose their benefits if their children lived with them, even though their children's wages would not provide for the family.

The writer, J. B. Priestly in his book *English Journey*, wrote about the depressed areas of the country, describing them as:

'Slums, … a cynically devastated countryside, sooty dismal little towns, and still sootier grim fortress-like cities. This England makes up the larger part of the Midlands and the North and exists everywhere; but it has not been added to and has no new life poured into it'.

In the depressed areas of the country hunger was a persistent factor in the lives of many unemployed families and a survey in 1933 concluded that unemployment benefits were insufficient to provide a minimum diet recommended by the Ministry of Health. It was only during the 1930s that a real scientific understanding about the effect of nutrition shortages emerged and the causes of deficiency diseases like rickets were understood. For many families in these areas meat was a rarity, as often were fresh vegetables. On average far more working-class women went hungry than men when there was insufficient food to go round. Mothers would ensure their children ate first and men as the primary breadwinners would eat too, meaning that women's health suffered disproportionately.

Instead staples like bread, margarine and tea made up most meals. Because most money was diverted towards food, there was little left for anything else, meaning that homes, clothes and possessions became progressively more worn and shabby and were irreplaceable if they were damaged or lost. While middle-class families during the 1930s might have been able to access consumer credit, many poorer working-class families managed to make ends meet by getting 'tick' from the local greengrocers and in poorer areas the local pawnbroker enabled families to borrow money.

'Tick' – An informal 'tab' or credit with a local shopkeeper, enabling customers to take goods and pay for them when they could afford them.

Hunger marches and the NUWM

The desperation of workers and their families in the most deprived parts of the country from 1921 onwards had led the Communist Party of Great Britain to establish the National Unemployed Workers' Movement. The organisation, which was boycotted by the Labour Party because of its links with the communists, organised a series of marches to protest the means test throughout the 1930s, which quickly came to be christened the 'Hunger Marches'. The protesters were unemployed men from the depressed regions of Britain who walked to London, encountering both support and opposition along the route. The most famous of the marches was from Jarrow in Tyneside in 1936, called by the marchers the 'Jarrow Crusade'.

The north-east of England felt particularly forgotten and ignored by the far wealthier south-east and London, and the marchers sought to bring to the attention of the Government the scale of the deprivation and poverty in which the region was mired. Many marchers recall an unsympathetic reception from members of the public and office workers when they arrived in London, who looked upon them as a troublemaking and potentially violent group.

George Orwell in his book *The Road to Wigan Pier*, remarked on the power that unemployment had on the working classes to quell dissent:

'During the past dozen years the English working class have grown servile with a rather horrifying rapidity. It was bound to happen, for the frightful weapon of unemployment has cowed them. Before the war their economic position was comparatively strong, for though there was no dole to fall back upon, there was not much unemployment, and the power of the boss class was not so obvious as it is now. A man did not see ruin staring him in the face every time he cheeked a 'toff', and naturally he did cheek a 'toff' whenever it seemed safe to do so.'

From *The Road to Wigan Pier* by George Orwell, (Penguin Classics), 2012, p.141.

▲ A hunger march from northern areas of England to London, May 1931.

The growth of the media

How did new forms of entertainment enhance the quality of life for British people between the wars?

Mass popular culture developed throughout the inter-war years. A large, predominantly working-class audience with a growing disposable income sought entertainment, escapism and excitement through the new medium of cinema. In addition to this, radio, publishing and popular music gave ordinary British people a far richer and more varied culture, accessible at a lower cost than at any other time previously.

The development of cinema

Cinema was the most popular form of mass entertainment during the inter-war period. In the 1920s and 1930s the British film industry came under pressure from the much larger and more powerful American industry based in Hollywood (in 1914 one-quarter of all films shown in Britain were made by British film companies, but just over a decade later in 1925 this had fallen to 5 per cent). Whereas in the nineteenth century British audiences might have enjoyed books about the adventures of imperial heroes by H. Rider Haggard and Rudyard Kipling, in the early twentieth century they were much more likely to enjoy American films about cowboys and gangsters. Many commentators reflected popular concerns that British culture was being 'Americanised'.

In 1927 the British Government passed the Cinematograph Films Act, ensuring that a certain percentage of films had to be British. The year 1927 was also significant because it was the year that 'talkies', movies with spoken word sound, were first produced. Most of the output of British film studios between the wars were films that provided entertainment for their audiences. Romances, thrillers, crime dramas and historical pictures dominated. In the popular press, many cinemas in the immediate post-war period were regarded as 'seedy' and dirty places. Throughout the 1920s, cinemas became more gentrified, 'respectable' places to visit. In the 1920s and 1930s hundreds of elaborate 'picture palaces' were built, attracting affluent middle-class audiences.

Cinema ticket sales grew during the post-war slump of the 1920s and again during the Great Depression. The cinema offered unemployed men and women one of the few chances of escapism from the mundane realities of unemployed life. In London a study in 1931 showed that unemployed people tended to watch films on average 2.6 times a week, normally being daytime showings because of the cheaper tickets. In Glasgow 80 per cent of the city's jobless saw a film once a week during the depression, indicating that visiting the cinema had become an important part of life for people caught in long-term unemployment and deprivation. In the South Wales valleys, the area of highest poverty in the country during the early 1930s, improvised cinemas were created in the miners' institutes. Some institutes only charged what out-of-work miners could pay for tickets.

NOTE-MAKING
The focus here in your note-taking is on quality of life, so one easy way to create clear notes is to draw up a table with one column featuring a form of entertainment or media, and a second column showing the impact it had on quality of life. You might want to focus on the size of audiences, or the availability of the medium.

Miners' institutes – Social clubs and educational institutions for miners within mining communities.

The development of radio and popular music

The inventor of modern radio technology Guglielmo Marconi found the government to be obstructive when he proposed setting up a radio station, but it eventually allowed the British Broadcasting Company (BBC) to form in 1922. It was licensed by the Government and so right from the start the organisation had a close relationship with the state, and this would often have an impact on the way news, music and entertainment was transmitted, first as radio programmes and later as television. This close relationship meant that radio programmes often reflected the values of the government and the BBC, not necessarily the interests of the listener. As a result, often BBC broadcasts did not reflect the quality of life experienced by many British people throughout the 1920s and 1930s.

In 1927 the corporation was given a royal charter and effectively became a publicly owned state broadcaster, though it retained independence over its editorial content, with John Reith becoming the first director-general.

The BBC's mission as set out by Reith was to 'inform, educate and entertain', and throughout the 1920s and 1930s the corporation broadcast lectures, concerts and programmes thought to be beneficial to ordinary people and to improve their understanding of the world they lived in. Reith claimed that the BBC should 'give the public slightly better than it thinks it likes'. The effects that this policy had on quality of life in Britain were mixed. First, Reith believed the BBC's role was to give working-class people access to the kind of culture that the upper and middle classes enjoyed. The extent to which this improved their quality of life is debatable. Many found the programmes they listened to interesting and informative, but from the 1920s onwards the kinds of popular culture pastimes millions of British people engaged in (listening to jazz and swing music, going to dance halls) shows a demand for entertainment that Reith did not wish to broadcast.

John Reith, 1889–1971

Reith was the first director-general of the BBC and later Minister of Information in Chamberlain's wartime government. He was viewed by his subordinates at the BBC as an autocratic and domineering personality who had strong beliefs about what the British public should be allowed to hear on the radio. He was deeply religious and conservative in his values, and strongly disapproved of King Edward VIII's decision to abdicate to marry Wallis Simpson. Reith wanted the BBC to be impartial in politics and clashed with the Government during the General Strike. He insisted that all news from both sides of the dispute was reported without comment and tried to arrange for a broadcast by the Labour Party, but this was vetoed by the Government. The Government also pressured him to refuse a request from the Archbishop of Canterbury to broadcast an appeal for a compromise. As with many important public figures during the early 1930s, he had a degree of sympathy for Italian fascism and German national socialism, though as war drew closer at the end of the decade his views changed. Reith served in the Government during the Second World War and was given a peerage for his services.

Dance halls

▲ *'That Haunting Melody'*, an artists' impression of a fashionable London club in the 1930s

The 1930s saw the first major introduction of American music into Britain with the success of jazz and swing music. There were some 20,000 dance bands in Britain by 1930 according to the magazine *Melody Maker*, and this demonstrated the immense popularity of the dance hall during the decade. American music only grew in popularity. British dance bands were influenced by American jazz band leaders like Duke Ellington and Count Basie.

The development of mass publishing

Improving rates of literacy throughout the first decades of the twentieth century meant that by the 1930s there was a much larger market for cheap fiction and non-fiction paperback books. A more informed public with a growing interest in world affairs, economics, philosophy, psychology and science bought books in far greater quantities during the 1930s than ever before. The return to prosperity in the second half of the decade and the growing concern over world events fuelled a desire for escapism in literature and popular fiction, which also benefited the growing market for cheap paperbacks.

Victor Gollancz

Gollancz was the son of European Jewish émigrés to Britain and before entering publishing he worked as a teacher. He established a mail order subscription service called the Left Book Club, which sent out to its members a monthly book that gave a socialist perspective on economics, politics or culture. By 1936 it had nearly 60,000 members and in 1937 it published the first interview in the West with Mao Zedong, the Chinese communist leader, in the book *Red Star Over China*.

Allen Lane

Allen Lane founded Penguin Books in 1935, first selling cheap paperback 'classics' from a vending machine at Victoria Station. Lane created a non-fiction imprint, Pelican Books, in 1937.

LOOK AGAIN

In this section we have seen how British society changed throughout the war years and the inter-war decades. Look back at the section and evaluate which groups benefited most throughout this period and which social groups were most disadvantaged between 1914 and 1939.

KEY DATES: SOCIAL DEVELOPMENTS, 1915–36

1915	Women enter war munitions work
1918 March	Representation of the People Act
1919 April	Addison Housing Act
1919 Dec	Sex Disqualification (Removal) Act
1922 Oct	BBC founded
1928 July	Representation of the People Act 1928
1936 Oct	The Jarrow Crusade

3 Social policies, 1914–39

The inter-war years were a period of economic instability and unemployment, but also a time in which there were significant improvements in the provision of healthcare, education, housing and social welfare.

Inter-war social reforms

How did social reform improve the lives of British people between the wars?

During the life of Lloyd George's post-war coalition government there was considerable demand for social reform in unemployment insurance, old-age pensions and housing. Lloyd George had talked about rewarding the men returning home from war and the Liberal Party before the war had been the pioneers of social reform.

The growth in popularity of the Labour Party offering wide-ranging social reform, which appealed to working-class voters, meant that the coalition Liberals had to introduce reforms or become obsolete. Between 1900 and 1918 there was a major shift in the political consensus about welfare provision. Until 1914, most welfare had been administered by a patchwork of local, voluntary and charitable organisations. This reflected the Victorian view that private charity was the best way of helping the poor. However, in the early part of the twentieth century, partly as a result of the growth of wartime state intervention, it became widely accepted that the state had a much bigger part to play in poor relief. This view was influential in the development of reforms in housing, education and welfare in the inter-war period.

Housing reform

The Housing Act 1919, introduced by the housing minister Dr Christopher Addison (christened the Addison Act), gave new powers to local authorities to build homes. The Act was based on a 1917 report which stated that in the post-war era new homes would be needed in order to improve the quality of public health among much of the population. The poor health of recruits who volunteered to fight in the war was blamed on the large numbers of slum houses across Britain.

In 1923 Baldwin's Minister of Health, Neville Chamberlain, passed a new housing act that provided state subsidies to private house builders to build new homes, adding 438,000 new homes by the end of the decade. The Wheatley Act in 1924 extended this policy to local councils to build new homes and in 1930 the Greenwood Housing Act gave councils subsidies to demolish slums and build new homes. By the eve of the war, a quarter of a million slums had been cleared.

House building became an important part of Britain's recovery. A 'Cheap Money' policy instituted by the National Government meant that interest rates were kept at low levels throughout the 1930s. This allowed more people to buy houses and the number of new houses built dramatically increased (see Figure 2).

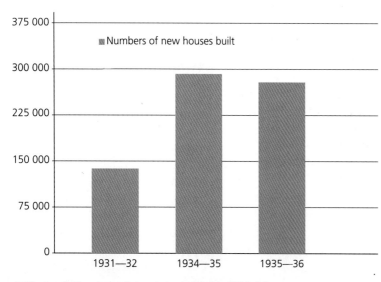

▲ **Figure 2** Number of new houses built, 1931–36.

The total value of mortgages taken out in 1930 was £316 million, but by 1937 it was £636 million, with an extra half a million borrowers buying new homes.

On average real incomes rose by 19 per cent between 1932 and 1937, industrial production rose by 46 per cent, Gross National Product rose by 23 per cent and exports increased by 28 per cent.

Education reforms, 1918–39

Education for most children in Britain by 1918 was provided by the Local Education Authorities (LEAs), which had been created in 1902 by the Balfour Education Act. There were 328 authorities which provided two types of schools:

- Elementary – providing children with a basic education up to the age of fourteen.
- Secondary and technical schools – educating children to the age of sixteen.

The authorities paid teachers' wages, provided free school meals to children from poor families, ensured the upkeep of school buildings and monitored teaching standards and qualifications.

The Act also created another kind of secondary education, grant-funded grammar schools. Grammar schools provided a higher standard of education and places were highly sought after. The schools used entrance exams to select the most talented pupils. Overall, secondary schools were the preserve of middle-class children, even on the eve of the Second World War only 13 per cent of working-class children aged thirteen and above were still in school.

In 1914 Local Education Authorities were permitted to offer free school meals to poor children. For many children from working-class families, the costs of schooling and the need to help provide for the family were such that after primary schooling the children were sent out to work.

In the aftermath of the First World War, the Government embarked on ambitious educational reforms. The Education Act 1918 was based on the Lewis Report compiled during the war. The report recommended:

- A school leaving age of fourteen.
- Thereafter eight hours a week of 'continuation' education up to the age of eighteen. A new tier of county colleges would be established in order to provide this training, however by 1959 they had not been created.
- Employers were obliged to release their young employees to attend college, normally on one day a week.
- The curriculum was divided between 'practical instruction' for less able children to prepare them for the workplace and 'advanced instruction' for more intelligent children.

Most of the costs of education were transferred away from the LEAs to central government, making the 1918 Act a watershed moment in the history of British education, as control over school financing was centralised. This process of centralisation would continue throughout the century. It resulted in an improvement in teachers' salaries and pensions, which the Government hoped would improve school standards.

Welfare reforms: unemployment insurance

The Unemployment Insurance Act of 1920 was Lloyd George's last major welfare reform. It extended social welfare in the following ways:

- It extended National Insurance from the 4 million workers covered in 1919 to 11.4 million in 1921.
- It increased benefits to 15s for unemployed men and 12s for unemployed women. These payments were still low compared to average wages. Low-paid workers such as bus drivers earned about 60s a week. Women were paid much less and had an average wage of about 10s a week.

In 1919, the existing National Insurance scheme covered only 2.5 million out of Britain's 20 million workers. The reforms extended that provision to 12 million workers. The state's role became significantly larger than originally envisaged. In 1911 Lloyd George assumed that insurance would be self-financing as payments were based on contributions from employers and employees. However, the 1920–21 Acts covered millions of non-contributors who had been affected by mass unemployment. Indeed, the Act created a state-funded 'dole' which was available to the unemployed without a means test. This extension of state spending was justified by:

- the need to support the unprecedentedly high levels of unemployment
- fears that extreme and widespread poverty might lead to revolution, as it had done in Russia in 1917
- the popular desire to support soldiers who had fought and risked their lives for Britain in the First World War.

Nonetheless, as unemployment receded during the 1920s, there was no reduction in the state's commitment to welfare provision.

In 1921 a second Act was introduced. Mass unemployment had placed such a huge burden on public finances that the amount paid out had to be reduced. Therefore payments to the unemployed under the age of eighteen were reduced and payments to unemployed women continued to be less than those of men.

The Conservative Party between 1924 and 1929 was keen to reduce the welfare bill and though official inquiries demonstrated that there was little abuse of the system, the welfare budget was £35 million in debt when MacDonald came to power.

Figure 3 Unemployment Insurance Acts throughout the 1920s.

Legislation	Impact on the unemployed
Unemployment Insurance Act (1920)	Unemployment insurance is extended to nearly all workers (11.4 million). Benefits for unemployed men and women increased.
Unemployment Insurance Act (1921)	Payments to under 18s were reduced, as were payments to unemployed women.
Unemployment Insurance Act (1924)	Means testing for benefits is not introduced in this bill, but claimants were obliged to demonstrate that they were actively seeking work.
Unemployment Insurance Act (1927)	Means testing for benefits introduced.
Unemployment Insurance Act (1930)	Abolished the need for claimants to demonstrate they were actively seeking work before they could receive benefits.

Public health reforms

In previous chapters we have seen the development of public healthcare provision by the state. The inter-war years saw a continued development in this provision. It was strongly influenced by the scientific advances that had been achieved by the end of the First World War.

Developments in healthcare, 1918–29

Throughout the period the fragmented system of healthcare provision and the antiquated Poor Law institutions increasingly became subject to local and national government coordination and control. Because enormous changes in the provision of healthcare took place after the Second World War (see Chapter 8), changes during the inter-war period are often overlooked. In the decade that followed the end of the First World War the role of government in healthcare provision significantly expanded.

In 1919, the government established a new Ministry of Health, shifting the responsibility for healthcare away from the Poor Law hospitals. The idea of centralising the provision of healthcare was first proposed by the socialist Fabian Society (see page 79) before the war. The Fabians believed that centralised, state-planned healthcare was the only way to significantly improve health in Britain.

Tuberculosis

The most serious public health problem in the immediate aftermath of the First World War was the deadly disease tuberculosis (TB). Before the war, the government had set up TB sanatoria funded by National Insurance in order to slow down the spread of the disease. The Ministry of Health Act 1919 also created the Medical Research Council, led by Lord Richard Haldane, which was established in order to research the causes of TB. The council was an official, publicly funded body but independent from government control – ministers had no power over the MRC's medical or scientific findings. The Tuberculosis Act of 1921 made the provision of TB sanatoria by local authorities compulsory.

The Dawson Report

The Labour Party in 1919 was the first British political party to advocate a free and comprehensive national health service. In the following year a major government study, the Dawson Report, was commissioned into the organisation of health services. It recommended a network of state-funded clinics and hospitals, organised by the government. The Dawson Report's recommendations were echoed by voices from the public and the medical profession. The report's recommendations were not implemented, ultimately due to their financial cost. Britain was no longer the wealthy country it had been before the First World War and had emerged from the conflict saddled with debt, making national healthcare provision prohibitively expensive.

Depression, recovery and public health

Between 1929 and 1939, overall public health seemed to be improving, with key indicators such as child mortality in decline. However, for areas afflicted by extreme poverty the picture was quite different. In the 'special areas' (see page 179), which were the poorest and most deprived in Britain, the number of women who died in childbirth was higher. This figure can be directly linked to poverty and malnutrition, because when a charitable body, the National Birthday Trust, distributed free food to expectant mothers in these areas in 1934 the number of deaths began to decline. The Ministry of Health did very little to alleviate health problems in the poorest parts of Britain during the depression; instead civil servants from the ministry avoided discussing the link between poverty and mortality. They placed responsibility for poor nutrition on housewives, claiming that poor health was the result of a lack of knowledge of basic nutrition, rather than a result of regional poverty.

In the second half of the decade there was an improvement in maternal mortality rates in general due to an overall improvement in the economy, but a study in 1936 showed that one-tenth of Britain's population was chronically underfed and half the population had some type of deficiency. Both these factors led to ill-health and shorter life expectancy among the poorest people in Britain.

Arguments for a national health service

By the mid-1930s ideas about the health system seemed to have shifted in favour of far greater state involvement in health provision. Campaigners for a universal system of healthcare argued that the complex system meant that different ailments were treated by different bodies in an almost arbitrary manner. For example, county councils provided healthcare for psychiatric patients, whereas district councils provided isolation hospitals for illnesses like tuberculosis. By 1938 voluntary hospitals accounted for one-third of all hospital beds, and the poorest and oldest of patients tended to end up in the worst kinds of hospitals, the workhouses.

Chamberlain's reforms in 1929, designed to force the Poor Law institutions out of healthcare provision, were only very gradually implemented throughout the 1930s. In 1937, 466 hospitals still remained under the control of the Public Assistance Boards. In London the council took the biggest steps towards taking over hospitals, with 76 hospitals being taken over by 1931 alone.

There was a growing awareness not just among campaigners but in government circles too, that healthcare provision in Britain on the eve of the Second World War was still very chaotic. A Political and Economic Planning (PEP) report published in 1937 entitled 'The British Health Services' stated that:

'a bewildering variety of agencies, official and unofficial, have been created during the past two or three generations to work for health mainly by attacking specific diseases and disabilities as they occur'.

The British Medical Association in 1930 and 1938 joined in the call for a nationally organised health service and there was a clear demand for change even before the war broke out.

By 1939 the Ministry of Health was discussing plans for regional health boards centrally managed by the government. Additionally, the medical journal *The Lancet* argued for a national system of healthcare.

Britain by 1939

By the eve of the Second World War British society was still divided along clear and unambiguous class lines. The Great Depression and the government's response to it had caused immense hardship in the poorest and most economically deprived parts of the country, but for many British people, the 1930s had been a decade of rising living standards. The introduction of health, education, housing and welfare reforms and the experience of a rapid economic recovery after 1934 saw many British people enjoying a significantly better lifestyle in 1939 than they had in 1914. In addition to this, greater leisure time enabled millions of people to enjoy new media such as cinema and the radio.

KEY DATES: SOCIAL POLICIES, 1914–39	
1914	LEAs authorised to offer free school meals to children from poor families
1918	Education Act raised school leaving age to 14
1919	Addison Act
1920–30	Four Unemployment Insurance Acts passed
1923	Chamberlain Housing Act
1937	British Health Services Report published

Chapter summary

- By the eve of the Second World War, Britain's economy and society had undergone a long period of transformation. Old staple industries had gone into decline and new light industries had developed, but this meant that areas dependent on coal, steel, cotton and shipbuilding became pockets of deep poverty and deprivation.
- The role of the state during wartime rapidly expanded in order to keep the army supplied, but following the end of the war, major state intervention in industry and society continued.
- Britain's economy was far more volatile after the war than it had been before; the stresses that the war had placed on the economy, along with huge debts, combined with longer term problems on under investment to create two economic depressions during the inter-war years.
- The 1920s and 1930s were not periods of universal economic gloom, however. Not only was there an economic recovery after 1934, but in many parts of Britain living standards improved. British people in the 1930s began to have access to greater leisure time and a wider range of consumer choices and leisure activities. Modern technology provided the population with access to radio, cinema and cheap mass publishing.
- A housing boom enabled hundreds of thousands of people to own their own homes for the first time. This suggests that the period between 1914 and 1939 can be thought of as one that featured a series of economic crises, but also a long period of transition and change.

CHAPTER SUMMARY DIAGRAM

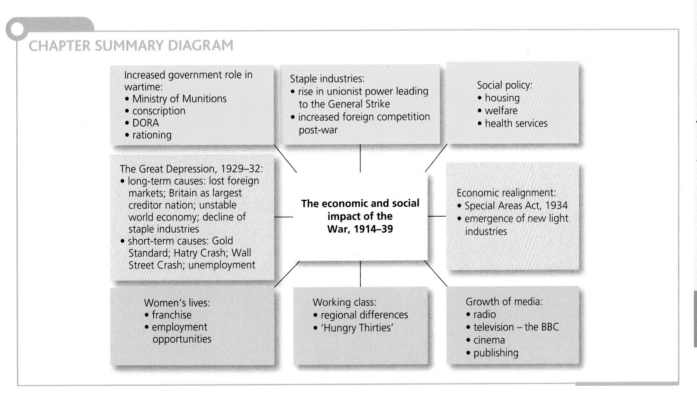

Working on interpretation skills: extended reading

How valid is the notion that the 1930s was a time of hardship and poverty in Britain?

Dr Emmett Sullivan assesseds the extent of prosperity and depression in the 1930s.

It is not possible to argue that the 1930s in Britain was the 'Devil's Decade'. Poverty and hardship persisted, but in a smaller measure than seen before. Rowntree's 1941 study of York estimated that one in ten of the working classes lived in poverty, an improvement over his 1899 study – which had 30 per cent of the working classes in poverty. That 'one-in-ten' figure is repeated for National Insurance (NI) unemployment: the figure never fell below 10, or 1.5m of those covered by the scheme in the 1930s. Unemployment was not the only cause of poverty and hardship, but it became the principle one. Yet after 1933 the majority of the British population enjoyed a growth in real wages, employment and consumption. 10 While never matching America's 1920s 'high mass consumption', the 1930s employed population in Britain enjoyed radios, vacuum cleaners and washing machines for the first time; and for a few of the wealthier working classes, a home telephone and a car. The 1930s also became an era of mass leisure – football on a Saturday afternoon, the morning paper and the 15 cinema. Freed of the Gold Standard, British import prices fell, meaning that for those employed the purchasing power of static nominal wages rose. 5

For those employed in an age before other modern economic statistics, the monthly NI unemployment figures coloured opinion, and became part of the inter-war historiography. The 1929–32/33 slump caused 20 much hardship, particularly in the export industries, and unemployment rocketed to the same levels seen a decade earlier. However, the 1929–32/33 slump was 'imported'. It was a product of Britain's high participation in the world economy, rather than anything fundamentally wrong with the British economy, and the 4 per cent to 5 per cent drop in 25 GDP 1929–32/33 was soon made up. That trend continued for most of the 1930s, 1937/38 aside, to the benefit of those in work.

Policy failure and inertia in the 1930s helps to explain the persistent negative view. The abdication crisis and appeasement added to a more general disillusionment. The fall of the second Labour government also heralded the 30 end of the Gold Standard and free trade. The National Government's cuts in benefits and civil service pay signalled a supposed austerity. International initiatives – such as the London Economic Conference 1933 – largely failed. Social policy reforms were as moribund in the 1930s as they were in the 1920s. The social surveys of the 1930s – by Llewellyn Smith, Caradog Jones, 35 Boyd-Orr and the Pilgrim Trust – portrayed a society failing the neediest. Topping this off was a number of socialist polemics, most notably Orwell's *Wigan Pier*. The dissatisfaction with this 'stagnation' was reflected in the popularity of the 1942 Beveridge Report, the 1945 Labour landslide, and was confirmed in the historical literature until the 1970s, and in popular culture 40 to the present day.

There was also a new negative trend in the 1930s. The First World War created a regional economic problem. The 1929–32/33 slump convinced exporters of the industrial staples that there would be no general revival in foreign markets. They made workers permanently unemployed, rather than simply 'temporarily stopped'. In contrast, access to electrical power meant new enterprises located near the most prosperous markets – London and the South East. Along with the Midlands, where firms took advantage of a skilled engineering workforce to staff their factories, they had low rates of unemployment in the late 1930s. The 1936 Jarrow Crusade typified the plight of the older industrial areas, and throughout the 1930s Scotland, Northern Ireland and Wales had unemployment rates twice that of London. Governments failed to address the regional problems. Industrial Transference and the Special Areas did little to bring new employment. Only deficit-financed rearmament expenditure from 1936 gave any possibility of the Government placing contracts in the worst affected areas.

Administration of the unemployed was also poorly done. Public Assistance Committees, which dealt with those who had exhausted their NI benefits, were simply the Poor Law Guardians in another guise. They now had the right to enter claimant's homes to apply a 'means test'. This was the final humiliation for many of the unskilled male unemployed who had not worked for twelve months or more – one in twenty of the unemployed were 'long-term'.

The prosperity of Britain was known of long before Feinstein and Crafts in the 1970s created historical GDP figures to show the extent of growth. However, in the absence of these estimates, the experience of the '10 per cent' cast dark shadows over the memory and history of the 1930s.

Dr Emmett Sullivan is Senior Lecturer in Economic History, Royal Holloway and Bedford New College, University of London.

ACTIVITY

Having read the essay on pages 198–99, answer the following questions.

Comprehension

1 What does the author mean by the following phrases?
   a) 'Gold Standard' (line 31).
   b) 'Public Assistance Committees' (line 57),
   c) 'Jarrow Crusade' (line 50).

Evidence

2 Using paragraphs 1–4, list the ways in which the author provides evidence suggesting that the effects of the Great Depression have been overstated.

Interpretation

3 Using your knowledge (and the essay), list evidence to suggest that:
   a) the depression was not a major economic catastrophe for Britain
   b) the depression did represent a major economic crisis.

Essay

4 Write an essay answer to the following question:

'The 1930s was not the "decade of hardship" of unemployment and poverty.' Assess the validity of this view.

Working on interpretation skills

ACTIVITY

The three extracts below give different interpretations of the extent to which British people experienced economic hardship between the wars. You should begin by reading each one and listing the main points made and the evidence used to support them. Then answer these questions:
- In what way do Extracts A and B agree and disagree?
- In what way do Extracts B and C agree and disagree?

Now answer the following practice A-level question:

Using your understanding of the historical context, assess how convincing the arguments in these three extracts are in relation to the development of economic hardship between the wars, 1918–39. (30 marks)

Extract A This extract is about the death of Annie Weaving, a 37-year-old housewife, who died of malnutrition.

Mrs Weaving had been struggling to keep her family going on the forty-eight shillings a week benefits her husband received. She did so by going without food herself and though the immediate cause of her death was recorded as pneumonia, the coroner concluded that this would not have proved fatal if Mrs Weaving had had enough to eat, rather than sacrificing her life for the sake of her children. At the inquest, the coroner was blunt: 'I should call it starvation to have to feed nine people on £2.8s a week and pay the rent.' The press took up the story, and the *Week-End Review* launched a 'Hungry England' inquiry in the spring of 1933 ... They found that unemployment relief payments were insufficient to provide the minimum diet for a family recommended by the recently established Advisory Committee on Nutrition set up by the Ministry of Health ... In London in 1929 unemployment and underemployment accounted for 38 per cent of families in poverty, and 55 per cent of the unemployed were living on the poverty line.

From *The 30s: An Intimate History of Britain*, by J. Gardiner, (Harper Collins), 2011, p. 68.

Extract B This extract refers to changes in unemployment insurance as a result of the immediate post-war recession of 1920–21.

In 1911 Asquith's Liberal government had passed a pioneering Unemployment Insurance Act, but this covered only 2.25 of Britain's 19 million workers, with limited benefits. New legislation in 1920–21 extended coverage to 12 million workers at a level of about one-third of the national minimum wage. The 1911 Act assumed a self-financing National Insurance Fund based on contributions from employers and employees, but this principle was eroded in 1920–21 amid the panic about mass unemployment: the government extended help to those in need, even if they had not paid contributions, and also made payments to wives and children. The result was a generalised 'dole', subsidised by the Treasury from taxation and justified by the unprecedented levels of unemployment. Attempts to limit the escalating cost through means tests and other devices were resisted during the 1920s by the two Labour governments. By 1931 unemployment benefits amounted to £120 million a year, nearly two-thirds of which were being paid for by the state.

From *The Long Shadow* by D. Reynolds, (Simon and Schuster), 2013, p. 145.

Extract C In this extract the author examines the extent to which women were able to contribute to the war effort during the First World War.

The total size of the female workforce in 1921, however, showed virtually no net change since 1911. Despite the wartime bulge, it was still around 5–7 million, compared with 13.7 million men. It is apparent that much wartime employment was a transient phenomenon, especially in fields where the intrusion of women had been most shocking and had attracted most publicity. Photographs of women driving trams, buses and ambulances became well known, not because of their typicality, but because of their novelty. In 1921 as in 1911 there were only 3,000 women employed on the railways, less than one percent of the total. During the war the workforce was diluted with women, only to be purposefully undiluted afterwards, just as the Treasury agreements had specified. The process was reinforced by the post-war slump, which likewise helped to solve the [lack of] servant[s] problem. The 1921 census showed 1.85 million women in personal service ... this represented a fall from the figure of 2.13 million in 1911. By 1931 it was back at 2.13 million, exactly the same as twenty years previously.

From *Hope and Glory, Britain 1900–1990* by P. Clarke, (Penguin), 2004, p. 95.

Working on essay technique

Remember the advice from Chapters 1–4 and the summary provided at the end of Chapter 5 and consider this A-level practice question:

'Overall, during the period between the wars, 1918–39, living standards improved.' Assess the validity of this view. (25 marks)

Avoiding convenient stereotypes

TV programmes and films that feature the inter-war period present it rather uniformly as a time of economic hardship and suffering for the British people. As we have seen in this chapter, this not just an over simplification, it is in many cases factually wrong. Try to avoid making oversimplified 'sweeping statements' that bear little relation to more complex realities. This is an opportunity to create a more nuanced and accurate response. This means examining the evidence, i.e. that in *some* parts of the country there was extreme poverty but this was not the case in the Midlands and the South East.

When writing this type of essay, it is possible to respond to the question by stating that 'to some extent' the statement is valid, but that overall a more varied and complex picture exists. You should aim to explain *why* some parts of Britain suffered poverty and low standards of living and others did not. A conclusion to the essay might offer some suggestions as to what this indicates about Britain's economy and society between the wars.

Embracing complexity

Any study of British economics, politics or society will inevitably result in complex and sometimes ambiguous conclusions. The evidence shows that the idea that Britain was a uniformly depressed and impoverished country throughout the 1930s is thin. It is important to grapple with more complex pictures of historical circumstances than seek to simplify them. Aim to be able to give a detailed description of Britain in the 1930s, but to remain concise.

For an answer to a question such as this, you should consider:

- the post First World War boom and recession, 1919–21
- the impact of the economic depression, 1929–34
- the growth of new consumerism during the 1930s
- the development of mass popular culture
- the end of the depression in 1934
- Government intervention in depressed areas, i.e. the Special Areas Act
- Government social reform (health, pensions, housing and slum clearance).

7

Political developments, 1939–64

Attempting to write a complete history of Britain's Second World War and the post-war decades up to 1964 is far beyond the scope of this chapter. Instead this section will focus on the impact that the war had on Britain's politics between 1939 and 1964.

The main focus of this chapter will be on the following areas:

- The impact of the Second World War on British politics.
- The role of Winston Churchill as wartime leader.
- The 'Labour landslide' of 1945 and the ideology of the post-war Labour Government.
- Conservative dominance from 1951 and political consensus.
- Labour's victory in 1964.

The key breadth questions covered in this chapter concern the development of democracy and political organisation, the importance of ideas and ideology, and the changes in Britain's relationship with Ireland.

For the period covered in this chapter the main issues can be phrased as a question:

Why did a political consensus emerge between 1945 and 1964?

CHAPTER OVERVIEW

For the second time in 25 years Britain experienced total war, but this time a coalition national government was already formed at the start of the war instead of developing half way through, as had happened during the First World War. The war saw the rise to power of Winston Churchill in 1940 and his crushing defeat by the Labour Party under Clement Attlee in 1945 at the war's end. In the aftermath of the war, it has been argued that a new kind of 'consensus' politics developed as the Conservatives accepted major parts of the Labour Party's policies on the welfare state and nationalisation. By 1951 Labour was voted out of office and spent the next thirteen years in opposition as the country enjoyed a 'golden age' of rising living standards and prosperity. This period in opposition was brought to an end with the election of a Labour prime minister, Harold Wilson, in 1964, promising a modern, meritocratic and classless Britain powered by new technology and science.

1 The impact of the Second World War on British politics

On 1 September 1939, Germany invaded Poland while Britain delivered an ultimatum to Hitler: withdraw or face war. On 3 September Britain declared war on Germany, but despite a number of small naval engagements very little occurred over the following seven months. In September 1939 Winston Churchill returned to government as First Lord of the Admiralty, a position he had held during the First World War. The decision by Chamberlain to invite Churchill to join the Government was interpreted by much of the press and the general public as a sign that Chamberlain was serious about combatting Germany. Churchill had a reputation as being the most outspoken opponent of appeasement. His track record as a war politician and soldier during the First World War also suggested that his presence in the Cabinet meant that Britain was prepared for a long war with Germany. The reality, however, was that there was little clear idea of how to defeat Germany or what strategy to employ and several of Churchill's initiatives met with early disaster.

The outbreak of war and the rise of Churchill

Why did Winston Churchill become prime minister in May 1940?

The BEF was sent to France, as it had been in 1914. This period was christened the 'Phoney War', but ended in April 1940 with an incompetent and disastrous British attempt to save Norway from German invasion and Norway's subsequent occupation by Germany.

In the resultant Norway debate in Parliament on 7 May, Chamberlain faced the full fury of both opposition and government benches for the poor handling of the war. He narrowly won a vote of no confidence, but recognised it in real terms as a defeat. The retired Admiral and Conservative MP Sir Roger Keyes criticised Chamberlain for his timidity during the debate.

'One hundred and forty years ago, Nelson said, "I am of the opinion that the boldest measures are the safest," and that still holds good to-day.'

Leo Amery, one of Churchill's allies, shouted down Chamberlain in the House, saying: *'In the name of god, go!'*

On 9 May Chamberlain attempted to form a new coalition government but the Labour Party refused to serve under him, leaving either Lord Halifax or Winston Churchill. Halifax realised he could not run the war from the House of Lords and stepped aside to give the job of prime minister to Churchill, who came to power on the day of Germany's invasion of France.

Churchill's wartime Cabinet was a mixture of Conservative, Labour and Liberal politicians. Churchill included Labour politicians, mainly from the centre and right of the party, who he believed were ready to place the national interest above party politics.

> **NOTE-MAKING**
>
> In this section, make notes on Churchill's personality and his role as wartime leader. Carry out further research to create your own profile on him.

The Battle of Britain

In the decade before the war, British politicians from both parties were concerned about the threat of aerial attack from Nazi Germany. Stanley Baldwin was pessimistic about Britain's air defences in 1932, stating that 'the bomber will always get through'. When France fell in June 1940, the German air force was able to use French airfields close to Britain to launch an attack across the Channel. From July to October 1940 the German air force (*Luftwaffe*) attacked British shipping, then attacked Royal Air Force bases, runways and radar centres. For the *Luftwaffe* the initial goal of the Battle of Britain was to gain air superiority over Britain in order to make a seaborne invasion possible. The creation prior to the war of a network of radar sites, underground telephone lines, operations centres and aircraft spotters called the 'Dowding System', meant that the RAF was aware of incoming *Luftwaffe* attacks. In addition to this, Britain's fighter aircraft production during the battle dramatically increased (see page 227), which meant that German hopes that the RAF would be ground down never materialised.

Churchill's premiership, 1940–45

On 13 May, as the situation deteriorated in France, Churchill made his first speech as prime minister to the House of Commons, offering 'blood, toil, tears and sweat'.

By the end of the month the situation had worsened. As the German army swept through France, the BEF withdrew to Dunkirk, trapped on the beaches and awaiting evacuation. German successes brought about a new political crisis in government as some ministers considered whether or not to make peace with Germany.

On 25 May Halifax proposed a negotiated settlement with Germany, clashing with Churchill. Churchill called a meeting of the whole Cabinet, arguing that Britain would be a 'slave state' if it agreed to German terms. Much of the popular view of Winston Churchill, his stoicism in the face of adversity, was formed during this debate and subsequent speeches to Parliament. However, Churchill himself had briefly considered making terms with Hitler, and it was only his belief that Britain had sufficient forces to continue fighting that made him reject the idea of negotiation.

Churchill's stature as a national war leader developed gradually over the next five years; he was not universally accepted as a 'saviour' in 1940. This was in part due to mistakes he had already made as First Lord of the Admiralty from 1939 onwards and errors he had made during the First World War.

Churchill was seen, even by those on the far left who were traditionally his political opponents, as the 'right man at the right time' to lead Britain. Furthermore, his standing with the general public was high, especially after he visited bombed-out districts of London and other major cities. He was credited with showing strong and determined leadership during the most difficult phases of the war and his colleagues in the wartime Cabinet saw him work tirelessly from his underground

Winston Churchill, Britain's wartime Prime Minister, who came to power during the darkest days of the war, in May 1940. ▶

war rooms located close to Downing Street in Whitehall. However, despite his drive, focus and determination, there was little belief that Churchill was a suitable peacetime prime minister. His time as chancellor of the exchequer during a period of economic problems and a reputation for being arrogant and elitist worked against him. Churchill was one of the oldest British prime ministers to take office, coming to power when he was 65 years of age. As a younger man, Churchill had been part of Asquith's reforming Liberal Government and had campaigned for the People's Budget in 1909. However, during the war he seemed to exhibit little of his earlier radicalism and instead had grown reactionary in his views on class. These views would seem quite anachronistic and out of date by 1945. Winston Churchill's over-riding interest during the war was the preservation of the British Empire and Britain's world role, but even he conceded by 1945 that Britain's power was receding and the empire was in decline.

Some Conservatives opposed Churchill because they believed that his policy towards Germany would fatally damage the British Empire, whereas Churchill announced that Britain would fight on for 'victory at all costs'. As both prime minister and minister of defence, Churchill had almost complete control over Britain's war strategy and paid little attention to civilian matters that were the responsibility of other ministers. His desire to be 'hands-on' in military strategy led him into conflict with several of his generals. The Chief of the Imperial General Staff, Sir Alan Brooke, remarked in his war diaries that he often had to intervene to prevent Churchill from devising schemes that would more than likely end in disaster. Churchill's wartime Cabinet of Conservative, Labour and Liberal MPs served under him until the war with Nazi Germany ended in May 1945.

Source A Winston Churchill, addressing the House of Commons following the evacuation of the British Expeditionary Force at Dunkirk on 4 June 1940.

Even though large tracts of Europe and many old and famous states have fallen or may fall into the grip of the Gestapo and all the odious apparatus of Nazi rule, we shall not flag or fail. We shall go on to the end. We shall fight in France, we shall fight on the seas and oceans, we shall fight with growing confidence and growing strength in the air, we shall defend our island, whatever the cost may be. We shall fight on the beaches, we shall fight on the landing grounds, we shall fight in the fields and in the streets, we shall fight in the hills; we shall never surrender, and even if, which I do not for a moment believe, this island or a large part of it were subjugated and starving, then our Empire beyond the seas, armed and guarded by the British Fleet, would carry on the struggle, until, in God's good time, the New World, with all its power and might, steps forth to the rescue and the liberation of the old.

1 What impression of Churchill do you obtain from Source A?
2 What is the context of this source? What might Churchill have been trying to achieve by making this speech?

Evaluating Churchill

More books have been written about Winston Churchill than nearly any other British prime minister. Overall, a largely positive consensus has emerged; historians like Martin Gilbert, Max Hastings and Andrew Roberts present him as a flawed, erratic genius who drank to excess, but who was 'in the right place at the right time' in 1940. A. J. P. Taylor wrote that the debacle in Norway that swept Chamberlain from power was largely Churchill's fault. In his book, *The War Lords*, he summed up Churchill as:

'[A] combination of the profound strategist, the experienced man and the actor. Not always the tragic actor; there was a rich comedy about him as well. No other war leader, I think, had the same depth of personal fascination as Churchill ... he combined, to the end, imperial greatness with human simplicity.'

Here is a summary of some of the many views on his legacy.

Winston Churchill

The first popular historian of Churchill's wartime legacy was Churchill himself, who wrote:

'History will be kind to me for I intend to write it'.

Churchill wrote an account of the war which received a Nobel Prize for Literature in 1953. He planned the series of books from 1940 onward, making sure that the documents that would support his views were stored at his private home at Chartwell. The books were written with the agreement of the post-war Labour Government and made sure that neither Churchill nor the British Government were embarrassed. This meant that many of his errors, oversights and diplomatic failings during the war were ignored. The historian Paul Addison agreed with the view that Churchill had skilfully controlled the debate over his wartime leadership, stating that in 1945 he won not only the war, but also the right to control the narrative of the war years.

Roy Jenkins

Jenkins, a former Labour Chancellor and Home Secretary in 2001, wrote an immensely popular and influential biography of Churchill. The book was very sympathetic in its approach and presented Churchill as a hasty and volatile character who, before 1940, had more political disasters than triumphs. Jenkins claims that 1940 was a moment of 'greatness' that Churchill had sought all his life. Jenkins makes it clear throughout the book that he has immense sympathies for his personal hero.

Richard Toye

Toye, in his book, *Churchill's Empire*, presents Churchill not as a defender of liberty but as an ardent imperialist. His racist rhetoric towards Asian and African subjects of the British Empire was the result of his formative years as a soldier in Africa and India. Churchill, in Toye's account, was interested in the preservation of the British Empire above all things, and his condemnation of Nazi tyranny was merely based on a recognition that Nazism was a grave threat to the Empire. He presents Churchill as an anti-democratic elitist figure, who, despite calling for national unity, had little time for the lower orders of British society.

Anthony Beevor

In his book *The Second World War* (2012), Beevor presents Churchill as an important unifying figure in 1940, but one whose constant meddling in military matters prolonged the war and delivered military disasters in the Middle East, Asia and Europe. He suggests that Churchill was unaware of Britain's declining world role during the war and was finally over-ruled by his generals in 1945 when he considered a further war with the USSR.

The Labour Government, 1945–51

Why did the Labour Party win a landslide victory in 1945?

At the end of the Second World War, the Labour Party won the biggest electoral victory in its history, an outcome at the polls that was a clear rejection of Winston Churchill's Conservative Party. The election led to a government coming to power that had more ambitious plans for social reform than almost any other in British history, and a parliamentary majority to carry them out. It resulted also in an acceptance by the Conservatives that social reform and nationalisation were firmly on the political agenda and any hopes they might have had of re-creating a pre-war *laissez-faire* style government were gone. This section examines the successes and failures of Labour after 1945 and addresses the question of why the party was voted out of power just six years later, despite the popularity of its reforms.

The government that came to power in July 1945 was the first majority Labour government ever to have been elected. The Government brought about huge changes to social security, healthcare, education and housing, its 1945 manifesto implementing many of the recommendations made in the Beveridge Report (see page 251). However, by 1951 the party was divided and the continuation of post-war austerity was deeply unpopular. The defeat of Labour in 1951 led to thirteen years of Conservative dominance. This section will explore Labour's successes and failings in the immediate post-war years.

The election of 1945 and Labour's victory

Figure 1 General election results, 1945.

Party	Votes (millions)	Share of the vote (%)	Seats	Change in the number of seats since 1935
Conservative	9.97	39.7	210	–219
Labour	11.97	47.7	393	+239
Liberal	2.25	9.0	12	–9
Other	0.91	3.6	25	+14

Source: House of Commons Library, UK Election Statistics: 1918–2012.

By May 1945, Winston Churchill had served as prime minister for five years, since he took power during the crisis of the fall of France in May 1940. Throughout the war the Labour Party had served in coalition with him and both Labour and the Conservatives had put aside partisan differences in order to win the war. In that month, following the defeat of Nazi Germany, the Labour Party signalled its intention to withdraw from the coalition. In July 1945, a general election was called, even though Churchill had hoped to keep the coalition going until the defeat of Japan.

Churchill believed that he would be rewarded by a grateful British public for his wartime service, and his manifesto focused heavily on foreign policy. There were bitter memories of the Conservative pre-war governments and economic hardship, not helped by Churchill's rather crass claims that a post-war Labour government would rely on a 'Gestapo' in order to police its planned social reforms. The Labour manifesto, 'Let us Face the Future', promised action on housing, jobs, social security and a national health service, and resulted in a landslide victory.

NOTE-MAKING

Use the headings in this section to make brief notes as you work through it. Set these notes out clearly using main headings, sub-headings and sub-points, using the headings and questions in the text to help you.

As you make your notes, consider the questions:
● Why was Churchill rejected in 1945?
● What was the appeal of Labour?
● What did the electorate appear to want?
● How significant was the experience of the Great Depression?

Star or highlight the points which seem important with respect to these questions.

Gestapo – The secret state police in Nazi Germany.

Labour ideology and policies

Labour's 1945 manifesto set out the party's plans for post-war Britain. Labour offered:

- full employment
- new homes and communities for working-class people
- a National Health Service
- free education for all children
- a comprehensive system of social security
- nationalisation of key industries like steel, shipbuilding and the railways.

Despite the promises by the Conservatives of a 'New Deal' on social policy, many voters clearly doubted that the party was committed to social reform. The policies Labour planned to introduce were the most extensive social reforms since the Liberal Government of 1906. Between 1945 and 1951 most of Labour's election promises were delivered. Unemployment had fallen to 281,350, compared to over a million at the start of the Second World War. In addition to this achievement, a welfare state had successfully been established (see pages 253–56). The party's most significant achievement, however, was the creation of the National Health Service (see page 254). By the end of the decade, it had also succeeded in changing the basic assumptions of British politics. It was taken for granted that the state now had a much larger role in people's lives than it had during the war and the Conservative Party was forced to accept this as well.

Nationalisation

In 1918, the Labour Party's Constitution contained a commitment to 'common ownership of the means of production', known as Clause Four. The clause was written by Fabian socialist Sidney Webb in November 1917 and was seen as a commitment to state socialism by the Party. The initial wording of Clause Four implied workers control industries, a process that appeared to be happening in Russia at the time that the constitution was written. In practice, Clause Four was interpreted by the Labour Party not as a commitment to workers' control over industry, but as state control on the behalf of the workers. By 1945, nationalisation of industries by the government was not seen by its supporters as simply the product of ideological dogma. It was believed that state control of industry could prevent a reoccurrence of the hardships of the 1930s, when foreign competitors had imported cheaper coal to Britain, resulting in job losses and wage cuts. A nationalised coal industry could rely on state subsidies to prevent job losses occurring. Similarly, the experience of the war seemed to demonstrate that state control of industries led to greater efficiency and organisation, so nationalisation appeared to be a modern, rational policy.

The Conservatives and the *Industrial Charter*

One of the most important documents of the post-war era was drafted not by the Labour Party but by Winston Churchill's Conservatives. The *Industrial Charter*, written in 1947, was a set of pledges to maintain many of the economic and social policies introduced by Labour. Nationalisation, the Charter stated, would not be extended but nor would it be rolled back. The welfare state and the increased role of the trade union movement in economic management would also be Conservative policies. Most members of the party opposed high-taxing and high-spending governments and believed that the state should have as limited a role in the economy as possible, but they were forced to accept new political realities after the catastrophic defeat of July 1945. The welfare state and a mixed economy were popular with the electorate and if the Conservatives stood any chance of getting back into power they needed to accept this fact. The *Industrial Charter* was a statement by the Conservatives that helped to forge the post-war consensus between the two parties (for more on consensus politics, see page 214).

Labour divisions

Why did the Labour Party experience divisions during its most successful period in government?

In 1950 simmering resentments within the Labour Party, which had long been suppressed, began to emerge. Left and right factions within the party had existed since the 1920s and the era of Ramsay MacDonald, but by 1950 they were engaged in bitter debates about the spending priorities of the Labour Party.

Election of 1950

Some of Labour's lost seats in 1950 were due to the House of Commons (Redistribution of Seats) Act 1949 which reduced the number of Labour safe seats by redrawing constituency boundaries, but it was also the decline of popularity with middle-class voters that saw Labour gain fewer votes. In addition to this, the overall size of the working class was shrinking, with 78 per cent of British society identifying themselves as working class in 1931 but only 72 per cent viewing themselves as working class in 1951. More people considered themselves to be living middle-class lifestyles as the 1950s began and they were less inclined to vote for the Labour Party or have membership of a trade union.

The main causes of dissatisfaction were:

- **Rationing**: wartime food and fuel rationing continued after the war, with some items such as bread that were not restricted during wartime becoming rationed in peacetime (see page 229 for more details).
- **Austerity**: the Labour Party seemed unable to revive Britain's struggling economy in the immediate post-war years (see pages 229–31 for more details).
- **Taxation**: the standard rate of taxation in 1949 was 9s in every pound (45 per cent), and the top rate of graduated tax for high earners was 90 per cent.

Following the 1950 election, Prime Minister Clement Attlee found it increasingly difficult to control the Labour Government. By 1951 he was exhausted by five years of government and many of his most able ministers fell ill or died in office. When Foreign Secretary Ernest Bevin died in 1951, the party lost one of its most able and talented ministers. In addition to this, the party had become divided over budget cuts. Labour's chancellor, Sir Stafford Cripps, had resigned the previous October due to ill-health, depriving Attlee of two of his most experienced ministers in just over six months.

In 1950 Britain became involved in the Korean War to protect South Korea, as part of the new United Nations force. The war resulted in a huge increase in military spending and an 'austerity Budget' in 1951 was announced by the new chancellor Hugh Gaitskell. This involved the introduction of prescription charges for glasses and dentistry, and resulted in the resignation of Aneurin Bevan, the minister for labour and the pioneer of the National Health Service (see page 254). Attlee had previously been skilled at defusing feuds within the party but by 1951 he lacked authority. Attlee called an election in October 1951 and lost to the Conservative Party.

Ernest Bevin, 1881–1951

Ernest Bevin was a working-class Labour politician and trade unionist. He was born in Somerset and worked as a lorry driver and labourer before becoming involved in Labour politics. He was on the right of the Labour Party and suspicious of communism. While he participated in the General Strike of 1926 he believed the strike was a mistake. After his wartime service as minister of labour and national service, he became foreign secretary and was highly regarded by the civil servants who served under him. He died in 1951.

Graduated tax – A tax by which people with different incomes are divided into 'tax brackets' and taxed at different rates, with higher incomes being taxed at higher rates.

LOOK AGAIN

In this section we have explored the effect of the Second World War on politics and the party system. How did British politics change between 1939 and 1951 as a result of war?

KEY DATES: THE IMPACT OF THE SECOND WORLD WAR ON BRITISH POLITICS

1939 3 Sept	Britain declares war on Germany
1940 4 June	Churchill makes his 'never surrender' speech
1945 8 May	Nazi Germany defeated
1945 June	Labour wins a landslide victory
1947 May	Conservatives publish the *Industrial Charter*
1951 Oct	Labour defeated by the Conservatives in the general election

Labour's defeat (Figure 2) was the result of:

- internal party splits
- a failure to end rationing
- a sense that the party had run out of steam and lacked new ideas
- a lack of enthusiasm from the electorate for further nationalisation
- boundary changes that benefited the Conservatives.

Figure 2 General election results, 1951.

Party	Votes (millions)	Share of the vote (%)	Seats	Change in the number of seats since 1950
Conservative	13.72	48.0	321	+24
Labour	13.95	48.8	295	-20
Liberal	0.73	2.6	6	-3
Other	0.2	0.9	3	-1

Source: House of Commons Library, UK Election Statistics: 1918–2012.

The Festival of Britain

▲ 'The Islanders', a huge sculpture, representing the strength and resilience of the British people, especially during the Second World War. The sculpture was shown as part of the Festival of Britain, 1951.

Prior to Labour's defeat in 1951, Britain celebrated the centenary of the Great Exhibition of 1851. A 'Festival of Great Britain' was held in order to help boost exports and showcase British manufacturing and science after six years of post-war austerity. The Government hoped that the exhibition would raise morale and would act as 'one united act of national reassessment, and one corporate reaffirmation of faith in the nation's future' (quoted from the official literature of the festival). The festival took three years to plan between 1948 and 1951 and saw events held across the country.

The focal point of the exhibition was London's South Bank, a former warehouse district that now featured a modern new riverside embankment and gardens. This reshaping of the South Bank of the Thames was meant to showcase what housing would look like in the Britain of the future, when modern new towns would be built and Victorian slums would be cleared away. The displays along the South Bank also showed the cutting edge of British architecture, science, engineering and design. Even though the exhibition came three years before the end of rationing and the start of mass consumption, it suggested that Britain's economy and consumer confidence were recovering.

2 Political developments, 1951–64

For the next thirteen years the Conservative Party would dominate British politics and win two further general elections in 1955 and 1959. Winston Churchill returned to Downing Street for four years, just as the final wartime rations and restrictions came to an end (see page 231). Churchill was 76 years old when he returned to power and many of his Cabinet colleagues observed that the dynamism and drive he had exhibited during the war years appeared to have gone. Instead, Churchill acted more as a 'caretaker' prime minister, while the ministers within his government gradually came to prominence.

Conservative dominance from 1951

Why was the Conservative Party so popular between 1951 and 1964?

Even though Churchill suffered a stroke in 1953, he managed to remain in office until retiring in 1955. His replacement was Anthony Eden, a relatively young and popular politician with an impressive wartime record as Churchill's foreign minister. He called a general election in May 1955 to ensure that he had a strong mandate. The election results indicated that the British public approved of the Conservative Party's management of the economy, which was experiencing a post-war consumer boom from 1954 onwards (see page 232). By July 1955 Britain had the lowest unemployment figures in its recent history, with only 215,000 people out of work, accounting for just over 1 per cent of the workforce.

Despite the Conservative Party's popularity and its dominance of the political system, the party was not immune from crisis. Within a year of taking office Eden was embroiled in the Suez Crisis, Britain's biggest post-war diplomatic disaster, which forced him to resign and demonstrated the weakness of Britain's position in the world. But despite the fact that Britain had experienced a humiliating defeat and its global standing was diminished, improving living standards and continued high employment meant that the Conservatives won a further general election in 1959.

NOTE-MAKING

As you work through this chapter, use the headings to make brief notes. Set these notes out clearly using main headings, sub-headings and sub-points. For example:

Main heading: Conservative dominance

Sub-heading 1: Eden's government

Sub-heading 2: Macmillan's government

Sub-heading 3: Home's government

When you have completed your notes on the first few pages, review the process and then devise your own sub-headings for the remainder of the chapter, using the headings and questions in the text to help you.

As you make your notes, consider the question: Why were the Conservatives so popular throughout the 1950s?

The Suez Crisis

Britain had maintained a presence in Egypt since the nineteenth century to protect the Suez Canal (which was part owned by Britain and France), which was its route to India. After Indian independence in 1947, the canal was used as a means of shipping oil to Britain, Europe and America.

The nationalist president of Egypt, Gamal Abdul Nasser, stated that the canal should be in Egyptian hands and that he would be willing to pay British shareholders a fair price for it. Eden reacted with suspicion and hostility, comparing Nasser to Mussolini and Hitler. Eden was one of the few politicians who spoke out against appeasement and was convinced that unless a tough stance was taken against Nasser history would repeat itself. Nasser occupied the Canal Zone on 26 July 1956; his close relationship with the USSR convinced the British that the canal would soon fall into Soviet hands.

When France and Egypt's enemy, Israel, invited Britain to take part in an invasion of the Suez Canal Zone, Eden agreed in secret to participate. He was motivated by a desire not to be humiliated by Nasser. He knew his standing in the Conservative Party depended on presenting a strong image as an international statesman.

When the invasion began on 5 November 1956, President Eisenhower, who had not been consulted on Britain's intentions, reacted angrily and felt deceived. He threatened to sell America's reserves of British currency and collapse the value of the pound. Faced with the possibility of economic crisis, Britain was forced to withdraw and Eden resigned in January 1957. The outcome of Suez was a significant reduction in British world power and a recognition that it could no longer act independently without seeking US approval.

Macmillan's government

Eden was replaced as prime minister by his chancellor of the exchequer, Harold Macmillan, who would preside over a period in post-war British history that is often seen nostalgically as a 'golden age'. A **mixed economy**, rising living standards, low unemployment and declining social inequality (in 1957 British wages and living standards were at their most equal in the twentieth century), made the Macmillan government very popular. In the 1959 general election the Conservatives increased their majority.

Night of the Long Knives

By 1962 the popularity of the Conservative Party was declining as the long period of economic growth from the mid-1950s onwards began to slow down. Macmillan's privileged background and the large number of upper-class Cabinet members (there were 35 former Etonians in his government) meant that many people perceived the Conservatives as out of touch. The Labour Party under Gaitskell and then Harold Wilson argued that privileged aristocratic Conservatives who had risen due to their connections, not their ability, were holding Britain back. The dramatic increase in consumer spending had resulted in a series of unforeseen economic problems (see pages 233–35) and Macmillan needed to demonstrate that he was in control of his government.

Macmillan sacked seven ministers from his Cabinet and replaced them with younger men. The press referred to this drastic measure as the 'Night of the Long Knives' – a sarcastic reference to an event in Nazi Germany in 1934 known by that title, when Hitler had ordered the murder of leading opponents in the Nazi Party. Part of Macmillan's reason for doing this was to resolve an image problem that the Conservatives had developed. They were seen as ageing and privileged, instead of young and meritocratic. In the early

> **Mixed economy** – An economy in which some industry is owned privately but other major industries are owned by the state.

Harold Macmillan, 1894–1986

Harold Macmillan was a moderate, aristocratic Conservative. He was part of the Macmillan publishing dynasty and, as an MP in the 1930s, spoke out against government inaction on unemployment. His parliamentary constituency was Stockton-on-Tees in the north-east of England, one of the most depressed parts of the country. When Macmillan became prime minister in 1957 he believed in the goal of full employment, and a mixed economy with a degree of nationalisation. His memories of the high unemployment of the 1930s made him determined not to risk this in Britain again. Throughout his term in office he benefited from favourable global economic conditions, but he was aware that inflation could be a consequence of the economic boom. Macmillan's tenure is seen popularly as an era of affluence.

1960s television and newspapers were dominated by youth culture and in America a young president, John F. Kennedy, had become very popular. Youth was thought to be in keeping with popular feelings among the electorate. Macmillan's actions were briefly perceived as ruthless, but the sudden and widespread sackings proved popular with the public, demonstrating that Macmillan was capable of taking action.

Scandal

Another area where the Conservatives were starting to be mistrusted was the issue of national security. At the height of the Cold War three high-profile spy scandals rocked the Government.

John Vassall

Between 1952 and 1962 John Vassall, a naval attaché at the British embassy in Moscow, was blackmailed by the KGB – the security agency for the Soviet Union. It used the fact that he was secretly homosexual (at that time homosexual acts were illegal), to force him to betray his country. He passed on large quantities of top secret information on the British Royal Navy and was caught when Soviet spies defected to the West and gave MI6 Vassall's name.

Harold 'Kim' Philby

In January 1963 one of Britain's most senior intelligence agents, Kim Philby, defected to the USSR. He was the head of British Counter Intelligence and had been under suspicion for spying for the USSR since the early 1950s. As foreign secretary in 1955, Macmillan had publicly announced that he had investigated Philby and exonerated him. Philby's defection was hugely embarrassing to Macmillan. Because of the Official Secrets Act, it was not revealed until 1968 that Philby had held such an important office within MI6.

John Profumo

Less than six months later, in June 1963, the Government's Secretary of State for War, John Profumo, admitted to having had an affair with a show girl, Christine Keeler. He had previously denied the affair to Macmillan, who had believed him. When it transpired that she had also had a relationship with a Russian attaché, Yevgeny Ivanov, the press focused on the spy angle to the story (though it is doubtful there was any security risk). Profumo was forced to resign.

Sir Alec Douglas-Home

Ill-health and the stress of mounting problems forced Macmillan to resign in October 1963. His replacement was Sir Alec Douglas-Home. Home was regarded by most of his party to be a skilled administrator and an astute politician, but he suffered from an image problem that would damage the Conservatives' chances in the next election. Home was a member of the House of Lords and had the title of Earl (which he renounced when he became prime minister). Satirists on television and in magazines like *Private Eye* ridiculed Home for his aristocratic manners and particularly his speech, though this was in fact partly due to an injury he had sustained to his mouth in the First World War.

Source B Harold Macmillan's statement about 'Kim' Philby, clearing him of wrongdoing, *Hansard*, Volume 545, 7 November 1955.

'Mr Philby had been a friend of Burgess [a Soviet spy in MI6] from the time when they were fellow undergraduates at Trinity College, Cambridge. Burgess had been accommodated with Philby and his family at the latter's home in Washington from August 1950 to April 1951 ... and, of course, it will be remembered that at no time before he fled [to the Soviet Union] was Burgess under suspicion. It is now known that Mr Philby had Communist associates during and after his university days. In view of the circumstances, he was asked in July 1951 to resign from the Foreign Service. Since that date his case has been the subject of close investigation. No evidence has been found ... to show that he was responsible for warning Burgess or Maclean [also a Soviet spy]. While in government service he carried out his duties ably and conscientiously, and I have no reason to conclude that Mr Philby has at any time betrayed the interests of his country, or to identify him with the so-called 'Third Man' [a suspected third spy in British intelligence, following the defection of two other senior intelligence officers, Guy Burgess and Donald Mclean] if indeed there was one.'

1 How far does the evidence against Philby given in Source B seem incriminating?
2 Was Macmillan being naive about Philby? Does the statement in Source B demonstrate his critics' claims that he was out of touch?

Post-war political consensus

To what extent did a post-war consensus develop between the Labour and Conservative parties?

One of the most contested aspects of post-war British politics is the idea that there were several decades of political consensus. This is the idea that there was a broad agreement between the two political parties on the fundamental aspects of economic, social and industrial policy. A commitment to full employment, the welfare state and cooperation with the trade unions were typically seen as policies that both parties agreed on. Some historians agree that there was a wide range of policies that both parties agreed upon, but others believe that this was largely illusory and there were in reality deep differences between the parties' economic and social goals. This section will explore three separate arguments about the post-war era.

In 1975 historian Paul Addison argued in *The Road to 1945* that the population shifted towards the left during the war, resulting in election defeat for the Conservatives. The most significant political development of the war years, he claimed, was the experience of wartime cooperation and collaboration between the Labour and Conservative parties. Addison argues that the post-war consensus emerged from the war years, and that the main beneficiary of the consensus was the Attlee Government of 1945–51, because for the most part, the Conservative Party was accepting Labour's social and economic policies, not the other way round.

However, two revisionist historians, John Barnes and Kevin Jeffrys, both argued in the 1990s and 2000s that Britain in the 1950s was far less politically consensual. Jeffrys in *Retreat from Jerusalem* argues that often the social democratic achievements of the two parties in the post-war decades was overstated and instead of providing welfare for all (supposedly the essence of the post-war consensus) instead simply facilitated a consumer boom. Historian Peter Hennessy argued that a British 'New Deal' took place after 1945 because of the legacy of the 1930s. He states that consensus went far beyond simply economic and social policy and saw both parties agree on defence and foreign policy, largely as a result of the Cold War. However, it was the historian Jose Harris in 1983 who provided the strongest and most convincing attack on the notion of consensus, when she argued that all the parties were agreed upon was the outcome they were trying to prevent. Neither party wanted to see a return to the 1930s, but as the 1950s and 1960s progressed the economic measures they took and their overall economic ethos began to diverge.

Source C From Peter Hennessy's lecture to the British Academy in February 2008, *The British Academy Review*, July 2008.

What was the post-war settlement? For the purposes of shorthand, one can probably call it the 'never again' impulse converted into policy. Never again 1930s, never again slump, social deprivation, plus a desire on the part of many, although not all, to put right permanently, if you could, the inequalities, injustices and deprivations bequeathed by the Industrial Revolution over the 180 years or so before the early post-war period. Much of the thinking had been done by the late 1930s but it took the impact of an all-in, total war, in which the entire British people were in the front line, to make it happen so swiftly and comprehensively. Its intellectual high priests and architects were neither Conservative nor Labour but Liberal, as everybody remembers (it is a standard feature of every essay on the subject) – John Maynard Keynes and William Beveridge – and extended state intervention was its primary instrument.

ACTIVITY

Sources C–E below and on page 215 give different interpretations of the extent to which there was a post-war consensus.

1 In what way do Sources C and D agree and disagree?
2 In what way do Sources D and E agree and disagree?
3 Using material from the sources and your own knowledge, state to what extent there was a consensus between the two main parties.

Source D From *The Road to 1945* by Paul Addison, (Pimlico), 1994, p. 5.

All three parties went to the polls in 1945, committed to the principles of social and economic reconstruction which their leaders had endorsed as members of the coalition. A massive new middle ground had arisen in politics … when Labour swept to victory in 1945, the new consensus fell like a branch of ripe plums, into the lap of Mr Attlee.

Source E From *Austerity Britain: 1945–51* by David Kynaston, (Bloomsbury), 2008 p. 238.

For the Conservative Party, so crushingly vanquished in 1945 … its first post-war conference in 1946 the mood on the platform was still pessimistic … on the conference floor there was a much greater sense of defiance – not least on the part of Margaret Roberts, newly elected president of the Oxford University Conservative Association. [Delegates] demanded a real Conservative policy instead of a synthetic socialist one.

The Labour Party from Gaitskell to Wilson

Why did the Labour Party not shift to the left during its thirteen years in opposition?

For thirteen years between 1951 and 1964 the Labour Party was in opposition, losing three consecutive general elections in 1951, 1955 and 1959. Part of the reason for these continued defeats was the party's inability to persuade middle-class 'floating voters' to defect from the Conservative Party. In addition to this, Labour appeared to have run out of ideas by 1951 – its major social reforms had been enacted and the party had little new to offer except further nationalisation, which was not a vote-winning idea. Labour was divided between two factions within the party: the Gaitskellites, who backed Hugh Gaitskell on the centre right of the party, and the Bevanites, who supported Aneurin Bevan on the left.

In 1956 the centre-right Labour MP Anthony Crosland wrote a book that would have a profound effect on the Labour Party, called *The Future of Socialism*. He argued that the conventional view that socialism could be achieved only by nationalisation was wrong. Nationalisation, he argued, had become an end in itself, rather than the means to an end, which should be a fair and prosperous society. If other economic practices such as the free market could fulfil that task, it was ideological folly not to employ them.

> **'Floating voters'** – Voters who do not have strong loyalties to any particular party and switch how they vote. Often floating voters decide the outcome of general elections.

Hugh Gaitskell, 1906–63

After two decades as leader of the Labour Party between 1935 and 1955, Clement Attlee stepped down when the party was defeated in 1955. He was replaced by interim leader Herbert Morrison in November 1955. In the leadership election that followed a month later, Morrison was replaced by Hugh Gaitskell. He was Bevan's main rival for leadership of the party and unlike Bevan he was middle class and did not owe his role as a senior member in the party to trade union sponsorship. He believed that there was no future for the Labour Party if it steered itself to a more left-wing, ideologically socialist position.

Gaitskell was aided in his bid for the party's leadership by the fact that Bevan, despite his important role in the development of the NHS, was disliked within the party. Gaitskell, on the other hand, was popular with the party and the electorate. He was fiercely critical of Eden's failures during the Suez Crisis and many political journalists and commentators thought that he would lead the Labour Party to victory in the 1959 general election. Gaitskell was regarded as being on the centre right of the Labour Party; many of his ideas were similar to those of Macmillan and his chancellor Rab Butler. When Labour lost the 1959 election a period of bitter internal feuding began. Gaitskell blamed the left of the party for demanding more nationalisation, which for many people enjoying new living standards was not seen as an important issue.

Crosland claimed that the worst aspects of capitalism, low wages, tyrannical bosses and impoverished workers had all but disappeared by the mid-1950s and therefore capitalism did not need to be opposed. Instead, it should be harnessed to provide the wealth that a welfare state required. The book was embraced by the centre and the right of the party and attacked by the left. In the left-wing Labour periodical the *Tribune*, Crosland was denounced and accused of betraying socialism. The book served to deepen the feud between the two wings of the Labour Party.

Harold Wilson's leadership

In 1955, Gaitskell appointed Harold Wilson as his Shadow Chancellor of the Exchequer. Wilson had been elected to the Lancashire seat of Ormskirk in the 1945 Labour landslide election victory. He had previously worked as a civil servant and had been a research assistant to William Beveridge, studying the causes of unemployment. Wilson freely admitted that he had never really seen himself as a socialist and while he did not abandon Clause Four of the constitution, committing the party to greater nationalisation, he was not anxious to promote it either. In his view, the keys to a fairer Britain were development using science and technology, and the erosion of class boundaries that kept talented and able people from poorer backgrounds from getting ahead. Wilson was a supporter of the royal family and had little interest in closer ties with either Europe or America, believing that the British Commonwealth was the country's best trading partner. One of Wilson's key advantages over his rivals, Macmillan and Home, was his understanding of the power of television. He was far more skilled in reaching voters using televised broadcasts and TV news than the Conservatives, a fact that made them seem old-fashioned and out of touch.

Wilson's government

Hugh Gaitskell died from a heart attack early in 1963 and Harold Wilson had been the new leader of the Labour Party for over a year by the time he won the general election of 1964. He presented the party as meritocratic and classless, comparing it to public perceptions of the Conservatives as aristocratic and out of touch. During the election Wilson effectively used television to present himself as the face of a modern Britain. However, despite the problems that the Conservatives faced, Labour won by a slender majority of just four seats (see Figure 3), meaning that if Wilson wished to bring about major policy changes, a new election would have to be called.

Figure 3 General election results, 1964.

Party	Votes (millions)	Share of the vote (%)	Seats	Change in the number of seats since 1959
Conservative	11.98	43.3	303	-62
Labour	12.21	44.1	317	+59
Liberal	3.10	11.2	9	+3
Other	0.37	1.4	1	-

Source: House of Commons Library, UK Election Statistics: 1918–2012.

Harold Wilson and his chancellor, James Callaghan, discovered within their first few days in office that Britain's economic problems were far worse than they had previously thought. The previous chancellor of the exchequer, Reginald Maudling, had delivered generous tax cuts and spending promises in the Conservative's last budget and left the country with an £800-million budget deficit. This presented Wilson with a dilemma. He had promised to improve

Budget deficit – A situation in which the government is spending more than it is raising through taxation.

pensions and build half a million new homes a year. In addition to this he was determined to maintain Britain's military presence overseas, which accounted for over one-fifth of all Britain's spending in the 1960s.

Wilson did not wish to abandon his commitments to either social reform or Britain's prestige. The only other option to lessen the pressure on the economy was to devalue the pound. This would have allowed the British Government to pay off its debts more easily and aided exports, but Wilson was unwilling to do this as he did not want Labour to be seen as the party of devaluation. However, in 1967 he was forced to take the decision to devalue, which was a huge embarrassment for the Government and led to the resignation of Callaghan as chancellor.

Conservatism and the Establishment

Wilson's victory had a lasting effect on the Conservative Party, which attempted to shed its aristocratic image, understanding the appeal of Wilson's modern and supposedly more meritocratic party. The next three leaders of the Conservative Party, between 1966 and 1997 – Edward Heath, Margaret Thatcher and John Major – were from lower middle-class and working-class backgrounds. The party in the 1960s and beyond tried to present itself as modern and egalitarian, as Wilson had.

Wilson's critics within both the Labour and Conservative parties accused him of being an opportunist with few ideals or scruples and no long-term vision for Britain.

Source F One of Wilson's Cabinet colleagues, Denis Healey, on Wilson's performance as party leader and prime minister, from *The Time of My Life* by D. Healey, (Politico's Publishing Ltd), 2006, p. 329.

Vaguely Liberal at Oxford, and a civil servant during the war, Harold Wilson had won fame as Attlee's President of the Board of Trade, by promising 'a bonfire of controls'. He applied himself seriously to Labour Party politics for the first time when he threw in his lot with Bevanism in 1951, as 'Nye's little dog', to use Dalton's words. Then, as Bevan's star faded, he moved far enough towards the centre to be elected leader of the Labour Party when Gaitskell died in 1962. By now he had become an accomplished speaker; he roused the Party Conference to wild enthusiasm by talking of 'the white heat of the technological revolution'. In the General Election of 1964 he made rings round the skeletal inadequacy of Sir Alec Douglas-Home. Unfortunately, since he had neither political principle nor much government experience to guide him, he did not give Cabinet the degree of leadership which even a less ambitious prime minister should provide. He had no sense of direction, and rarely looked more than a few months ahead. His short-term opportunism, allied with a capacity for self-delusion which made Walter Mitty appear unimaginative, often plunged the government into chaos.

British politics in 1964

By 1964 the consensus in British politics was still strong, with both parties committed to achieving full employment, funding the NHS and a welfare state. Where the parties differed was less about the substance of their policies and more to do with the style of their presentation. Wilson was skilful in using the media to present Labour as modern, dynamic and classless. The Conservatives were slow to realise the importance of television as a force in modern politics and were unable to present their party in quite the same way. Despite this, Wilson won an exceedingly narrow victory in 1964 with an overall majority of four. The Conservative Party since 1954 had presided over a post-war boom and rising living standards had secured them two further election victories. Even though the Labour Party had been associated most closely with social reform, the building of the welfare state and the creation of a new and arguably more egalitarian Britain, the Conservatives were seen as the party of economic stability and rising living standards. Their willingness to accept the post-war economic and social consensus meant that many British people who had benefited from the establishment of a welfare state voted for the Conservatives throughout the 1950s, believing that new institutions like the NHS would be protected. The Conservatives were also credited with providing Britain with over a decade of relative economic and social stability after the crisis years of depression, war and recovery. When the party handed over the reins of power to Harold Wilson, the boom, and with it an era of relative political and social peace in Britain, was coming to an end.

KEY DATES: POLITICAL DEVELOPMENTS, 1955–64

1955 Churchill replaced by Eden

1955 Conservatives win a second successive general election

1956 Suez Crisis

1957 Macmillan becomes prime minister

1959 Conservatives win third election term

1963 Macmillan replaced by Douglas-Home

1964 Conservatives defeated by Labour; Wilson becomes prime minister

Figure 4 Governments from 1939–64

Dates	Prime Minister	Party
1937–40	Neville Chamberlain	National Government
1940–45	Winston Churchill	National Government
1945–50	Clement Attlee	Labour
1950–51	Clement Attlee	Labour
1951–55	Winston Churchill	Conservative
1955–57	Anthony Eden	Conservative
1957–63	Harold Macmillan	Conservative
1963–64	Alec Douglas Home	Conservative
1964–70	Harold Wilson	Labour

LOOK AGAIN

In this section a consensus developed in British politics in the 1950s and 1960s. Looking back at the section evaluate the main causes of the development of this consensus.

3 Anglo-Irish relations after the Second World War

Northern Ireland had been a very useful part of Great Britain during the Second World War. It had been an ideal place to fly anti-submarine aircraft from and helped to protect shipping during the Battle of the Atlantic. The contribution made by tens of thousands of Northern Irishmen to the war effort was matched by the 50,000 men from Ireland who also volunteered for Britain. A generation of British politicians felt a special loyalty to Northern Ireland in the post-war era, partly as a result of these sacrifices. This sentiment was felt far stronger and deeper with many British prime ministers and Cabinet ministers than it was in the British general public, among whom lingered a widespread anti-Irish prejudice. In this section we will explore how life changed for people north and south of the border in Ireland in the two decades after the end of the Second World War.

Life for Protestants and Catholics in Northern Ireland

Why were Catholics in Northern Ireland the victims of discrimination?

Since the creation of Northern Ireland, the Protestant Ulster Unionist Party had dominated the six counties politically and economically. The unionists were afraid that the Catholic population was growing faster than that of the Protestants in Northern Ireland and this would result in the ability of Catholics to eventually outvote Protestants. Even though this was unlikely, it was an anxiety that led Protestant politicians and civil servants in the 1940s and 1950s to try to concentrate Catholic populations into certain small constituencies where their votes would not change the outcome of elections. In 1949 the Ireland Act recognised the right of Northern Ireland to remain within the United Kingdom unless the government of Northern Ireland decided otherwise. The Act was a response to the Irish Free State's decision in 1948 to declare itself a republic. This created an even greater incentive to isolate Catholics into relatively poorer communities wherever possible. The Ulster Unionist Party attempted to maintain its dominance of politics by rewarding its Protestant power base, diverting subsidies and government contracts to businesses in Protestant areas and awarding well-paid government jobs to Protestants. Foreign companies setting up factories in Northern Ireland, such as American chemical giant Du Pont in 1957, were encouraged to employ a majority of Protestants. The police service, the Royal Ulster Constabulary, was almost exclusively made up of Protestants and they were supported by an auxiliary service of volunteers called the B-Specials. They were recruited specifically to fight the IRA, but had a poor reputation for discrimination and violence against the Catholic population.

Housing

The supply of council housing in Northern Ireland was also controlled by the Ulster Unionists, who ensured that it was distributed in a way that benefited the Protestant community. Catholics were allocated a sufficient number of houses, but they were normally in poorer areas and placed away from Protestant communities. Protestant politicians often did not want Catholics housed in their constituencies or wards, knowing that they would more than likely vote for a Catholic candidate. The Housing Trust, a non-sectarian branch

NOTE-MAKING

Escalating tensions

Violence between Catholic and Protestant communities in Northern Ireland emerged over decades, but there were short-term factors that escalated tensions by the early 1960s. Divide your notes in this section into long-term and short-term causes of tension, and evaluate which factors were more significant in making conflict by the 1960s more likely.

of the civil service of Northern Ireland which distributed houses, was accused (falsely) of active discrimination against Protestants when it allocated homes on the basis of need, not religion. Plans to develop a new city at Craigavon with thousands of new houses was proposed in the early 1960s, leading to fears of a mass migration from the Republic of Ireland of Catholics seeking jobs and new opportunities. Even though the plans to build the new city largely failed, it was still an alarming moment for the Ulster Unionists, who saw that the domination of housing and urban development was crucial to retaining political control over the six counties.

Harland and Wolff

Northern Ireland boasted the largest shipyard in the world, famous for building the ill-fated *Titanic*. The Harland and Wolff shipyard in Protestant East Belfast was Northern Ireland's largest employer and its skilled, well-paid jobs were dominated by Protestant workers. By the mid-1960s, of the 10,000 workers at the site, only 400 were Catholic. Job applicants were often turned down before their applications were read if their address was in a predominantly Catholic area.

Ian Paisley

Since the formation of Northern Ireland in 1921, many Protestants had lived with a siege mentality, believing themselves to be constantly under threat from the Catholics in the Irish Free State and later the Republic. They believed that the IRA, even though it barely had any members throughout much of the period between the 1920s and 1960s, was a deadly threat to their way of life.

Siege mentality – Feeling surrounded by enemies and constantly under threat.

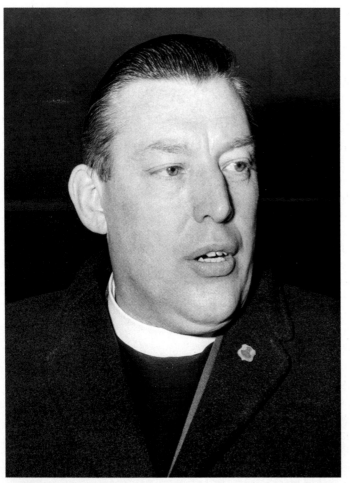

▲ Ian Paisley, a staunchly anti-Catholic Church leader in the Belfast Protestant community.

Above all, there was a widespread suspicion among many Protestants of the minority Catholic community in Northern Ireland and a fear that they supported and helped the IRA. These fears were largely fictitious, as was the fear that Northern Ireland would eventually be abandoned by the British government and handed over to the Republic. However, one Protestant church and community leader began to articulate and amplify these fears from the 1950s onwards. His name was the Reverend Ian Paisley and he had widespread power and influence within Protestant Northern Ireland between the 1950s and his death in 2014. Paisley spoke to the deeply religious Protestants in Northern Ireland in an angry and impassioned manner, warning of the dangers of ecumenicalism (the attempts by the Catholic and Protestant Churches to find some areas of common ground and understanding), believing it was the first step towards Northern Ireland being 'sold out' to Dublin. He used his own newspaper the *Protestant Telegraph* to propagate his ideas, though often it printed lurid tales of Catholic sexual degeneracy and condemned the Pope as an agent of Satan. Paisley established his own Presbytarian Church in the 1950s and by the 1960s it had become a powerful political organisation in Northern Ireland, largely because Paisley was able to play on the anxieties of the Protestant community.

Terence O'Neill

In 1963 a new prime minister, Captain Terence O'Neill, was elected in Northern Ireland. He was an Ulster Unionist and had been selected by his party to prevent the rise of the Northern Ireland Labour Party (NILP). The NILP was separate from the UK Labour Party, which traditionally had a policy of not standing for election in Northern Ireland. O'Neill had a far wider plan to end sectarianism in Northern Ireland; he was from the liberal end of the Ulster Unionists and believed that he could appeal to Catholics to abandon the nationalist parties and embrace unionism. This could be done by offering Catholics better jobs and living conditions. Already, the provisions of the British welfare state were far more generous than anything offered by the Republic of Ireland and many Catholics secretly had little real desire to be reunited with a less prosperous south. However, O'Neill's attempts to offer attractive inducements to the Catholics failed. The Unionist-dominated government continued to discriminate and ignore O'Neill's requests for greater fairness. When in 1963 Pope John XXIII died and O'Neill sent a letter of condolence to Cardinal Conway of the Catholic Church and lowered the Union Flag to half-mast on Belfast City Hall as a mark of respect, Paisley accused him of treason. Paisley made it clear that he was determined to force O'Neill from office and sabotage any attempt to end sectarianism in Northern Ireland.

The IRA and the border campaign

During the Second World War, the IRA had launched a couple of ineffective attacks on England and Northern Ireland, but the police forces in Northern Ireland, Ireland and Britain prevented the organisation from having any real successes. By 1945, the IRA's goal was to overthrow the government of the Republic of Ireland that had accepted the Anglo-Irish Treaty and to destroy Northern Ireland itself, reuniting the entire island. In 1948, the IRA changed its policy and no longer targeted the Republic, recognising the legitimacy of the government in Dublin. The following year the IRA, which had previously viewed itself as separate from party politics, formed links with Sinn Fein (see page 155) and the party gradually became the IRA's political wing. The IRA managed to rearm itself by raiding and taking weapons from British military barracks in Northern Ireland and England. These guns were used to fight a guerrilla campaign against Britain in Northern Ireland which lasted from 1956 to 1962. The IRA's plan was to attack police stations, government buildings and centres of industry until the Unionists and British were unable to govern large parts of Northern Ireland.

The first wave of attacks was followed by the decision of the Northern Ireland government to bring back internment. Despite numerous attacks, the IRA succeeded only in killing six Royal Ulster Constabulary policemen for the loss of eleven of their own men throughout the campaign (four were killed when a bomb-making 'factory' exploded). By 1959 the campaign had run out of steam and the IRA were short of weapons and volunteers, but it was not until 1962 that it was formally called off. Despite the failings of the IRA, Ulster Unionists took the border campaign as evidence that the IRA was a major threat to their future and this led to the formation of Protestant armed groups called 'loyalists'. By 1966 a terrorist group called the Ulster Volunteer Force, named after the original UVF led by Sir Edward Carson (see page 86), was formed. Its members murdered hundreds of Catholics between 1966 and 1994 when a ceasefire was called.

Gerrymandering – To manipulate the outcome of elections by drawing constituency boundaries in a way that disadvantages one side.

The civil rights movement

The example shown by Martin Luther King in America during the 1950s and early 1960s inspired the development of a civil rights campaign for Catholics in Northern Ireland. The IRA, following its decision to suspend the border campaign, hoped that the developing movement would create widespread disruption which could later be exploited. The campaign began in 1964 with the creation of the Campaign for Social Justice in Northern Ireland. The movement was formed partly in response to a visit by Prime Minister Alec Douglas-Home to Northern Ireland in 1963, where he stated that the legal system and the courts were the solution to religious discrimination. The Government of Ireland Act 1920, however, placed the decisions of local authorities beyond the reach of the courts.

The organisation was led by Dr Conn McCluskey and his wife Patricia and was based in the town of Dungannon where there was a Catholic majority (53 per cent of the inhabitants), but where the electoral rules enabled twice as many Protestant councillors on the town council as Catholic. The manipulation of the electoral system to produce a Protestant majority was known as gerrymandering and was even more pronounced in the city of Derry, where 14,000 Catholics were able to elect eight councillors, whereas 9,000 Protestants elected twelve. Votes were allocated only to householders or leaseholders, therefore the poorer Catholics who rented their homes in greater numbers had less electoral strength. Dr McCluskey visited the new Labour Government in London in 1964 to try to persuade Harold Wilson that there was a potential disaster brewing in Northern Ireland. It was hoped that the Labour Party might be more sympathetic to the cause of Catholic civil rights than the Conservatives were, but Wilson was largely disinterested in the problems of the six counties. The complacency of both the Conservative and Labour governments in the early 1960s presented both the IRA, the UVF and other nationalist and loyalist terrorist groups with an opportunity to recruit supporters. By the late 1960s when Northern Ireland exploded into violence, Wilson's Labour Government had missed a historic opportunity to defuse tensions. For the next three decades both parties would have to live with a civil war within the province fought by terrorist groups which claimed the lives of 3,530 people and saw tens of thousands injured in bombings and shootings.

Source G This is a source from a book on the conflict in Northern Ireland. It tells the story of a prominent Northern Irish Protestant, John Beresford-Ash, who returned to the province in 1959. From *Loyalists* by P. Taylor, (Bloomsbury Paperbacks), 1998, p. 32.

When he [John Beresford-Ash] returned to Northern Ireland and the family home at Ashbrook in 1959 ... he was not happy at what he found, in particular in his home town of Derry where, although nationalists were in a majority, the electoral boundaries had been so gerrymandered that unionists ran the city. 'It was an extraordinary situation,' he said. 'There was blatant discrimination against the Roman Catholic population. They were kept in certain wards so that regardless of their numbers, they could never have proper representation at local government level.' John also saw that however hard they tried, many Catholics found it difficult to escape the poverty to which they had long been consigned because of the discriminatory nature of employment.

1 Read Source G. Why might a Protestant be concerned about the treatment of Catholics in Northern Ireland?
2 Consider this source alongside the information in the rest of this section. What were the consequences of the discrimination that Beresford-Ash described?

The Tricolour Riots, September 1964

In the general election of October 1964 one of the IRA veterans of the border campaign, Billy McMillen, ran as an independent republican candidate for Belfast. In late September his campaign office displayed the tricolour flag of the Irish Republic. While this was illegal in Northern Ireland at the time, the police were not inclined to remove the flag, knowing that it would inflame tensions and lead to violence. When Ian Paisley demanded that the flag be taken down, and threatened to lead a large group of his supporters to invade McMillen's offices to remove it, the police acted. Armed officers raided the campaign headquarters, but the IRA put the flag up again the next day. Now the authority of the law was called into question and the police raided the offices again, only to be met by angry demonstrators who attacked them. The rioting in 1964 ended a period of relative calm on the streets of Belfast that had lasted since the 1920s and would be followed by further, far bloodier rioting in 1969.

Northern Ireland by 1964

Despite pleas by the leaders of the province's Catholic civil rights leaders, the two main parties in Westminster paid relatively little attention to the problems of Northern Ireland. The gradual increase in tensions between the two communities was not addressed throughout the post-war period by either Labour or Conservative governments. Instead, the political initiative in Northern Ireland shifted from moderate politicians like O'Neill, to extremists like Paisley on one side and the IRA on the other.

KEY DATES: ANGLO-IRISH RELATIONS AFTER THE SECOND WORLD WAR

1949 June	Ireland Act
1962 Feb	Border campaign ends without success
1956 Dec	IRA's border campaign begins
1963 March	O'Neill elected as prime minister of Northern Ireland
1964 Jan	Campaign for Social Justice in Northern Ireland established
1964 Sept	The Tricolour Riots

▲ A republican protester raises the Irish tricolor flag at Billy McMillen's campaign office in October 1964.

7 Political developments, 1939–64

223

Chapter summary

- The Second World War saw the rise of Winston Churchill in 1940, who led Britain to victory by 1945.
- The Labour Government won office in 1945, promising social reform, nationalisation and a National Health Service.
- In the post-war era a new political consensus emerged between the Conservative and Labour parties.
- By 1951 splits within the Labour Party and a failure to end rationing led to the party's defeat at the polls.
- Between 1951 and 1964 the Conservative Party dominated politics, enjoying widespread popularity during a long economic boom.
- By the early 1960s the Conservative Party was increasingly seen as outdated, upper class and out of touch.
- The Conservatives were faced with a series of embarrassing spy scandals in the early 1960s.
- In 1964 Labour leader Harold Wilson was elected to power after presenting the Labour Party as modern and egalitarian.
- Throughout the post-war period Catholics faced discrimination in housing and jobs in Northern Ireland.
- By the early 1960s a civil rights movement was developing in Ireland, and fierce resistance was mounting from Protestants like Ian Paisley.

Chapter summary diagram

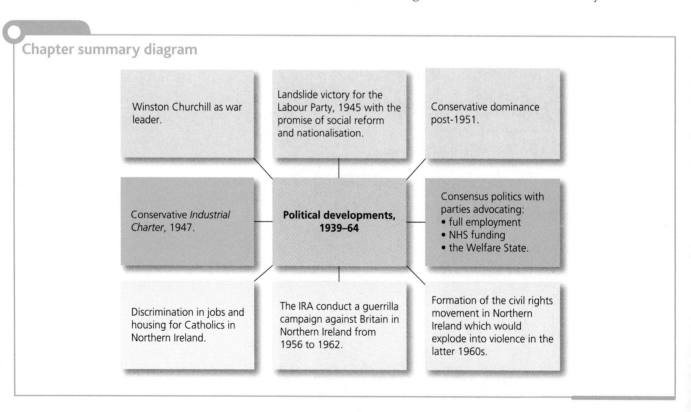

Working on essay technique

So far in the advice given the skills being developed could help a student to write a good essay. To write an outstanding essay though all the same skills are needed. In addition:

- all those skills should be shown at a high level
- there should be a good understanding shown of issues and concepts (which might on this breadth paper include showing awareness of longer-term perspectives)
- an excellent understanding demonstrated of the historical context, with precise factual information conclusion that contains a well-substantiated judgement.

Try to demonstrate these skills in answering the following A-level practice question:

'Between 1939 and 1964 Britain developed a political consensus.'
To what extent is this a valid interpretation of Britain throughout the period?
(25 marks)

This question is inviting you to assess the validity of competing arguments. This means that simply reciting a narrative about wartime cooperation between the parties and the post-war consensus will only enable you to reach low mark scheme levels. Instead you need to understand the key debates (as put forward by historians such as Hennessy, Addison and Kynaston, see pages 214–15) and assess their relative merits.

With each competing argument you might want to follow the process below:

- **Explain**, in brief, what the historian thinks (for example, 'Addison argues that all parties were agreed that state intervention was necessary because of the huge task of post-war reconstruction, and this helped forge a 'left' consensus that benefited Labour over the Conservatives or Liberals').
- **Discuss** the extent to which this is a valid point of view (for example, 'While many British politicians believed that there was a greater role for the state in the economy and the welfare state was a positive development, the population tended to vote for more individual reasons and were less socialist in their outlook. Labour was defeated in 1951, for example, by popular discontent at their failure to end rationing').
- **Compare** with other perspectives such as those of David Kynaston and Peter Hennessy.

8

Economic and social change, 1939–64

This chapter covers the economic and social developments that took place between the start of the Second World War and the mid-1960s, where your study ends. It covers:

- Britain's war economy.
- The post-war economic boom.
- Changes in the position of women and youth.
- Immigration and racial tensions.
- The growth of the welfare state.
- Changes to healthcare and education.

When you have read this chapter and worked through the assignments, you should be able to address the following breadth issues:

- How important were ideas and ideologies?
- How and with what effects did the economy develop?
- How and with what effects did society and social policy develop?

The main focus of this chapter can be summarised by the following question:

In what ways did austerity and affluence change British life between 1945 and 1964?

CHAPTER OVERVIEW

In this chapter we will explore the ways in which Britain changed socially and economically over two decades following the end of the Second World War. The Britain of 1964 had undergone a profound transformation since 1945. An era of rationing, austerity and hardship had been replaced by an age of mass consumerism, rising living standards and increasing leisure time. Britain developed a welfare state and a National Health Service during the first Labour government from 1945–51. Subsequent Conservative administrations chose to retain much of the social reforms Labour had pioneered. A broad consensus developed between 1945 and 1964 as to the role of the state and the extent of government management of the economy. The most important economic aspect of the consensus was a commitment by both parties to attempt to achieve full employment. The years of mass unemployment during the 1930s cast a long shadow over the politics of the post-war decade and no party could entertain policies that would see a return of joblessness. Instead both the Labour and Conservative parties accepted a higher than normal rate of inflation in return for low unemployment. In addition to this, social attitudes appeared to have changed by the early 1960s. Deferential attitudes towards the upper classes and the establishment were in decline and in films, books and plays working-class life and culture was celebrated and glamourised. The purpose of this chapter is to help explain these social and economic shifts.

1 Economic developments, 1939–64

Britain underwent several major economic transitions between 1939 and 1964. During the war, the state once again intervened in the economy on an unprecedented scale, rationing food and other essential resources. Following the war, British people experienced several years of post-war austerity, followed by a long post-war economic boom.

The mobilisation of resources in wartime

How did rationing affect the lives of British people during the war?

At the outbreak of war in 1939 the Government extended controls over most of the economy. Britain was under direct attack from bombing and was fighting a war of national survival. This meant that most British people were willing to accept shortages and privations quite willingly during the conflict.

Rationing and living standards

In the First World War, rationing was introduced only in the final year of the conflict, but in the Second World War it began from the start. Petrol was rationed from September 1939 onwards, and the first food rationing began in 1940. As with the First World War, rationing represented a dramatic increase in the involvement of the state in the economy. The production, price and distribution of goods was controlled by the government, which represented a fundamental break with the government's traditional *laissez-faire* role. Because the price of goods no longer determined their availability (i.e. it was impossible for wealthier customers to pay more for scarce luxuries as they would have been able to do under normal economic conditions), a black market emerged. Wartime black marketeers or 'spivs' broke rationing rules to sell sought-after goods at high prices.

Within three years of the outbreak of war, spending on food had fallen by 15 per cent and the amount of clothes purchased had fallen by nearly 40 per cent. Consumers were issued with a ration book of coupons with strict allowances for foodstuffs such as cheese, meat and eggs. They were required to register with local grocers and shopkeepers to prevent fraudulent attempts to beat the ration quotas.

In January 1940 the Cabinet agreed that domestic consumption had to be the economy's 'lowest priority' and that the public needed to be informed of the need for 'effort, suffering and sacrifice'. The subsequent propaganda employed appears to have been successful in that government surveys found that British people were unwilling to make 'voluntary sacrifices' for the war effort, but accepted compulsory ones as inevitable.

Britain's war economy

A key factor in Britain's ability to resist Nazi Germany was its ability to mass produce the weapons of war necessary to continue the struggle. Even during the initial stages of the war such as the Battle of Britain (see page 204), the British were able to out-produce Germany, especially in the field of aircraft production. In 1940, when Britain appeared to be losing the war, the growth of state intervention resulted in a huge increase in war production and military expenditure (see Figure 1). Britain produced 15,000 aircraft in 1940, rising to 47,000 in 1944, and an average of between 6,000–8,000 tanks per year

> **NOTE-MAKING**
>
> The ability of Britain to harness its economic potential and to find allies with vast resources is a key reason for Britain's victory during the war. Use a mind-mapping technique (see page x) in this section to identify economic challenges and economic achievements faced by Churchill's government.

Figure 1 Government military expenditure, 1939–45.

Year	Military expenditure (as percentage of national income)
1939	15%
1940	44%
1941	53%
1942	52%
1943	55%
1944	53%
1945	51%

Aircraft production

During the Battle of Britain, Lord Beaverbrook was appointed to head the new Ministry of Aircraft Production, applying quotas for fighter aircraft.

In the six months before his appointment, of the nearly 3,000 aircraft built only 638 were the badly needed Hurricanes and Spitfires to defend British airspace, but in the following four months 1,875 were built, tripling British output. The rate of *Luftwaffe* losses and Germany's slower rate of replacement meant that the RAF could win the fighter war of attrition that was being waged in the skies over Britain.

between 1939 and 1945. Military spending as a whole leapt from 15 per cent of GDP in 1939 to 51 per cent in 1945.

In 1939 a new piece of far-reaching legislation, the Emergency Powers (Defence) Act, was passed, replacing the DORA passed in 1914. It gave the government powers to intervene in nearly every aspect of public and private life in Britain and, if need be, to direct the entire economy.

Lend Lease

Between 1939 and 1941 the USA offered Britain considerable economic help, despite the USA's position of neutrality. The American Neutrality Act 1939 initially allowed the British to buy supplies with cash only but, by December 1940, Britain's cash and gold reserves were spent. Winston Churchill arranged a credit agreement with the USA, known as the Lend Lease Agreement. America would supply Britain with the resources it needed but the bill would be paid after the war.

Equally as important was the support the USA gave to the British economy which was facing strangulation from German U-Boats in the Atlantic, preventing British merchant ships from bringing goods to Britain. American 'Liberty Ships', large cargo vessels full of oil, coal, timber, foodstuffs and essential raw materials for the war effort provided Britain with an economic lifeline throughout the war.

Compared to Germany, damage from bombing was limited and little of Britain's economic infrastructure was permanently destroyed. Civilian evacuations and refugees from bombing presented the wartime civil authorities with logistical headaches, but the long-term impact on Britain of the *Luftwaffe* was minimal.

One of the keys to Britain's victory in the Second World War was the role that the state played in the economy. Organising aircraft production, instituting rationing and arranging economic aid from the USA were as essential to victory as the war's military campaigns and battles.

Source A From the autobiography of Labour politician Barbara Castle, in which she discusses rationing. *Fighting all the Way* by Barbara Castle, (Pan Books), 1994, p. 92.

An Emergency Powers (Defence) Act was rushed into law (May 1940) under which all citizens were required to place 'themselves, their services and their property' at the disposal of the government. Those not serving in the forces were mobilized in a nationwide Home Guard. Food rationing was tightened up. The butter ration was cut to 2 ounces, sugar to 8 ounces and uncooked bacon to 4 ounces. Margarine and other fats were included at last and – the cruellest blow of all – tea rationing was introduced at the devastating rate of 2 ounces per week. We were all exhorted to dig for victory. Exotic fruits like oranges, lemons and bananas almost disappeared from our diets.

1 What was the impact of the Emergency Powers Act on the British people according to Source A?
2 How did the relationship between citizens and the state change?
3 Use Source A and your own knowledge to explain briefly the significance of government intervention in the economy during the Second World War.

Austerity and boom, 1945–64

At the end of the Second World War, Britain was bankrupt. The cost of the war had crippled the economy and left Britain economically dependent on the USA, whom it was heavily indebted to. By the early 1950s, however, an economic boom developed which lasted for a decade, prompting Prime Minister Harold Macmillan in 1957 to state that the British people had 'never had it so good'. This section explores Britain's bust-and-boom economy over a twenty-year period.

Rationing and austerity, 1945–51

Why did Labour continue with rationing long after the end of the war?

By the end of the Second World War Britain had accumulated over £4 billion of debt with the USA. Repaying this debt and the mounting interest accruing on it cost £70 million every day.

Once again, British trade had been seriously disrupted and damaged by the war. Not only had British shipping been sunk by German U-Boats, but many of the countries in Europe and Asia that had previously bought British exports were devastated by war. American wartime aid to Europe and China helped US manufacturers dominate post-war markets with their products. Brands like Hershey's chocolate and Studebaker cars now competed with Cadbury and Morris. The British economy had contracted by one-quarter as a result of the war and trade had declined by two-thirds. In the immediate aftermath of the war, the rationing of food, clothing, fuel and consumer essentials such as soap continued for several years. The Labour Government believed that continued rationing was essential. Following the abrupt end of the Lend Lease Agreement with America, a now bankrupt Britain had to devote its industries to creating products to export and goods were diverted away from domestic consumption.

Not only was food rationed but other essential items such as clothing, soap, paper, fuel and kitchen utensils were controlled by rationing until the end of the war. The Labour Government had been forced to introduce bread rationing between 1946 and 1948, a move described by the *Daily Mail* as 'the most hated measure ever to have been presented to the people of this country'. Other non-food stuffs were rationed after the war: clothing was rationed until 1949, along with wood. 'Utility furniture', designed using as little wood as possible, and new furniture was restricted to newly married couples or people who had been 'bombed out' during the war. In 1947, as part of the conditions placed on Britain by the USA in 1945 when the British had negotiated a large American loan, the pound became fully convertible. This meant that controls over the quantity of British pounds that could be exchanged for US dollars were lifted. Instantly the value of the pound plummeted as international financiers who were dubious about the British economy bought US dollars in order to trade in America, which was booming. The result was a run on the pound similar to that which occurred in 1931 (see page 146). As the economy deteriorated rationing intensified, with cutbacks to the supply of meat, dairy and fats.

> **NOTE-MAKING**
>
> Here we have two contrasting economic periods: an age of austerity and an age of affluence and wealth. Divide your notes into two sections, one focusing on austerity 1945–54 and the other on the economic boom 1954–64. You might want to show how in both periods living standards were affected so use sub-headings on 'rationing', 'the winter of 1947', and then in the second section 'the consumer boom'. See if you can also add some sub-headings of your own.

Cold War commitments

The realities of the Cold War meant that raising the standard of living in the immediate aftermath of the war was very difficult. The Government's commitments to feeding parts of Germany that were under British control and to continue fighting in Greece and re-establishing British control in Asian countries like Malaya, had an impact on limited food stocks at home. Expensive British defence commitments grew again in 1950 with the start of the Korean War, diverting resources away from the civilian consumer economy and into rearmament (defence spending was 23 per cent in 1950).

In 1948 George Marshall, US secretary of state, proposed offering extensive loans to war-ravaged Europe. He believed that unless America acted and helped the continent to recover, it might fall to communism. Britain was one of the biggest recipients of this Marshall Aid in 1948 (consuming up to £2.7 billion in loans). Britain failed to use Marshall Aid to reinvest in industry and used it instead to pay for general expenses at home and overseas.

The Labour Government believed that a planned economy would eventually result in raised standards of living. Its 1950 manifesto stated:

'There can be no advance without planning. Exports must be sold in the right markets at the right price, and imports arranged according to our needs. Only by price control and rationing can fair shares of scarce goods be ensured.'

The Conservatives campaigned to end rationing as quickly as possible, but in 1950 Labour proposed to continue it. Labour won the election that year with a greatly reduced majority, a reduction in votes that many blamed on continued rationing. The slender victory in 1950 meant that a second election in 1951 had to be called, which the Labour Party lost.

In its manifesto the Labour Party accepted shortages in food and other essential items and luxuries as an inevitability. It stated that 'many Tories still cry "Scrap controls". Nothing could be more disastrous'.

Winter of 1946–47

During the winter of 1946–47 extremely heavy snow exposed the extent of Britain's post-war economic fragility and had a significant effect on the quality of life for British people. From December 1946 to March 1947 the country was partially paralysed by snow and ice. This would normally not have been such a problem, but because coal stocks had been depleted by the war it led to coal shortages for Britain's homes. Families who relied on coal to heat their homes instead used electric fires, placing an increased strain on the national electric grid. Electricity supply to industry and homes was cut by the minister for fuel and power, Emmanuel Shinwell, to nineteen hours a day, resulting in cold homes, factory closures and unemployment. The Government feared that it would start to run out of food. One-quarter of all Britain's sheep were lost, root vegetables were frozen into the ground and food reserves declined to such an extent that Canadian and Australian citizens began to post food parcels to British families. The electoral defeat of Labour in 1951 was partly attributed to the failure of the Government to ensure food and energy distribution.

Source B British housewife, Judy Haines, wrote in her diary about the shortages of meat in 1945. From *Austerity Britain* by D. Kynaston, (Bloomsbury), 2007, p. 105.

Got ahead with ironing and then felt I must go in quest of meat as that little chop left over from our Sunday joint will not make a very nourishing shepherd's pie. Dyson's [the butchers] very empty. I enquired tenderly if the van had called and they informed me 'no' and there should be some rabbits. I have had my hopes raised like this before, falsely. But I went home out of the cold, made myself a cup of cocoa and then half way through it saw the van. Hastily finished my drink and set off again. Yes, there were some rabbits but they weren't ready yet. O.K. I'll come back again.

1 In Source B, how has rationing affected the standard of living of the diarist?
2 What effect might this have had on support for the Government in the long run?

The end of rationing

The Conservatives had campaigned in 1951 to end post-war rationing, but the final restrictions on the commodities people could purchase were not lifted until 1954. On 4 July 1954 restrictions on purchasing meat were lifted by the Conservatives. The previous year sugar and butter had been released from rationing controls. When meat rationing ended the increase in demand for beef, lamb and poultry saw prices initially rise steeply as the supply of foodstuffs could not keep up. Most rationing had gradually ended under Labour including:

- flour in 1948
- clothes in 1949
- chocolate and biscuits in 1950
- petrol in 1950
- soap in 1950.

Nationalisation

A major economic change undertaken by the new Labour Government in 1945 was the introduction of the nationalisation of Britain's essential industries. A commitment to the state ownership of industries had been set out in Clause Four of the Labour constitution in 1918, which suggested that the workers themselves might own industry.

Nationalisation – The policy of taking private industries into state ownership, which runs them on behalf of the population.

By 1945 it was clear that workers would not control British industry but instead the state would, taking control of coal, power, railways, shipbuilding and banking into public ownership. It was hoped that nationalisation would give the government the ability to create full employment in the economy: nationalised industries that were financed by government would not have to shed jobs during economic downturns. The main priority of Labour and later Conservative governments was not to return to an age of mass unemployment like the inter-war years. Nationalised industries would also be the recipients of state subsidies, insulating them from foreign competition and protecting jobs.

During the first Labour ministry a series of nationalisation Acts brought large sections of industry under government control:

- Coal Industry Nationalisation Act 1946
- Bank of England Act 1946
- Transport Act 1947 (nationalising the railways, road haulage and buses)
- Electricity Act 1947 (nationalising electricity production and the national grid)
- Gas Act 1948 (nationalising the gas industry)
- Iron and Steel Act 1949 (nationalising the iron and steel industry).

The shareholders of the industries taken into public ownership were compensated by the Government. The private rail companies were bought from their owners. The total bill for nationalisation exceeded £2 billion, which left little money for the important modernisation needed. This stored up economic problems for the future: many of Britain's post-war economic problems stemmed from lack of investment in new manufacturing and industrial processes.

Interpretations of the Labour Governments

Historians have been divided about the merits of the 1945–51 Labour Governments. Some argue that nationalisation, the welfare state and a cooperative approach to working with the trade unions stored up major economic problems for the future. Others suggest that Labour ushered in a more humane, compassionate and caring society.

Corelli Barnett

Historian Corelli Barnett argues that instead of investing Marshall Aid (see page 230) carefully in new industries, the Labour Party squandered it. He argues that Labour assumed that Britain was still a global superpower in 1945 and could spend the money on supporting large numbers of troops overseas and paying for an expensive welfare state instead of rebuilding a bankrupt economy. Loan money was also used to prop up the value of the pound, by 1945 a much weakened currency, and by purchasing reserves of gold and currencies. Barnett points out that in 1945 Britain's world power status was an illusion and had been throughout most of the war. It had been based on the American lend-lease agreement (see page 228).

Peter Hennessy

Historian Peter Hennessy argues that Labour's achievements should not be denigrated and that, compared to previous decades, Britain was a fairer and more humane place than it had ever been: He stated that:

'In 1951 Britain, compared to the UK of 1931 or any previous decade, was a kinder, gentler and a far, far better place in which to be born, to grow up, to live, love, work and even die.'

From *Britain in the 20th Century* by I. Cawood, (Routledge), p.254.

In his history of the first Labour Government, *Never Again: Britain 1945–51*, Hennessy presents the six years of Labour as a time of optimism, full of new ideas and with a widespread sense of equality and egalitarianism.

Conservative dominance and post-war boom, 1951–64
Why did standards of living improve during thirteen years of Conservative rule?

The Conservative Party dominated British politics between 1951 and 1964 and during that time full employment, high wages, growing leisure time, low prices and abundant consumer choice led to many British people experiencing better standards of living than any generation before them. In addition to this, the welfare state introduced by Labour provided a 'safety net' that prevented millions from slipping into destitution.

NOTE-MAKING

The 1950s were a decade dominated by the Conservative Party. Create a flow chart that shows the changes in the party's fortunes throughout the decade. You might want to include the consumer boom, the growth of 'Butskellism', stop-go policies and the revolt on the right.

The consumer boom

The post-war decades in Britain saw the longest sustained increase in living standards in British history. At the end of each decade from the 1950s to the 1970s the British people's spending power had risen. Even during the 1970s when inflation reached double figures, the overall standard of living grew. This rapid growth in living standards was based on several key factors:

- a global economic boom throughout the post-war era; new technologies pioneered in wartime and a global population boom created the conditions for economic prosperity internationally
- Britain's welfare state, which ensured a basic standard of living for most of the population
- relatively low energy prices until the 1970s
- a commitment by both political parties to full employment
- strong trade unions able to negotiate high wages for their members
- the increasing availability of consumer credit
- the rise in average wages since 1945.

In 1957 Prime Minister Harold Macmillan famously declared that 'most of our people have never had it so good'. A decade earlier there had still been food shortages, but by the late 1950s the economy had recovered. One factor that allowed working-class families to access consumer goods such as household furnishings, televisions, fitted kitchens and cars, was the relaxation of rules surrounding consumer credit in 1954. Being able to borrow in order to buy luxuries increased at such a rapid pace in 1955 (the demand for television sets rose by 10 per cent) that shopkeepers selling electrical goods announced delays of up to three months while new stock was ordered.

In the inter-war years, credit had been popularly seen as far less morally acceptable, particularly in working-class communities. 'Respectable' people lived within their means and did not borrow. The 1950s saw an inversion of this idea and respectability often came through the ability to buy new and desirable products.

In 1957 Britain spent just over £1 billion on consumer goods and by 1960 £1.5 billion, showing that the rate of consumption of luxuries was rising, and with wages in 1959 being on average twice what they were in 1950 there was far more spending power.

Economic consensus

The degree of agreement over economic policy during Macmillan's time in office was satirised by the media. R. A. Butler, Macmillan's chancellor and Hugh Gaitskell, the Labour shadow chancellor, both of whom served in their respective roles between 1951 and 1955 gave rise to policies collectively described as 'Butskellism'. The term was used by *The Economist* magazine in 1954, suggesting that the policies of the two men were virtually identical. The main economic priority of both Butler and Gaitskell was full employment. The Government was quick to use Keynesian-style public works schemes when unemployment began to rise. Throughout the period unemployment averaged at 500,000, with lows of 300,000. There was no return to the mass unemployment of the 1930s. In addition they supported:

- a mixed economy of nationalised and private industries
- high state spending on welfare, education and health
- consultation with the trade union movement.

Source C From *The Peoples of the British Isles: A New History from 1870 to the Present* by T. Heyck and M. Veldman, (Lyceum), 2015, p. 218.

Despite continuing popular fear that 1930s-level unemployment might reappear at any moment, the number of jobless people never rose above a million between 1945 and the early 1970s. So strong was employment that 'full employment' came to be defined as an economy with only a 2 percent unemployment rate – a concept that was beyond the fondest hopes of inter-war economists. The causes of full employment over the two decades of the 1950s and 1960s were (1) the post-war rebuilding from wartime destruction and expansion of exports; (2) low interest rates inspired by Keynesian financial policies; and (3) the influence of the huge American economic expansion. As the American economy grew, it pulled much of the world economy with it. In Britain, full employment allowed wages to rise, and although wages pushed prices up with them, real earnings improved for Britons by 80 percent between 1950 and 1970.

1 According to Source C, how did the economy improve between the end of the Second World War and the early 1970s?

2 What factors in Source C explain this improvement?

Stop-go policies

Both the Conservative and Labour parties agreed that in order to have full employment, a degree of inflation was acceptable. Keeping unemployment down at all costs inevitably led to a gradual rise in prices. However, Macmillan did not want prices to rise too rapidly and periodically had to slow the economy down. In a bid to balance economic growth against excessive price rises, he was forced to adopt 'stop-go' economic policies. Macmillan and his Chancellor of the Exchequer, Peter Thorneycroft, were forced to introduce deflationary measures by 1957 to cope with the overheating of the economy caused by Butler's Budget in 1955. These measures involved raising taxes and cutting state spending. Macmillan has been described by economists as 'expansionist', meaning that he was in favour of increasing levels of state spending and disliked being forced to cut back. This was due to the fact that he had been MP for Stockton-on-Tees in the north-east of England during the depression, one of the poorest and most deprived unemployment blackspots in Britain. Stop-go economic policies led to investors in the financial markets that determined the value of the pound gradually losing confidence in the British economy.

The revolt on the right

In 1958 Chancellor Peter Thorneycroft, Treasury Minister Nigel Birch, and Financial Secretary to the Treasury Enoch Powell all resigned. The three men believed that Macmillan's government was spending too much and storing up economic problems for the future. They were convinced that inflation, not unemployment, posed the greatest threat to the economy; these views differed to those held by most economists and politicians in the late 1950s. They proposed spending cuts, tax rises, an end to subsidies to nationalised industries and other measures to take excess money out of the economy that they claimed was the cause of inflation.

The resignation of the three men was an embarrassment to the Government, but during a period of low unemployment and relatively low inflation, their exit made little impression on the wider public.

Figure 2 General election results, 1959.

Party	Votes (millions)	Share of the vote (%)	Seats	Change in the number of seats since 1955
Conservative	13.75	49.4	365	+21
Labour	12.22	43.8	258	-19
Liberal	1.64	5.9	6	-
Other	0.26	1.0	1	-2

Source: House of Commons Library, UK Election Statistics: 1918–2012.

Corporatism

In the 1950s and 1960s the Labour and Conservative parties were both willing to cooperate with the trade union movement and a policy of corporatism emerged. This meant that the government invited unions, to agree to participate in the setting of pay scales for workers in nationalised and private industries in order to prevent inflation and strikes. Throughout the war, union leaders had been appointed to numerous government bodies on wages, industry and social policy and this continued after 1945. It meant that union leaders had more access to decision-making than at any point in their history and their views were frequently heard within government. In 1939 union leaders sat on twelve government committees, but by 1949 they sat on 60.

In 1945, 120 Labour MPs were sponsored directly by the unions, of which 26 became ministers and six sat in the Cabinet, including Ernest Bevin, the foreign secretary. Between 1945 and 1951 the TUC and the Labour Party shared similar views on economic and social priorities. Labour repealed the 1927 Trades Disputes Act imposed after the General Strike, restoring to the union movement much of their power in industrial disputes (see page 170 for more details on the General Strike). Unions could once again picket employers they were in dispute with, and they were able to organise sympathetic strikes (see page 171). The 1950s was an era of high employment and high trade union membership (by 1962 there were 9 million unionised workers).

New technology

In the two decades after the Second World War the British economy was transformed by new technologies. British people enjoyed improved standards of living with new consumer goods such as televisions and cameras and access to cheaper goods that had previously been out of their price range, like fridges. These were now made more affordable through mass production. The development of jet travel and car ownership in the 1950s and 1960s enabled British people to visit and experience both their own country and overseas in ways that would not have been conceivable for previous generations. One of Britain's wartime inventions, the computer, gradually became integrated into the working of government departments and large corporations, meaning that organisations could work with increasingly accurate data to predict future trends or plan for the future. There was a popular fascination with technology throughout the period which was often reflected in popular culture (the early 1960s saw a profusion of science-fiction-based shows such as *Doctor Who* and *The Avengers*), which featured science and technology as prominent themes. Labour leader Harold Wilson repeatedly referred to his plans to make Britain a modern and meritocratic society by using technology, and in 1964 established a Ministry of Technology.

Economic problems by 1964

By 1964 the Government was encountering economic problems:

- Unemployment in 1963 grew to its highest level since the end of the war: 878,000.
- Increased consumer spending increased demand for foreign goods and Britain experienced a balance of payments problem, causing a threat to the value of the pound.
- Macmillan and Douglas-Home both refused to devalue the pound and instead borrowed £714 million from the IMF in order to support it.

By 1964 a decade-long economic boom was gradually beginning to tail off. During this period, the majority of British people had seen unprecedented improvements to their standard of living. However, by 1964 both inflation and unemployment were starting to rise, though job losses would not rise above a million until the 1970s.

LOOK AGAIN

This section examined a period of immense economic contrasts. The British economy experienced rationing, austerity and, later, a post-war economic boom. Look again at this section and examine why, in 25 years, there was both economic hardship and affluence in Britain.

KEY DATES: ECONOMIC DEVELOPMENTS, 1939–57

1939 Sept	Second World War begins
1940 Jan	Food rationing introduced
1940 Dec	Britain forced to seek credit for arms from USA
1945 May	Second World War ends
1946–47	Cold winter causes economic crisis
1954	Rationing ends
1954–64	Economic boom
1957	Macmillan makes his 'Never had it so good' speech

IMF – The International Monetary Fund is a global organisation of which Britain is a member. It was created after the Second World War to ensure global economic stability and has been used by Britain several times in the post-war decades as a source of loans.

NOTE-MAKING

It was clear by the 1960s that British society had changed for women, the working classes and immigrants, but how far was this a result of the war? As you make notes in this section create a column on each page where you can add evaluations and judgements about how far the war was actually responsible for bringing about social change.

2 Social changes and divisions, 1939–64

In the period between the start of the Second World War and the mid-1960s, British society underwent a series of dramatic transitions. Attitudes towards class and deference changed, the position of women and young people in society altered, and after 1947 Britain experienced Commonwealth immigration.

Wartime unity, law and order, and social class

How united were the British people during the war?

The wartime Ministry of Information presented the British people as a united and determined population, committed to seeing the tough years of the war through. The Ministry also suggested that a spirit of solidarity across class boundaries had resulted from the external threat of Nazi Germany.

While these sentiments did exist, historians in the post-war decades have presented a far more complex picture of social relations in Britain during the war. Many onlookers at the time, according to historian Arthur Marwick, were sure that the experience of the war would make Britain a classless society. Some historians in the post-war era have argued that a social revolution took place as Britons of all classes endured the Blitz (for more on the 'social revolution thesis' of Arthur Marwick, see page 249).

Contrasting views of the Blitz

Angus Calder

Calder was a revisionist social historian, and argued that the idea of the 'spirit of the Blitz' was a myth. In his two books on the subject, *The People's War* and the *Myth of the Blitz*, Calder argues that the war brought about more social difference than solidarity. The wealthy were able to circumvent rationing and the poor were disproportionately affected by bombing and the loss of housing. The wealthy, he claims, were far more reluctant to bear the sacrifices of the war years than has been suggested by the official propaganda of the wartime Ministry of Information.

Juliet Gardiner

Gardiner believes that the Blitz brought out many positive qualities in ordinary British people. She argues that a spirit of resilience and determination were the main responses to bombing. The start of the bombing led to panic and fear among much of the population of London and other cities, but the government was surprised by how calm and resolute the public were, according to Gardiner. In her book *The Blitz: Britain Under Attack*, she does highlight social differences and divisions, claiming that often, well-to-do communities were less than welcoming to poorer evacuees. In Windsor, in 1940, the local council announced that they were not willing to accept from the East End of London 'children or Jews'.

The experience of being made homeless as a result of wartime bombing, along with the hardships of rationing, caused people of all social classes to cooperate and interact in ways they had never done before and this, it has been argued, caused class barriers to diminish. Studies carried out by the social research foundation Mass Observation suggest that very little social change occurred during the war and that class distinctions remained. Many men and women who volunteered to fight found that the branches of the armed services that they had joined were deeply divided along class lines. Deferential attitudes seem to have survived the war relatively unchanged; across much of Europe, war was also accompanied by social upheaval and revolution, but in Britain the class system, and in particular the monarchy, were largely unaffected.

The Conservative Party had been deeply suspicious of working-class organisations and political movements throughout the inter-war period. However, during the Second World War not only did Churchill have to share power with the Labour Party, but the trade union movement also had a key part to play in the management of the war effort. It was these compromises that made some British people believe that a united and inclusive sense of 'Britishness' existed during the wars that transcended class boundaries.

British public opinion may have become more united in 1940 behind Winston Churchill and the Government's resolve to fight on. However, this does not necessarily mean that the country became more socially united or classless. Between 1939 and 1945 there was a 57 per cent increase in recorded crime in Britain, suggesting that some people were less concerned with solidarity and more interested in black market racketeering and looting bombed-out houses. By 1945 there had been 114,000 prosecutions for black marketeering and abuses of the rationing system.

Post-war boom, affluence and consumerism, 1945–64

How did improving living standards change culture in the 1950s and 1960s?

In the two decades after the Second World War, Britain underwent rapid cultural and social changes. The advent of television, mass consumerism, mass car ownership and the development of youth culture all had a significant impact on the quality of life in Britain. These changes were possible due to rising living standards, growing incomes, increased leisure time and consumer choice.

In the late 1950s and early 1960s a series of writers depicted working-class life in a way that had not been popular or mainstream before. In the inter-war years, depictions of poverty and deprivation in writing about working-class experience were common (writers such as J. B. Priestly, Patrick Hamilton and George Orwell, who wrote the harrowing account of poverty in depression England, *The Road to Wigan Pier*, for example), but in the 1950s and 1960s novels featuring working-class heroes and rebels became popular.

The importance of radio

In Chapter 6 we saw how radio became a powerful medium for education, entertainment and news during the inter-war years. In the 1950s and 1960s its role developed as its audience changed. After the war three channels, the *Home Programme*, the *Light Programme* and the *Third Programme* made broadcasts similar to those heard in the 1930s, but by the 1950s and 1960s they began to lose ground to unlicensed and illegal broadcasters. The BBC had the only licence to broadcast in the UK, but 'pirate' radio stations such as 'Radio Caroline', based on ships moored just outside British territorial waters, broadcast programmes that proved to be immensely popular.

ACTIVITY

Research

In pairs, find out about one of the following working-class writers or playwrights from the early 1960s (you can refer to the Further Research section, on page 268 to help you with this):
- Alan Sillitoe
- John Osborne
- Joe Orton
- Shelagh Delaney.

Answer the following questions:
1 What was the book or play they were famous for?
2 What did it say about Britain's changing society?

Clean Up TV!

In 1964 a school teacher with devout Christian values, Mary Whitehouse, launched a campaign group called 'Clean Up TV'. She believed that television was the most corrupting medium in modern life and was introducing un-Christian ideas to the youth of Britain. The sections above have already shown that far from engaging in promiscuity, British teenagers tended to have conservative attitudes towards sex and relationships. The rapid popularity of Whitehouse's new organisation indicated that this was not how many British people perceived the climate of sexual morality in the mid-1960s. At the first meeting of 'Clean Up TV' over 70 coaches full of campaigners filled Birmingham Town Hall and most of their criticism was directed against the BBC. Not only did Mary Whitehouse condemn scenes of a sexual nature on television, but also images of drinking, criticism of the Royal Family and references to crime and lawlessness. Her views were often far more extreme than those of her supporters; she believed that television and consumerism were eroding faith in God in Britain and that her task was to bring the country back to what she believed were its original Christian roots.

The problem for the BBC and the government was that there was no effective way of stopping the broadcasts and because they played the latest music they developed a huge teen audience. Because of the post-war baby boom and growth in affluence, the large teenage market had more disposable income than ever before and were a keenly sought after demographic that the BBC did not want to lose.

Pirate radio resulted in the reorganisation of the *Light*, *Third* and *Home Programmes* into Radio 2, 3 and 4 respectively. A new Radio 1 was launched which focused exclusively on catering for a youth market and broadcasting pop music. Many of the DJs who had become famous on pirate radio were hired by Radio 1 and became national celebrities.

The importance of television

In 1953 the coronation of Queen Elizabeth II was the first major royal event to be televised and attracted massive audiences; the BBC filmed the event live and broadcast it to nearly 8 million viewers. Following the coronation broadcast the number of TV licence holders doubled to 3 million.

Within ten years (1953–63) television had taken up an ever-increasing share of people's leisure time at home and became a fundamental aspect of family life as the price of TV sets dramatically decreased and television was no longer a pleasure for a minority. Instead, Britain was increasingly defined by its choice of programming.

Commercial TV

In 1954, just a year after the BBC's coronation triumph, the Government passed the Television Act which allowed for a commercial rival to the BBC. The following year ITV was established and was financed not as the BBC was, through a licence fee, but through commercial advertising. ITV offered a different type of broadcasting from the BBC, one which attempted to be more classless and modern. It did not try to impose values on the viewer that were thought to be good for them, but offered entertainment that the viewer wanted. The result was that within five years the company was so financially successful that its advertising revenues were greater than all the major national newspapers put together. ITV was made up of a consortium of regional TV broadcasters and the station had a predominantly working-class audience that enjoyed the quiz shows and variety shows it broadcast. The station imported American sit-coms to Britain for the first time which were immensely popular, such as the *Phil Silvers Show* and *Lassie*, but attracted criticism from some commentators that it was enabling British culture to become Americanised. Even so, the most successful programme on ITV was *Coronation Street*, depicting life in an urban Manchester community, which began broadcasting in 1960. Middle-class viewers tended to prefer the BBC and looked upon ITV broadcasts as 'vulgar' or 'common', demonstrating that in the nation's TV watching, class distinctions and elitist attitudes were developing. More socially traditional radio programmes such as *The Archers*, which followed the lives of a farming community, and *Mrs Dale's Diary*, which viewed life through the eyes of a doctor's wife, remained popular with the middle classes and older working-class listeners.

The importance of cinema

In the immediate aftermath of the Second World War Britain's film industry produced a series of immensely popular comedies from the Ealing film studios. Between 1947 and 1957 the 'Ealing Comedies' entertained but also explored the changing quality of life in a Britain still struggling with the economic aftermath of the war. As austerity ended and Britain's world role also declined, a generation of war films in the late 1950s and early 1960s served to remind cinemagoers of Britain's war triumphs and disasters – though understandably the emphasis was very much on the former. While entertainment was unquestionably the primary purpose of these productions it may be that for many British people this was important because relative economic decline, the loss of world power status, the end of empire and the growth of immigration left them with a sense of uncertainty.

Carry On films

One of the most successful film franchises of the 1960s were the *Carry On* films, made at Pinewood Studios. They featured a regular cast of actors, including Sid James, Barbara Windsor, Kenneth Williams and Charles Hawtrey. The films were innuendo-laden comedies, but they represented the economic realities of the British film industry, with tiny budgets and stars that worked for a fraction (£5,000 per film) of their Hollywood counterparts. The *Carry On* films were a uniquely British type of humour and were not easy to export to America.

The importance of pop music

Popular song had been a feature of British life since the nineteenth century and the development of working-class music halls. The development by the 1950s of copyright laws on sheet music, vinyl records, record players and radios created an environment where a mass market in recorded popular music could exist. The American army's radio service broadcast popular swing, jazz and blues music in Britain during the war, and a decade later British musicians and performers had combined these musical traditions to make an authentically British music sound.

Rock 'n' roll

In the late 1950s and early 1960s American rock 'n' roll music found an enthusiastic following in Britain. American performers like Elvis Presley, Buddy Holly and Chuck Berry reinvented black blues music and popularised it for a youth audience, and the market for American records grew. A homegrown style of rock 'n' roll, skiffle, was also extremely popular. The most successful skiffle artist, Lonnie Donegan, was the biggest-selling British performer throughout the 1950s, with 31 top-30 singles and three number ones by 1962. At this time new groups like the Beatles, the Kinks, the Rolling Stones and the Who replaced skiffle and American blues with their own rock sound and, from 1963 onwards, 'invaded' America, making British pop music world famous.

One pop music genre in the 1960s that had a close relationship with consumerism and fashion was Mod music. Bands like the Who, the Kinks and the Small Faces attracted mainly working-class fans who spent their wages on acquiring the Mod 'look'. Smart Italian suits and shoes, Lambretta scooters and duffle coats were all part of Mod style. In many music subcultures of the 1960s and 1970s consumerism, which was only possible through rising living standards, played an integral part. Being able to buy the right clothes or accessories became as important to fan subcultures as the music itself.

Beatlemania

The Beatles formed in 1957 and had their first major commercial success in 1963. The following three years of their career have been described as 'Beatlemania'. Their fourth single 'She Loves You' (1964) sold 750,000 copies in just under a month. The four members of the group were greeted by screaming fans at their concerts and eventually stopped touring for good in 1966, exhausted by the popularity they had achieved. The enormous appeal of the Beatles should be seen within the context of rising living standards in the early 1960s. Their music between 1963 and 1966 was cheerful, optimistic pop music that seemed to capture the times.

▲ Harold Wilson with the Beatles – (*l to r*) Paul McCartney, George Harrison, John Lennon and Ringo Starr – at a show business awards luncheon in London in March 1964.

▲ Young Mods with their scooters, Tower Bridge Road, London, in 1963.

Mods, Rockers and Clacton

On Whitsun weekend in May 1964 at Brighton, Margate and Clacton, groups of Mods and Rockers clashed. The press reported an 'orgy of hooliganism', and particularly focused on Clacton as a town that was 'beaten up' by the teenagers. The reports wildly exaggerated the events and while there were fights between the rival gangs, the riots that were reported were largely in the imaginations of headline writers.

The 'riots' themselves are of less significance than the reaction to them in the press and among the readership of Britain's tabloids. The lurid tales of anarchy struck a chord with many readers who felt that, overall, young people during an age of affluence were less respectful and that society was less law-abiding.

Youth culture

Teenage culture was first recognised by the media in the post-war years, but instances of it have been identified by social historians as far back as the 1920s. In the post-war decades a baby boom, along with an increase in leisure time and disposable income, created a large market for clothes, records, hairstyles, magazines and all the accessories that were essential to developing a distinctive 'look', which enabled teenagers to fit into a particular subculture. As mentioned above 'Mod' was a dominant look in the 1960s, but before Mod culture developed other subcultures such as the 'Teddy Boy' (young men who dressed in a mock Edwardian style and listened to American rock 'n' roll music such as Elvis Presley) emerged. Often the Teddy Boys were associated with violence and hooliganism, though there was nothing to suggest that they or any other music subcultures were any more criminal than other young people from their communities.

The British tabloid press was important in turning otherwise minor groups like the Teddy Boys into a cause for alarm among older readers, many of whom were confused and worried about the decline in deference these subcultures represented. Newspapers frequently whipped up moral panics about the actions of young people.

> **Moral panics** – Popular anxieties about social or cultural change; often the subject of the 'panic' is relatively harmless.

For most young people in Britain the reality was far more mundane. Opinion polls taken in the 1950s and 1960s demonstrated that young people, far from being radical or subversive, had traditional views on law and order, sex, marriage and the family. A majority aspired to live comparatively normal lives and hoped to marry, have children and work hard for a living.

'Swinging' London

By 1964 the popularity of the Beatles and other pop groups, film stars and celebrities had focused media attention on London. From this period onwards the capital appeared to be the epicentre of fashion, glamour and style. In 1964 the opening of the fashion store Biba in Kensington was a significant moment in the style and fashion of the decade, offering the latest looks made popular by pop stars like Sandy Shaw and Petula Clark. Fashion designer Mary Quant popularised the mini skirt and fashion photographers like David Bailey photographed models Leslie Hornby (Twiggy) and Jean Shrimpton.

This, of course, was not the experience of most people in Britain during the 1960s. In subsequent decades, the early 1960s has been portrayed as a time of glamour, excitement and sexual promiscuity. For most people in Britain, the 'Swinging Sixties' were only experienced through the pages of the tabloid press or on the television.

Decline of deference

An end to rationing in 1954 and the relaxation of consumer credit enabled working-class households to enjoy a level of prosperity they could scarcely have dreamt of a decade earlier (see page 233). It also meant that traditional ideas about community, social class and social mobility became increasingly challenged: people began to question the class system not from a position of poverty and radical socialist ideas, but from a place of prosperity, surrounded by the comforts that consumer capitalism could afford them.

Television and cinema exposed audiences to satirical entertainment which ridiculed ideas about social class, while writers and filmmakers questioned the class system, and tabloid newspapers exposed scandals involving the ruling classes.

The 'satire boom'

One of the clearest examples of a decline in deference came with the 'satire boom' of the late 1950s and early 1960s. In 1960 a subversive and popular stage show *Beyond The Fringe*, starring among others Peter Cook, Dudley Moore, Jonathan Miller and Alan Bennett, played to packed audiences. It made fun of Britain's establishment, the government, army and the upper classes, attracting fierce controversy.

One sketch titled 'The Aftermyth of the War' satirised Britain's war effort, even though for most people the war was a recent memory and a victory to feel proud of. The success of the stage show led to a satirical TV programme *That Was The Week That Was*, starring David Frost, which combined satirical humour with interviews of leading politicians. It was the first time that the British public had seen elite political figures on the television being questioned rigorously by journalists, and it represented a clear change in public attitudes to authority.

Source D From a history book examining British culture in the post-war era, *British Culture and the End of Empire* by S. Ward, (Manchester University Press), 2001, p. 91.

From the late 1950s, changing tastes in popular British comedy had begun to generate an unprecedented appetite for mockery and ridicule of the manners, pretensions and pomposity of Britain's ruling elite – the so called British 'establishment'. It was the 1960 Edinburgh stage revue Beyond the Fringe, that launched the new satire craze into the public sphere, featuring an array of highly innovative sketches on contemporary issues and institutions such as capital punishment, the Cold War, the nuclear threat, the class system, the legacy of war, religion, politics and, above all, politicians ... The satire boom has generally been interpreted as a symbol of profound changes in the dominant values of post-war British society. In particular, it has been understood in terms of the decline in tradition and deference, the rise of the 'permissive society', and the emergence of a cynical contempt towards politicians and public figures generally.

1 What values does the author of Source D suggest were under attack from satire from the late 1950s onwards?
2 What other factors might have had an effect on the decline in deference?

Changing life for women

By 1964 how far had opportunities improved for women in Britain?

The period 1939 to 1964 was one of advances for women in Britain but also of setbacks. The war presented British women with unprecedented opportunities to work in men's roles and to develop skills, experience and confidence. However, throughout the post-war years women continued to face problems such as unequal pay, unequal working conditions and often the frustration of suburban tedium, even during periods of growing prosperity.

Women and the Second World War

As with the First World War, the demands of total war on most of the population of Britain meant that there was an increase in opportunities for women. There was also an increase in hardships and dangers, not just for women who served in the armed forces, but also on the home front as a result of rationing and bombing.

The Second World War saw women conscripted for war work unless they were already employed in reserved occupations. Civil servant Sir William Beveridge wrote a secret report in 1940 that showed that there would be insufficient volunteers to cater for Britain's needs at war. By the spring of 1941 women aged 18–60 were required to register, were interviewed and offered a range of jobs that did not involve front-line combat. In December that year the National Service Act made conscription the law.

Women engaged in a wide range of military and civilian roles between 1939 and 1945:

- Many women found themselves far from home on farms as part of the Women's Land Army, working to grow enough food to keep the country from starving during the U-Boat blockade.
- Munitions factories, aircraft construction, parachute packing and uniform manufacture required a predominantly female workforce.
- The Women's Voluntary Service, which supported the civil defence forces and offered shelter and comfort to bombing victims, offered an essential wartime service. Women assumed non-combat roles as drivers, cooks, intelligence analysts, clerks, radar plotters and mechanics in all three of the auxiliary services during the war:
  - The Women's Auxiliary Air Force
  - The Women's Auxiliary Army Corps
  - The Women's Royal Naval Service.
- Women cryptanalysts and translators worked breaking enemy codes and a small number of British women spies carried out wartime intelligence work.

Women who did not serve in the armed forces or who were not working in the munitions industries still experienced rationing and many saw their families split up by evacuation and the enlistment of their husbands in the army. Despite the hardships caused by rationing, the war years brought practical benefits to the lives of many women:

- Many were better paid as a result of their employment during the war.
- They acquired new skills and confidence in their abilities.
- Many reached levels of importance and seniority that were not available to them in civilian life.
- Overseas postings and relocation gave women opportunities and experiences they had never had before.
- The opportunity to work alongside men towards the defeat of Germany, Italy and Japan gave many women a sense of participation and contribution that they found missing in everyday civilian life.

Reserved occupations – Jobs considered so important that workers in them should not be removed from them – this derived from the First World War, when many men enlisted from occupations such as mining and engineering leaving serious shortages of labour in key industries.

Cryptanalysts – A code breaker.

Evacuation

Throughout the war some 1.5 million British people, mainly children, were evacuated away from major towns and cities to the countryside. Some children who were sent to live in the countryside came from poorer inner-city neighbourhoods and lived with more affluent families. Some of these children were frightened and distressed and were often treated unsympathetically by their hosts. They were inclined to look upon incidents such as crying and bedwetting as evidence of the poor child rearing standards of working-class people in the inner cities. This suggests that, in some cases, the experience of evacuation did little to develop social solidarity. On the other hand, many children had positive experiences and some were even reluctant to return home.

Women's position in post-war Britain

At the end of the Second World War the Government hoped that the social upheavals caused by the war would not result in social change in the post-war era and that women who had worked throughout the war would resume their roles at home as wives and mothers. It offered few inducements in terms of pay or working hours to encourage women to remain in the workplace.

Working life for women

Those women who remained in employment worked in fields that were almost exclusively reserved for women: 86 per cent of working women in 1951 were in industries such as nursing, teaching, factory work, waitressing and clerical work. Before 1944 most women were required to give up work once they were married and in the majority of industries a 'marriage bar' was applied. From 1946 onwards major employers began to remove the requirement for women to leave their jobs when they got married. The practice ended in:

- the teaching profession, 1944
- the civil service, 1946
- the Bank Of England, 1949.

Throughout the 1950s and 1960s the bar was gradually removed from most businesses, but the attitudes of women recorded by Mass Observation in the 1940s and 1950s show that many were ambivalent about their working lives. Some analysts believed that working women who anticipated their jobs ending when they got married had inherited the values of previous generations. A 1948 study of 100 women in three different locations found:

- a widespread desire to end work after marriage
- the need for extra income as the main motivation for working
- that most women interviewed didn't define themselves by their work or see it as an important part of their identity.

The minority of women who wanted to build careers for themselves in the 1940s and 1950s were seen as unusual and were often thought to have failed in some way to fulfil their primary role of 'homemaker' and mother.

The end of the marriage bar meant that in the three decades after the war, more and more women worked for longer with 50 per cent of married women retaining their jobs by 1972. Until the late 1950s in nearly all workplaces unequal pay was an established norm for women, who received, on average, 40 per cent less pay than their male counterparts. In 1958 the civil service introduced equal pay for all employees, along with the education system and the NHS, but there was no government legislation on pay until the Equal Pay Act of 1970.

Family life and personal freedoms

As we have seen, the Second World War involved the majority of Britain's adult female population in war work or active service. This fragmentation caused by wartime experiences meant that in the immediate post-war period many were happy to return to their primary role of 'homemaker' and mother. However, by the late 1950s surveys were starting to paint a different picture, with women feeling isolated and becoming increasingly discontent with their role and status in society. The 1960s and 1970s saw the rise of women's groups and movements to challenge the existing status quo.

Isolation of the 1950s housewife

One study in the late 1950s showed that 40 per cent of women interviewed were content with their lives at home, but the remaining 60 per cent admitted to feelings of boredom, frustration and loneliness. One possible explanation for these changes in attitudes from the late 1940s to the late 1950s was the rapid growth of a consumer society (see page 233), the expansion of leisure time and the improvement in educational opportunities (see page 257), presenting women with far greater choices than they had previously had.

Advertising and consumerism helped to shape the perceptions and expectations of women at home. The 'housewife' was portrayed in newspaper and television adverts as the controller of the domestic sphere, utilising modern technology to run the kitchen. The role of the woman was not simply to cook and clean but to be the decision-maker in day-to-day purchasing decisions (though men normally made big purchases such as cars or televisions). As a result advertisers and product makers in Britain's consumer boom were keen to market their goods to women. Labour-saving devices like washing machines and vacuum cleaners, it was suggested by advertisers, would leave more time for a woman to focus on her family and her husband.

In 1960 a journalist for the *Guardian* newspaper, Betty Jerman, wrote an article that highlighted the frustrations of many women who lived at home. In the article 'Squeezed in Like Sardines in Suburbia', she presented domestic life for middle-class women as dull and suffocating, stating that:

'This example of suburbia is an incredibly dull place to live in and I blame the women. They stay here all day. They set the tone. Many of them look back with regret to the days when they worked in an office … I cannot help wondering what effect the mental atmosphere will have on our children.'

One reader, Maureen Nichol, responded to the article, suggesting that:

'Perhaps housebound wives with liberal interests and a desire to remain individuals could form a national register, so that whenever one moves, one can contact like-minded friends.'

The Housebound Housewives Register was created as a result, and was subsequently renamed the National Housewives Register. It was the first organisation to cater for isolated women at home.

Birth control

In 1961 the contraceptive pill was introduced but doctors were only allowed to prescribe it to married women, fearing that it might encourage promiscuity among single women. This showed the extent to which doctors were seen (and saw themselves) as guardians of public morality. Within a decade a million women were using the pill, demonstrating its popularity and the needs of many women to limit the number of children they had. The pill offered women sexual freedoms that had been unknown and was seen by conservative critics as a cause of Britain's 'permissive society'. Women were now able to enjoy sex without the fear of an unwanted pregnancy. Previously it was common for men to consider themselves in charge of contraception. The pill gave women the ability to control their own fertility and was far more effective than other contraceptive devices.

The permissive society

Rising living standards, a growth in education and more leisure time saw attitudes to sex and marriage gradually change throughout the 1950s and 1960s. It was suggested by some commentators that a 'permissive society' had developed in Britain, meaning that young people were having sex before marriage more often, resulting in 'illegitimate' babies being born. The evidence collected by social researchers throughout the 1960s did not support the idea that a permissive society had really emerged. Young people on the whole had conservative attitudes towards sex, a limited number were sexually active, and most were in relationships or hoped to get married before having sex.

1 What problems does the news report (Source E) suggest the pill might pose to the government and to women?

2 What does the language of the report suggest about attitudes towards women's rights in the early 1960s?

Commonwealth – The organisation of nations that had previously made up the British Empire.

Source E From a BBC news report in 1961 on the day the contraceptive pill was made available.

Several companies are busy manufacturing the product [contraceptive pill] in Britain which will cost the NHS just over one shilling a pill – 17s a month. And some politicians are anxious that the drug could be a huge financial burden on the Treasury which currently spends £90m a year on drugs provided by the health service. Sir Charles Dodds, Britain's leading expert on the drugs contained in the Pill and who heads a research institute at Middlesex Hospital, has said the pills could have long-term side-effects. He compared a woman's body with a clock mechanism. 'Even if you thoroughly understand the mechanism of a clock, provided it is going well it is very much better to leave it alone. To interfere with it if you do not understand it can be disastrous', he said. The Family Planning Association, which runs clinics all over Britain, is still deciding whether or not to give the go-ahead to its physicians to issue the Pill to married women.

Immigration and race relations

Why did Britain experience mass immigration between 1945 and 1964?

In 1947, at the Commonwealth Conference, it was decided that each member state of the Commonwealth would be responsible for creating its own citizenship laws. For decades, there had been a loose understanding between member states that their citizens were all British subjects, irrespective of where they were from. The Labour Government in 1948 passed the British Nationality Act which gave people from across the Commonwealth the status of 'citizen of the United Kingdom and Colonies', and allowed mass immigration to Britain. This immigration was seen as essential to the long-term development of Britain by the Labour Government. Acute labour shortages in the aftermath of the war were a concern to government planners, particularly as Labour had such expansive housebuilding plans and a new and growing health service. Despite this, the Government seemed genuinely surprised by the flow of immigrants from 1947 onwards.

Mass immigration, 1947–58

In June 1948 the *SS Empire Windrush* was one of the first ocean liners to bring Jamaican people to Britain. Its arrival at Tilbury Docks was well-documented by the media and the 492 new British citizens found homes in Brixton. The lure of good jobs and a better future drew immigrants from the newly independent India and Pakistan and migrants from both east and west were shocked to find the 'mother country' impoverished and still affected by rationing, with a worn-down infrastructure and bombed-out cities. They were equally unprepared for the degree of racial abuse that they experienced, not just from gangs of young men in the East End of London who were verbally and sometimes physically abusive, but also from employers, landlords and shops that refused to employ, rent to and serve the new immigrants.

SOME OF THE JAMAICANS ON BOARD THE " EMPIRE WINDRUSH " : They are here to seek for work which their own island cannot provide.

◀ Jamaicans on board the *SS Empire Windrush*, June 1948.

In the decade following the Second World War, Britain actually saw more emigration than immigration. White British families who despaired of the bleak austerity of the post-war years left for Canada, Rhodesia, South Africa, Australia and New Zealand in search of a better life. In Australia 80,000 British people resettled between 1945 and 1969. They took advantage of a heavily subsidised scheme, the '£10 Passage'. It enabled an adult to travel to Australia (children travelled free) with some resettlement help to the equivalent of £350 in today's money.

As Britain became gradually more affluent in the 1950s, the new cultures that had made Britain their home found opportunities to benefit from the rise in disposable income. The first Chinese restaurants, run by Hong Kong Chinese, offered new and 'exotic' tastes to the traditionally unadventurous British diet. By the 1950s there were already dozens of Indian restaurants that had opened in Britain since the turn of the century, but the arrival of Punjabis in the 1950s, many of whom found a home in Southall, meant that there was a massive expansion of Indian restaurants. The significance of ethnic foods, markets, restaurants and shops on British race relations was that it was in these settings that many ordinary white Britons first encountered other cultures.

Sir Oswald Mosley, the leader of the former British Union of Fascists, tried to revive his movement in 1948, following five years of wartime internment. The new party he formed was called the Union Movement and among its aims was its opposition to mass immigration, which by 1957 had reached 35,000 people a year. While his bid to be elected to Parliament as a candidate for the Union Movement in 1959 was a dismal failure, members of the movement managed to attack, harass and provoke black and Asian Londoners, leading to a riot in Notting Hill in 1958.

Immigration and unrest, 1958–64

By 1960 the Macmillan Government was becoming increasingly worried that mass immigration was resulting in racial tensions and proposed to limit the numbers of migrants, particularly those without skills. This led to a surge in immigration over the next two years as people from Asia, the Caribbean and East Africa sought to enter Britain before the law changed. Richard A. 'Rab' Butler, the home secretary, created the Commonwealth Immigration Act in

1962, which limited the immigration of Commonwealth passport holders (though not those with British passports). It placed conditions on those looking to come to Britain, forcing them to apply for a work voucher and those without sufficient skills were rejected. Despite the Labour Party's criticism of the scheme while in opposition, Harold Wilson's government backed it when it came to power in 1964. Pro-immigration Labour MPs in staunchly working-class seats had been voted out in the 1964 election, demonstrating that immigration was a key issue for working-class voters who were worried about jobs and who found themselves struggling to adapt to living in multi-ethnic communities.

At Smethwick in the Midlands, a safe Labour seat, the Conservative Party candidate ran an openly racist campaign. The town had seen a rapid increase in black and Asian residents throughout the previous decade; by 1964 they made up one in ten of the population. Pubs barred black drinkers and a housing shortage raised tensions in the white community, whose members believed immigrants were being favoured by the council for scarce homes. Conservative Peter Griffiths won the seat from the incumbent Labour MP Patrick Gordon Walker, a leading figure in the party. His campaign slogans included: 'If you want a nigger neighbour, vote Labour.' The campaign was successful and even though nationally there was a 3 per cent swing in votes to Labour, in Smethwick the shift to the Conservatives was 7 per cent. This showed both the Labour and Conservative parties that immigration was an issue that was very sensitive with Britain's working-class communities, who felt it threatened their jobs and communities.

The first attempt to address racial discrimination following Smethwick was the Race Relations Act 1965. Passed by Wilson's government, it stated that it was unlawful to refuse service, overcharge or delay service to a person based on their ethnic origin. The practice of placing announcements in shops or boarding houses that 'coloured' or Irish customers were unwelcome was commonplace up to that point, and the Act's main weakness was that it excluded both shops and boarding houses, so it was largely ineffective.

Source F An extract on the politician Patrick Gordon Walker: 'Walker, Patrick Chrestien Gordon, Baron Gordon-Walker (1907–1980)' by Robert Pearce, *Oxford Dictionary of National Biography*, (Oxford University Press), 2004, pp. 88–90.

Labour won the 1964 general election and Gordon Walker duly became foreign secretary, on 16 October, but in fact he had lost the contest at Smethwick by 1174 votes after a racist campaign by his opponents. A national swing to Labour of 3.5 per cent was transformed, in Smethwick, into a 7.2 swing to the Conservatives. The Tory candidate, Peter Griffiths, refused to condemn the slogan 'If you want a nigger neighbour, vote Labour' and called for a complete ban on coloured immigration. This was the first major eruption of racism in modern British politics, and many considered the election result to be a major national scandal. The fact that Gordon Walker had opposed the limitations on immigration imposed by the 1962 Commonwealth Immigrants Act was used against him ... A seemingly safe seat was hastily found for the foreign secretary at Leyton, whose incumbent MP was sent reluctantly to the Lords. But on 21 January 1965 Gordon Walker again lost, by 205 votes. Immigration was not a key issue in Leyton, though the National Front campaigned violently against him and the press gloried in portraying – unrealistically but effectively – a lugubrious patrician [a member of the upper classes who views themselves as being responsible for the poor] statesman too disdainful to beg the votes of the plebs [derogatory word for working-class people]. He resigned as foreign secretary the following day.

1 How did the issue of race and immigration affect Gordon Walker's career (Source F)?
2 To what extent does Source F show that politicians were using race and immigration to further their own political goals?

Interpretations: a cultural revolution?

To what extent did Britain experience a major cultural change in the 1950s and early 1960s?

How far did attitudes, ideas and values really change during the 1960s? Did Britain become less deferential and did the image of 'Swinging' London have anything to do with reality? Many historians agree that many assumptions held about social and cultural change in the 1960s have been proved to be exaggerated or false. Popular attitudes towards immigration, women's rights, homosexuality, the death penalty, family life, the monarchy and Britain's youth were still highly conservative by the end of the period. The historian Arthur Marwick claimed that there was a cultural revolution in the 1960s. He argues that the period that can be classed as the 1960s actually ran from 1958–74 (the notion of a 'long decade' or 'long century' is often used by historians to describe particular eras that cannot be confined to strict time slots). Marwick believed that there were several signs of a cultural revolution during the decade:

- the development of new subcultures that were opposed to the establishment (a women's movement, gay rights movement)
- a growth in entrepreneurialism and the setting up of numerous fashion shops, theatres, book shops, photographic agencies and other enterprises that were 'bohemian' (see page 241 on 'Swinging' London)
- the development of new technologies such as telephones, record players, jet travel and consumer goods
- the development of television
- an unprecedented wave of international cultural exchange (British Mods wearing Italian fashions; the Beatles 'conquering' America)
- upheavals in class and family relationships
- new attitudes to sex and 'permissiveness'.

Historian Dominic Sandbrook more recently has suggested that the radical changes that occurred in the lives of British people were not ideological or moral ones, but consumerist. As available wealth and leisure time grew, along with consumer choice, British people found themselves grappling with social and cultural change brought about by mass affluence. It was rising living standards, he argues, that defined the 1950s and 1960s, far more than new ideas about identity, politics or society. These ideas were certainly present in the 1950s and 1960s, but were not dominant or central to daily life. He argues that most people in Britain did not experience any kind of 'cultural revolution', but simply enjoyed unprecedented prosperity and leisure time.

Source G From 'Experimental Theatre in the 1960s' by Arthur Marwick, *History Today*, October 1994.

Much attention has been focused on pop groups and film stars, on directors, designers, photographers and models, on hippies and druggies; but the important transformation was in the way that ordinary people, of whatever class or race, gained a freedom in basic relationships and everyday living, non-existent in the mid-1950s.

What happened between 1958–59 set the social and cultural agenda for the rest of the century; it also had a special character of its own, arising from the unique interaction of innovation pushed to extremity, with the persistence of the traditional liberal humanist values of tolerance and respect for cultural diversity … Films, legitimizing new moral standards and new modes of behaviour in front of mass audiences, rock music, its liberating forms being danced to in every corner of every country: there is little difficult in seeing these as agents of change.

> **Cultural revolution** – A fundamental shift in the way that individuals perceive themselves, the society around them and the way in which they communicate these new ideas and outlooks to others.

ACTIVITY

The three extracts below and page 250 give different interpretations of the extent of a cultural revolution in the 1960s. Begin by reading each one and listing the main points made and the evidence used to support them. Then answer these questions:

1 In what way do Sources G and H agree and disagree?
2 In what way do Sources H and I agree and disagree?
3 Using material from the sources and your own knowledge, write two paragraphs in answer to the following question: 'To what extent did Britain experience a cultural revolution in the 1960s?'

Source H From 'The Swingers Who Never Were' by Dominic Sandbrook, *New Statesman*, 21 March 2005.

Where they once saw a 'cultural revolution', historians now see much stronger evidence of continuity, caution and conservatism. We often think of long-haired guitar-toting students … But just one in ten young people in the late 1960s went to university. Most did not join communes or have orgies or march against the Vietnam war; indeed, almost anywhere you look you can find evidence that belies the myths of permissiveness and revolution. Was there really a cultural revolution? A million people rushed out every Saturday to buy the latest hit singles; but two million men and boys went in pursuit of fish, and a staggering 19 million people pottered about the garden. Far from transforming the lives of the nation, the Pill was largely unknown: in 1970, a survey found that only nine in a hundred single women had ever taken it, and in any case, birth control had been widespread for years anyway in the form of the humble condom. Far from losing themselves in a whirlwind of orgies and affairs, young people were marrying and settling down earlier than ever before: in 1970, the average age of a bride fell below 23 for the first time. According to every survey, most people still had the same number of sexual partners as their parents had had before them, which is to say just two or three.

Source I From *Hope and Glory* by P. Clarke, (Penguin), 2000, p. 291.

The sexual behaviour of young people was escaping traditional controls, not least among students living away from home. This stereotyped impression of the 'swinging sixties' was often linked with the introduction of the new birth-control Pill for women. But there is evidence indicating that changes in conduct in fact precede – by as much as a decade – the widespread availability of the Pill in the late 60s, a development which was more a response to new sexual mores than the cause … Whether there was as much sexual activity among the young as talk about the permissive society suggested, is not easy to establish … the sixties raised timeless issues of inter-generational conflict to new levels, partly because, with growing prosperity, economic independence was more quickly achieved by teenagers in a tight labour market.

LOOK AGAIN

This section focused on how British society changed between 1939 and 1964. Look back at this section and particularly the interpretations section and evaluate the main reasons why society changed. Did attitudes and values among the British public really change dramatically throughout the period?

KEY DATES: SOCIAL CHANGES AND DIVISIONS, 1939–64

1939 Sept	First evacuation from cities takes place
1947	Immigration from the Caribbean to the UK begins
1953 June	Queen Elizabeth II's coronation
1958	Notting Hill riot
1961	Contraceptive Pill becomes available
1963	The Beatles dominate the charts
1964	Smethwick by-election

WORK TOGETHER

Working in pairs, debate and develop arguments that either support or challenge Marwick's claims (Source G). Decide which partner is going to support Marwick's argument and who will oppose it. Before you begin a discussion, make notes on the strengths and weaknesses of your chosen argument.

You might want to focus on the following areas in this chapter in order to find evidence to support or undermine the Marwick thesis:
● the decline in deference
● popular music and film
● women's rights
● youth culture.

3 Developments in social policy, 1939–64

The Labour Government that came to power in 1945 was elected on a mandate of far-reaching social reform. This section explores the origins of these social reforms, their implementation and their impact on the British people.

Planning for the post-war era: the Beveridge Report

What was the significance of the Beveridge Report?

During the Second World War, government became increasingly interventionist, even taking action to improve the diet of British people. The Government's Food Policy Committee, chaired by Clement Attlee, the Labour leader, authorised subsidised milk and heating fuel for mothers with small children. Finally, in 1940, supplementary pensions were introduced for the elderly. The war years, therefore, were actually a period in which one-third of the population who had been unable to eat enough during the depression, found their standards of living improve, even during a period of rationing.

The Beveridge Report

In 1945, Labour argued that state planning should continue in order to rebuild Britain and solve the problems of deprivation and unemployment. Labour politicians such as Clement Attlee, Herbert Morrison and Stafford Cripps had been senior ministers in the wartime National Government, and had been involved in government planning. They argued that the methods that had won the war should be used to win the peace. Outside the Labour Party, an enlarged role for the state also seemed like a good idea. Indeed, it seemed perfectly natural to apply the same methods that had led to victory in war to public welfare. Initiatives to deal with education and health will be addressed later, but in this section the focus will be on how the Beveridge Report affected welfare provision.

The Beveridge Report set out a vision of post-war Britain in which state welfare had conquered the five evils of squalor, ignorance, want, idleness and disease. It was written by the social reformer William Beveridge in 1942 as part of broader attempts by the Government to plan the reconstruction of Britain after the war.

The report advocated a new relationship of cooperation between the state and the individual. Beveridge was not suggesting that the state should take over responsibility for the running of people's lives. He was keen to provide welfare, referring to it as a 'safety net', but also to preserve the independence of the British people. He argued that government action:

'*should not stifle incentive, opportunity, responsibility. In establishing a national minimum, it should leave room and encouragement for voluntary action by each individual to provide more than that minimum for himself and his family'.*

The report advocated universal benefits, meaning that they would be paid to everyone regardless of income level, rejecting the means tests introduced in the 1930s. In essence, Beveridge argued for a flat rate of contributions from all wage earners to pay for welfare benefits and a flat rate of benefit irrespective of individual circumstances.

NOTE-MAKING

Where did the welfare state come from? This is a question that has dominated much thinking on British post-war history. In your notes create a timeline from the 1900s to the 1950s and focus on key governments:

- The 1906 Liberal Government (see pages 71–73).
- Lloyd George's Coalition 1918–22 (see pages 135–37).
- The Governments of Ramsay MacDonald 1924 and 1929–31 (see pages 142–43 and 145).
- Stanley Baldwin's Government (see pages 144–45).
- The National Government (see pages 146–47).
- The 1945 Labour Government (see pages 207–08).

Sir William Beveridge, 1879–1963

Beveridge was a member of the Liberal Party and a social reformer. His career had been focused on the development of social security since the start of the twentieth century. By the Second World War he was a leading expert on unemployment and pensions and he had come to believe that only strong centralised planning could provide Britain with a welfare state.

Ministry of Information – The wartime government ministry created to communicate government policy and propaganda to the general public.

British Medical Association – The professional body representing doctors and their interests.

White Paper – A report that explains an issue and presents possible solutions to the problem, used by government to help plan policy and new laws.

Beveridge's vision was extremely popular. Indeed, the report sold several hundred thousand copies. It was also used as propaganda. British troops stationed overseas were sent copies to encourage them to fight for a better Britain. The Beveridge Report seemed to articulate the hopes of most Britons of a Britain free of poverty. The Ministry of Information monitored public opinion and found the report to have support from all elements of society. It was well-received by all of Britain's newspapers too, including the *Times* and *Telegraph* which traditionally supported small government and low taxes.

The Government decided not to implement the recommendations immediately. Moreover, Prime Minister Winston Churchill spoke out against introducing excessive welfare provision after the war. It became clear, however, that the post-war general election would be fought over the recommendations in the report and the Conservative, Liberal and Labour parties all adopted the report to differing degrees.

The Emergency Medical Service

In 1939 the Emergency Medical Service was founded to provide first aid and casualty clearing stations for people wounded in air raids. It allowed the government to dictate a hospital's activities, a power it had never previously possessed. Between 1939 and 1940 an entire national service had been created in anticipation of German attacks.

The Emergency Medical Service resulted in the pooling of resources, skills and expertise, and the creation of a national system. Very quickly, government planners adopted the national framework as the basis for plans for a post-war healthcare system.

War also led to a change of attitude within the medical profession. Previously many doctors and hospital administrators had preferred to stay independent of government. However, the central organising power of the state, along with additional funding, proved to be attractive. Consensus in favour of a national state-run system did not emerge immediately, but in 1941 Medical Planning Research, a group of 200 doctors, endorsed provisional plans for a nationwide health service.

Negotiations with the British Medical Association (BMA)

The creation of a post-war health system required intense negotiation between doctors, represented by the British Medical Association, and managers of local authority, private and voluntary hospitals. All groups were willing to collaborate, but also concerned about the loss of autonomy that a national state-run health system required.

Negotiations between 1942 and 1943 resolved many of the major issues. Consequently, the Government published a White Paper on health in 1944 recommending a new national system paid for from general taxation. By the end of the Second World War a huge shift in thinking about health had taken place. All three main parties committed themselves to state-provided, centrally funded healthcare.

Building the welfare state

How successful was Labour in creating a welfare state by 1951?

Some historians argue that the welfare state was the product of Britain's experience in two world wars; others that it was the culmination of social reforms that had been developing since the 1870s (see Chapter 2). The clearest expression of Labour's post-war reforms had come in the form of the Beveridge Report in 1942, which advocated a comprehensive system of welfare benefits for all from 'the cradle to the grave'.

The biggest achievement of the Labour Government was the establishment of a National Health Service, but it was accompanied by a raft of other acts that offered the social 'safety net' envisaged by Beveridge. Figure 3 below lists the major social reforms of the government and the impact they had on the British people.

Figure 3 Welfare legislation 1945–48 and its impact.

Legislation	Impact
National Assistance Act, 1948	The Victorian poor law system was finally abolished in 1948 by the National Assistance Act and it offered welfare to those who were not covered by national insurance. The homeless, disabled and unmarried mothers were all able to claim, as were pensioners living on the poverty line. The Act abolished the unpopular Public Assistance Committees and replaced them with a centralised National Assistance Board.
National Insurance Act, 1946	Levied as a 4s 11d weekly charge on wages, but it ensured that unemployment and sickness benefits were paid and a state pension was available at the age of 65 (or 60 for women).
Industrial Injuries Act, 1946	Gave workers the right to be compensated for accidents and injuries in the workplace. The national insurance fund paid out the compensation and the Act was popular with the more dangerous professions such as mining. An average of 2,425 people were killed each year at work in the 1940s, and even more injured, with mining accounting for over a quarter of the total number of deaths and injuries.
New Towns Act, 1946	New towns were designed to relieve the overcrowded working-class districts of major cities like London, Birmingham, Glasgow and Newcastle. New towns like Stevenage, Cwmbran, Cumbernauld and Hatfield were designed using modern architecture and town planning and for many working-class families who had lived in crowded slums before the war, they represented a considerable improvement in living conditions. It was the first time that many working-class people had lived in suburban estates.
Family Allowances Act, 1945	Created child benefits for the first time, which came into effect the following year. The Act gave an allowance of five shillings a week for all children (with the exception of the family's eldest child), payable to their parents. Initially the trade unions opposed the introduction of family allowance as they believed it would be used by the government as an excuse not to increase wages.

The NHS

The Labour Party's landslide victory of 1945 led to the creation of the National Health Service. The party's manifesto had promised a comprehensive healthcare system:

'In the new National Health Service there should be health centres where the people may get the best that modern science can offer, more and better hospitals, and proper conditions for our doctors and nurses. More research is required into the causes of disease and the ways to prevent and cure it.'

Labour was not alone in promising a National Health Service. The Conservative manifesto offered:

'A comprehensive health service covering the whole range of medical treatment from the general practitioner to the specialist, and from the hospital to convalescence and rehabilitation.'

When the new prime minister, Clement Attlee, formed his Cabinet he gave the position of minister for health to the Labour left-winger Aneurin Bevan. Between August 1945 and July 1946 he devoted himself to the creation of the National Health Service Act (England and Wales) with a separate act for Scotland the following year. The Act was designed to establish a comprehensive health service that was largely free of charge. NHS hospitals would be run by regional hospital boards with executive committees managing GPs, dentists and opticians, and local health authorities providing services such as ambulances, vaccinations and community nursing. The Act also specified that the NHS would be paid for by direct taxation rather than insurance. For two years until the foundation of the NHS in 1948, Bevan struggled to get the cooperation of doctors. In order to win their support, Bevan agreed to a series of compromises:

▲ A group of student NHS nurses learning how to bandage a head properly at Milford Hospital in the 1960s.

- Consultants were allowed to continue working privately and were allocated beds in hospitals for private patients.
- GPs were able to avoid becoming local authority employees and therefore subject to local authority pay controls – their preserved status as self-employed also brought significant income tax advantages.
- Regional health boards were appointed, not elected, and were dominated by consultants who tended to be upper middle class.

As a result of these compromises, the new NHS was run by privileged groups from the outset. Nonetheless, Bevan achieved much of what he intended, although he claimed that the concessions to consultants amounted to bribery and he had 'stuffed their mouths with gold'. Section 21 of the National Health Act called for the establishment of health clinics where GPs, consultants and nurses would carry out all kinds of healthcare from preventative health advice to acute care. This was opposed by the BMA, who thought that it would downgrade the status of doctors. Because doctors' practices were private businesses, the BMA feared that the changes would affect each doctor's ability to earn. By 1958 only ten of these health clinics had been built, showing how powerful the BMA was in deciding the fate of healthcare in Britain.

Source J From *Bevan* by C. Beckett and F. Beckett, (Haus Publishing), 2004, p. 73.

Bevan's first act on entering his ministry [of Health, in 1945] was to remove the large soft leather chair. 'This won't do' he said. 'It drains the blood from the head and explains a lot about my predecessors.' He was a working minister, identifying closely with his civil servants. Bevan's Chief Medical Officer, Sir William Wilson Jameson (1885–1962), says Bevan 'sold himself to the ministry within a fortnight'. This was vital if the department was to work with him during the years ahead, but it was also part of Bevan's approach to the job. He saw himself as a member of the work-force.

'Never once during the 1945–50 government', said Jennie [Lee, his wife] 'did he come home and complain about his permanent officials. On the contrary, he was full of gratitude to them and was worried only by the strains he was imposing on them.'

> 1 What view of Bevan does the author of Source J present?
> 2 What else might a historian need to know about Bevan's ideas, beliefs and outlook to create a complete picture of his views?

Aneurin Bevan, 1897–1960

Bevan was the son of a South Wales miner from Tredegar, one of the poorest and most deprived parts of Britain. He was one of ten siblings and worked as a miner from the age of thirteen after underachieving at school, later learning to read at the Tredegar Miner's Institute. He protested against the First World War, and by the age of nineteen he was chairman of the local miners' lodge and stood out to mine owners as a troublemaker and potential revolutionary. At the end of the First World War he was sponsored by the South Wales Miners' Federation to study politics and economics in London and during the General Strike in 1926 he became one of the miners' leaders in south Wales. He became an MP in 1929 and was an outspoken critic of the Conservative Party, reserving particular vitriol for Winston Churchill. He was also a critic of Ramsay MacDonald, especially after the formation of the National Government. Bevan later visited Spain during the Spanish Civil War and had sympathies for the left-wing Republican Government there and the British volunteers who fought in the International Brigade (see page 151). Bevan was as outspoken as Churchill by 1939 and after the war began he actively campaigned for Churchill to replace Chamberlain. Bevan believed that the war presented a unique opportunity to change British society and build a welfare state.

Benefits of the NHS

The establishment of the NHS gave British people free healthcare paid from National Insurance and taxation. However, because of Bevan's disputes with the medical profession, the service was still fragmented when it was created in 1948 and in many parts of the country there were inequalities in the provision of healthcare. Some areas saw new hospitals built, whereas others had to rely on older voluntary hospitals that were able to avoid central government control. The NHS provided three tiers of service (known as the tripartite system):

- hospital services: accident and emergency service and in-patient treatment for serious illnesses
- primary care: GPs, dentists, opticians and pharmacists all operated as independent contractors (private businesses, not run by the NHS but who sold their services for a profit)
- community services: health visitors, vaccination services, health education, midwives and ambulances were all managed by local authorities, not directly by the NHS.

The new service was a huge expansion in health coverage in the lives of many ordinary people in Britain. The combination of better healthcare and increased affluence saw life expectancy increase from 65.8 years for men and 70.1 years for women in 1948 to 71 years for men and 77 years for women in 1979.

In 1952 Bevan outlined his ideas about public health in a book *In Place Of Fear*. He wrote:

'When we consider the great discoveries in medicine that have revolutionised surgery and the treatment of disease, the same pattern appears. They were made by dedicated men and women whose work was inspired by values that have nothing to do with the rapacious bustle of the stock exchange.'

Bevan did not believe there was any room within the NHS for markets or free enterprise, even though GPs were allowed to be self-employed contractors to the NHS. This was a view that was shared not only in much of the Labour Party, but by moderate or left-leaning MPs and ministers within the Conservatives as well.

Within the first half decade of the NHS's existence, the service's costs had risen significantly beyond the levels that were anticipated. In addition to this, Britain's other major spending commitment, defence, grew rapidly after 1950 due to the Korean War. The result was a decision by Labour chancellor Hugh Gaitskell in 1951 to increase charges on prescription glasses and dentures, resulting in Bevan's resignation. The amount that was effectively cut from the NHS was tiny, £13 million out of an overall budget of £4 billion, and Bevan (who had already left the Ministry of Health for the Ministry of Labour) resigned in part because of his dislike of Gaitskell. The loss of Bevan from the Government divided the party and contributed to its downfall in the 1951 general election. No Labour chancellor until James Callaghan in 1968 made cuts to the healthcare budget, in part because of how unpopular it would be with the public, but also because of the potential for internal party conflict.

Despite increased levels of spending on healthcare after 1948, studies found that the actual practice of medicine often did not improve as a result. The health foundation the Nuffield Trust reported in 1952 that:

'The overall state of general practice is bad and still deteriorating ... some conditions are bad enough to require condemnation in the public interest.'

NHS spectacles

Glasses and eye tests were provided free of charge on the NHS and as a result the numbers of spectacle wearers after 1948 dramatically increased. Initially £2 million was set aside to pay for free glasses, but within a year £15 million of glasses had been claimed. By 1950, £22 million a year was being spent on publicly funded eye tests and glasses, with 7.5 million pairs per year being dispensed. NHS glasses were prescribed to many wearers who barely needed them at all and they were famously unattractive, but even so there were long waiting lists to get them.

Education

The Beveridge Report of 1942 identified ignorance as one of the great 'evils' that affected Britain. The war exposed the failings of the British educational system as many branches of the armed services had to teach basic literacy and numeracy to the lower ranks. The Second World War required educated troops as the technological complexity of modern warfare had dramatically increased. An educated civilian workforce and a civil defence and auxiliary service was also required, not just during the war but after it as well. As the tide of war turned against Nazi Germany, Britain approached a new and uncertain world – one in which it could not afford to be complacent. It was for these reasons that a new Education Act was passed in 1944 to prepare for a post-war educational system.

The 'Butler Act', 1944

The Education Act 1944 and the later Scottish Education Act 1945 were both major extensions to working-class children's access to education. State secondary schools would no longer charge fees and the cost of mass education would be paid for out of general taxation, making schools, like healthcare, the responsibility of central government. Compulsory education was extended to the age of fifteen. Local Education Authorities were obliged to provide 'instruction and training as may be desirable in view of their different ages, abilities and aptitudes'. However, both Acts created an education system that reflected, and critics argued perpetuated, Britain's rigid class structure. The Acts were created by R. A. Butler, the education minister, and established a 'tripartite' system of schools for secondary education closely matching Britain's class system: grammar schools, secondary modern schools, and secondary technical schools. Grammar schools continued to be the preserve of the middle classes and produced, along with private schools and Britain's elite public schools like Eton, the country's political, economic and institutional leadership. They were, however, also a conduit for working-class children who were able to pass the Eleven Plus exam. The access to grammar schools for working-class children was a key factor in social mobility in the post-war era, as many were able to proceed to university as a result. Secondary moderns tended to educate lower-middle-class and working-class children and the technical schools educated the middle classes for a life in scientific or engineering work, to create a technocratic class that could help the country to adapt in an age of high technology and nuclear power.

Civil defence – The fire service, rescue teams, air-raid wardens and others who limited the impact of German bombing or helped to rescue survivors.

Auxiliary service – Services that helped the front-line troops, such as the Women's Army Corps.

Technocratic class – Skilled engineers, managers and scientists who can make society function effectively.

The Eleven Plus exam

In order to determine which secondary school a child attended children sat the Eleven Plus exam. Initially the drafters of the Butler Act had intended for the exam to filter children to the three types of school:
- academic ability: grammar schools
- technical ability: technical colleges
- functional ability: secondary moderns.

Technical ability was eventually left out and instead of the test being a means of channeling pupils to schools that suited them, it became a test to decide whether pupils could enter grammar school or not. Critics argued that it was impossible to tell how a child would develop intellectually at the age of eleven. Opponents of grammar schools in the Labour Party argued that the Act deepened class divides by sending a majority of working-class children to secondary moderns.

Butler did not anticipate how few technical schools would be built. The majority of children who did not pass the Eleven Plus exam found themselves joining secondary modern schools instead.

The effect of the Butler Act was that for the first time millions of working-class children had a free and compulsory secondary education up to the age of fifteen. Social change in the 1960s and 1970s was in part the result of the 1944 Act, as it enabled more children than at any other time in the nation's history to become educated.

However, there were limits to the Act's egalitarianism. Children attending secondary modern schools were unable to take public exams such as the school certificate. There was an influential movement of politicians and public figures, including the poet T. S. Eliot, who argued that education should remain elitist and that secondary modern pupils should not have access to examinations. The result of this discrimination was that it was far more difficult for secondary modern pupils to be accepted to university or to join 'white collar' professions.

In 1947 a General Certificate of Education (GCE) replaced the school certificate. It was divided into ordinary (O) and advanced (A) levels, but again, only grammar school pupils were allowed to sit the exam. In 1965, Harold Macmillan's Government introduced a new qualification, the CSE, that was sat by 40 per cent of pupils (20 per cent sat the GCE) and the remaining 40 per cent still had no access to an exam. The CSE was seen as less intellectually demanding and was not as attractive to universities and employers.

Source K From 'Social Insurance and Allied Services', a report by Sir William Beveridge, (HMSO), 1942.

Benefit in return for contributions, rather than free allowances from the State is what the people of Britain desire. This desire is shown both by the established popularity of compulsory insurance, and by the phenomenal growth of voluntary insurance ... It is shown in another way by the strength of popular objection to any kind of means test.

Most men who have once gained the habit of work would rather work – in ways to which they are used – than be idle ... But getting work ... may involve a change of habits, doing something that is unfamiliar or leaving one's friends or making a painful effort of some other kind. The danger of providing benefits which are both adequate in amount and indefinite in duration, is that men as creatures who adapt themselves to circumstances, may settle down to them...

[The unemployed] should be required, as a condition of continued benefit to attend a work or training centre, such attendance being designed as a means of preventing habituation to idleness and as a means of improving capacity for earnings.

New universities

The Second World War demonstrated the need for large numbers of science graduates. Innovations like radar, code breaking, jet technology and computing had developed as a result of the pressures of war and in the post-war era there was still a huge demand for such skills. The 1945 Attlee government believed that universities should become centres for science and engineering, creating the technologically skilled generation that would run the country's economy in the 1950s and 1960s. In the same year a government paper, the Percy Report, recommended that the privileged position of classical education (Latin, the Classics) in university curricula be challenged in favour of Science and Engineering, and that universities be dramatically expanded to cater for the large numbers of students that would be created as a result of the Butler Act 1944. The following year a second paper, The Barlow Report, confirmed that there were far too few scientists and engineering students and also argued for a government funded expansion of universities. Despite this recommendation, by the 1960s there were still far too few science courses and many universities

When the Government published the Beveridge Report at the end of 1942, some traditionalists in the Conservative Party opposed it, believing that a welfare state would encourage idleness and dependence. How far does Source K support that view?

prioritised arts subjects, indicating that universities were institutions that were resistant to change.

By 1951 there were 84,000 students and two new 'red brick' universities had been established. The first was set up in Nottingham in 1948 (developed from an existing college) and a second, the University College of North Staffordshire (later Keele University), in 1949. A third, Southampton, was built in 1952.

In 1961, despite the huge increase in school pupils and the recommendations of Percy and Barlow, only 15 per cent of applications to university were successful. By the end of the decade, however, a revolution in British university education appeared to have taken place.

In 1961 the Robbins Committee met and two years later produced some dire warnings for the government. Britain was being overtaken by other countries in terms of university performance and the only option was to guarantee a university place for all who were eligible to attend. A goal of five times more student places by the year 1980 was recommended by the committee's report. The committee's paper stated that university education should achieve four main goals:

● Universities must give 'instruction in skills' to ensure the country had a competent workforce.
● Universities must develop in their students, 'general powers of the mind' to make sure that they were broadly well educated.
● Teaching academics should still continue to carry out research because 'the process of education is itself most vital when it partakes of the nature of discovery'.
● Teaching also had a social role and should impart 'the transmission of a common culture and common standards of citizenship'.

One of the new universities opening in 1961, just as the Robbins Committee met, was the University of Sussex. The university was described as a 'plate glass' campus, because of its modern buildings and architecture.

The final university innovation that was planned in 1964 (and which finally opened in 1971) was the Open University, established by the Wilson Government under Arts Minister Jenny Lee. The Open University was an institution based almost exclusively on distance learning, where people could study degrees at home. It ensured that people of any age who had missed out on higher education could become qualified and it was a key part of Wilson's modernising and democratising goals.

British society in 1964

By 1964, British people enjoyed a better standard of living, on average, than at any other point in British history. A century of social reform and improvements in medical care had led to increased average life expectancy of 71, compared to a range between 26 (recorded in inner-city Manchester) and 57 in 1851. British children had better educational opportunities than they had ever had before as a result of the 1944 Butler Education Act, and there was an effective social security 'safety net' of welfare payments, ensuring that families and individuals did not sink below the poverty line. The British had experienced a decade of unparalleled consumer choice since 1954. Rising wages and low prices ensured that the 1950s and 1960s were seen at the time as a golden age of affluence. Ideas about the role of women and young people in British society and traditional ideas about class and deference were beginning to be questioned in the two decades after the war, but, as with mainstream British prejudices about race and immigration, they were slow to change. While there may have been a desire for change in some parts of British society in the treatment of women, the working classes and ethnic minorities, British people on the whole had conservative attitudes towards social and cultural change.

KEY DATES: DEVELOPMENTS IN SOCIAL POLICY, 1942–64	
1942 Dec	Beveridge Report published
1944 Aug	(Butler) Education Act published
1945 July	Labour landslide election victory
1947	Establishment of GCE exams
1948 July	NHS established
1951	Prescription charges introduced
1954	End of rationing, start of consumer boom
1964	Commencement of planning for the Open University

Chapter summary

- Between 1939 and 1964 Britain underwent a series of major social and cultural changes.
- Some historians argue that the war brought about fundamental change in British social attitudes, while others dispute this.
- The blueprint for Britain's post-war welfare state was created in 1942 in the guise of the Beveridge Report.
- In 1945 a Labour Government introduced sweeping social reform, including the introduction of a National Health Service.
- By 1951, the Labour Government was replaced by the Conservatives, who ruled for the next thirteen years. Labour's divisions and its inability to end rationing led to a decline in support for the Party.
- By the mid-1950s a consumer boom had begun, fuelled by available credit and rising wages.
- In 1947, mass immigration from the Caribbean, and later Asia, began. By the late 1950s there were growing racial tensions which exploded into violence in Notting Hill in 1958.
- During the Second World War women experienced new freedoms and opportunities.
- In the aftermath of the war, many women returned to domestic life, but the law began to change in order to allow women greater access to the workplace.
- Historians have debated the extent to which a 'Swinging Sixties' really happened. Some believe there was a revolution in attitudes towards social class and sex; others argue that British popular attitudes were conservative throughout the period 1945–64.

CHAPTER SUMMARY DIAGRAM

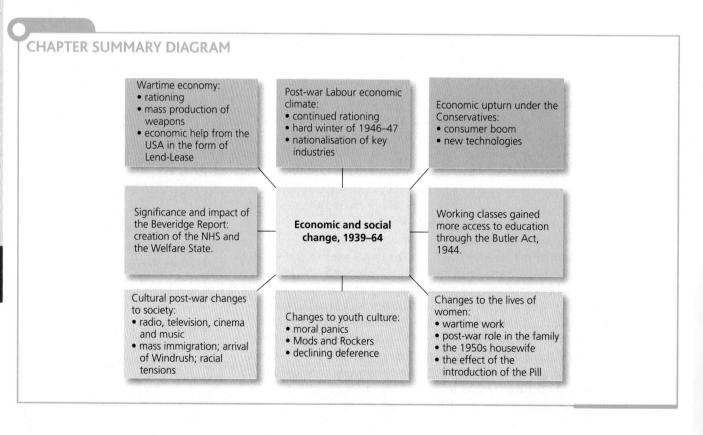

Working on interpretation skills: extended reading

How had total war changed British society by 1951?

Angela Davis considers the effects of war on welfare, class, family and race.

During and after World War Two total war – including rationing, conscription, bombing and evacuation – was said to have transformed British society. Since the 1970s historians have questioned this view. They have, according to Jose Harris, expressed doubts about the war's revolutionary impact; challenged the image of consensus; and demonstrated the range of ideologies and interest groups which shaped Britain's post-war Welfare State. The experience of total war and its aftermath did bring changes to British society though, and this essay considers four areas where its effects can be seen: welfare, class, family and race.

The wartime coalition asked a committee led by William Beveridge to look into Britain's social insurance schemes and make recommendations. In his 1942 report Beveridge proposed a system of social security based on three 'assumptions': family allowances, a comprehensive health service and high employment. Two of Beveridge's assumptions were realised before the war's end: in 1944 the Government committed itself to maintaining high employment and the Family Allowance Act was passed in June 1945. In July 1945 Labour, led by Clement Attlee, was elected on a manifesto of social reform and fulfilled Beveridge's third assumption with the introduction of the NHS in 1948. Other reforms were also implemented: the National Insurance Act (1946); the Town and Country Planning Act (1947); the Children Act (1948); and the National Assistance Act (1948). This series of reforms, together with the 1944 Education Act, was the basis of the Welfare State. Its implementation was not without difficulties, but the Labour Government completed its welfare reforms and maintained full employment in the face of serious problems at home and abroad. The post-war Welfare State was built on pre-war institutions, but it was transformative.

Arthur Marwick argued that during the war the gulf between classes narrowed. In contrast Harold Smith believes class conflict continued: evacuation led to tension between middle-class hosts and working-class evacuees; the public was aware the wealthy had access to more and better food despite rationing; and unofficial strikes increased each year from 1940 through 1944. Social and economic inequality remained after Labour's election victory. The late 1940s were blighted by poor housing and, for many, worsening living standards. At times, food restrictions were tighter than during the war – bread was rationed for the first time in 1946. However, although not always successful, the Attlee Government tried to tackle inequalities of wealth and property, supported by voters who believed there should be a fairer society after the hardships of war.

5

10

15

20

25

30

35

40

Family life was greatly disrupted by total war. Fathers were either away in the forces (some never returned) or occupied in essential war work. Many mothers were also juggling family responsibilities with employment: 7.75 million women were in paid work by June 1943. The *45* participation of mothers in war work was only ever seen as a temporary measure by the government, industry and women themselves. By June 1947 the numbers in paid work fell to six million, but quickly started to rise again. Evacuation led to thousands of children leaving their parents to live with host families. It also focused new political attention on *50* children's wellbeing. However, while post-war reconstruction sought to return Britain to pre-war patterns of family life, changes were already underway.

The arrival of the ship *Empire Windrush* in 1948, carrying Jamaicans who had served in the British forces or factories during the war, is often used *55* to show how the war proved a turning point in attitudes towards race and immigration. In reality Afro-Caribbeans did not arrive in significant numbers until the early 1950s. Most foreign workers came from Europe. Much of the debate about minority groups in the immediate post-war period continued to concentrate on the Jews. However the war did bring *60* changes. Before 1939, black communities were traditionally linked to the ports. The war opened up opportunities and there was a move 'inland', which intensified after 1945. The Attlee Government was also responsible for beginning the process of decolonisation of the Empire, starting by granting independence to India in 1947. *65*

Traditional histories of World War Two portrayed total war as transforming British society. While this essay agrees with revisionists who argue there were limits to the scale of change, it has also shown developments did occur in many areas of British social life.

Dr Angela Davis, University of Warwick.

ACTIVITY

Having read the essay, answer the following questions.

Comprehension
1 What does the author mean by the following phrases?
   a) 'Total War' (line 1)
   b) 'Welfare State' (line 27)
   c) 'Full employment' (line 26).

Evidence
2 Using paragraphs one to six, list the arguments that contradict the idea that the Second World War brought about revolutionary social change.

Interpretation
3 Using your knowledge (and the essay), list evidence to suggest that:
   a) there was a wartime social revolution
   b) radical change did not really occur.

Essay
4 Write an essay answer to the following A-level practice question:

'The period 1939–64 saw little real social change in Britain.' Assess the validity of this view.

Working on interpretation skills

ACTIVITY

The three extracts below give different interpretations of the extent to which life for women improved between 1945 and 1964. You should begin by reading each one and listing the main points made and the evidence used to support them. Then answer these questions:

1 In what way do Extracts A and B agree and disagree?

2 In what way do Extracts B and C agree and disagree?

3 Now answer the following practice A-level question:

Using your understanding of the historical context, assess how convincing the arguments in these three extracts are in relation to the development of women's employment rights between 1945 and the 1960s. **(30 marks)**

Extract A

So now that university educated women in this post-1945 era had the option of entering the labour market, regardless of their marital position, what opportunities awaited them? The evidence suggests that university women were faced with limited career options. From school through to graduation, a lack of careers advice and choice was evident, it was believed that a woman's career did not matter because it would be so short lived ... Women were excluded not only from positions advertised for science/engineering graduates, which may have been more understandable given the smaller number of female graduates from these disciplines, but also from positions directed at arts students. In essence, 'it was the man who mattered', and the use of the male pronoun was also effective in placing limitations upon the career choices of university women ... the adverts were actually specifically referring to men. Those advertisements that were directed at male students emphasised the managerial positions that would be attained in a short space of time, carrying with them 'real responsibility'.

From 'A Good Job for a Girl' by S. Aiston, *Journal of Twentieth-Century British History*, (Cambridge University Press), 2004, p. 364.

Extract B

Was the woman's place still, as it had been before the war, in the home? A sharp if short lived anxiety about Britain's apparently declining population proved a key 'pro-natalist' [a person in favour of women devoting themselves to pregnancy and childbirth] weapon for the 'home and hearthists', even persuading two well-known progressives, Margaret Bondfield and Eva Hubback to argue publicly in November 1945 that 'domestic work in a modern home will be a career for educated women'. Unsurprisingly women's magazines seldom deviated from upholding the domestic *status quo ante bellum* [before the war]. 'If men and women fail to take their traditional positions in the dance of life', declared *The Lady* [a women's magazine] in January 1946, 'only a greater dullness is achieved.' Soon after a fictional heroine in *My Weekly* put it succinctly: 'I've spent a week discovering I'd rather be Mrs Peter Grant, housewife, than Rosamund Fuller, dress designer' ... By September 1946 the number of married women at work (including part time) was, from a wartime peak of more than 7.2 million down to 5.8 million.

From *Austerity Britain 1945–51* by D. Kynaston, (Bloomsbury), 2008, p. 99.

Extract C

At the beginning of the 1950s, most married men and women generally lived separate lives. A wife was expected to concentrate on her duties as a mother and homemaker, while it fell to her husband to earn enough money for the family to live in the expected style. Most observers agreed that the most inflexible separation was found in isolated industrial areas. One survey of a mining village found that husband and wife lived 'separate and in a sense secret lives' with the woman being regarded as decidedly inferior ... the wife conducted her social life over the washing line, at the corner shop, visiting relatives at a moderate distance occasionally and perhaps now and again going with her husband to his pub or club ... the life of a girl after school followed a pre-determined path: 'Daughter follows mother in her main occupations of child rearing and housekeeping'. In both working and middle class households little girls were groomed to be both housewives and mothers.

From *White Heat* by D. Sandbrook, (Abacus), 2006, p. 689.

Working on essay technique

One effective technique that successful essay writers employ is to examine the presumptions in a question and then ask whether they are valid. If it can be argued that the statement in the essay question itself is too simplistic, limited or that it ignores far more important issues, you can challenge the question and in doing so build a strong line of argument.

Consider the following A-level practice question:

'The post-war welfare state, 1945–64, was built on the foundations of Asquith's Liberal reforms 1906–10.' Assess the validity of this view. (25 marks)

This question is inviting you to participate in a debate that has been ongoing throughout much of the post-war era between historians: to what extent was the welfare state solely the creation of the Labour Party and how far could earlier governments take credit?

If we challenge the presumptions in the question, then we can ask: Did the Liberals create the foundations of the welfare state or did it develop from later events such as the depression, inter-war social reform or the Second World War?

From earlier chapters in this book we can see that there were significant social reforms throughout the late nineteenth and early twentieth centuries. It might therefore be argued that the welfare state that emerged after the Second World War was the result of a far longer historical process. However, inter-war social reforms in education and healthcare and the expansive wartime role of the state also suggest that there were more short-term factors at play.

In order to fully address this question you will need to review your knowledge of the Liberal reforms and assess whether they formed the basis of a future welfare state or not. To recap, read pages 115–23 in Chapter 4.

Key questions: Britain, 1914–64

The specification you have been studying on Britain highlighted six key questions. We reviewed these at the end of Part 1 (page 128), providing opportunities for you to think about themes running through your study of the period. Now there is the opportunity for you to review this for Part 2 and the whole period of your study.

In the examination the essay will be focused on broad areas of the content and will reflect one or more of the six key questions. Therefore, this section should be of great help to you in your revision, both looking at themes and also revisiting the detailed content you have studied.

KEY QUESTION 1
How did democracy and political organisations develop in Britain?

Questions to consider

- What was the long-term significance of the Representation of the People Act 1918?
- How and why did Britain see the development of National Government from 1931 to 1945?
- Why did some British people gravitate towards fascism and communism during the 1930s?
- In what ways did Britain's main political parties transform themselves between 1945 and 1964?

Working in groups

Considering the period as a whole:
1 Discuss the view that British party politics between 1851 and 1964 was dominated by Britain's wealthy elites and worked in their interests.
2 Discuss the view that without the introduction of mass democracy Britain faced a possible revolution between 1851 and 1928.
3 Discuss the idea that of all the factors that changed politics, the Second World War had the biggest impact in the period 1851–1964.

KEY QUESTION 2
How important were ideas and ideologies?

Questions to consider

- What were the main differences in ideology between the Conservative and Labour parties after 1918?
- How did ideas and ideologies shape the outcome of general elections between 1918 and 1964? What were the key ideological debates of the period focused on?
- To what extent was there a post-war political consensus?
- Why did extreme political ideas develop during the inter-war period?

Working in groups

Considering the period as a whole:
1 Discuss the popularity of the Liberal Party and Labour's social reforms between 1851 and 1964.
2 Discuss the divisions in the Liberal and Labour parties 1851–1964. What similarities are there between the divisions within both parties?
3 Discuss the appeal of Conservative ideas to the British public between 1851 and 1964.
4 Discuss why extreme and violent political parties failed to dominate British politics between 1851 and 1964.

Questions to consider

- What was the effect of the First World War on the British economy?
- What were the main economic developments between 1918 and 1964? Why did Britain experience a shorter economic depression than most countries in the 1930s?
- What impact did the Second World War have on Britain's economy and finances?
- Why was there an economic boom lasting from 1954 into the 1960s?

Working in groups

Considering the period as a whole:
1 What was the effect of warfare on the British economy 1851–1964?
2 To what extent was Britain a declining economic power throughout the period 1851–1964?
3 What was the link between Britain's economic performance and the government's relationship with the trade unions?
4 What were the causes of:
   a) economic booms
   b) economic slumps between 1851 and 1964?

· ·

Questions to consider

- How far had British social attitudes towards class, deference, private life, sexuality and morality changed between 1914 and 1964?
- How did the class system work in the post-war era?
- Why was there social mobility throughout the period 1914–64?
- How did social reform affect living standards between 1914 and 1964?

Working in groups

Considering the period as a whole:
1 Discuss what factors encouraged change in British society 1851–1964.
2 Discuss what factors encouraged class conflict in British society 1851–1964.
3 Discuss why class identity became such a powerful issue during the period 1851–1964.

How and why did Britain's relationship with Ireland change?

Questions to consider

- Why did the Easter Rising in 1916 occur?
- Think of key figures between 1914 and 1964 like de Valera, Collins, Redmond, O'Neill and Paisley. How did they affect the relationship between Britain and Ireland?
- What impact did the IRA and the UVF have throughout the period 1914–64?
- Why was there a civil rights movement in Northern Ireland by 1964?

Working in groups

Considering the period as a whole:

1 Evaluate the contribution of British prime ministers in finding a solution to the 'Irish Question' 1851–1964. How effective were they?

2 How important were nationalist leaders in advancing the cause of Irish independence?

3 What was the overall impact of war on Ireland between 1851 and 1964?

How important was the role of key individuals and groups and how were they affected by developments?

Questions to consider

- Think of the key individuals, for example Herbert Kitchener, Ramsay MacDonald, Stanley Baldwin, Neville Chamberlain, Winston Churchill, Aneurin Bevan, John Maynard Keynes and Harold Wilson. Summarise their contributions to the government of Britain and/or to changes that took place in the period.
- Think of key groups, for example the Conservative Party, Sinn Fein, the British Union of Fascists, the Peace Pledge Union. What impact did groups have on the development of Britain throughout the period 1914–64?
- How were key individuals affected by developments over which they had little control?
- Which individuals seemed more in control of events?
- To what extent did groups determine events? To what extent did they react to events?

Working in groups

Considering the period as a whole:

1 Compare the contributions of two British prime ministers of the period, one Liberal and one Labour, for example Gladstone and MacDonald. Who made the more important contribution to constitutional and social reform, and why?

2 Compare the political decisions of two Conservative prime ministers, for example Disraeli and Macmillan. Which prime minister appears to have had better political judgement, and why?

3 Discuss what you understand by 'groups' that influenced politics and government in Britain. Which group had the greatest influence across the period 1851–1964, and why?

Further research

General recommendations

There are many excellent books on Britain during the period 1851–1964, some more detailed than others. Some are written specifically with A-level students in mind. Other academic books are written for more specialist audiences, but many are very accessible to students who already possess the necessary background knowledge.

Listed in this section are a number of novels and films which are recommendations intended to extend your overall sense of the period.

Lowe, N. (2009) *Mastering Modern British History*, Palgrave Master Series. London: Palgrave Macmillan.

A detailed and comprehensive study guide to Britain in the nineteenth and twentieth centuries, written accessibly for students.

Pearce, R. (2000) *Britain: Domestic Politics, 1918–39 1880–1929*. Access to History. London: Hodder Education.

A detailed and well-written guide to British politics between the two World Wars.

Clarke, P. (2004) *Hope and Glory: Britain 1900–2000*. London: Penguin.

Very accessible account of British society, politics, economics and culture throughout the twentieth century.

Gardiner, J. (2011) *The Thirties: An Intimate History of Britain*. London: Harper Press.

An excellent and in-depth account of Britain in the 1930s, featuring Britain's society, culture, politics and economics throughout the period. Exceptionally well researched and objective.

Griffin, E. (2013) *Liberty's Dawn: A People's History of the Industrial Revolution*. New Haven: Yale University Press.

A history of working-class life in the nineteenth century, told from the letters of working-class people, an excellent source of primary evidence.

Flanders, J. (2012) *The Victorian City: Everyday Life in Dickens' London*. London: Atlantic Books.

A detailed and readable exploration of life in Victorian London across all the social classes, giving valuable context.

Waller, S. (2008) *AQA History AS Unit 2. A Sixties Social Revolution? British Society 1959–1975*: Student's Book. London: Nelson Thornes.

A comprehensive and well-written guide to exploring the debates about the extent of social change in the 1960s.

Brunskill, I. (2007) *The Times Great Victorian Lives*. London: Times Books.

The obituaries of eminent Victorians such as Gladstone, Disraeli, Peel, Ruskin and Darwin. It gives a valuable insight into how these public figures were seen at the time.

Morgan, K.O. (2001) *Britain Since 1945: The People's Peace* (2nd edn.) Oxford: Oxford Paperbacks.

An excellent exploration of Britain's post-war economic and social changes.

Hennessy, P. (2012) *Distilling the Frenzy: Writing the History of One's Own Times*. London: Biteback Publishing.

A reflective and fascinating exploration of post-war Britain and the challenge of relative economic decline faced by both Labour and Conservative governments .

Marwick, A. (2003) *British Society Since 1945: The Penguin Social History of Britain*. London: Penguin.

A partisan but compelling discussion of the roots of social change in Britain.

Jackson, A. (2004) *Home Rule: An Irish History, 1800–2000*. Oxford: Oxford University Press.

A comprehensive history of modern Ireland, focusing on Home Rule and the struggle for independence.

Books relevant to particular chapters

Chapter 1

There are several excellent books published on this period in recent years.

Rappaport, H. (2012) *Magnificent Obsession: Victoria, Albert and the Death That Changed the Monarchy*. London: Windmill Books.

An examination of the relationship between Victoria and Albert and the devastating effect his death had on her and on Victorian society.

Jenkins, R. (2012) *Gladstone*. London: Pan Books.

A detailed and enlightening biography of Gladstone, though ultimately written from a sympathetic perspective.

Aldous, R. (2012) *The Lion and the Unicorn: Gladstone vs Disraeli*. London: Vintage.

The classic text on the struggle for supremacy between the two party leaders. Their respect and disdain for one another is fully explored here.

Blake, R. (1966) *Disraeli*. London: Eyre & Spottiswoode.

Still the essential starting point for any serious study of Disraeli – while Blake is sympathetic he is prepared to recognise his subject's limitations.

Chapter 2

Arnold, C. (2009) *Bedlam: London and Its Mad*. New York: Pocket Books.

General history of psychiatry in London in the modern era, but has plenty of interesting points about asylums in the Victorian era.

Hall, C., McClelland, K. and Rendall, J. (2000) *Defining the Victorian Nation: Class, Race, Gender and the British Reform Act of 1867*. Cambridge: Cambridge University Press.

A brilliant dissection of social, ethnic and gendered responses to the 1867 Reform Act that gives important insights into life in mid-Victorian Britain.

Forman Peck, J. (ed.) (2003) *New Perspectives on the Late Victorian Economy: Essays in Quantitative Economic History, 1860-1914*. Cambridge: Cambridge University Press.

A very comprehensive, though quite complex work, that explains the realities of the Victorian economy.

Chapter 3

Harrison, R. (2010) *Life and Times of Sidney and Beatrice Webb 1858–1905*: The Formative Years. London: Palgrave Macmillan.

One of many excellent biographies of the Webbs, focusing on their early political and economic thought.

Hattersley, R. (2010) *David Lloyd George: The Great Outsider*. London: Little Brown.

A largely sympathetic account of Lloyd George's radicalism and the People's Budget.

Jenkins, R. (2011) *Mr Balfour's Poodle*. London: Bloomsbury Reader.

Roy Jenkin's account of the constitutional crisis over the People's Budget, largely critical of the Tories and the House of Lords.

Adams, R. (2013) *Balfour: The Last Grandee*. London: Thistle Publishing.

An excellent biography of Arthur Balfour, focusing on the often detached and enigmatic nature of the man.

Hibbert, C. (2007) *Edward VII: The Last Victorian King*. London: Palgrave Macmillan.

A general all-round description of Edward VII's reign, highly accessible and full of illuminating detail about his bon viveur lifestyle.

Chapter 4

Mann, T. (2009) *Tom Mann's Memoirs*. Charleston: BiblioBazaar.

A fascinating journey through the life and thoughts of syndicalist Tom Mann. Presents an interesting counterpoint to the biographies of the political elites of the Victorian and Edwardian era.

Pankhurst, E. (2014) *Suffragette: My Own Story*. London: Hesperus Press.

Detailed if partial account of the career and struggles of Emmeline Pankhurst and the development of the WSPU.

Meeres, F. (2013) *Suffragettes: How Britain's Women Fought and Died for the Right to Vote*. Stroud: Amberley.

Accessible general introduction to the struggle for women's suffrage.

Pugh, M. (2013) *The Pankhursts: The History of One Radical Family*. London: Vintage.

Thorough biographical account of the Pankhurst family's political journey, from suffrage to flirtations with communism and fascism.

Chapter 5

Overy, R. (2010) *The Morbid Age: Britain and the Crisis of Civilisation, 1919–1939*. London: Penguin.

A brilliant intellectual history of the inter-war years, focusing on the sense of pessimism and decline that seemed to grip inter-war intellectuals and writers.

Wilson, T. (1966) *The Downfall of the Liberal Party*. London: Collins.

A classic work on the Party's decline.

Baxell, R. (2012) *Unlikely Warriors*. London: Aurum.

A fascinating and illuminating history of the British volunteers to the international brigades in the Spanish Civil War. It charts their motivations, anti-fascist beliefs and the role played by the Communist Party of Great Britain.

Pugh, M. (2006) *Hurrah for the Blackshirts*. London: Pimlico.

A revealing examination of the popularity of the fascist movement among Britain's elite in the mid-1930s, especially Lord Rothermere of the *Daily Mail*.

Rose, N. (2011) *The Cliveden Set*. London: Vintage.

An exploration of the political and aristocratic elite who converged on the Astor family's home at Cliveden and their attempts to support a pro-appeasement policy during the 1930s.

Burk, K. (2014) *War and the State: The Transformation of British Government, 1914–1919*. Oxford: Taylor & Francis.

A well-researched discussion of the rapid growth of British state power during the First World War. This is a large book and expensive to purchase, but you may be able to view a copy at your local library.

Lynch, R. (2015) *Revolutionary Ireland, 1912–25*. London: Bloomsbury Academic.

A comprehensive history of the establishment of an independent Ireland and a particularly detailed exploration of the aftermath of the Easter Rising

Chapter 6

Hattersley, R. (2009) *Borrowed Time: The Story of Britain Between the Wars*. London: Abacus.

An accessible and concise history of inter-war Britain focusing on memories of the First World War and anxieties about future conflict.

Maloney, A. (2012) *Bright Young Things: Life in the Roaring Twenties*. London: Virgin Books.

An interesting overview of cultural and social change during the 1920s, focusing on the new hedonistic freedoms experienced by the upper and middle classes.

Taylor, D. (2009) *Bright Young People: The Rise and Fall of a Generation 1918–1940*. London: Vintage.

The lives and loves of an inter-war generation scarred by memories of conflict. A very revealing and fascinating social history.

Gardiner, J. (2009) *The Thirties: An Intimate History.* London: Harper Press.

The most thorough and comprehensive social, economic and political history of the 1930s, meticulously researched.

Pugh, M. (2009) *We Danced All Night*. London: Vintage.

An excellent and concise social history of the inter-war years, focusing on new affluence, leisure time and popular culture.

Chapter 7

Addison, P. (1994) *The Road to 1945: British Politics and the Second World War*. London: Pimlico.

One of the most important texts on the subject of the development of post-war Britain, Addison's arguments have informed British historians over the next two decades.

Kynaston, D. (2008) *Austerity Britain*. London: Bloomsbury.

A ground breaking social history, part of a series that focuses on social change throughout the period. Kynaston's book is based on Mass Observation reports and contains real gems of empirical evidence.

Thomas Symonds, N. (2014) *Nye: The Political Life of Aneurin Bevan*. London: IB Tauris.

A new and detailed biography of Bevan, focusing on his political life in the run up to, during and after the 1945 Labour Government.

Davenport-Hynes, R. (2012) *An English Affair: Sex, Class and Power in the Age of Profumo*. London: Harper Press.

A brilliantly researched and detailed account not just of the Profumo Scandal but of the wider questions of class, propriety, sexuality and privilege in 1960s Britain.

Thorpe, D. (2010) *Supermac: The Life of Harold Macmillan*. London: Vintage.

The standard work on the life of Macmillan. Well researched, largely impartial and accessible.

Chapter 8

Gardiner, J. (2005) *Wartime: Britain 1939–1945*. London: Headline Review.

A thorough and detailed account of social attitudes and social change during the Second World War.

Calder, A. (1992) *The People's War*. London: Pimlico.

Groundbreaking work on social attitudes during the war, tearing down long held assumptions about solidarity and cohesion during the war years.

Longmate, N. (2002) *How We Lived Then: History of Everyday Life During the Second World War*. London: Pimlico.

A detailed and incisive account of life during the war, well researched and accessible.

Rose, S. (2004) *Which People's War? National Identity and Citizenship in Wartime Britain 1939–1945*. Oxford: Oxford University Press.

A challenging but important exploration of national identity during the Second World War, a notion that had profound implications for the post-war period.

Timmins, N. (2001) *The Five Giants: A Biography of the Welfare State*. London: Harper Collins.

An excellent account of the origins, development and growth of the Welfare State, along with changing attitudes towards the provision of welfare.

Harris, B. (2004) *The Origins of the British Welfare State: Society, State and Social Welfare in England and Wales, 1800–1945*. London: Palgrave Macmillan.

A longer view on the roots of welfare from the nineteenth century onwards, focusing on the Gladstonian reforms, the 1906 Liberal Government and social reform in the inter-war years.

Hennessy, P. (2006) *Never Again: Britain 1945–51*. London: Penguin.

A positive account of the post-war Labour Government, well researched and excellently argued and explored.

Sandbrook, D. (2010) *Never Had It So Good: Britain from Suez to the Beatles: 1956–1964*. London: Abacus.

An excellent and incisive cultural, social and political history of Britain in the age of affluence.

Novels and biographies

There are hundreds of novels about the period 1851–1964 to choose from, below is just a small selection. A student of nineteenth-century Britain would of course read the works of both Charles Dickens and Thomas Hardy, the two greatest novelists of the period. In the twentieth-century, Virginia Woolf, H. G. Wells, George Orwell, Graham Greene, Evelyn Waugh and Muriel Spark are all well worth exploring.

Hamilton. P. (1941) *Hangover Square*. London: Penguin.

A bleak thriller set during the depressed 1930s, capturing the struggles of the poor and dispossessed during the inter-war period.

Brittan, V. (2004) *Testament of Youth: An Autobiographical Study of the Years 1900–1925*. London: Virago Classic Non-fiction.

The autobiography of Vera Brittan, who served as a nurse during the First World War, but suffered the loss of her brother, fiancé and best friend during the war.

Orwell, G. (2004) *Keep the Aspidistra Flying* (new edn.) London: Penguin.

A satirical novel by George Orwell that is critical of the new, empty consumerism and careerism of the 1930s.

Waugh, E. (2000) *Brideshead Revisited (new edn.)*. London: Penguin Classics.

A novel set during the inter-war years, charting the gradual decline of an English aristocratic family. Ever present throughout the novel is the memory of the First World War and the growing inevitability of the second.

Tomalin, C. (2012) *Thomas Hardy: The Time-torn Man*. London: Penguin.

A revealing and insightful biography of the great writer, placing him in meaningful historical context.

Tomalin, C. (2012) *Charles Dickens: A Life*. London: Penguin

Similar to the Thomas Hardy biography, Dickens' political views and activism are explored, along with his writing.

Orwell, G. (2001) *The Road to Wigan Pier* (new edn.) London: Penguin Modern Classics.

Orwell's best known work of non-fiction, an exploration of poverty in 1930s Britain.

Levy, A. (2004) *Small Island*. London: Headline Review.

The story of West Indian servicemen and nurses who fight for Britain during the Second World War, only to experience racism when they settle in Britain during the 1940s and 1950s.

McCourt, F. (2005) *Angela's Ashes*. London: Harper Perennial.

An autobiographical account of life in impoverished Ireland and the Irish community in New York. It gives a clear picture of the immense hardships faced by impoverished Irish families between the wars.

Llewellyn, R. (2001) *How Green was my Valley* (new edn.) London: Penguin Classics.

Set at the end of the nineteenth century, this novel focuses on the lives of a mining family in South Wales, their hardships, aspirations and the tensions in a mining community.

Films

Victorian and Edwardian Britain

Far From The Madding Crowd Thomas Vinterberg (dir.) 2015.

Adaptation of Thomas Hardy's novel of hardship and sacrifices made by Bathsheba Everdene in poverty stricken rural England.

Topsy Turvy Mike Leigh (dir.) (1999)

Biopic of the lives of Victorian musical writers and producers Gilbert and Sullivan.

The Importance of Being Ernest Oliver Parker (dir.) (2002)

Adaptation of Oscar Wilde's classic farce; an amusing exploration of Victorian manners.

The Young Victoria Jean-Marc Vallée (dir.) (2009)

A dramatisation of the turbulent first years of Queen Victoria's rule, and her enduring romance with Prince Albert.

Howard's End James Ivory (dir.) (1992)

An adaptation of E. M. Forster's classic novel. When a young working-class intellectual falls in love with the daughter of a middle-class socially conscious family he has to fight class prejudice to be accepted.

Hobson's Choice David Lean (dir.) (1954)

An adaptation of a play by Harold Brighouse, set in Lancashire in the 1880s (Brighouse was born in Salford in 1882). The film is classified as a 'romantic comedy', but actually deals with themes of class intolerance, alcohol abuse, the changing role of women, sexual morality and the entrepreneurial spirit of the late Victorian period.

First World War

There are numerous films about the First World War (for example *Lawrence of Arabia* or, more recently, *War Horse*). The films below are less about the chaos of the battlefield and more related to the impact that the war had on all aspects of Britain.

Regeneration Gillies MacKinnon (dir.) (1997)

The story of soldiers and famous war poets, consigned to Craiglockhart psychiatric hospital during the war for refusing to fight. Based on the novel by Pat Barker.

Oh What A Lovely War (dir.) Richard Attenborough (1969)

Taken from a satirical musical, this film presents the politicians and generals as buffoons and the ordinary soldiers as cannon fodder. Much of the way in which the war is remembered results from this film.

My Boy Jack Brian Kirk (dir.) (2007)

The tragic story of Rudyard Kipling's son Jack, who he had admitted to the British army despite being declared unfit due to his eyesight. When Kipling's son goes missing in battle, the famous writer searches for answers as to his fate and struggles with his own guilt.

Inter-war Britain

The following films capture the inter-war decades between 1918 and 1939. Some were made at the time, others are 'period' movies that skilfully re-create the atmosphere of the times.

The King's Speech Tom Hooper (dir.) (2010)

Compelling tale of the divorce crisis and King George VI's struggle with public speaking. Discount the enormous factual error in the film – Churchill is presented as being anti-Edward VIII; much of the rest of the film helps to explore class, privilege and politics throughout the period.

Remains of the Day James Ivory (dir.) (1993)

The story of Mr Stevens, a butler at a stately home in the inter-war period who is witness to secret diplomatic overtures by the British aristocracy to the Nazis.

Land and Freedom Ken Loach (dir.) (1995)

Based on true accounts of the Spanish Civil War, this film tells the story of a young British working-class man who travels to Spain to fight with Spanish anarchists against the Francoist *coup d'état*.

Sing As We Go Basil Dean (dir.) (1934)

A musical made during the Depression, it is dated but should be seen as an example of morale-boosting propaganda. Much of it was shot on location –unusual at that time – and it therefore has a real sense of time and place. The main lead is played by Gracie Fields (one of the best-known British film and stage performers of the twentieth century), a working-class girl laid off from her job at a mill in Lancashire and seeking work in a seaside resort.

Second World War

There are, of course, innumerable Second World War films that deal with the war itself (*A Bridge Too Far*, *The Longest Day*), but here is a selection of films about how the war was experienced on the home front.

The End of the Affair Neil Jordan (dir.) (1999)

The tale of a doomed, illicit love affair set during the Blitz and in the immediate aftermath of the war.

The Imitation Game Morten Tyldum (dir.) (2014)

An exploration of the wartime work of mathematician Alan Turing and his suicide, following his prosecution for homosexual acts in the 1950s.

Hope and Glory John Boorman (dir.) (1987)

John Boorman's autobiographical recollections of life as a young boy in wartime Britain.

Land Girls David Leland (dir.) (1998)

The story of three girls working on a farm during the war, focuses on social class and shared sacrifice.

Post-war Britain

The following films capture the two post-war decades between 1945 and 1964. Some were made at the time, others are 'period' movies that skilfully re-create the atmosphere of the times.

A Hard Day's Night Richard Lester (dir.) (1964)

The first of several musical feature films starring the Beatles, capturing the energy and optimism of Britain in the early 1960s.

A Taste of Honey Tony Richardson (dir.) (1961)

A groundbreaking film set in the North West of England in the early 1960s, featuring themes of mixed race relationships, sex before marriage, single motherhood and homosexuality.

Passport to Pimlico Henry Cornelius (dir.) (1949)

A classic British comedy from Ealing Studios that sees Pimlico in London find the legal right to declare itself independent after the war. The film was seen at the time as making a thinly veiled commentary on post-war rationing.

Scandal Michael Caton-Jones (dir.) (1989)

An accurate re-telling of the Profumo Scandal, which also explores British society, racial tensions and corruption in the early 1960s.

Nowhere Boy Sam Taylor-Wood (dir.) (2009)

A biopic of the formative years of John Lennon, accurately capturing the 'look' of post-war Liverpool and life during the mid- to late-1950s.

An Education Lone Scherfig (dir.) 2010

A coming-of-age tale in the early 1960s, taken from the memoirs of journalist Lynne Barber. A schoolgirl has an affair with an enigmatic con man and is introduced to the exciting and decadent world of early 60s London.

Glossary of terms

Autocratic Where absolute power is concentrated in the hands of one leader and they can rule without a constitution or parliament. In Russia, the Tsar had allowed a parliament, the Duma, to exist but it had little power and the Tsar was free to ignore and dissolve it at will.

Auxiliary service Services that helped the front-line troops, such as the Women's Army Corps.

Baby boom A dramatic increase in the number of babies born during and after the Second World War.

British Medical Association The professional body representing doctors and their interests.

Budget deficit A situation in which the government is spending more than it is raising through taxation.

Catholic Emancipation MPs and Peers have to take an oath of allegiance to the crown before being allowed to enter parliament. Before 1829 this oath was worded so that Roman Catholics could not say it without renouncing their faith. The 1829 Act removed these parts, making the oath one that all Christians could accept.

Civil defence The fire service, rescue teams, air-raid wardens and others who limited the impact of German bombing or helped to rescue survivors.

Civil service The paid advisors, officials and clerks who work in government departments to implement the policies of the government of the day.

Closed shop The practice among trade unions of preventing any non-unionised worker from having a job in a factory or workplace dominated by the union.

Coal seams Strata of coal underground that are large enough to be cut out and sent to the surface.

Coercion Acts These Acts made it legal for individuals to be detained in prison without being charged and brought to trial for a specific offence.

Coffin ships Ships that were basically unseaworthy and were sent to sea with the intention that they would sink and allow an insurance claim to be made.

Commonwealth The organisation of nations that had previously made up the British Empire.

Concentration camps These camps were so-named because they 'concentrated' elderly men, women and children in areas that were under military control. Once there they could not leave without permission.

Conscription The compulsory drafting of men into the armed services.

Co-operative schemes These schemes involved the principle of working together rather than in competition and working to share in group rather than individual prosperity.

Cryptanalyst A code breaker.

Cultural revolution A fundamental shift in the way that individuals perceive themselves, the society around them and the way in which they communicate these new ideas and outlooks to others.

Demobilisation The return of conscripted soldiers to civilian life at the end of the war.

Democratic Democracy can be generally defined as a political system in which those considered to be adults have the right to vote for their political representatives and through them to have a significant influence over government policies. Beyond this general principle however there is no precise formula about the specific details of the political system and democratic systems vary in form around the world.

Dominion status A self-ruling part of the British Empire, such as Australia or Canada.

Emergency Powers Act A piece of post-war legislation that gave the government similar powers to DORA. It enabled the government to use force to restore order, particularly with regard to industrial disputes.

Endemic and epidemic diseases Endemic diseases are those that are always present but not running out of control – in the 1850s measles and diphtheria would fit this category. An epidemic disease is one that is spreading rapidly such as cholera in 1831 and again in 1848–49.

English Bar The legal profession in England and Wales.

'Floating voters' Voters who do not have strong loyalties to any particular party and switch how they vote. Often floating voters decide the outcome of general elections.

Free trade An economic policy that allows imports and exports to enter and leave the country without imposing taxes or limitations on quantities.

General strike A situation in which all trade union workers go on strike to support a particular cause, regardless of whether they are directly involved in the dispute.

Gerrymandering To manipulate the outcome of elections by drawing constituency boundaries in a way that disadvantages one side.

Gestapo The secret state police in Nazi Germany.

Go-slows Workers deliberately being as unproductive as possible as a form of protest.

Graduated tax A tax by which people with different incomes are divided into 'tax brackets' and taxed at different rates, with higher incomes being taxed at higher rates.

Guerrilla tactics Fighting using ambushes, bombs and snipers. Guerrilla soldiers do not wear uniforms and often hide among the civilian population.

IMF The International Monetary Fund is a global organisation of which Britain is a member. It was created after the Second World War to ensure global economic stability and has been used by Britain several times in the post-war decades as a source of loans.

Imperial preference A policy of tariffs that favoured imports from the empire into Britain over other trading nations like the USA.

Invisible earnings So-called because they are purely paper transactions covering the fees charged for professional services rendered rather than actual products being sold.

Khaki election Khaki is a Hindustani word meaning 'soil-coloured' and used in English to describe the light yellow-brown colour of army uniforms.

Light manufacturing The industrial production of consumer goods such as furniture, radios and bicycles.

Locked out The practice by employers of locking the factory gates and keeping workers out of their jobs until they agree to accept lower wages.

Mass picketing The use of hundreds or thousands of union members to prevent workers from entering a factory or business that is the subject of an industrial dispute.

Miners' institutes Social clubs and educational institutions for miners within mining communities.

Ministry of Information The wartime government ministry created to communicate government policy and propaganda to the general public.

Mixed economy An economy in which some industry is owned privately but other major industries are owned by the state.

Moral panics Popular anxieties about social or cultural change; often the subject of the 'panic' is relatively harmless.

Morganatic marriage A royal wedding where the husband or wife marrying into the royal family does not take on the title of king or queen, but instead has the lesser title of duke or duchess. It ensures that the non-royal can never become monarch if the royal dies, and, crucially, that children of the marriage are excluded from the line of succession.

National Executive Committee of the Labour Party The governing body of the party that ensures that the party's constitution is upheld.

National government [definition to come]

Nationalisation The policy of taking private industries into state ownership, which runs them on behalf of the population.

Net creditor A country or an institution that lends more money than it borrows.

Partition The splitting up of Ireland into two separate parts.

Piece work The practice of paying a worker for every item they create, not on an hourly rate. This can result in lower wages but conversely piece work helped improve the standard of living in agriculture in the 1930s. It was often used in industry as a temporary incentive to increase productivity on big orders without needing to take on extra workers who did not have the skills needed. This could increase earnings substantially while such an order was being filled.

Pocket boroughs Boroughs controlled by individual landowners (the borough being 'in their pocket'). They were also known as 'nomination boroughs' because the landowners effectively nominated the MPs.

Poverty line The level of income below which it is difficult to secure the basic necessities of life: shelter, food, clothing, etc.

Private Member's Bill A bill introduced by an ordinary MP rather than the government. In the nineteenth century this was much more common than today and sometimes governments could not stop such a bill passing even if they wished to. However, more usually they were passed because the government agreed not to oppose them.

Ratepayers Rates are taxes payable to local authorities rather than the central or national government. Such taxes therefore varied locally. The only local rate that was universal was the Poor Rate which, under a law dating from 1601, had to be paid in order to support those who could not support themselves.

Real wages Defined as the value of goods or services that wages can actually buy. For example, if wages remain the same while food prices increase, their 'real' value has gone down. On the other hand if food prices fall the 'real' value of wages has risen.

Reserved occupations Jobs considered so important that workers in them should not be removed from them – this derived from the First World War, when many men enlisted from occupations such as mining and engineering leaving serious shortages of labour in key industries.

Rotten boroughs Boroughs which had once been large and populours and which had declined in population, but which still retained the right to MPs. These MPs 'purchased' their seats from landowners.

Royal Commission A formal public inquiry into a specific issue that is of major importance and usually an issue of controversy. It operates independently of the government that sets it up and once begun cannot be ended except by its own decision. The Commission must produce a report with findings, evidence and recommendations for a course of action, though the government can choose to ignore these if it wishes.

Short-hours contracts A contract that does not guarantee fixed hours each week, meaning that workers' wages are never secure.

Short-time working When the amount of time worked in the week is reduced because there is not enough work available for a full week – it is an alternative to reducing the workforce and keeping those still employed on full time.

Siege mentality Feeling surrounded by enemies and constantly under threat.

Speaker of the House of Commons The person who chairs Commons debates and is the final authority on rules of procedure.

Speculative boom An economic boom based on the stock market, often unstable and short-lived.

Staple industries Industries producing essential products for which there is a high and continuous demand and on which large-scale employment can be based.

Sympathetic strikes Strike action by a union that has no direct involvement in an industrial dispute, in solidarity with workers from unions who are on official strike.

Technocratic class Skilled engineers, managers and scientists who can make society function effectively.

'Tick' An informal 'tab' or credit with a local shopkeeper, enabling customers to take goods and pay for them when they could afford them.

Trade gap A negative difference between the value of exports and the cost of imports.

U-Boats German submarines that attacked British shipping during the First and Second World Wars.

War bond A war bond is essentially an IOU or a 'promise to pay' from the government. Governments that have to raise large sums of money to pay for armaments offer bonds to the public on the promise they when they are repaid they will have increased in value.

White paper A report that explains an issue and presents possible solutions to the problem, used by government to help plan policy and new laws.

Workhouse A place of refuge where paupers could receive food and shelter (known as 'relief') in return for doing work of some kind. The earliest reference we have to one comes in 1631. In 1723 Parliament passed an Act confirming that it was legal for parishes to demand that paupers enter a workhouse to get relief. By the 1770s there were 1,800 such workhouses, meaning roughly one in seven parishes had one.

Index